EMPLOYMENT PROTECTION ACT 1975

By

S. D. ANDERMAN, B.A., LL.B., M.Sc.
Senior Lecturer in Law
School of Law
University of Warwick

LONDON
BUTTERWORTHS
1976

Annotated Legislation Service Volume 235

ENGLAND
Butterworth & Co. (Publishers) Ltd.
London: 88 Kingsway, London WC2B 6AB

AUSTRALIA
Butterworths Pty. Ltd.
Sydney: 586 Pacific Highway, Chatswood, NSW 2067
Also at Melbourne, Brisbane, Adelaide and Perth

CANADA
Butterworth & Co. (Canada) Ltd.
Toronto: 2265 Midland Avenue, Scarborough, M1P 4S1

NEW ZEALAND
Butterworths of New Zealand Ltd.
Wellington: 26–28 Waring Taylor Street, Wellington 1

SOUTH AFRICA
Butterworth & Co. (South Africa) (Pty.) Ltd.
Durban: 152–154 Gale Street, Durban

U.S.A.
Butterworth & Co. (Publishers) Inc.
Boston: 19 Cummings Park, Woburn, Mass. 01801

ISBN 0 406 54750 5

PREFACE

The Employment Protection Act 1975 (EPA) marks the second and more innovative stage of the current reform of the legal framework for industrial relations. The first stage, the Trade Union and Labour Relations Act 1974, repealed the Industrial Relations Act 1971 and re-established a legal framework based on extensive legal immunities for trade unions whilst retaining and improving statutory protection for employees against unfair dismissal. The 1974 Act gave little positive legal support to trade unions and collective bargaining. It pointed to voluntary measures such as negotiation backed up by conciliation, arbitration and inquiry, rather than legal sanctions, as the most effective method of resolving collective industrial disputes.

The EPA introduces a more positive look to the legal framework in two quite distinct respects. It extends and develops existing employment protections which apply to employees regardless of trade union membership, the statutory "floor" of rights which has been built up to give protection to employees in their contractual relationship with their employers. The Act also provides a new charter of legal rights for trade unions and trade unionists which are designed to promote new, and strengthen existing, collective bargaining arrangements. This introduces a more novel element into the legal framework and moves it into the largely uncharted waters of a new law of industrial democracy below company board level.

At the same time these new legal measures do not mark a complete break with the past; they are built on the foundations of previous legislation and they continue to share certain of the basic values of the traditional legal framework. They continue to be viewed as essentially ancillary to collective bargaining in that they either provide machinery designed to encourage its growth or set minimum substantive standards above which collective bargaining may provide more favourable terms. Moreover, the Act continues to endorse the importance of voluntary measures by placing the Advisory, Conciliation and Arbitration Service on a statutory footing.

The purpose of this book is to offer a detailed commentary on the provisions of the new Act. Each part has been looked at in the context of any preceding legislation or the common law position it was designed to alter. The commentary emphasises possible sources of future litigation, and where possible looks at the legislative policy underlying each part of the Act.

February 1976

S. D. ANDERMAN

NOTE

The following abbreviations have been used in the text:

CEA Contracts of Employment Act 1972
EPA Employment Protection Act 1975
HSWA Health and Safety at Work etc. Act 1974
RPA Redundancy Payments Act 1965
TULRA Trade Union and Labour Relations Act 1974

IMPLEMENTATION

At the time of going to press, three Commencement Orders had been made (the Employment Protection Act 1975 (Commencement No. 1) Order 1975, S.I. 1975 No. 1938, the Employment Protection Act 1975 (Commencement No. 2) Order 1976, S.I. 1976 No. 144, and the Employment Protection Act 1975 (Commencement No. 3) Order 1976, S.I. 1976 No. 321), which brought parts of the Act into force on six dates: 1st January, 1st February, 1st March, 8th March, 30th March and 20th April 1976. Full details are given in the notes to the sections and schedules which are affected.

The Employment Protection Act 1975 (Commencement No. 4) Order 1976, S.I. 1976 No. 530, was made after this book was at press, bringing further provisions of the Act into force on 6th April, 20th April and 1st June, 1976.

CONTENTS

TABLE OF STATUTES

References in this Table to "*Statutes*" are to Halsbury's Statutes of England (Third Edition) showing the volume and page at which the annotated text of the Act will be found. Paragraph numbers printed in bold type indicate where the Employment Protection Act 1975 is set out.

TABLE OF CASES

In the following Table references are given to the English and Empire Digest showing where a digest of the case will be found

PARA.

E

F

G

H

I

J

K

L

CHAPTER ONE

INTRODUCTION

1. THE BOOK AND THE ACT IN OUTLINE

[**1**] This book is divided into two parts, reflecting the basic division that runs through the Act itself. Part I is concerned with the extension of the statutory floor of individual employment protections. Part II examines the new charter of rights for trade unions and trade unionists.

Part I

[**2**] The new individual employment protections are essentially a continuation of an existing trend in British labour legislation, the growth of protective legislation designed to provide certain safeguards for employees against their rather vulnerable legal position at common law. The forerunners of this development were the various Truck Acts and Factory Act of the 19th century. In more recent years, since 1963, a series of statutes have been enacted which have concentrated on the provision of safeguards which provide protections for employees when the employment relationship ends. Thus, the Contracts of Employment Act 1963 (now 1972) provided minimum periods of notice of termination or pay in lieu of notice of dismissal, the Redundancy Payments Act 1965 provided a lump sum payment to a qualified employee who lost his job owing to redundancy and the Trade Union and Labour Relations Act 1974 retained the remedies for unfair dismissals introduced by the Industrial Relations Act 1971.

[**3**] One major feature of the Employment Protection Act is its reinforcement and development of existing statutory safeguards which gives employees protection upon the termination of their jobs. The Act makes the following changes:

—increases the minimum periods of notice required by the 1972 Contracts of Employment Act
—re-defines the requirements for continuous employment in the 1972 Act (Chapter Two)
—amends the law of redundancy *inter alia* to provide for a trial period in cases where the employer offers alternative employment (Chapter Three)
—alters the law of unfair dismissal by introducing a right to a written statement of the reasons for dismissal for dismissed employees
—strengthens the remedies for unfair dismissal
—eases the preliminary requirements for the presentation of a valid complaint of unfair dismissal

—provides new tests of fairness in cases of employees dismissed for pregnancy and for participation in industrial action (these are considered in Chapter Four)

—creates new protections for employees in the event of the insolvency of their employers (Chapter Five).

[**4**] In addition to safeguards upon termination, the statutory floor in recent years has begun to extend protections to employees which apply while the employment relationship remains in being. The earlier protections of the Truck Acts and Factory Act have been augmented by the Health and Safety At Work etc. Act 1974, the Equal Pay Act 1970 and the Sex Discrimination Act 1975. The EPA introduces a variety of new rights for employees that apply more comprehensively to regulate the continuing employment relationship. The Act provides:

—an expansion of the right of employees to information in the written statement of terms and conditions and in an itemised pay statement (Chapter Six)

—a new right of employees to a guarantee payment for workless days (Chapter Seven)

—a right of employees to paid suspension from work on medical grounds (Chapter Eight)

—new rights for female employees to paid maternity leave and to return to work after maternity leave (Chapter Nine)

—new rights of employees to time off work (Chapter Ten).

[**5**] To meet the need for an enforcement procedure that is "informal speedy and accessible", the Act extends the jurisdiction of the Industrial Tribunals to encompass all complaints or infringements of the "individual" rights created by the statute. It also makes provision for conciliation in connection with complaints to tribunals (s. 108). As well, the Act creates a new appellate court for the tribunal system, the Employment Appeals Tribunal which will have the informality and accessibility of the now defunct National Industrial Relations Court. However unlike the National Industrial Relations Court, the new Employment Appeals Tribunal will have no original jurisdiction in respect of issues involving collective labour relations. Its jurisdiction will be largely restricted to the appellate stage of complaints of infringements of individual employment rights.[1]

Part II

[**6**] The second part of the Act consists of the new collective rights, those provisions which provide positive legal rights for trade union members and trade union organisations and legal support for the extension of collective consultation and negotiation.

In particular the Act provides:

—legal support for trade union recognition (ss. 11–16 discussed in Chapter Twelve)

[1] For a more detailed description of this new institution, see chapter Nineteen.

—legal support for disclosure of information to trade unions (ss. 17–21 discussed in Chapter Thirteen)

—legal support for advance notification to the Government and prior consultation with trade unions in the event of redundancies (ss. 99–107 discussed in Chapter Fourteen)

—new rights for trade union members and trade union officials (Chapter Fifteen).

[**7**] Moreover the Act adds to existing positive legal support for the lower paid and weakly organised worker by:

—strengthening Wages Councils and creating statutory Joint Industrial Councils (ss. 89–97 discussed in Chapter Sixteen)

—expanding existing machinery for extending the unilateral arbitration procedure of s. 8 of the Terms and Conditions of Employment Act 1959 in Sch. 11 of the EPA (s. 98 discussed in Chapter Seventeen).

[**8**] In addition to placing the ACAS on a statutory footing, the EPA creates two institutions designed to administer the new charter of trade union rights. A Central Arbitration Committee has been formed to provide enforceable arbitration awards as part of the enforcement machinery for many of the new rights. A Certification officer has been established to produce a certificate of independence for trade unions. As well, the jurisdiction of the industrial tribunals and hence the appellate jurisdiction of the EPA have been enlarged to allow complaints by trade union members and trade unions in respect of some of the above rights.[2]

2. THE EMPLOYMENT PROTECTION ACT AND THE NEW LEGAL FRAMEWORK

[**9**] Although the EPA employs legal means to effectuate employment protections at both individual and collective levels, it quite noticeably eschews the use of legal restrictions against employees and independent trade unions. In almost all cases, the new legal rights are given to employees and trade unions whilst the legal restrictions and liabilities are applied to employers and employing organisations. In part this may reflect an appreciation that legal restrictions on industrial action are not always effective. However, it may also be viewed as an indication that both elements of the new Act have a common purpose, notably the creation of wider restrictions on the exercise of unilateral managerial prerogative and the provision of an alternative source of rule which is fairer to the ordinary employee. Neither the common law of the employment contract nor the economic forces of the labour market have ever provided an assurance that employment decisions would be jointly taken by parties with equivalent bargaining power.

[**10**] Though they jointly pursue the aim of creating an alternative, the two parts of the Act are different in kind. The new individual rights are intended to create minimum substantive standards for employees; they are legislative rights designed to be adjudicated by tribunals. In contrast, the new "collective" rights

---

[2] For a more detailed description of the new institutions, see Chapter Eighteen.

are designed to replace unilateral managerial prerogative with decisions either by agreement between trade union representatives and management or with the views of the former taken into account before decisions are taken. The rights themselves are largely procedural in character, designed to produce a dialogue between the two parties to collective bargaining. They contain little direction as to the substantive results the parties should produce in an agreement arising out of that bargaining. As a consequence these results may vary with the relative bargaining strength of the parties. The one exception to this is that of the noticeably lower paid and weakly organised working groups. They receive the support of a statutory extension of collectively negotiated substantive terms.

[**11**] At the same time the two parts of the Act are designed to be complementary in character. The individual rights are designed to be a floor of rights not only in the sense of providing a safety net below which employees may not fall, but also a "floor" in the sense of a platform above which collective arrangements may raise standards. Thus the Act makes explicit provision in several places that where collective arrangements provide substantive terms which are more favourable, the employee may enjoy the best parts of both protections—statutory or voluntary. And where the parties to collective bargaining can provide terms which are at "least as favourable" and procedures which entail certain specified safeguards, they may if they wish obtain approval to exclude the employees covered by agreements from the particular statutory protections as an incentive to providing a voluntary procedure.

[**12**] There is a second and more subtle way in which the new collective rights complement the individual protections, that is, in the use made of the potentially stronger "remedial" powers of collective bargaining. Whatever aspirations may have been read into individual employment rights, for example, the provision of security of employment or the recognition of job property rights for employees, the actual effect of such rights has inevitably been limited by the fact that they are enforceable ultimately only by financial sanctions. Only in so far as an employer has willingly abided by the legal norm or has been prompted so to do by the financial disincentive contained within the legal sanction will an individual employment protection succeed in producing a reversal of a managerial decision once taken. Otherwise, the impact of this type of employment protection is effectively limited to the provision of a form of compensation to employees for the failure to reverse an improper managerial decision, in other words compensation for a loss of a property right or the loss of job security.

[**13**] In Britain, the legal framework has traditionally expected "free" collective bargaining, backed up by the social sanction of industrial action, to go beyond the more limited remedial possibilities of individual employment rights. In so far as the EPA introduces the use of legal means to promote the growth of collective bargaining and participation by trade union representatives in decisions taken by management, it may be viewed as adopting a new legislative strategy for employment protection. According to this new strategy, individual employment rights are to continue to be used as far as they are capable of providing protection but now legal support is offered to collective bargaining and trade unions to further these protections where it is possible to do so.

[**14**] In so far as the Act uses legal means to support employee participation

through trade unions and collective consultation it may be viewed as sowing the seeds of a new law of industrial democracy, even if the participation is concerned predominantly with managerial decisions below the level of company Boards of Directors.

[**15**] There are three features of this element in the new legal framework that give to this nascent British law of industrial democracy a rather distinctive look. First, there is the clear emphasis on participation through trade union representatives: the law is to be used essentially to support a "single channel" of participation and communication in managerial decisions rather than dual structures involving trade union representation on the one hand and employee representation on the other. Secondly, the legal obligations placed on managers are essentially procedural. The new collective rights create a range of obligations for managers which take the form of a duty to disclose, a duty to engage in prior consultation and a duty to negotiate in the sense of participating in a bargaining process. In their present form these legal requirements act essentially to prompt managers to follow certain prescribed procedures; on the whole they are not being used to affect the balance of bargaining power as long as the procedural proprieties are observed.

[**16**] Thirdly, the legal framework asks no direct *quid pro quo* of trade unions or trade unionists for the legal support in terms of a no-strike obligation: there is no statutory duty not to strike whilst the new legal machinery is being used to process industrial disputes. The intention behind this feature of the legal framework may need some clarification; it assumes that if appropriate procedures, whether legal or voluntary, can be provided by the State to deal with the causes of industrial disputes, this will effect a reduction in industrial action more successfully than laws designed simply to restrict strikes.

[**17**] In this sense, the new legal framework regards strikes essentially as symptoms of underlying disputes and the proper role for the law should be to provide machinery to deal with the underlying cause rather than attempting to repress the symptom.

[**18**] Whether British labour legislation retains any or all of these features in subsequent stages of reform ultimately depends on the results of the experiment with this type of legal framework. In more proximate terms, however, the direction of the next step and the third stage of reform of the legal framework is dependent upon the results of the report of the Bullock Committee of Enquiry on Industrial Democracy, which is unlikely to take a form that will be incompatible with the strategic thinking underlying employment protection.

PART I

INDIVIDUAL EMPLOYMENT PROTECTION

CHAPTER TWO

CONTRACTS OF EMPLOYMENT

[**19**] The Contracts of Employment Act 1972[1] makes four main contributions to the modern law of employment as well as to the law of termination. It prescribes minimum periods of notice of termination for employees which vary with the length of continuous service of employees. It clarifies the rights of employees during the period of notice.[2] It defines the elements of the concept of "continuous employment" which constitutes a qualification for most forms of statutory protections for employees including safeguards against termination. Finally the Act requires employers to provide recently hired employees with a written statement of terms and conditions of employment which may have certain implications for an employee's rights on dismissal.

[**20**] The EPA makes three important changes[3] in the Contracts of Employment Act by:

—increasing the minimum periods of notice
—easing the requirements of continuous employment which apply to almost all employment rights
—adding to the list of written particulars required be given to employees. These are discussed in Chapter Six.

INCREASED MINIMUM NOTICE OF TERMINATION

[**21**] Under the Contracts of Employment Act 1972 employees who were continuously employed for thirteen weeks were entitled to a minimum period of notice of termination regardless of any provisions for shorter notice in the

---

[1] The 1972 Act is itself a consolidation of the Contracts of Employment Act 1963 as amended by the Redundancy Payments Act 1965, together with certain amendments which were introduced by ss. 20, 21 and Sch. 2, Part II of the Industrial Relations Act 1971 and left largely unrepealed by TULRA 1974. The one provision repealed by TULRA was s. 20 (2) which required the employer to indicate to the employee the nature of his right under s. 5 of that Act.

[2] Contracts of Employment Act 1972, Sch. 1.

[3] The Act also introduces minor changes in the calculation of normal working hours and a "weeks' pay" (see ss. 85–6 and Sch. 4) and substitutes its own Sch. 5 for Sch. 2 of the Contracts of Employment Act 1972 (Rights of Employee in Period of Notice).

contract. This statutory minimum period of notice varied from one week after thirteen weeks of service to eight weeks after fifteen years' continuous service.

[**22**] Under the EPA these statutory minima are increased in two respects. Generally, one week's notice is required after only four weeks of continuous service (Sch. 16, Part II, para. 1).[4] After two year's continuous service, the minimum period of notice of termination required amounts to one week for each year of continuous employment from the end of the second year until the beginning of the twelfth year. The new minimum notice periods are:

Length of continuous service	*Minimum period of notice*
4 weeks	1 week
2 years	2 weeks
3 years	3 weeks
4 years	4 weeks
5 years	5 weeks
6 years	6 weeks
7 years	7 weeks
8 years	8 weeks
9 years	9 weeks
10 years	10 weeks
11 years	11 weeks
12 years	12 weeks

After twelve years of continuous service the minimum period of notice remains fixed at twelve weeks.

[**23**] There is no change in the statutory minimum period of notice required of employees. That remains fixed at one week.

[**24**] For most employees, the periods of notice required under the Act are an improvement upon the common law position, which tended to construe reasonable notice as increasing with job status rather than length of service. The provision of longer periods of notice for longer-serving employees does correspond to the degree of difficulty older employees experience in obtaining new employment, and this use of minimum notice periods as an adjunct of manpower policy is reinforced by the introduction of a right of employees to time off during the notice period to look for new employment or training facilities.[5]

CONTINUOUS EMPLOYMENT

[**25**] The individual employment protections that make up the statutory "floor" benefit only employees who satisfy certain qualifications. Many individual rights require that the employee must have been "continuously

---

[4] A new exception to this and the 1972 Act generally is added by the EPA to s. 9 of the 1972 Act, that is where a person is employed under twelve weeks on a contract for a specific task. See the EPA, Sch. 16, Part II, para. 10.

[5] Section 61 is discussed in Chapter Ten.

employed" for a specified period.[6] The method of determining the period for which an employee has been continuously employed is set out in Sch. 1 to the Contracts of Employment Act 1972. This schedule suggests that the statutory concept of continuous service consists of three distinct elements. First, service must remain unbroken, that is to say, continuity must be maintained. Secondly, the employee must have worked for the requisite length of time. Thirdly, the employee must have worked a certain number of hours in any week for it to be counted as a week of continuous employment.

[**26**] The EPA amends the 1972 Act in all three respects. First, in order for a week to count as a period of continuous employment, the minimum number of hours which the employee must work each week or be employed under a contract normally involving work has been reduced from twenty-one hours to sixteen hours. Moreover there are two special cases where the qualifying number of hours to be worked are further reduced. Thus, where an employee has been working under a contract normally involving sixteen hours work per week and this contractual arrangement is replaced by one normally involving eight hours work per week, the employee shall be entitled for twenty-six weeks to be treated as if he were working for sixteen hours weekly. And where an employee has been continuously employed for five years or more under a contract normally involving eight hours' employment per week, he shall be treated as if his contract normally involved sixteen hours of work per week (Sch. 16, Part II, paras. 7 and 8). Finally, these reductions in the requisite hours to be worked in a week for it to qualify as a week of continuous employment are to apply retrospectively once the provisions come into force.

[**27**] Secondly, under the EPA, any week in which an employee is absent from work wholly or partly because of pregnancy or confinement shall count as a period of employment and not break continuity of employment for a period of up to twenty-six weeks if the employee returns to work at the start of the twenty-seventh week (Sch. 16, Part II, paras. 15 and 16).

[**28**] Thirdly, if an employee returns to work after maternity leave in accordance with her rights under the Act, every week of her period of absence shall count in calculating a period of employment (Sch. 16, Part II, para. 17).

---

[6]

Employment protections	*Period of continuous employment required*
Minimum period of notice of dismissal	4 weeks*
Guarantee payments	4 weeks*
Medical suspension	4 weeks*
Written particulars of employment	13 weeks
Unfair dismissal	26 weeks†
Written reason for dismissal	26 weeks
Maternity pay	2 years
Right to return to work after maternity leave	2 years
Time off to look for work	2 years
Redundancy payment	2 years

*Except where a person is initially employed under a contract for a specific task which is expected to last for no more than 12 weeks (EPA, Sch. 16, Part II, para. 10).

†Except for dismissals for medical suspension rights (EAP, s. 29 (4)) or trade union membership activity (TULRA, Sch. 1, para. 11).

CHAPTER THREE

REDUNDANCY PAYMENTS

[**29**] Prior to 1975, there were two major legislative stages in the development of the law of redundancy: the enactment of an entitlement to a lump sum redundancy payment for employees dismissed owing to redundancy in the Redundancy Payments Act 1965, and the introduction of a right to complain of an "unfair redundancy", that is, unfair dismissal for reasons of redundancy, under Sch. 1, paras. 6 (7) and 6(8)[1] of TULRA.

[**30**] The EPA makes two types of contribution to the law of redundancy. It provides a third stage of major legislative reform by creating a statutory procedure requiring employers to notify the Government of impending collective redundancies of any consequence and to engage in prior consultation with trade union representatives concerning all and any redundancies. This reform will be discussed in Chapter Fourteen. In addition, the EPA amends the 1965 Act in three respects:

—it introduces a trial period where an employer offers alternative employment to a redundant employee

—it redefines "constructive" dismissal, making it identical to constructive dismissal under TULRA, Sch. 1

—it provides new rules to determine the "relevant date of dismissal".

THE TRIAL PERIOD

[**31**] Under the 1965 Act, subject to qualifications and exclusions, an employee who is dismissed by reason of redundancy is entitled to be paid a redundancy payment by his employer. The payment varies with "normal weekly earnings",[2] age and continuous service from a minimum of two weeks' pay to a maximum of £2,400.

[**32**] The determination of an entitlement to a redundancy payment involves four principle questions:

—was the employee eligible to present a complaint or was he precluded by the various qualifications and exclusions relating to length of service, classes of employment etc. (*e.g.* RPA, s. 16)

—was there a dismissal of the employee and if so when? (RPA, s. 3)

—was the dismissal by reason of redundancy, that is to say, was it attributable wholly or mainly to the fact that the employer's requirements for employees to carry out their work at the place where they have been employed has ceased or declined? (RPA, s. 1 (2))

[1] See, *e.g.*, *Vokes, Ltd.* v. *Bear*, [1973] I.R.L.R. 363; *Bessenden Properties, Ltd.* v. *Corness*, [1973] I.R.L.R. 365.

[2] See now EPA, Sch. 4.

—did the employer make a timely offer of suitable alternative employment and did the employee unreasonably refuse that offer (RPA, ss. 2 (3) and 2 (4)).

[**33**] Even if an employee is dismissed by reason of redundancy, he could be disentitled to a redundancy payment under that Act if his employer prior to the ending of the employment offers in writing to renew his contract of employment or re-engage him in suitable alternative employment.

[**34**] Where an employee accepts the offer of alternative employment, the 1965 Act provides that he should be treated as if he had not been dismissed. His length of service in the original employment will be "tacked on" to that in the new employment with no break in continuity for the purpose of qualification for and calculation of a future redundancy payment (RPA 1965, s. 3).

[**35**] However, if an employee is unhappy with the offer and refuses it, he must either be able to convince a tribunal that it is not suitable, that is, it is not substantially equivalent in terms to his old job,[3] or he must show that his refusal was not unreasonable, otherwise he will be disqualified from a redundancy payment.

[**36**] It need hardly be said that the subsequent testing of disentitlement creates grave risks for an employee unattracted by an offer of alternative employment. The only way he may obtain a final assessment of whether the offer is thought suitable or his refusal is deemed reasonable is by allowing himself to be dismissed and later discovering from an industrial tribunal whether redundancy compensation is payable or whether he has lost his entitlement to a redundancy payment as well as his job. The risks of a refusal of alternative employment thus often far outweigh the distaste of acceptance. The 1965 Act makes some concession to the precariousness of the employee's position by requiring the employer to disclose the main terms of the offer of proposed alternative employment in writing to the employee (s. 2 (4)),[4] and it has been held that the offer must set out with some particularity the capacity and place of employment and the other terms and conditions of employment.[5]

[**37**] It is doubtful, however, whether a mere written statement of the main terms of employment is always adequate to allow an employee to evaluate the desirability of a job. The EPA attempts to give an employee a better idea of the prospective job before compelling him to make his decision. It introduces a trial period of four weeks where the employer offers to re-engage an employee or renew his employment contract and the terms of the new contract as to the capacity and place in which he is employed, or as to the other terms and conditions of his employment differ, wholly or partly, from the provisions of the previous contract and the employee commences work under the new contract. At the same time, it removes the requirement and safeguard that the offer must be in writing.

[3] *Taylor* v. *Kent County Council*, [1969], 2 Q.B. 560; [1969] 2 All E.R. 1080, D.C.

[4] *Toolan* v. *Beck and Pollitzer Engineering, Ltd.*, [1975] I.R.L.R. 183, Q.B.D. in which it was held that a tribunal may not take account of provisions of an oral offer by the employer in deciding whether an offer of alternative employment is suitable in relation to an employee.

[5] *Marriott* v. *Oxford and District Co-operative Society, Ltd.*, [1969] 1 All E.R. 471 Q.B.D. *Maher* v. *Fram Gerrard, Ltd.*, [1974] 1 All. E.R. 449; [1974] I.C.R. 31, but see, *Kaye* v. *Cooke Finsbury, Ltd.*, [1973] 3 All E.R. 434; [1974] I.C.R. 65.

[**38**] During the trial period the employee is entitled to work in the employment offered without any risk of appearing consensually to vary his employment contract.[6] Should he decide that the alternative employment is unacceptable he may terminate the trial period with or without notice. He will then be treated as having been dismissed on the date on which his employment under the original contract ended for the reason he would have been dismissed at that time as long as the employer makes no further offer of employment (Sch. 16, Part I, para. 3 (8)). In the event, the employees' entitlement to redundancy compensation for dismissal under the original contract is still subject to the test of whether the alternative employment offered was suitable and whether the decision to terminate the contract, in effect, to refuse the offer, was reasonable (EPA, Sch. 16, Part I, para. 2 (6)). However the employee's experience during the trial period may well provide useful evidence to establish the suitability or non-suitability of the alternative job as well as the reasonableness or unreasonableness of his refusal to accept the offer. Should the employer terminate the new contract for a reason connected with the change to the new employment, the employee may qualify for a redundancy payment since in effect the offer of alternative employment has been withdrawn.[7]

[**39**] The trial period may be extended for a period longer than four weeks by agreement between employer and employee for the purpose of retraining the employee for employment in the new job,[8] as long as this agreement is in writing and specifies both the date at which the trial period will end and the terms and conditions that will apply after the end of that period.[9]

[**40**] The Act also changes the definition and timing of dismissal to take account of the trial period. Thus, where an employer makes an offer of renewal or alternative employment to a redundant employee before the ending of his employment and the job is to commence within four weeks of that date, the employee shall not be regarded as dismissed by the employer by reason of the ending of his employment under the previous contract. It should be noted that the employee shall be deemed not to have been dismissed not only during the actual trial period in the new job but also during the four-week interval that might arise between the ending of the old job and the start of the new.

[**41**] If the employee ultimately accepts the employer's offer and work begins within the requisite time period, the entire period of the interval will count as a period of employment for the purpose of compiling the employee's length of continuous employment.[10] Again, if at any time during the trial period or at its end the employee or employer terminates the contract and the employer does not make a further appropriate offer to renew or re-engage, the employee shall be treated as having been dismissed on the date *when the original contract ended*[11] for the reasons he would have been dismissed at that date.

---

[6] Cf. *Marriott* v. *Oxford and District Co-operative Society, Ltd.* (No. 2), [1970] 1 Q.B. 186; [1969] 3 All E.R. 1126 (C.A.); *Saunders* v. *Paladin Coachworks, Ltd.* (1968), 3 I.T.R. 51; *Sheet Metal Components, Ltd.* v. *Plumridge*, [1974] I.R.L.R. 86; *Shields Furniture, Ltd.* v. *Goff*, [1973] 2 All E.R. 653; [1973] I.C.R. 187.

[7] See s. 2 (8) of the amended Act.

[8] See s. 2 (6) of the amended Act.

[9] See s. 2 (7) of the amended Act.

[10] RPA 1965, s. 8 (3).

[11] This would be true even if more than one trial period had occurred because of more than one offer by the employer. (See the EPA, Sch. 16, Part I, para. 3 (8)).

[**42**] If however the employee continues to work after the end of the trial period he runs the risk of not being entitled to a redundancy payment because he has consensually varied his contract and has not been "dismissed" from his old employment.[12]

THE NEW DEFINITION OF "CONSTRUCTIVE" DISMISSAL

[**43**] In the 1965 Act the definition of dismissal includes a form of constructive dismissal or justified resignation. Under that Act an employee is "dismissed" where he terminates the contract *without notice* in response to conduct by the employer which entitled him so to terminate it. The requirement that the employee must terminate the contract without notice has been referred to as a "trap" for the unwary[13] although it was always open to an employee to argue that his notice to the employer was an "acceptance" of the employer's repudiation under s. 3 (1) (*a*).[14] Nevertheless the "trap" was omitted from the definition of dismissal in the unfair dismissal provisions of TULRA. The EPA 1975 creates consistency between the two types of employment protection by amending the definition of dismissal in the 1965 Act to allow the employee to leave either *with* or without notice in response to treatment by the employer which would entitle the employee to leave without notice.

THE RELEVANT DATE OF DISMISSAL

[**44**] The exact date upon which the employee is dismissed, that is to say the "relevant date of dismissal" for the purposes of the 1965 Act, can affect many of the issues comprising the test of dismissal by reason of redundancy. The qualification to claim, the timeliness of the claim, the timeliness of the offer of alternative employment and the calculation of the redundancy payment are all dependent upon the timing of the "relevant date of dismissal". The 1965 Act provides that the relevant date of dismissal in the case of a contract terminated by notice is the date on which the notice expires. In the case of a contract terminated without notice it is the date on which the termination takes effect. That Act is silent on the question of what the relevant date of dismissal may be where the employer fails to give the employee due notice. Judicial interpretation tended to attach some weight to the view that even though a dismissal might be a breach of contract, it none the less had the effect of terminating the contract, leaving the ex-employee a right of action for damages.[15] This interpretation however tended to allow a wide discretion to employers to determine the relevant date of dismissal and hence affect the entitlement of the employee to statutory protection.

[**45**] The EPA re-defines the "relevant date of dismissal" in the 1965 Act to ensure that it is the date upon which the contract would have expired if notice

[12] See *Marriott, Saunders, supra*. But *cf. Sheet Metal Components* v. *Plumridge*, [1974] I.R.L.R. 86.

[13] See, *e.g.*, *G.K.N. (Cwmbran), Ltd.* v. *Lloyd*, [1972] I.C.R. 214 (NIRC).

[14] See discussion of the relationship between the two sections in *Sutcliffe* v. *Hawker Siddeley Aviation, Ltd.*, [1973] I.R.L.R. 304; [1973] I.C.R. 560.

[15] See, *e.g.*, *Nightingale* v. *Biddle Bros. Builders, Ltd.* (1967), 2 I.T.R. 624. See also fuller discussion on this point in connection with effective date of termination under Sch. 1, para. 5 of TULRA in paras. 59–63.

required by the Contracts of Employment Act had been duly given by the employer, whether or not in fact the employer had given such notice.[16] Consequently, it is only where the employer dismisses without notice in circumstances in which he is contractually entitled to do so that he may advance the relevant date of dismissal.

---

[16] Schedule 16, Part I, para. 10. The interval between the new relevant dates of dismissal shall count as a period of employment for the purposes of calculating whether the employee has been continuously employed for the requisite period.

CHAPTER FOUR

UNFAIR DISMISSALS

[**46**] The EPA expands and develops the statutory protections against unfair dismissal that were introduced in the Industrial Relations Act 1971 and substantially re-enacted and modified in Sch. 1 of TULRA 1974. Under that Schedule a suitably qualified employee who is dismissed may complain to an industrial tribunal that the dismissal was unfair and if the tribunal finds the complaint well founded it may recommend the reinstatement or re-engagement of the employee if this would be practicable and in accordance with equity. Otherwise it must award compensation.

[**47**] A tribunal determination of a complaint of unfair dismissal involves four principle tests. The first two concern the preliminary requirements which are necessary for the presentation of a valid complaint of unfair dismissal.

(1) Was the employee eligible to present a complaint, or was he precluded by the various qualifications and exclusions relating to classes of employment, length of service, age, etc.?
(2) Was the employee dismissed and if so when?

If the employee's claim meets the preliminary requirements the tribunal then goes on to pose the question of the fairness of the dismissal.

(3) Was the dismissal fair or unfair, that is, has the employer satisfied the tribunal that in the circumstances he acted reasonably in treating his reasons as sufficient to justify the dismissal?

Finally if the employee has been found to be unfairly dismissed the tribunal must decide:

(4) To what remedy is the employee entitled, reinstatement, re-engagement or compensation.

[**48**] The changes to these statutory safeguards against unfair dismissal introduced by the EPA include:

(A) The introduction of a requirement that the employer must provide a dismissed employee on request with a written statement of the reasons for dismissal (s. 70).

(B) An easing of the preliminary requirements necessary for the presentation of a valid complaint by:

—reducing the categories of excluded classes of employment
—allowing employees to bring complaints during the period of notice
—re-defining the effective date of dismissal

—re-defining the employee's entitlement to serve a counter-notice to the employer.

(C) A reinforcement of the remedies for unfair dismissal by:

—strengthening the remedies of reinstatement and re-engagement
—increasing the measure of compensation
—providing a new form of interim relief for dismissals for trade union membership and activity (this is discussed in Chapter Fifteen).

(D) The introduction of new standards for the test of fairness in the special circumstances of:

—dismissals for participation in industrial action
—dismissals for pregnancy.

A. THE WRITTEN STATEMENT OF REASONS FOR DISMISSAL

[**49**] For all employees dismissed after twenty-six full weeks of continuous service, whether the dismissal was with or without notice or consisted of the expiry and non-renewal of a fixed term contract, the EPA introduces a right upon request to a written statement of particulars of the reasons for the dismissal within fourteen days of the request (s. 70). If the employer unreasonably refuses to provide a written statement or if the written particulars are inadequate or untrue, the employee may present a complaint to an industrial tribunal.[1] To meet the statutory test of adequacy, the employer's written statement will be required to go further than a classification of the dismissal under one of the statutory heads listed in TULRA, Sch. 1, para. 6 (2), that is, conduct, capability or qualifications, redundancy, etc. The employers must give particulars of the reasons, that is to say, a statement of the main factual grounds for the dismissal. Where a tribunal decides that an employee's complaint concerning the inadequacy of the written statement is well founded, it may in its discretion make a declaration as to what the employer's reasons for the dismissal were[2] as well as an award to the employee of a sum equal to the amount of two weeks' pay (s. 70 (4)).

[**50**] An award against the employer in respect of an inadequate written statement is additional to any compensation the employee might receive for unfair dismissal. However, an employee must present the complaint for the failure to provide a written statement at a time when he would be entitled to present a claim for unfair dismissal to a tribunal, that is, no later than the date of his complaint or if no complaint is made three months after the effective date of dismissal (s. 70 (5)).

[**51**] Whilst the immediate financial penalty for an inadequate written statement may be limited to two weeks' pay, a poorly prepared written statement may have more serious financial implications since the statement is "admissible in evidence", *inter alia*, in any unfair dismissal hearing (s. 70 (3)).

---

[1] The time limit for presenting the complaint is the same as that for a complaint of unfair dismissal for that dismissal (s. 70 (5).

[2] *Cf.* Contract of Employment Act 1972, s. 8.

B. WAS THE EMPLOYEE ELIGIBLE TO PRESENT A COMPLAINT?

[**52**] Under Sch. 1 of TULRA employees in certain classes of employment have been excluded from an entitlement to complain of unfair dismissal. The EPA reduces these exclusions by removing the exclusions of small firms of less than four employees and employees of close relatives other than spouses and teachers in Scotland. The EPA also explicitly provides that the death of the employee does not extinguish an employee's claim for unfair dismissal (EPA, Sch. 12, Part II).

[**53**] The excluded classes of employment that remain after the amendments of the EPA are:

—employment by spouse
—dock workers
—part-time employees (normally of less than 16 hours); see the EPA, Sch. 16, Part II, paras. 7 and 8 for exceptions.[3]
—shore fishermen
—overseas employment
—employees covered by a designated dismissal procedure agreement; see TULRA, Sch. 1, para. 13).

[**54**] The qualification of six months' continuous service and the disqualification of normal retiring age continue to apply to all dismissals other than dismissals for an inadmissible reason. As well, the exclusion on employees on fixed-term contracts of two years or more in certain circumstances continue to apply (TULRA, Sch. 1, para. 12).

[**55**] A third test of eligibility is whether the complaint was presented at the proper time. Under TULRA the complaint must be presented within three months of the date of dismissal but may not be presented before the effective date of dismissal. Thus in the case of a dismissal with notice the employee must wait until the notice period expires. The EPA expands the jurisdiction of tribunals to consider complaints by allowing an employee to present a complaint of unfair dismissal at any time after notice of dismissal has been given even though the notice period has not expired. In the event the employee in receipt of the notice of dismissal may have the case heard during the notice period and the order of reinstatement could take the form of an order to the employer to withdraw the notice of dismissal (EPA, Sch. 16, Part III, para. 21).

Dismissal with notice

[**56**] The types of dismissal that entitle an employee to complain of unfair dismissal include termination by the employer with notice, termination without notice, expiry of a fixed-term contract without renewal and constructive dismissal (TULRA, Sch. 1, para. 5). The EPA introduces two changes to the rights of employees in the event of dismissal with notice, a category of increasing importance given the lengthening periods of obligatory notice. One change affects the date on which the dismissal is deemed to occur, the other concerns the special case of the employee who serves counter-notice.

[3] See para. 26, *ante*, for a fuller discussion of the part-time employee exclusion.

Counter-notice

[**57**] Under TULRA, Sch. 1, paras. 5 (3) and 5 (4), an employee under notice of termination could serve a counter-notice of termination during the obligatory notice period in writing, leave before the notice period expires and nevertheless be deemed to have been dismissed for purposes of presenting a complaint for unfair dismissal. This statutory right to serve a counter-notice was restricted to the obligatory notice period. If an employer gave a period of notice that was longer than the statutorily required notice and the employee served his counter notice during that part of the notice period that fell prior to the obligatory period, the employee would lose the advantage of para. 5 (3) and could be held to have resigned.[4]

[**58**] The EPA changes the rules of counter-notice in two respects. An employee may serve counter-notice of termination at any time during the period of notice whether within or outside the obligatory period of notice. It is still the case, however, that any notice given must either specify the date of termination or contain material from which the date is positively ascertainable.[5] A mere warning will not be adequate. Secondly, however, the Act deletes the requirement that the counter-notice be in writing. This removes a potential technical disqualification which might occur under the TULRA if the employee gave a purely oral counter-notice.[6]

The effective date of dismissal with notice

[**59**] An important element in determining an employee's right in a complaint of unfair dismissal is the exact date on which the employee is dismissed, that is, the "effective date of dismissal". This date is applicable in determining the employee's length of continuous service. It also is relevant for the purpose of deciding whether he meets the qualifying period for a complaint (TULRA, Sch. 1, para. 10) or calculating a basic award of compensation (EPA, ss. 74 (3) and 75 (6)). As well, the date helps to define the time when an employee is entitled to a written statement of reasons and whether an employee's claim is presented within the three-month time limit. It was somewhat surprising therefore that the definition under the 1974 Act of the effective date of dismissal for dismissals with notice contained a major ambiguity. That Act defines the effective date of dismissal in a case where the employee was dismissed with notice as the date on which the notice expired.[7] It also states that where an employee is dismissed without notice, the effective date of termination is the date on which the termination takes effect. It is silent on the question of what the effective date of dismissal may be when an employee has been dismissed without due notice.

[**60**] This statutory language has been interpreted to allow the timing of the effective date of dismissal to be determined by the action of the employer in ending the employment prematurely rather than by the employee's statutory entitlement to notice. As long as the employer gave a clear notification that

---

[4] See, *e.g.*, *Oldham & Son, Ltd.* v. *Heyd-Smith* (1973), 16 K.I.R. 177.
[5] *Cf. Morton Sundour Fabrics, Ltd.* v. *Shaw* (1967), 2 I.T.R. 84.
[6] *Cf. Meger* v. *Green's Food Fare, Ltd.* (1966), 1 I.T.R. 244.
[7] This was held to apply to a notice period that "straddled" a qualification date. See *Brindle* v. *H. W. Smith (Cabinets), Ltd.*, [1973] 1 All E.R. 230; [1972] I.R.L.R. 125.

the contract should terminate on a particular day, that notified day has been held to be the effective date of termination even if the employer's premature termination of the contract was wrongful.[8]

[**61**] Under the 1974 Act if an employer dismissed an employee without notice when he should have given notice or dismissed him with less notice than the amount to which he was entitled, the effective date of dismissal was the date when the employment actually ceased not the date when notice would have expired if properly given. The timing of the effective date of dismissal was not affected by the fact that the employee could recover damages for breach of contract. Nor was it affected by the fact that the employer paid wages in lieu of notice, since these were viewed as damages for breach of contract.[9]

[**62**] The EPA redefines the effective date of dismissal to ensure that in a case where notice is required to be given to the employee under the Contracts of Employment Act 1972 (as amended) the date at which that notice would expire if duly given is the effective date of dismissal regardless of whether the employment was terminated by the employer without notice or without proper notice[10] (Sch. 16, Part III, para. 10).

[**63**] Consequently it is only where the employer is contractually entitled to dismiss without notice that the effective date of dismissal will be the date when employment actually ceases for the purpose of determining the employee's statutory entitlements in a complaint of unfair dismissal.

C. THE NEW REMEDIES FOR UNFAIR DISMISSAL

[**64**] Under Sch. 1 of TULRA 1974, employees who were found by industrial tribunals to have been unfairly dismissed were entitled to a recommendation of reinstatement or of re-engagement if this was practicable and in accordance with equity. Otherwise the tribunal was required to award compensation for loss of earnings and other benefits up to a maximum of two years' pay or £5,200, whichever is the less. The EPA introduces new measures which strengthen the remedy of reinstatement and increase the measure of compensation for unfair dismissal. It also introduces a new type of interim relief for the dismissed employee in the special case of a dismissal for alleged trade union membership or activity.

The new remedy of reinstatement

[**65**] Under the EPA the remedies of reinstatement and re-engagement have been altered in three respects.

—The remedy that will issue from the tribunal will take the form of an order of reinstatement or re-engagement rather than a recommenda-

[8] *British Building and Engineering Appliances* v. *Dedman*, [1973] I.C.R. 82; *affirmed*, [1974] 1 All E.R. 520; [1973] I.R.L.R. 379; *Cf. Lees* v. *Arthur Greaves (Lees), Ltd.*, [1974] 2 All E.R. 393; [1974] I.R.L.R. 93 in which an employee was merely told to leave and this was interpreted to mean that he was still employed but no longer required to work.

[9] See *Dedman supra*; *Lees supra*; see also *Hackwood* v. *Benross Trading Co., Ltd.*, [1975] I.R.L.R. 2.

[10] This redefinition may not affect the effective date of dismissal in the rare instance where the employment is terminated by "mutual agreement" *Lees* v. *Arthur Greaves (Lees), Ltd.*, [1974] 2 All E.R. 383; [1974] I.R.L.R. 93.

tion for re-engagement or reinstatement. That this is more than merely a change in form is ensured by two other accompanying changes.

—A new set of statutory provisions have been added to "guide" the tribunals in the exercise of their discretion in awarding reinstatement and re-engagement.

—The penalty for non-compliance with a tribunal order, although continuing to take the form of a financial award that is "additional" to compensation, is greater than the previous penalties for non-compliance with a tribunal recommendation.

The new guidelines for tribunal discretion in respect of remedies

[**66**] Under TULRA, Sch. 1, the two main issues which a tribunal had to determine before making a recommendation of reinstatement or re-engagement were the practicability and the fairness of making such a recommendation. In practice in most cases this involved the tribunal in an investigation of the employer's and the employee's views as to the desired remedy as well as some attempt to determine whether the job was still vacant and whether any suitable alternative jobs were vacant or were likely to become vacant. However, the tribunals were not consistent in their approach to these issues. Some probed far more deeply than others to determine the practicabilities of securing re-employment for the unfairly dismissed employee. As well, the remedies of reinstatement or re-engagement were surprisingly rarely applied in tribunal hearings. The percentage of all unfairly dismissed employees who received recommendations of re-employment has remained about 5 per cent during the 1971–75 period.

[**67**] The EPA quite unambiguously indicates that re-employment in some form is the preferred remedy for unfair dismissal. It provides that where a complaint of unfair dismissal is well founded an industrial tribunal must first consider whether the employee is entitled to a reinstatement order and if it decides not to make such an order it must next consider whether to make an order for re-engagement (EPA, s. 71 (6) and (7)).

[**68**] An order of reinstatement is defined as an order that the employer restore the employee to his former position treating him in all respects as if he had never been dismissed. This would include arrears of pay, any rights or privileges including seniority and pension rights and improvements in terms and conditions of employment that would have benefited the employee had he not been dismissed. An order of re-engagement can consist of an order to the same employer, his successor or any associated employer to take the employee back on the same job or other suitable employment. The tribunal has discretion to specify the terms upon which the employee is to be re-engaged including arrears of pay for the interim period and any right which must be restored to the employee.

[**69**] The Act introduces three specific considerations which a tribunal must take into account when determining whether to make an order for either reinstatement or re-engagement:

—the wishes of the employee must be given weight in the determination of the appropriate remedy

—the impracticability of an employer to comply with an order for reinstatement must be determined under new assumptions where the employer claims that the employee has been permanently replaced
—the determination of the fairness of an order must include a consideration off whether the employee caused or contributed to some extent to the dismissal (EPA, s. 71 (3)–(5)).

The wishes of the employee

[**70**] Once an industrial tribunal finds an employee to be unfairly dismissed, it must give the individual an explanation of the possible orders of reinstatement or re-engagement that may be made in his case and ask him if he wishes such an order to be made. Only if the employee expresses a wish for the tribunal to make a particular order is the tribunal empowered to exercise a discretion to do so (EPA, s. 71 (1)).

Practicability of compliance by the employer

[**71**] In cases where the employer claims that reinstatement is impracticable because the employee has been permanently replaced by another, the tribunal may not take this fact into account unless the employer shows the impracticability of a temporary replacement or that a reasonable period of time had elapsed after the dismissal without word from the employee that he wished to be reinstated and that it was no longer reasonable to re-arrange the work (EPA, s. 71 (8)).

Contributory fault and re-employment orders

[**72**] Where the employee has caused or contributed to the dismissal the tribunal must consider whether it is just to order reinstatement or re-engagement and if so on what terms. However, where a tribunal takes into account contributory fault and orders re-engagement rather than reinstatement it must do so on terms which so far as reasonably practicable are as favourable as reinstatement (EPA, s. 71 (6) (*c*) and (7) (*c*)).

[**73**] This requirement appears to preclude a tribunal from ordering re-engagement on terms which include a loss of arrears of pay. It thus prompts the tribunal to use a finding of contributory fault either to order the re-engagement of the employee in another job rather than his reinstatement in the same job or to refuse altogether to give him a remedy of re-employment in one form or another. However, in the case of an order of either reinstatement or re-engagement, back pay may be reduced by any amounts the employee has earned in employment or received in social security or other benefits.

Penalties for non-compliance

[**74**] Although the remedies of reinstatement and re-engagement take the form of orders, the penalty for a failure or refusal to comply with such orders continues to consist of an award of compensation that is additional to the normal award of compensation for unfair dismissal.

[**75**] Where the employer complies in part with the tribunal's order, the tribunal may make an award of compensation having regard to the loss sustained by the employee as a consequence of the employer's failure fully to comply with the terms of the order. The amount of compensation under this head may not exceed £5,200 (TULRA, Sch. 1, para. 20 (1) as amended by the EPA, Sch. 16, Part III, para. 17).

[**76**] Where the employer's non-compliance extends to a failure to reinstate or re-engage on any terms, the tribunal may award compensation in the form of an additional award over and above the other elements of compensation. The additional award is a form of exemplary damages and consists of either an award of from thirteen to twenty-six weeks' pay in most cases or an award of from twenty-six weeks to fifty-two weeks' pay in cases of dismissal involving trade union membership or activities, racial discrimination or sex discrimination (EPA, s. 72 (2) and (3)).

[**77**] Where the tribunal has made an order of reinstatement or re-engagement and the employer does not comply, the tribunal may not make an additional award if the employer satisfies it that it was not practicable to comply with the order (s. 72 (2) (*b*)). However, where the employer's claim of impracticability is based upon his engagement of a permanent replacement, the tribunal must ignore the claim unless the employer can show that it was not practicable for him to have the employee's work done by a temporary replacement or other temporary arrangement (s. 72 (4)).

[**78**] Finally, where an employee has expressed a wish to be reinstated or re-engaged and this is communicated to the employer within seven days of the hearing the tribunal can require the employer to pay the costs and expenses of any adjournment or postponement of the hearing caused by his failure without special reason to give evidence of the availability or unavailability of the job from which employee was dismissed or of comparable or suitable employment (Sch. 16, Part III, para. 19).

Compensation: the basic award and compensatory award

[**79**] Where the tribunal makes a finding of unfair dismissal and makes no order of reinstatement or re-engagement it must make an award of compensation to be paid by the employer to the employee. The measure of compensation has been changed to include a new basic award and modifications have been introduced to the compensatory award for loss of earnings and other benefits.

[**80**] The new basic award is itself a combination of two award elements; a minimum award of two weeks' pay in all cases of unfair dismissal; and an award to compensate for loss of accumulated entitlement to statutory protection against loss of employment. Thus the basic award is calculated as an equivalent to an employee's full entitlement to a statutory redundancy payment. Under the present statutory rules this could amount to a maximum of £2,400 over and above any compensatory award. The basic award can be reduced (but not below the minimum award of two weeks' pay) by any proportion which the tribunal considers just and equitable having regard to the extent the dismissal was caused or contributed to by the employee. Moreover, the basic award could be reduced by the amount of any redundancy payment received by the employee from the employer either under a tribunal award or otherwise.

[**81**] The compensatory award consists of an amount representing the loss sustained by the employee in consequence of the dismissal and including expenses as well as loss of expected benefits. It is based on the measure of compensation for unfair dismissal under TULRA Sch. 1, para. 19, with certain minor modifications made to take into account the introduction of the basic award. In particular, any loss of entitlement to redundancy payment must be excluded from the calculation of loss of expected benefit except where the amount of such loss would exceed the basic award (s. 76 (3)). This could occur for example where a contractual redundancy scheme provided a payment in excess of the amount due under the 1965 Act. In calculating this expected loss, no amount is to be added to compensate for a deduction from the basic award owing to the contributory fault of the employee (s. 76 (3)). Moreover, where the employer has actually made a redundancy payment in excess of the basic award entitlement, that excess goes to reduce the compensatory award (s. 76 (3)). In determining how far the loss sustained by the dismissed employee was due to the employer, no account may be taken of an industrial pressure to which he may have been subjected (s. 76 (5)).

[**82**] The common law concept of mitigation of loss continues to apply in the calculation of the compensatory award (s. 76 (4)). The EPA adds the possibility of further reductions where the employee has unreasonably precluded an order of reinstatement or re-engagement being complied with (s. 76 (6)). As well, where an employee has obtained compensation for the dismissal under the Sex Discrimination Act 1975, that amount goes to reduce compensation for unfair dismissal (s. 77 (1)).

[**83**] The maximum amount of a compensatory award taken together with compensation under s. 76 (1) is £5,200 (TULRA, Sch. 1, para. 20 (1), as amended by the EPA, Sch. 16, Part III, para. 17). Both the additional award and the basic award have their own maxima. Before a tribunal may apply the maximum limit to a complainant who has suffered actual financial loss in excess of that figure it is required first to make any proportionate deductions for contributory fault (s. 76 (6) or any deduction for payments made by the employer (s. 75 (8)) from the actual financial loss suffered and then apply the statutory maximum as a limit to the award of compensation (EPA, Sch. 16, Part III, para. 7).

D. INDUSTRIAL ACTION: THE NEW PROTECTION FOR EMPLOYEES

[**84**] TULRA contained special provisions for deciding the fairness or unfairness of employees dismissed for participating in strikes or other industrial action (TULRA, Sch. 1, para. 8) or not offered re-engagement after a lockout (TULRA, Sch. 1, para. 7).

[**85**] These provisions had two purposes. In general where an employer dismissed the entire group of employees who participated in the industrial action or refused to offer re-engagement to any of them after a lockout, the tribunal was not to decide whether the employer's action was a fair or unfair industrial sanction. Secondly, however, where an employer acted selectively, either by choosing only some of the striking employees for dismissal or by refusing to re-engage some of the employees after a strike or lockout, and his action was

prompted by reasons which were "inadmissible", the employee could be deemed to be unfairly dismissed.

[**86**] The EPA amends these provisions in two respects. It helps to clarify the first purpose by spelling out that in general the tribunal shall not determine the fairness or unfairness of certain of the industrial sanctions applied by an employer including a lockout even though it might involve breach of contracts, a dismissal of all employees taking part in a strike or other industrial action, or a refusal to offer re-engagement to all employees after a lockout or strike.

[**87**] In such cases the employer's action is not to be regarded as fair or unfair; the tribunal's jurisdiction is simply withdrawn (EPA, Sch. 16, Part III, para. 13). Certain limits to this withdrawal of jurisdiction remain in the case of a strike. The dismissal must occur in response to the employee taking part in industrial action—if he has ceased taking part in the action,[11] and possibly if he has only threatened to take industrial action, the fairness of the dismissal could be tested by a tribunal under TULRA, Sch. 1, para. 17.

[**88**] Secondly and most importantly, it provides that where an employer exercises industrial sanctions selectively—whether by dismissing fewer than all of the employees who were participating in an industrial action or by offering re-engagement after a strike or lockout to fewer than all the relevant employees —the tribunal must determine the fairness of the employer's sanction, whether or not the employer was motivated by trade union activities or another inadmissible reason.

[**89**] The Act thus establishes the principle that *all* cases of selective dismissal or non-re-engagement for participation in industrial action can be heard by an industrial tribunal, whether or not that dismissal was for an "inadmissible" reason. However, it leaves open to industrial tribunals what criteria to use to determine when discrimination or selectivity is fair or unfair.

Dismissal for pregnancy

[**90**] Where a pregnant employee is dismissed partly or wholly owing to or in connection with her pregnancy, the Act introduces a special test of the fairness of the dismissal. There are two elements in this special test. First, the employee will be treated as having been unfairly dismissed under Sch. 1, of TULRA unless she has been dismissed for one of the following specified reasons:

(*a*) that she was incapable of adequately doing her job;
(*b*) that she could not continue to work without contravening a statutory duty or restriction (s. 34 (1)).

[**91**] Secondly, even if she is dismissed for one of the specified reasons, where a suitable alternative vacancy exists in the employing company, the employer must offer her the vacancy or the employee will be treated as unfairly dismissed under Sch. 1, of TULRA (s. 34 (2)).

[**92**] Finally, there appears to be nothing in the language of these sections to preclude a residual test of "reasonableness in the circumstances" under the

[11] See, *e.g.*, *Heath* v. *J. F. Longman* (*Meat Salesmen*), *Ltd.*, [1973] 2 All E.R. 1228; [1973] I.R.L.R. 214; *cf. Seed* v. *Crowther* (*Dyers*), *Ltd.*, [1973] I.R.L.R. 199.

general test of fairness in TULRA, Sch. 1, para. 6 (8), as long as an employee has the requisite length of continuous service to be qualified under that paragraph.

Dismissal for incapability

[**93**] An employer may dismiss a pregnant employee if she is incapable of adequately doing the work she was employed to do or at the effective date of termination she will become so incapable (s. 34 (1) (*a*)). However, the onus is on the employer to show that the incapability of the pregnant employee was sufficient to warrant dismissal (*cf.* TULRA, Sch. 1, para. 6 (8)).

Dismissal for contravention of a statutory restriction

[**94**] An employer may dismiss a pregnant employee where because of her pregnancy she cannot or will not be able to work without contravention of a statutory duty or restriction (s. 34 (1) (*b*)). In addition to any other specific restrictions relating to pregnant women, the duties imposed on employers by the Health and Safety at Work etc. Act 1974 would be applicable, in particular, the employer's general duty to ensure the health, safety and welfare at work of all his employees (HSWA, s. 2 (1)).

An offer of suitable alternative employment

[**95**] In addition, even if a pregnant woman has become incapable of adequately performing her work or precluded by a statutory restriction from continuing to work, her dismissal will be treated as unfair if a suitable alternative job was available in the firm and the employer failed to make an offer of that job in accordance with the following requirements:

—the offer to re-engage the employee must be made on or before the effective date of termination (s. 24 (2))
—the new contract of employment offered must take effect immediately on the ending of employment under the previous contract (s. 34 (3) (*a*))
—the work offered under the new contract must be suitable in relation to the employee and appropriate for her to do in the circumstances (s. 34 (3) (*b*))
—the provisions of the new contract must be not substantially less favourable than corresponding provisions of her previous employment. This would apply to the provisions as to capacity and place in which she is employed as well as to the other terms and conditions of employment (s. 34 (3) (*c*)).

[**96**] It is to be noted that the test of suitability and appropriateness are to be applied taking into account the "circumstances of the employee". Presumably this would include not only the fact of pregnancy but also, where it is the case, that the offer of alternative employment is not meant to be a permanent change of employment. This is reflected in the test of the terms of alternative

employment. Unlike the test under the Redundancy Payments Act which concerns a more permanent change of employment, the test for the terms of suitable alternative employment for a pregnant employee is whether they are not substantially less favourable. This test presupposes the possibility of some decline in basic terms and conditions such as status or pay.

[**97**] The potentially wider field of suitable alternative employment for pregnant employees is a two-edged sword. It increases the possibility that the employer may find alternative work but at the same time it increases the possible number of jobs of which it may later be said that a suitable alternative vacancy existed in the firm. The point is particularly apposite since the Act places on the employer the onus of proving not only that an offer of alternative employment complied with the requirements listed above but also that in the event of no offer there was no suitable vacancy for the employee (s. 34 (4)).[12]

[**98**] To allow the employer some scope for his investigations, the pregnant employee dismissed with notice has no right to serve a counter-notice to the employer to terminate employment during the notice period (s. 34 (5)).

[**99**] An exclusion of the right to complain of unfair dismissal for pregnancy contained in a fixed-term contract of two years which is signed before the commencement of s. 34 will apply to an employee treated as unfairly dismissed under that section (s. 34 (6)). However, the exclusion of rights not to be unfairly dismissed that might otherwise apply if a designated dismissal procedure agreement is in force does not apply (s. 34 (7)).

---

[12] This rather unusually places a burden on the employer of proving a negative. In practice it might well come down to a requirement that the employer show the steps he took to investigate the possibilities of suitable alternative vacancies in the firm.

CHAPTER FIVE

RIGHTS ON INSOLVENCY

[**100**] The statutory rights enjoyed by employees are enforceable largely by means of an action against the employer. When an employer becomes insolvent, a statutory entitlement may have no more enhanced status than that of a debt of the insolvent employer. To avoid this potential debasement of statutory remedies, the Act provides two types of protections for the employee of the insolvent employer. First any amounts owed by an employer in respect of guaranteed payments, pay for medical suspension, payment for time off or pay under a protective award shall be treated as wages payable by the employer and thus receive priority over other debts in a claim against the remaining assests of the firm[1] (s. 63).

[**101**] Secondly, the Act provides that the Redundancy Fund may pay an employee where his employer has become insolvent and is unable to pay debts owing in respect of arrears of pay up to a maximum of eight weeks, pay owing for a notice period, holiday pay of up to six weeks, a basic award of compensation for dismissal or fees or premiums paid in by an apprentice or an articled clerk (s. 64). The Redundancy Fund may also be used to pay unpaid contributions by the employer into the resources of an occupational pension scheme (s. 65).

[**102**] The total amount that is payable by the Redundancy Fund in respect of any of these debts is subject to a maximum of £80 for any one complete week. In the case of unpaid contributions to occupational pension scheme, the maximum amount is the amount contributed by the employee to the pension scheme during the twelve months prior to the insolvency.

[**103**] To obtain a payment from the Redundancy Fund the employee must make an application in writing to the Secretary of State for Employment. Where an officer is required to be appointed in connection with the employer's insolvency such as a trustee in bankruptcy, a liquidator, receiver or manager or a trustee under a composition agreement, trust deed or other arrangement between the employer and his creditors, the Secretary of State may not make a payment until he has obtained a statement from the officer of the amount of the pay owing or a period of six months has elapsed from the receipt of the application.

[**104**] If the Secretary of State has failed to make a payment from the Redundancy Fund to which the employee is entitled he may bring a complaint to an industrial tribunal normally within three months of the date of the Secretary of State's decision was communicated to him or within such further period as the tribunal considers reasonably practicable. If the complaint is well founded

---

[1] In their new status as wages payable by the employer, these debts would enjoy a priority claim over all other debts of the firm including repayment of debentures and floating charges. However, they would be subject to a maximum of £200 for each claimant and limited to debts which had accrued in the four weeks prior to the insolvency.

the tribunal must make a declaration to that effect and indicate the amount of the payment which the Secretary of State ought to make.

[**105**] If the Secretary of State makes a payment from the Redundancy Fund either directly in response to an application by the employee or in response to a declaration by an industrial tribunal he is subrogated to any of the rights and remedies of the employee for the purpose of recovering such sums to be paid into the Redundancy Fund (s. 67).

CHAPTER SIX

NEW RIGHTS TO INFORMATION

[**106**] The Act takes a few small steps forward in the area of providing employees with more information about their employment and employment rights by:

—adding to the list of written particulars required to be given to recently hired employees or to employees whose terms and conditions have been changed (Sch. 16, Part II, paras. 4 and 5)
—giving employees a right to an itemised pay statement (ss. 81–84)
—giving employees a right to a written statement of reasons for dismissal (discussed in Chapter Four).

THE NEW WRITTEN PARTICULARS

[**107**] The Contracts of Employment Act 1972 requires employers to provide particulars in writing to employees of the more important terms of the contract. An employer usually provides the specified information in a written contract (CEA, s. 6). Alternatively, he may leave the contract of employment unwritten in which case he must provide the employee with a written statement not later than thirteen weeks after the start of the employment which either contains a list of certain specified terms and conditions (CEA, s. 4 (1)) or refers the employee to some other reasonably accessible document which contains all or any of the specified terms (CEA, s. 4 (5)). The employer must specify the terms applicable as at the specified date not more than one week prior to the date the statement is given. Moreover, should there be any subsequent change in such terms, the employer must similiarly notify the employee within one month of the change (s. 5).

The EPA adds four new requirements to the information which the employer is obliged to give to the employee, whatever the chosen form of communciation. First, in addition to identifying the parties and giving employees the date when the employment began the employer must now state whether any employment with a previous employer counts as part of the employee's continuous period of employment with him and if so specifying the date on which the continuous period of employment began (EPA, Sch. 16, Part II, para. 4 (*a*)).

[**108**] Secondly, in addition to giving written particulars of the terms of employment in respect of the rate and terms of remuneration, hours of work, holidays and holiday pay, sickness and sick pay, pensions and minimum periods of notice, the employer must now set out the title of the job which the employee is employed to do (EPA, Sch. 16, Part II, para. 4 (*b*)).

[**109**] Thirdly, the requirement that the employer must include a note

within the written statement specifying elements of a grievance procedure has been expanded to include the specification of any disciplinary rules applicable to the employee or the reference of the employee to an accessible document which specifies such rules. As well, the note must specify a person to whom the employee can apply if dissatisfied with any disciplinary decision relating to him, the manner which such application should be made and any further steps to the disciplinary procedure if any. The note referring to disciplinary rules, grievance procedures and disciplinary procedures is not required to include any rules, disciplinary decisions, grievance or procedures relating to health and safety at work (EPA, Sch. 16, Part II, paras. 5 and 6).

[**110**] In its origin the written statement was designed primarily to enable employees to know more about their contractual rights. If an employer provides no written statement or omits a required particular an employee may complain to an industrial tribunal which has the power to determine what the particulars ought to be. Similarly if there is a dispute as to the correctness of the particulars, either the employee or the employer may refer the matter to the tribunal. The tribunals have been given no powers to enforce their determinations. This has been left to the ordinary courts.

[**111**] Whilst the original intent of the legislation may have been to improve the employee's knowledge of the terms of the contract, the actual effect of the requirement of a written statement has also been to provide an important source of evidence of contractual terms in subsequent employment disputes. The terms contained in the written statement may be shown by other evidence to be an incorrect statement of the actual terms.[1] However, in one Court of Appeal decision *Gascol Conversions, Ltd.* v. *Mercer* [1974] I.R.L.R. 155, [1974] I.C.R. 420, the contents of a written statement for which the employee signed a receipt was held to constitute the "sole evidence that is permissible of the contract and its terms".

[**112**] The new terms required in the written statement may therefore have certain contractual implications. For example, the job title specified in the written statement will have some evidentiary weight in any subsequent attempt to define the nature of the work the employee is required to perform under the contract for the purposes of deciding whether an employee has been "constructively dismissed" and other issues in a complaint of unfair dismissal or claim for a redundancy payment.[2] As well the specification of "any disciplinary rules" may help to define the contractual entitlement of employers to dismiss employees without notice for gross misconduct. However, whilst the contents of the written statement may help to define the contractual position in respect of termination without notice, the statutory test of unfair dismissal without notice must include a test of the reasonableness of the disciplinary rule,

---

[1] See, *e.g.*, *Parkes Classic Confectionery, Ltd.* v. *Ashcroft* (1973), 8 I.T.R. 43 (Div. C4). Section 109 of the EPA provides a power by Ministerial order to confer jurisdiction on industrial tribunals in respect of *inter alia* damages for breach of contract of employment. However, until this power is exercised the present dual system of enforcement continues to apply.

[2] Naturally other terms of the contract will also be relevant to define the work required performed, the status and the place. For example, "flexibility" or "mobility" clauses may be particularly influential, see *e.g.*, *United Kingdom Atomic Energy Authority* v. *Claydon*, [1974] I.R.L.R. 6; *Sutcliffe* v. *Hawker Siddeley Aviation, Ltd.*, [1973], I.R.L.R. 304.

whatever its contractual status.[3] It remains to be seen whether a failure to specify disciplinary rules will affect the fairness of a dismissal in a complaint of unfair dismissal. The absence of a relevant disciplinary rule in the written statement may possibly be "cured" by a carefully worded warning to the employee in the case of a termination with notice. However, the omission of a relevant disciplinary rule might affect the fairness of a termination without notice unless the employer can show that an employee should otherwise have known that his action amounted to gross misconduct.

[113] Finally, the requirement placed upon the employer to indicate to employees whether their period of continuous service includes a period with a previous employer is likely to affect subsequent claims under various statutory enactments. A representation in the written particulars that service with a previous employer counts as part of the employee's continuous service in his new employment could give rise to an estoppel which would prevent the employer from denying that representation in any claim for statutory protections which control rights and liabilities purely between employer and employee, such as entitlement to minimum periods of notice, length of service, qualification for unfair dismissal as well as a claim by the employee for a redundancy payment, despite the possible complication that the Redundancy Fund might be regarded as a third party.[4] Moreover, the employee might be entitled to damages for the misrepresentation.[5]

THE RIGHT TO AN ITEMISED PAY STATEMENT

[114] The Act gives to all employees a right to an itemised pay statement in writing at the same time as or before he is paid. The statement must contain the following particulars:

(*a*) the gross or total amount of wages or salary;
(*b*) the amount of any variable deductions;
(*c*) the amount of any fixed deductions unless a standing statement in writing of fixed deductions has been separately provided in accordance with the Act,[6] in which case a statement of aggregate fixed deductions will be sufficient;
(*d*) the net amount of wages or salary payable;
(*e*) where different parts of the net amount are paid in different ways, then the amount of and method of payment of each part-payment must also be stated.

[115] Where an employer fails to provide a pay statement as required, an employee may require a reference to industrial tribunal to determine what particulars ought to have been included in the itemised pay statement (s. 84). And where a question arises as to the particulars which ought to have been

[3] See, *e.g.*, *Jones* v. *London Co-operative Society, Ltd.*, [1975] I.R.L.R. 110.
[4] See, *e.g.*, *Evenden* v. *Guildford City Association Football Club, Ltd.*, [1975] Q.B. 917; [1975] 3 All E.R. 269; [1975] I.R.L.R. 213.
[5] *Ibid.*
[6] That is issued at intervals of not more than 12 months (s. 82 (3) and (4)) and counting the amount of each deduction, the intervals for deductions and the purpose for each deduction (s. 82 (1)).

included, but not simply the accuracy of a stated amount, the question may be referred for determination by an industrial tribunal by either employer or employee (s. 84 (2) and (3)). Any reference must relate to an employment which has not ceased more than three months prior to the date the application is made (s. 84 (4)).

[**116**] Where the tribunal finds that an employer has failed to give an employee a pay statement or that the pay statement is deficient the tribunal must make a statement to that effect and in the case where the employer has made unnotified deductions from the employee's pay during the thirteen weeks prior to the date of the application the tribunal may order the employer to pay the employee a sum up to the aggregate of the unnotified deductions made during that period (s. 84 (5)). The amount of unnotified deductions for which compensation could be given would include any fixed deductions for which the employer had given the employee no notice in a pay statement or in an effective standing statement.

CHAPTER SEVEN

GUARANTEE PAYMENTS

[**117**] At common law the duty of the employer to pay remuneration in exchange for the employee's willingness and ability to work is thought to constitute the core of his obligation in the employment relationship as long as the contract continues.[1] The duty to pay extends into the notice period even to the point of requiring the employer to provide work so as to allow piece workers to earn their normal remuneration[2] and ceases only when the contract is terminated by dismissal, resignation or frustration.

[**118**] However, where the employer fails to provide work for the employee for a limited period during the continuance of the employment relationship, the duty to pay wages may sometimes be excluded expressly or by implication of either custom or practice.[3] It may also be reduced by an implied term where the cause of the failure to provide work is beyond the control of the employer.[4] The uncertainty of the legal position for many hourly-paid employees has given rise to collective "guaranteed week" agreements and "shift completion payment" agreements which are often incorporated within individual contracts of employment.

[**119**] The EPA introduces a statutory right to a guaranteed payment for workless days (s. 22) designed to operate alongside existing contractual guaranteed pay arrangements unless the latter have qualified under an exemption order (s. 28).

[**120**] Under the Act, with some exceptions, an employee is entitled to a guarantee payment for any day on which he could normally be contractually required to work and the employer fails to provide work throughout that day. This payment is subject to a maximum of £6 in respect of any one day and a maximum of five days in any "relevant" three-month period, that is to say, any period between 1 Febuary, 1 May, 1 August and 1 November in each year.

[**121**] The employer's obligation to pay a guarantee payment is defined quite widely in terms of the reason for a failure to provide work. An employee has a right to a guarantee payment where he is laid off owing to a reduction in the firm's manpower requirements or to "any other occurrence" that affects his normal working (s. 22 (1)) which would include some causes beyond the control

---

[1] The failure to pay wages over an extended period could entitle the employee to treat the contract as repudiated. *Duckworth* v. *P. F. Farnish & Co., Ltd.* (1970), 5 I.T.R. 17.

[2] *Devonald* v. *Rosser & Sons.*, [1906] K.B. 728.

[3] *Ibid.* The attempt to prove custom failed upon the strict test of *Sagar* v. *H. Ridehalgh & Son, Ltd.*, [1931] 1 Ch. 310. However, this would not preclude an argument based on a term implied by practice, *e.g.*, *Marshall* v. *English Electric Co., Ltd.*, [1945] 1 All E.R. 653.

[4] *Browning* v. *Crumlin Valley Collieries, Ltd.*, [1926] 1 K.B. 522.

of the employer, such as an interruption in the supply of fuel or power. The only cause for a workless day that excludes the employee's entitlement to a guarantee payment is a trade dispute[5] involving another employee of the employer or an associated employer[6] (s. 23 (1)).

[**122**] To qualify for a guarantee payment the employee must have been continuously employed for four weeks (s. 22 (3)). To avoid disentitlement the employee must not unreasonably refuse to perform suitable alternative work provided by the employer on that day.

[**123**] Suitable alternative work could include work which the employee is not employed under the contract to perform and indeed any work which is suitable in all the circumstances (s. 23 (2) (*a*)).[7] Moreover, the employee could lose his entitlement to a guarantee payment if he does not comply with the reasonable requirements which his employer imposes to ensure that his "services are available" (s. 23 (2) (*b*)).

[**124**] It should be noted that the guarantee payment is payable only on a day where the employer has failed to provide work "throughout the day". Thus, an employee would be entitled to a payment on a day where he has been laid off, that is, not provided with work which is necessary to his entitlement to any remuneration under the contract.[8] This entitlement would extend to a day on which the employee would normally be working short-time, if no work were provided throughout the day.[9] However, where an employee begins work on any day and is sent home before the end of a shift, his entitlement to a guarantee payment would be precluded.

[**125**] The calculation of the guarantee payment has two elements: the calculation of the statutory entitlement and the reconciliation of this entitlement with contractual remuneration. The statutory entitlement is calculated by ascertaining the employee's "guaranteed hourly rate" and muliplying it by the number of the employee's "normal working hours" for that day.

[**126**] Where the employee has the same number of normal working hours each week the "guaranteed hourly rate" is the hourly rate of pay for the employee, that is, one week's pay, divided by the normal working hours in a week, but where the number of normal working hours differ from week to week an average or "fair" hourly rate must be calculated (s. 24 (2)). The employee's "normal working hours" is defined as the number of hours "fixed" by the employment contract and will include overtime only if the overtime is itself a minimum number of hours fixed by the contract, that is to say, a "bilateral obligation", the employer to provide it, as well as the employee to work it (Sch. 4).[10]

[**127**] The statutory entitlement constitutes a minimum right upon which contract and collective agreement may improve. Any contractual remuneration paid or payable (s. 26 (3)) by the employer to an employee for a workless day

---

[5] Trade dispute is defined in TULRA 1974, s. 29 (1).

[6] Associated employer is defined in TULRA 1974, s. 30 (5).

[7] This test is sufficiently wide to apply to work which might otherwise be viewed as unsuitable under the test of s. 2 (4) of the Redundancy Payments Act 1965.

[8] See Redundancy Payments Act 1965, s. 5.

[9] In which case the employee's entitlement to a guarantee payment is calculated as if the employee were working whole-time (s. 24 (4)).

[10] See *Tarmac Roadstone Holdings, Ltd.* v. *Peacock*, [1973] 2 All E.R. 485; [1973] I.R.L.R. 157.

(s. 26 (2)) under a guaranteed pay scheme goes towards discharging the employer's liability for the statutory payment for that day. Consequently when an employee has exhausted his contractual rights, if they are as favourable as statutory benefits, he has also exhausted his statutory entitlement. Moreover where a voluntary guarantee remuneration scheme provides a sum to be paid without work actually being done for a period greater than a day, that sum if paid for the period could be applied proportionally to the workless day to reduce the statutory payment (s. 26 (3) (*b*)).

[**128**] Where an employer fails to pay the whole or any part of a guarantee payment to which an employee is entitled, the employee may present a claim to an industrial tribunal within three months of the day or within such time as is reasonable in any case where it was not reasonably practicable to present a timely complaint. If the complaint is well founded, the tribunal must order the employer to pay the employee the amount to which he is entitled (s. 27). Unlike redundancy and maternity payments, there is no fund set up for guarantee payments.

[**129**] Finally, where a collective agreement or wages order is in force which provides a right to guaranteed remuneration, it may under certain conditions be exempted from the statutory payment scheme by order of the Secretary of State or appropriate minister (s. 28).

CHAPTER EIGHT

MEDICAL SUSPENSION

[**130**] Where an employee, having been continuously employed for four weeks, is suspended from work under certain specified statutory enactments because his health is or appears to be affected by a production process or other working condition, the EPA provides a right to be paid remuneration for a period of up to twenty-six weeks. This right to suspension with pay on medical grounds is carefully circumscribed. It applies only to medical suspensions based on an enactment specified in Sch. 2 of the Act or on a recommendation of any code of practice issued and approved under s. 16 of the Health and Safety at Work etc. Act 1974. Schedule 2 of the EPA now specifies fifteen statutory rules and orders, including the Factory Acts 1961. The Secretary of State may by order add provisions to the list.

[**131**] An employee is regarded as suspended from work only in so far as he continues to be employed by his employer without being provided with work or not performing work he normally performed before the suspension. Should an employer dismiss an employee owing to the statutory requirements, the dismissed employee may complain of unfair dismissal after having been continuously employed for only four weeks instead of the customary twenty-six weeks.

[**132**] If an employee is incapable of work for a period of time through disease or bodily or mental disablement he is disqualified from payment for that period (s. 30 (2)). Similarly he loses his entitlement to payment for any period in which he unreasonably refuses suitable alternative work offered by the employer whether or not that work is part of his original contract. He also loses his entitlement to pay for any period during which he has not complied with the reasonable requirement imposed by his employer with a view to ensuring that his services are available.

[**133**] The remuneration payable during a period of medical suspension is calculated on the basis of a week's pay for normal working hours on the day before the suspension began, that is, not including overtime unless it is a fixed obligation of both parties to the contract, (Sch. 4, Part II). The statutory entitlement of twenty-six weeks' pay is a minimum. If there is any contractual remuneration payable for medical suspension it goes towards discharging the employer's liability for the statutory entitlement. As well, the payment of the statutory entitlement goes towards discharging the employer's contractual liability for the period (s. 31).

[**134**] If the employer fails to pay the whole or any part of the remuneration to which the employee is entitled under the provisions for medical suspension, the employer may present a complaint to an industrial tribunal within three months or any further period the tribunal considers reasonable where it is satisfied that it was not reasonably practicable to bring such a complaint within the

three-month period. Where the tribunal finds the complaint well founded, it must order the employer to pay the employee the amount of pay owing to him (s. 32).

[**135**] An employee who is dismissed because of a suspension from work by reason of a specified statutory enactment may bring a claim for unfair dismissal and the normal requirement of continuous employment for an unfair dismissals claim is reduced to four weeks. If the employer has engaged a replacement for a job where the employee had been medically suspended, a dismissal of the replacement in order to make it possible to allow the suspended employee to resume work will be a substantial reason for dismissal under Sch. 1, para. 6 (1) (*b*) of TULRA as long as the replacement employee on engagement was informed in writing that this would occur. The dismissal would continue to be subject to the test of fairness in the circumstances under Sch. 1, para. 6 (8) of TULRA.

CHAPTER NINE

MATERNITY RIGHTS

[**136**] In addition to protection against dismissal owing to pregnancy (see paras. 90–99, below), the Act creates two new rights for employees who are absent wholly or partly because of pregnancy or confinement:

—a right to a maternity payment equivalent to six weeks' pay (s. 35 (1) (a) and ss. 36–38)

—a right to return to work at any time within six months (29 weeks) after confinement (ss. 35 (1) (*b*), 48–50, Sch. 3).

QUALIFICATIONS

[**137**] Both rights are hedged with numerous conditions and qualifications. Yet on closer inspection they appear to apply widely to employees who do not *voluntarily* leave their employment owing to pregnancy until the eleventh week before the period of confinement.

[**138**] The first requirement is that at the beginning of the eleventh week before confinement the employee must have been continuously employed by the employer for at least two years.[1] This requirement itself has two elements; the necessary length of continuous employment at the beginning of the eleventh week; and the requirement that the employment lasted until immediately before the beginning of the eleventh week (s. 35 (2) (*a*) and (*b*). However, as far as the condition of continuous employment is concerned, where an employee has been away from work owing to pregnancy during the preceding two years and that time away from work has been taken in accordance with the provisions of the Act, it will neither break her continuity of employment nor be deducted from the total of her period of continuous employment (Sch. 16, Part II, para. 13).

[**139**] Moreover, as regards the requirement that the employment must last until the beginning of the eleventh week, where the employee is not actually at work during the period preceding the eleventh week prior to the expected week of confinement (for example, because of illness), as long as she continues to be contractually employed by her employer she remains qualified for both maternity rights (s. 35 (2) (*a*)). Where an employer dismisses an employee because owing to her pregnancy she has become incapable of adequately doing her work and does not re-engage her in suitable alternative work, the dismissal will not preclude her entitlement to either maternity right as long as she would,

---

[1] The requisite period of continuous service may be varied from time to time by order of the Secretary of State (s. 35(5)).

but for the dismissal, have been continuously employed for two years at the eleventh week before confinement (s. 35 (3)).

[**140**] An employee is required to inform an employer, in writing if so requested, three weeks before the beginning of her absence (if possible) that she is or will be absent from work owing to pregnancy (s. 35 (2) (*c*) and (3)).[2] In the case of the right to return to work, the employee must also include notification that she intends to return to work with her employer (s. 35 (2) (*c*) (ii)). As regards maternity pay, the failure to notify the employer does not completely disentitle the employee, it merely delays the employer's obligation to pay until he receives the required information (s. 36 (4)). However, the failure to provide proper notification of an intention to return to work *will* disentitle an employee from her right to return under the Act (s. 35 (3)).

MATERNITY PAY

[**141**] A pregnant employee is entitled to a maternity payment for a maximum of six weeks for the first six weeks of absence starting on or after the beginning of the eleventh week before the expected week of confinement. An employee's absence owing to pregnancy prior to the eleventh week will not advance the period of payment, but continued working beyond the eleventh week may delay it (s. 36 (2)).

[**142**] The amount of the maternity payment consists of nine-tenths of "a week's pay", less any maternity allowance payable for the week under social security legislation[3] or any contractual remuneration paid by the employer to the employee in respect of a day within the payment period (s. 37 (1)). "A week's pay", as defined in the Act (Sch. 4, Part II) consists of the payment the employer is contractually required to make for the normal working week of the employee. This would include overtime only if the overtime were itself a minimum number of hours fixed by the contract for both parties, the employer to provide it, as well as the employee to work it.[4]

[**143**] Where the employer pays a maternity payment in accordance with the Act, he will be able to claim a rebate of the full amount from a new Maternity Payment Fund.[5]

[**144**] Where an employer fails to pay the whole or any part of a maternity payment to an employee, she may present a claim to an industrial tribunal normally within three months of the last day of the payment period or within such further period as the tribunal considers reasonably practicable (s. 38 (1)). If an industrial tribunal finds the complaint well founded, it must order the employer to pay the employee the amount of the maternity payment which is due.

[**145**] The employee may apply directly to the Secretary of State for a payment from the Maternity Pay Fund, where she has taken all reasonable steps (short of proceedings to enforce a tribunal award) to recover payment from the

[2] As well, an employee must also produce an authoritative certificate stating the expected week of confinement if she is requested by the employer to do so (s. 35 (4)).

[3] Social Security Act 1975, Sch. 4, Part I.

[4] *Tarmac Roadstone Holdings, Ltd.* v. *Peacock*, [1973] 2 All E.R. 485; [1973] I.R.L.R. 157.

[5] Section 42. See also ss. 39–47.

employer and has failed to do so or where her employer is insolvent (s. 43).[6] If the Secretary of State makes a payment from the Maternity Pay Fund in respect of the employer's default (s. 44) and it appears that the employer's default was without reasonable excuse, the Secretary of State may recover a sum from the employer up to the amount of the maternity payment and pay it into the Maternity Pay Fund (s. 44 (1)). If the Secretary of State decides to refuse a rebate to the employer (s. 42) or a payment to the employee (s. 43), or pays over less than the amount claimed, either may present a complaint to the industrial tribunal normally within three months of the decision (s. 46). The employer may appeal to an industrial tribunal where the Sectretary of State has determined that an amount is recoverable from the employer owing to his unreasonable default (s. 46 (4)).

[**146**] Where a tribunal finds any claim well founded, it may determine the amount to which the complainant is entitled and the Secretary of State must comply with that determination (s. 46 (3) and (4)).

THE RIGHT TO RETURN TO WORK

[**147**] Where an employee has been absent from work owing wholly or partly to pregnancy, she has a right to return to work with her original employer or his successor in the "job" in which she was previously employed and on terms and conditions "not less favourable than" those which she would have enjoyed had she remained in employment diring the period of absence (s. 48 (1)).

[**148**] Strictly speaking, this right cannot be said to be a right to reinstatement in the original job. For the Act defines the "job" as "the nature of the work which she is employed to do in accordance with her contract and the capacity and place in which she is so employed" (s. 48 (2) (*a*)). Therefore depending upon the contents of the employee's contract of employment her right to return could be satisfied by an offer of a number of alternative jobs of a similar contractual nature.

[**149**] Moreover, whilst the Act states that the employee is entitled to return to work on terms and conditions "not less favourable" than those which would have been applicable to her if she had not been absent, it also explicitly provides that as regards seniority, pension rights and other similar rights, the period or periods of employment prior to the employee's absence will be regarded as continuous with her employment following that absence (s. 48 (2) (*b*)). In other words, for purposes of any service-based contractual entitlement, the total amount of period of continuous service will exclude the period of her absence although that period will not operate to break her continuity of service.

[**150**] On the other hand in respect of the continuous service qualification for statutory protections, *e.g.*, unfair dismissal, redundancy, etc., a female employee who has "returned to work" in accordance with the Act is entitled to include every week during the period of absence from work within her aggregate period of continuous service (Sch. 16, Part I, para. 17).

---

[6] If the Secretary of State makes a payment to an employee of an insolvent employer out of the Redundancy Fund under s. 64 and it would have attracted a rebate from the Maternity Pay Fund had it been paid by the employer, then the Maternity Pay Fund must make a payment of a corresponding amount to the Redundancy Fund (s. 45).

[**151**] These rules of continuous service have two noteworthy implications. In the first place, the fact that continuity of service is not broken by absence owing partly or wholly to pregnancy or confinement means that an employee who returns to work after maternity leave in accordance with this Act is immediately qualified to another round of maternity benefits. Secondly, the creation of two standards for continuous service and seniority is likely to produce certain anomalies in the application of statutory employment protections along with contractual employment benefits. Thus, in calculating the amount of redundancy payment or the basic award of compensation for unfair dismissal, the employee's length of service will be longer than the calculation of service for pension rights, holidays, sick leave, and possibly service-based increments, etc. Moreover, in calculating a woman's entitlement to benefits that have been introduced during the period of absence or changes that have been made to existing benefits during the absence, such as a salary increase or a new bonus scheme, the employee's entitlement would exclude the period of absence and begin only from the date she returns to work.

[**152**] It is, of course, open to an employer to remove these anomalies by providing by contract a right to return to work more akin to reinstatement at least in respect of seniority. Where an employer provides a right to return to work under a contract of employment, an employee is entitled to take advantage of whichever right, statutory or contractual, is in any particular respect more favourable (Sch. 3, para. 5 (1)).

THE TIMING OF THE RETURN TO WORK

[**153**] If she has fulfilled all other statutory requirements,[7] an employee may exercise her right to return to work within twenty-nine weeks of the start of the week in which her actual confinement occurred (s. 48 (1)). All she is required to do is to give notice to the employer at least one week before the date of her intended return (s. 49 (1)).

[**154**] An employer is entitled to postpone the actual date of return for up to four weeks as long as he notifies the employee before the day of her return of the postponement and indicates the date at which she will be entitled to return to work with him (s. 49 (4)). An employee may postpone her return to work as well as the day of notice of return for one period (s. 49 (4)) of a maximum of four weeks owing to illness or disability as long as she gives prior notification to the employer and provides him with a medical certificate (s. 49 (3)).

[**155**] Finally, if there is an interruption of work because of industrial action or otherwise, which makes it unreasonable to expect the employee to return to work either before the end of the twenty-nine weeks after confinement or on the notified day of return, the Act allows a further extension of time for the employee. If the interruption occurs on the notified day of return, the extension may last until work resumes or as soon as reasonably practicable thereafter (s. 49 (5)). If the interruption occurs to the twenty-ninth week, the extension may last until within fourteen days of the end of the interruption of work even if this extends beyond the twenty-ninth week (s. 49 (6)).

---

[7] See paras. 137–140.

[156] To ensure that the right of an employee to return to work after pregnancy is not precluded by the costs of dismissing an employee who acted as a temporary replacement, the Act provides special rules for the dismissal of a replacement. As long as an employer informs a replacement employee upon engagement that the work will end upon the return to work of the pregnant employee, a subsequent dismissal of the replacement employee when the original employee returns from maternity leave will be viewed by the Act as a dismissal for a substantial reason. This is not to say that the dismissal will automatically be fair. Under the Act, even a decision to dismiss for a substantial reason must be "reasonable in the circumstances". This test is likely to include an obligation upon the employer to offer any suitable job vacancy to the replacement employee and to use some diligence in investigating the possibilities of alternative employment within the company. It might also extend to a duty not to select the employee unfairly for dismissal where other employees in comparable employment have been hired more recently.

[157] However, in the normal way, the dismissal of a replacement employee from a particular job on the return of the original employee from maternity leave in accordance with the Act is likely to be fair. It should be noted that a dismissal of a replacement employee is a dismissal for a substantial reason only where the first employee returns from maternity leave. Should the original employee fail to return to work, the replacement employee's status in respect of any statutory safeguards reverts to that of an ordinary employee.

REMEDIES FOR THE RIGHT TO RETURN TO WORK

[158] Where an employee refuses to allow an employee to return to work after maternity leave in accordance with the Act, she may present a complaint to an industrial tribunal. The complaint must be made normally within three months of the refusal. The remedies which the tribunal may apply to a well-founded complaint are an adaptation of the normal remedies for unfair dismissal and compensation for redundancy. The employer's refusal to permit the employee to return to work is treated as a dismissal on the notified day of return. The employee is presumed to have been continuously employed until that day and to be treated as if she had been dismissed for the reason for which she was not permitted to return. In determining whether a failure to allow the employee to return may be treated as if it was an unfair dismissal under the 1974 Act as amended or redundancy under the 1965 Act, the tribunal must take into account certain new grounds for entitlement.[8]

[159] Where an employer's reason for not permitting an employee to return to work in her original job is that it is not practicable so to do because the job has disappeared owing to redundancy, the employee is entitled to be offered alternative employment under a new contract of employment if a suitable vacancy is available with the employer, his successor or an associated employer. Should the employer fail to offer the employee any existing suitable vacancy, the employee will be treated as unfairly dismissed and entitled to the remedies

[8] There are also special rules applicable for a dismissal by the employer at any time during the period of maternity leave. See Sch. 3, para. (4).

for unfair dismissal. This will be true "notwithstanding anything in paragraph 6 of Schedule 1", for example even if she was dismissed in accordance with an agreed redundancy procedure (s. 48 (4) and Sch. 3, para. 2 (2)).

[**160**] Any alternative employment offered by the employer under a new contract must be suitable in relation to the employee and appropriate for her to do in the circumstances. As well, the contractual terms relating to her capacity, the place of work and other terms and conditions must not be substantially less favourable than those of the original job (s. 43 (5)).

[**161**] These provisions create a two-edged sword for the employer. They allow an offer to be made of alternative work which is of a lower standard than a job would be required to be under the test of suitable alternative employment under s. 2 (4) of the Redundancy Payments Act 1965. However, they also widen the scope of the vacancies that the employer must look for before refusing to permit the employee to return to work.

[**162**] The Act omits a clear expression of who must bear the onus of proof such as is provided in the case of dismissal for pregnancy.[9] Since the Act makes it an infringement for the employer not to offer a suitable alternative vacancy, the impression is created that the employee must assert and hence bear the burden of proving the infringement. However, in so far as the refusal to permit an employee to return is to be treated as a dismissal for the reason for which the employee is not permitted to return, the refusal for redundancy is likely to be subject to the residual test of unfair dismissal under TULRA, Sch. 1, para. 6 (8) as revised in EPA, Sch. 3, para. 2. And this requires the employer to satisfy the tribunal that it was reasonable in the circumstances for him to treat his reason for refusal as sufficient for dismissal. This in turn would require at least a showing that he met his duty to investigate suitable alternative vacancies for the employee returning from maternity leave whose job had disappeared.

[**163**] In the case of a failure to permit a return to work, unlike a dismissal owing to pregnancy, the search for suitable available vacancies must be made among associated employers as well as in the firm of the original employer or its successor (s. 48 (4)).[10]

[**164**] Where the employer refuses to permit the employee to return to work for any reason other than redundancy, the test of the employee's entitlement to the remedies of unfair dismissal is whether in the circumstances the employer acted reasonably in treating his reason for refusal as a sufficient reason for dismissing the employee had *she not been absent from work* (Sch. 3, para. 2 (1)). Here, too, the onus of proof is placed squarely upon the employer to satisfy the tribunal of the reasonableness of his actions. Clearly under this test there are few actions which an employee could take during this period which could give the employer a justified reason for dismissal. These would be limited to a few extreme situations, for example where the employee committed a crime, contracted a permanent or long-lasting illness or became severely disabled during the period of maternity leave. Equally clearly the fact that the employer has replaced the employee during the period of absence will not justify a refusal to

---

[9] See s. 34 (4).
[10] Associated employer is defined in TULRA, s. 30 (5).

permit her to return to work even if the employer had failed to take the necessary steps to ensure that the temporarily engaged employee could be fairly dismissed.

[**165**] The overall design of the remedies is to persuade the employer wherever the possibility exists to offer the employee alternative work if her original job disappears. If a vacancy were available and no offer was made, the guidelines for the exercise of discretion in awarding remedies for unfair dismissal suggest that the tribunal will order re-engagement. On the other hand an offer of alternative employment by the employer will tend to reduce the monetary remedies available to the employee. If the terms of the new job are not substantially less favourable than the original job the employee loses her entitlement to the remedies of unfair dismissal. If the new job is a suitable alternative job in accordance with the Redundancy Payments Act, s. 2 (4) and the employee unreasonably refuses to accept it, she is excluded from her entitlement to compensation for redundancy.

CHAPTER TEN
TIME OFF WORK

[**166**] Although the Act creates four types of right to time off work, only two apply to all employees regardless of whether or not they are trade union members. These are time off for public duties (s. 59) and time off to look for work or make arrangements for training in a redundancy situation (s. 61). The other two types of rights—time off for carrying out trade union duties (s. 57) and time off for trade union activities (s. 58)—are discussed in Chapter Fifteen on new rights for trade unions and trade unionists.

TIME OFF FOR PUBLIC DUTIES

[**167**] Under the Act an employer is required to allow an employee who holds a specific public office or is a member of a specified public authority to have time off during working hours to perform any of the duties of his public position (s. 59 (1)). This is a right to time off without pay. The duties include attendance at meetings including committee and subcommittee meetings and any other activity approved by the public body for the purpose of discharging its functions (s. 59 (3)). This right is limited to time off which is reasonable in the circumstances (s. 59 (4)). An employee may present a complaint normally within three months to an industrial tribunal that his employer has failed to allow him time off as required (s. 59 (6)). In considering the reasonableness of the amount of time off, the tribunal must consider three factors. First, how much time off is required for the employee's public office as well as how much time off is required for the particular duty. Secondly, it must also have regard to the time off the employee has been permitted in respect of trade union duties and activities. Finally, it must take into account the circumstances of the employer's business and the effect of the employee's absence on the running of that business. There is no Code of Pactice expected on this issue. The public offices which are specified under the Act as entitling an employee to time off are:

(*a*) Justice of the Peace;
(*b*) a member of a local authority;
(*c*) a member of any statutory tribunal;
(*d*) a member of, in England and Wales, a Regional Health Authority or Area Health Authority or, in Scotland, a Health Board;
(*e*) a member of, in England and Wales, the managing or governing body of an educational establishment maintained by a local education authority or, in Scotland, a school or college council or the governing body of a central institution or a college of education;

(*f*) a member of, in England and Wales, a water authority or, in Scotland, a river purification board (s. 59 (1)).

However, the Secretary of State may by order add to or remove any office or body from this list (s. 59 (5)).

[168] Finally the remedy to which an employee is entitled in the event of a well-founded complaint is a declaration by the tribunal and an award of compensation which the tribunal considers just and equitable in the circumstances taking into account the employer's default as well as the loss suffered by the employee which was attributable to the failure to grant time off.

TIME OFF TO LOOK FOR WORK OR MAKE ARRANGEMENTS FOR TRAINING

[169] An employee who has been given notice of dismissal has a right to reasonable time off with pay during the period of notice in order to look for new employment or to make arrangements for training for a future job. To qualify for such a right an employee must have been continuously employed for a period of at least two years either on the date on which notice is due to expire or the date which notice would expire if it were given in accordance with the period required by the Contracts of Employments Act 1972, as amended.

[170] The appropriate hourly rate at which the time off allowed is required to be paid is the "normal" hourly rate, that is the normal weekly wage divided by normal working hours. "Normal working hours" would exclude overtime which was not a contractually "fixed" obligation of both employer and employee, the former to provide it and the latter to work it.[1]

[171] There are few guidelines to the amount of time off which is likely to be viewed as reasonable. Presumably that could vary with an employee's particular skill, the condition of the local labour market and the success or failure of the employee's efforts to find new work or arrange for training courses as well as the amount of time off already allowed.

[172] Where an employer refuses to allow time off an employee may present a complaint to an industrial tribunal that the refusal is unreasonable. The complaint should be presented normally within three months beginning with the date on which the time off was refused. If the tribunal finds the complaint well-founded, it must make a declaration to that effect and award compensation subject to a maximum of two days' pay for a particular notice period. The maximum is subject to any payment already made for time off in accordance with the employer's liability under this section of the Act. Furthermore any pay given to the employee for time off under the statutory obligation shall go towards discharging an employer's contractual obligation and vice versa.

---

[1] See *Tarmac Roadstone Holdings, Ltd.* v. *Peacock*, [1973] 2 All E.R. 485; [1973] I.R.L.R. 157.

PART II

THE NEW RIGHTS FOR TRADE UNIONS

CHAPTER ELEVEN

STATUTORY RIGHTS AND TRADE UNION STATUS

[**173**] The new rights given by the EPA to trade unions and the extension of collective consultation and collective bargaining are wide in their application. They extend into six different areas:

—legal support for trade union recognition (Chapter Twelve)
—legal support for disclosure of information (Chapter Thirteen)
—legal support for consultation about redundancies (Chapter Fourteen)
—legal protection for trade union membership and activity (Chapter Fifteen)
—Wages Councils (Chapter Sixteen)
—The extension of existing collective agreements (Chapter Seventeen).

[**174**] However, these new rights do not apply equally to all trade unions. Whilst the EPA does not require trade unions to "register", it does qualify the new legal rights in other respects. There are three different types of statutory status for trade unions, each constituting a qualification for some or all of the new legal rights:

(1) "Independent" trade unions.
(2) "Recognised" trade unions.
(3) "Specified" trade unions.

It is useful to consider these in some detail before examining the new types of legal support.

"INDEPENDENT" TRADE UNIONS

[**175**] The most important status for a trade union is that of "independence". To be entitled to any of the new legal rights a trade union must be independent, that is to say, "neither under the domination or control of nor liable to interference leading towards control by an employer or employer group arising out of the provision of financial or material support or by any other means" (TULRA, s. 30). In case of doubt, it is conclusive evidence that a trade union

is independent if it obtains a certificate from the Certification Officer that it is an "independent trade union" (EPA, s. 8 (11)). To obtain a certificate of independence a trade union must first have its name entered on the list of trade unions maintained under s. 8 of TULRA. If its name is removed from that list the Certification Officer must cancel any certificate of independence in force (s. 8 (1)). If a trade union is refused a certificate of independence, it may appeal on questions of fact or law (s. 88 (3)) but the right of appeal is limited only to a trade union who has been refused certification (s. 8 (9)).

[**176**] The concept of independence was offered by the CIR in its study of trade union recognition.[1] The Commission concluded that the essence of "independence" and a pre-condition for effectiveness, especially in representing employees, is freedom from employer influence. Established trade unions, the report stated, demonstrate their independence by membership of the TUC, political action and a willingness to take some form of industrial action in their members' interests, and a history of vigorous negotiations resulting in reasonable settlements. The criteria used to test independence in borderline cases, it suggested, should include an examination of the history of an organisation to discover the part played by employers in establishing it and their influence on the way it has developed and operates.

[**177**] This diagnosis was accepted by the Government; it attempted to amend the Employment Protection Bill at its Third Reading in the House of Lords to include a list of criteria which were based on the specific criteria for independence recommended by the CIR. The criteria suggested in the amendment were as follows:

(*a*) any relevant conditions applied by any organisation to which the trade union is affiliated;
(*b*) whether and to what extent an employer was involved in the establishment of the trade union or continues to be involved in the conduct of its internal affairs;
(*c*) whether the trade union receives financial support or other material support from any employer and the extent of such support and the manner of its provision;
(*d*) whether meetings held by the trade union are attended by an employer or by representatives of an employer otherwise than by invitation;
(*e*) whether it is the practice for the trade union to submit minutes of its meetings or to supply other confidential information to an employer;
(*f*) whether and to what extent the policy of the trade union is influenced by an employer otherwise than through the normal processes of collective bargaining;
(*g*) whether membership of the trade union is confined to employees of a single employer or to employees of associated employers and the effect of such a restriction in the circumstances of the case;
(*h*) whether the trade union has engaged in collective bargaining with any employer or has shown its intention of doing so.

---

[1] CIR Study 5 *Trade Union Recognition*: *CIR Experience*, HMSO, p. 59.

Although these criteria were not introduced in the Statute, they are likely to be influential in the decisions of the Certification Officer.

THE RECOGNISED TRADE UNION

[**178**] A trade union may be said to be "recognised" in two different respects. First, it may be recognised by the employer to any extent for the purpose of collective bargaining. Secondly, it may be recognised in the sense that it has received an "operative recommendation" for recognition by the ACAS. The test of whether a trade union is recognised in the latter sense is a fairly easy one to apply. A recommendation for recognition must take the form of a request in writing, be available to all trade unions and employers concerned in the recognition issue and include a specification of the trade unions and employers affected, the employees covered, the issue for which recognition is recommended and the levels at which it is recommended (s. 14).

[**179**] In contrast, the first test of recognition is dependent entirely upon evidence as to the arrangements betwen employer and trade union with little restriction on the degree of formality or little indication as to the minimum degree of recognition that will be necessary to meet the requirement that the trade union has been "recognised" for the purposes of collective bargaining.

[**180**] The two relevant statutory definitions suggest that recognition is likely to be given a wide interpretation. Thus recognition is defined as recognition of the union by an employer or two or more associated employers[2] *to any extent* for the purposes of collective bargaining. "Collective bargaining" is defined as negotiations relating to or connected with one or more of the matters specified in TULRA, s. 29 (1) which provision in turn specifies a wide variety of matters ranging from substantive terms and conditions to procedural arrangements for negotiation, consultation or other procedure.[3] A trade union that has obtained even a minimum form of recognition from an employer, for example, "recognition for representational purposes", would appear to qualify as recognised along with trade unions which have obtained full recognition.

[**181**] Finally, in Part IV of the Act—Procedure for Handling Redundancies—use is made of the term "appropriate trade union" (s. 101 (1)). This, however, is defined as a trade union recognised by the employer in respect of that description of employee (s. 101 (7)).

"SPECIFIED TRADE UNIONS"

[**182**] The third legal status of trade unions defined under the new charter of legal rights is the most restrictive. It embraces trade unions which are either specified in a union's membership agreement or deemed to be so specified by the Act. The first category includes a trade union which is specified in the agreement or is accepted by the parties to the agreement as being the equivalent of a specified union. The second category includes a trade union which has either received an operative recommendation of the ACAS in respect of the employee group in question or has referred a recognition issue covering that employee group to the ACAS and the result is still pending (s. 53 (5)).[4]

---

[2] Defined in TULRA, s. 30.
[3] See para. 198, *post*.
[4] See the discussion in Chapter Fifteen.

CHAPTER TWELVE

RECOGNITION

[**183**] Legal support for increasing the size and strength of trade unions and for promoting the establishment of new collective bargaining arrangements is not entirely new to British labour legislation. A legal recognition procedure was a major element in the Industrial Relations Act 1971.

[**184**] The type of legal support provided by the EPA for recognition, however, has certain features which are quite different from its predecessor. In the first place, the procedure for determining a trade union's recognition rights does not require the trade union concerned to refrain from engaging in industrial action pending the results of the procedure. Secondly, the right to legal support for recognition is generally available to independent trade unions[1] against an employer or an associated employer, but not an employers' association, and any independent trade union may refer any recognition issue to the ACAS as the first step of the procedure, (s. 11). On the other hand, the procedure is not generally available to employers. An employer may only make a reference to the statutory recognition procedure in respect of an application for withdrawal or variation of recommendation of recognition (s. 13).[2] Thirdly, and perhaps most importantly, the types of recognition issue for which legal support is to be given to trade unions have been increased. The provisions of the Act are designed to assist trade unions to obtain recognition not only for the purpose of representing particular groups of employees; they also offer support to trade unions to obtain recognition by employers in respect of particular matters of collective bargaining.

[**185**] If the provisions of the Act are new in these respects, they have certain other features which are not unfamiliar. The duty to recognise is defined largely in procedural terms in that the employer is required to be "ready and willing to carry on such negotiations as are envisaged by a recommendation for recognition" (s. 15 (2)). As well, the enforcement procedure for any of the new recognition rights consists of the same two stages. There is a preliminary stage designed to produce a voluntary settlement if at all possible. This involves separate stages of conciliation, investigation and a report with recommendations by the ACAS (ss. 14 and 15). The second stage provides for compulsory arbitration by the Central Arbitration Committee on a claim for an improvement in substantive terms in the event of persistent non-compliance by an employer with an ACAS recommendation (s. 16).

---

[1] Of course, an employer may also ask the ACAS to inquire into or conciliate upon a recognition dispute as part of the Service's voluntary inquiry and conciliation functions.

[2] The measures giving legal protection to trade union membership and activity are also related to recognition (see the discussion in Chapter Fifteen).

[**186**] These rather complex provisions may usefully be examined in detail under the following four heads:

(1) The scope of the new recognition procedure: to what issues may it apply?
(2) The criteria to be used in recognition issues.
(3) The duty to recognise: what does it entail?
(4) The sanction for non-compliance with the duty to recognise.

THE SCOPE OF THE NEW RECOGNITION PROCEDURE: TO WHAT ISSUES MAY IT APPLY?

[**187**] The measures contained in the EPA are designed to give legal support for trade union recognition in an extremely wide sense. Some indication of this extent can be obtained by the definitional sections. Thus at one end of the scale recognition is itself defined as meaning, "the recognition of the union by an employer . . . to any extent for the purposes of collective bargaining" (s. 11 (2)). At the other end of the scale a "recognition issue", that is, an issue which may be referred by an independent trade union to the ACAS is defined to include not only "a request by a trade union for recognition by an employer" but also "where recognition is already accorded to some extent, a request for further recognition" (s. 11 (3)).

[**188**] The statutory procedure extends to two distinct types of recognition issue. The first type of issue is the more familiar one of a trade union claim for recognition in order to represent and negotiate on behalf of a particular *group of employees*. This type of issue is itself multifarious. It includes an application for initial recognition, that is where no other trade union represents any of the employees in the group. It encompasses an application for recognition in which other trade unions are involved in possibly competing claims. It also extends to an application for recognition for new groups of employees, where recognition has already been obtained for some groups. Finally it includes a procedure for the withdrawal of recognition, that is a procedure whereby any of the parties to an existing recognition agreement—employers or trade unions—can apply to vary or revoke that arrangement in respect of a given group of employees (s. 13).

[**189**] The second type of issue with which the recognition sections of the Act are designed to deal is one that entails a significant innovation in statutory machinery for British collective bargaining. This is the issue that arises where an independent trade union wishes to extend or specify the *subjects* for which they are recognised to negotiate on behalf of their members. This may include, for example, new substantive terms such as pensions or other new fringe benefits. As well, it may apply to particularly contentious areas of managerial policy hitherto left exclusively to managerial prerogative, such as transfer arrangements, etc.

[**190**] As the Act indicates a recommendation by the ACAS in respect of recognition must specify whether the recommendation is for recognition generally *or in respect of one or more specified matters* (s. 12 (5)). Thus, the recognition procedure relating to subjects of collective bargaining is avaliable in connection with an initial claim by a trade union for recognition in respect of a particular group of employees. It may also be used for a claim for further

recognition by a trade union which has already obtained recognition from any employer to negotiate on behalf of a particular group of employees and wishes to extend the range of subjects (s. 11 (3)).

THE CRITERIA TO BE USED IN RECOGNITION ISSUES

[**191**] Whatever the type of recognition issue referred, the statutory procedure involves essentially the same two stages.

[**192**] The first stage consists of the reference by the trade union (s. 11), or in the one special case the employer (s. 13), of the recognition issue to the ACAS for inquiry and report. Where the service considers the issue referred to be substantially the same as a previous reference, it may decline to proceed upon it. Otherwise it must proceed to investigate the issue and in order to prepare a report and recommendation and consult all parties who will be affected by the outcome of the reference. This stage requires the ACAS first to attempt to produce a conciliation settlement by, conciliating between the parties (s. 12 (3)). If conciliation is unsuccessful the next step is an inquiry and investigation by the ACAS with the aim of producing a report and recommendation that can provide a basis for a mediated settlement. That is perhaps why the report and recommendation become operative only after fourteen days after they have been made and received by the employer (s. 15).

[**193**] In making its determination of the extent to which the employer has a legal duty to recognise, or the extent to which existing recognition arrangements may be altered, the ACAS is given wide discretion. Its recommendation which must be presented in a report together with its findings, advice and reasons, must specify four items:

(1) The parties, that is employer(s) and trade union(s), to whom it relates.
(2) The group of workers for whom recognition is recommended.
(3) The extent of recognition—whether generally or for one or more specified matters.
(4) The level at which recognition is granted, *e.g.*, workshop, works, company, group.

[**194**] However, there is little in the statute that gives any indication of the criteria that the ACAS should use in deciding upon its recommendation under any of these heads. Unlike previous legislation which set out specific statutory guidelines along with a set of recommendations in an Industrial Relations Code of Practice, the EPA places few explicit limits on the discretion of the ACAS. The only guidance contained in the statute is limited to two points. The service must ascertain the opinion of workers to whom the recognition issue relates, (s. 14)[3] and is charged with a general duty to promote the

[3] Moreover, whilst it may ascertain the opinions of workers by any means it chooses, if it decides to take a formal ballot of these workers it must meet certain statutory requirements in respect of giving equal and fair opportunity for employees to vote, a secret ballot, prior notification to employers and trade unions affected, and opportunity to such organisation to make representations in respect of the ballot proposals. The Service must arrange for the question or questions on the ballot and the results of the ballot to be notified to employer and trade union affected and the employer is required to notify his employees of the results (s. 14).

improvement of industrial relations and in particular to encourage the extension of collective bargaining and the development and where necessary reform of collective bargaining machinery (s. 1 (2)).

[195] What specific criteria is the Service likely to apply to claims for:

(*a*) recognition for groups of workers
(*b*) recognition in respect of specified matters.

Recognition for groups of employees

[196] In the main where recognition issues concern either a claim to represent a group of employees or an application for withdrawal of recognition rights, the criteria used by the ACAS are likely to be similar to those used by the CIR during its period as a Royal Commission (1969–71) and to some extent during the period under the 1971 Act.[4] Where a claim is made by a single union on behalf of a relatively well-defined group of employees in a particular establishment, the main issue will be the determination of the support enjoyed by that union amongst that group of employees and is likely to be a test of support enjoyed in terms of potential membership rather than existing membership. So where the ACAS through its inquiries obtains evidence of the intentions of employees it could recommend recognition to a trade union with an actual membership consisting of a small minority of the employee group.

[197] Where a trade union's claim for recognition impinges upon existing collective arrangements, there is a question of which employees ought to be grouped together for negotiating purposes. This question of what is the relevant bargaining unit often strongly influences the secondary question of who is entitled to represent the employee groups.[5] In determining the bargaining units, the factors that give rise to common interests among groups of employees must be considered. At this stage, the wishes of employees, whilst of great importance, are likely to be balanced against other objectives such as the longer-term viability of arrangements, the maintenance of existing bargaining arrangements where they are working well, matching bargaining arrangements with management and trade union structures. Until a new code is published with guidance and the recommendations of the ACAS are published, it is difficult to predict which of the above objectives are likely to be emphasised. However the existing Industrial Relations Code of Practice offers some guide as to the factors that are likely to be taken into account when bargaining units are defined.[6]

---

[4] As the CIR commented in its Study No. 5 *Trade Union Recognition*: *CIR Experience*, the introduction of the Industrial Relations Act did not lead to any changes in the techniques which had been developed for determining recognition reference (p. 6).

[5] Interestingly, the Act allows a recommendation by the ACAS in respect of groups of workers but restricts the arbitration award by the CAC to employees. "Worker" and "employee" respectively are defined in TULRA, s. 30.

[6] The following factors are listed in the Code (paras. 74–81):

(i) the nature of the work; (ii) the training experience and professional or other qualifications of the employees concerned; (iii) the extent to which they have interests in common; (iv) the general wishes of the employees concerned; (v) the organisation and the location of the work; (vi) hours, working arrangements and payments systems; (vii) the matters to be bargained about; (viii) the need to fit the unit into the pattern of union and managerial organisation; (ix) the need to avoid disruption of any existing arrangements which are working well; (x) whether separate bargaining arrangements are needed for particular categories of employees such as supervisors or employees who represent management in negotiation.

Recognition in respect of specified matters

[**198**] The criteria to be used by the ACAS in deciding upon recognition to trade unions in respect of specified matters is even less easy to predict. A trade union may submit a claim for recognition in respect of any issue for the purpose of collective bargaining (s. 11). Collective bargaining is defined as negotiations relating to or connected with one or more of the matters specified in s. 29 (1) of the Trade Union and Labour Relations Act 1974. These include the following:

(*a*) terms and conditions of employment, or the physical conditions in which any workers are required to work;
(*b*) engagement or non-engagement, or terminations or suspensions of employment or the duties of employment, of one or more workers;
(*c*) allocation of work or the duties of employment as between workers or groups of workers;
(*d*) matters of discipline;
(*e*) the membership or non-membership of a trade union on the part of a worker;
(*f*) facilities for officials of trade unions;
(*g*) machinery for negotiation or consultation, and any other procedures, relating to any of the foregoing matters, including the recognition by employers or employers' associations of the right of a trade union to represent workers in any such negotiations or consultations or in the carrying out of such procedures.

[**199**] This definition is sufficiently wide to allow unions to use the recognition machinery to expand the content of collective bargaining into new forms of fringe benefits—pensions, sick pay schemes, supplementary employment benefit schemes, safety, manpower planning, etc. At the same time, however, the definition is sufficiently specific to preclude certain types of issues, such as investment plans, if they are found to be neither related to nor connected with one of the matters specified above.

THE DUTY TO RECOGNISE: WHAT DOES IT ENTAIL?

[**200**] Once the ACAS produces a recommendation and it becomes operative under s. 15, the employer is placed under a duty to recognise the trade union in the sense that he must take action by way of or with a view to carrying on negotiations as might reasonably be expected to be taken by an employer ready and willing to carry on such negotiations as are envisaged by the recommendation. A failure by the employer to meet this standard within the two months after the recommendation becomes operative could lead initially to an entitlement by the trade union to make a complaint to the ACAS which must attempt to settle the matter by conciliation. If conciliation fails and the employer persists in his non-compliance, the trade union may present a complaint to the Central Arbitration Committee. At this stage it is the Committee which will have the discretion to determine whether the complaint by the trade

union is well-founded. What criteria is it likely to apply? Until the Committee's decisions and reasons for those decisions are available, it is possible only to speculate.

[**201**] The test of readiness and willingness in the statute appears to be predominantly a procedural test. It is likely to require the employer at the very least to have an exchange of views with the trade union. Thus he must be willing to meet with union representatives and engage in discussion with them. This would include considering representations made by the trade union representatives and replying to these representations giving reasons for any rejections.[7]

[**202**] Willingness to bargain would also include an element of good faith. The employer's representative who attends a meeting should have some authority to conclude agreements. Moreover an employer who engages in tactics of delay, or a frequent change of position without any apparent reason might well be held to show evidence of unwillingness to bargain. Further, where the employer makes a unilateral change in terms in an area for which a trade union has received an operative recommendation this may be evidence of lack of readiness and willingness to recognise.

[**203**] Must the employer grant a substantive concession to meet the new statutory test? Strictly speaking, as long as the employer enters into a reasoned exchange with the trade union over the issues, in most instances he would not be required to concede on any particular point. Thus, to take an extreme example, if he made an offer on a "take it or leave it" basis and refused to discuss the issues with trade union representatives, he might be found to be not ready and willing to bargain, whereas if he carefully considered the trade union's representations and rejected them *in toto* with an explanation for his rejection he could be found to be acting in accordance with his statutory obligations.

[**204**] The one possible exception to this interpretation is an instance where an employer has already conceded a substantive term to a comparable group of workers which is similar to the one claimed by the trade union in the recognition procedure. In that case, it might be difficult to preclude the suspicion that there is an underlying motive of unwillingness to negotiate. Moreover in general whilst a concession may not be required, employers may find that an offer of a substantive concession is a relatively easy way to meet the statutory standard of readiness and willingness to negotiate. Hence, whilst the statutory requirements may be largely procedural in character, they may well have the effect of producing substantive changes for groups of employees generally as well as for specific subjects of collective bargaining for which recognition is granted.

THE SANCTION FOR NON-COMPLIANCE WITH THE DUTY TO RECOGNISE

[**205**] Where a trade union makes a complaint to the Central Arbitration Committee (CAC) that the employer has not complied with an operative recommendation of the ACAS in respect of recognition, it must also submit a claim

[7] *Cf.* The definition of consultation in s. 99 (7).

to the CAC for an arbitration award for an improvement in terms and conditions for employees covered by the recommendation (s. 16 (1)).[8] The threat of arbitration is designed rather crudely to act as a deterrent to non-compliance.

[**206**] If the Committee finds the complaint well founded, it must make a declaration to that effect and specify the employees affected by the finding and the matters in relation to which the employer has failed to comply with the recommendations (s. 16 (5)).

[**207**] In addition the Committee may convene an arbitration hearing at which both sides may appear and make an award on the claim submitted by the trade union. The award may require the employer either to observe the improved terms and conditions for his employees that the trade union has claimed or any other terms and conditions which the Committee considers appropriate. However, the award may only alter terms and conditions which fall within the scope of the matters specified in the declaration of the CAC in accordance with s. 16 (5) (*b*).

[**208**] The award has effect as part of the contract of employment of any employee in the group affected from the specified date and may be superseded or varied only by a subsequent CAC award, collective agreement or agreements between employee and employer which effects an improvement in the employee's position under the award (s. 16 (7)). The award may also effect an improvement of the contractual position of employees covered by statutory minimum remuneration arrangements in so far as the CAC award is more favourable than the prescribed terms under another enactment (s. 16 (8)) although the award may not be made in respect of terms and conditions which are fixed by statute (s. 16 (8)).

---

[8] Where a trade union has received or has refused a previous award in respect of the employer's non-compliance, a new claim may not be entertained until twelve months have elapsed (s. 16 (3)).

CHAPTER THIRTEEN

DISCLOSURE OF INFORMATION

[**209**] Along with legal support for independent trade unions wishing to obtain recognition for the purposes of collective bargaining, the EPA introduces a legal right for recognised independent trade unions to obtain information to assist them through all stages of their collective negotiations with the employer. This would apply to preparations for negotiations, and negotiations over the interpretation and implementation of agreements as well as discussions during the actual course of negotiations for the purpose of making new agreements.

WHAT INFORMATION MUST BE DISCLOSED

[**210**] The Act places upon the employer a duty to disclose on request to trade union representatives all such information that meets the following requirements:

(1) The information must either relate to his undertaking and be in his possession or relate to any associated employer.

(2) The information must concern collective bargaining about matters and in relation to groups of workers for whom either the trade union has been recognised or has received an operative recommendation for recognition.

(3) The information must be such that trade union representatives would be to a material extent impeded in carrying out collective bargaining without it.

(4) The information must be such that it would be in accordance with good industrial relations practice that the employer should disclose it for purposes of collective bargaining.

[**211**] The employer is entitled to request that the trade union representative put his request in writing or confirm in writing. Similarly the trade union representative is entitled to require the employer to disclose information in writing or confirm it in writing. However, even where the information requested is of a kind which the employer has a duty to disclose, the employer is not required to disclose such information in the form of original documents or even to make copies of or extracts from original documents; he is required only to produce information in the form of a document prepared for the purpose of conveying or confirming the information. Nor is the employer required to disclose such information where its compilation or assembly of the information would involve work or costs which are disproportionate to the value of the information for collective bargaining.

[**212**] In addition there are six further circumstances in which the employer is not required to disclose information even where non-disclosure might impede collective bargaining: *viz.*

(*a*) any information which if disclosed would be against the interests of national security;
(*b*) any information which if disclosed might contravene a statutory protection;
(*c*) any information which has been communicated in confidence or which has been obtained in consequence of a confidence reposed on the employer by another person;
(*d*) any information relating to an individual without his consent;
(*e*) any information which if disclosed would cause substantial injury to the employer's undertaking for reasons apart from its effect on collective bargaining;
(*f*) any information obtained by the employer in connection with legal proceedings (s. 18).

[**213**] The last four restrictions clearly reflect the fact that the statute places no legal obligation on trade union representatives not to disclose any information received under the disclosure procedure and this fact is likely to influence the interpretation of these restrictions. For example, in restriction (*e*) it is somewhat unclear whether it is the disclosure of information to trade union representatives or the possibilities of disclosure of such information to a wider audience that must be considered when assessing the potential substantial injury to the firm. However, given the omission from the statute of a duty of confidentiality for trade union representatives, it is fairly clear that the latter prospect cannot be ignored. As well this omission helps to explain the inclusion of restrictions on "confidential" information.

[**214**] This is certainly true of the requirement that the consent of the individual must be obtained before disclosure of information relating to him. What is less clear is how the restriction on the employer's duty to disclose will be applied in cases where information which has been communicated to the employer in confidence. This subsection implies a restriction which could apply as widely as is subjectively desired by the person conveying the information to the firm in the first place. Yet clearly some sort of objective standard will have to be applied so that "confidential" information in the meaning of the first limb of (*c*) is confined to that which is reasonable in the circumstances.

[**215**] The ACAS is required to "have regard" to the six specific restrictions in formulating any Code of Practice relating to the disclosure of information.

DISCLOSURE TO WHOM?

[**216**] The employer's duty to disclose information extends to the authorised representatives of a trade union who is either recognised by him for purposes of collective bargaining or who has received an operative recommendation for recognition from the ACAS in respect of any grade of his employees. A trade union representative is considered to be authorised if he is an official or other

person who is authorised by his trade union to carry on such collective bargaining. Again this could extend to shop stewards and other work place representatives as well as full-time officials.

ENFORCEMENT

[**217**] The enforcement machinery for the duty to disclose information consists of a two-stage complaint procedure followed by an arbitration award. The first complaint of a failure to disclose information or confirm it in writing is presented to the Central Arbitration Committee. The Committee may refer the complaint to the ACAS where it appears to be reasonably likely to be settled by conciliation. If the case cannot be settled by conciliation the Committee must hear the complaint[1] and make a declaration stating whether the complaint was well founded wholly or in part giving the reasons for its finding in respect of the information which the employer should have disclosed and the date on which the employer should have disclosed that information. The Committee must also specify a period of not less than one week from the date of the declaration within which the employer must disclose the required information.

[**218**] If the employer fails to disclose the required information in the period specified by the CAC, the trade union may make a second or "further" complaint to that effect and the Committee must make a declaration stating whether this further complaint is well founded in whole or in part and giving the reasons for its finding. It must also specify the information in respect of which the complaint is well founded.

[**219**] If the second complaint has no effect a trade union is entitled to present a claim to the CAC for an arbitration award improving the terms and conditions of employees for when disclosure of information was sought. Such a claim may be presented along with or after the further complaint of non-disclosure.

[**220**] There seems little logical connection between this sanction for non-compliance and the purposes of the disclosure procedure, apart from the possibility that the claim might relate to the terms for which disclosure was sought. The possibility of an arbitration award by the CAC is designed to act as a deterrent to non-compliance. If the employer discloses the information at any time before the CAC makes its award, he can ensure that the trade union's claim will be treated as withdrawn (s. 21 (2)).

[**221**] If the employer fails to disclose in accordance with the CAC declaration the Committee may hold a hearing and make an award that requires the employer either to observe the terms and conditions for his employees that the trade union has claimed or any other terms and conditions which it considers appropriate.

---

[1] During the first complaint stage the Committee has wide discretion to allow any person which it considers to have a proper interest in the complaint to be heard. However a failure to allow a hearing to a person other than the trade union and employer directly concerned will not affect the validity of the Committee's decision (s. 19 (5)). As well, in cases concerning the interests of national security where the validity of a certificate signed by or on behalf of the Minister of the Crown is called into question the certificate is to be considered authentic unless the contrary is proved (s. 19 (7)).

[**222**] The award may date back to the date specified in the declaration upon the original complaint but may not apply at any time before that date. Moreover the award must apply only to a group of employees for whom and relate only to substantive issues for which the trade union has been recognised by the employer or received an operative recommendation for recognition by the ACAS.

[**223**] The award has effect as part of the contract of employment of any employee in the group affected for whom the trade union is recognised. It applies from the specified date and may be superseded or varied only by a subsequent CAC award, collective agreement or an agreement between employee and employer which effects an improvement in the employee's position under the award (s. 21 (6)).

CHAPTER FOURTEEN

PROCEDURE FOR HANDLING REDUNDANCIES

[**224**] In addition to changed rights for individuals who are dismissed owing to redundancy,[1] the EPA 1975 contains two new requirements for employers of a collective nature in the event of redundancies; advance notification of collective redundancies to the Government and prior consultation with appropriate trade unions.

NOTIFICATION OF REDUNDANCIES

[**225**] The requirement of advance notice to the Secretary of State for Employment, presumably the local employment exchange,[2] is concerned with medium-sized and larger-scale redundancies. Thus where more than 100 employees at one establishment are to be dismissed for redundancy in a 90-day period from the date of the first dismissal, at least 90 days' notice must be given to the Department before the first dismissal takes effect. And where more than 10 employees at one establishment are to be dismissed for redundancy in a 30-day period, then 60 days' notice must be so given before the first dismissal takes effect. If special circumstances render it not reasonably practicable for the employer to comply with any of these requirements, he must nevertheless take all steps towards compliance with the requirements that are practicable in the circumstances. A failure to comply with this requirement of notice to the Secretary can result either in a reduction of up to one tenth of a redundancy payment rebate to which the employer may otherwise be entitled or to a fine of up to £400 on summary conviction.

[**226**] There is an important link between the two procedures. Wherever prior consultation on redundancies with trade unions is required, the notification to the Government must include an identification by the employer of the trade union concerned and the date when consultations began (s. 100 (3) (*b*)). In addition, although this has not yet been explicitly required by direction of the Secretary of State for Employment, the employer is likely to be required to include the numbers and descriptions of employees whom it is proposed to dismiss as redundant and the method of carrying out the dismissals including the period over which the dismissals are to take effect. Whether the Secretary of State will direct, as he is entitled to do, that the notice to the Government shall

---

[1] These include the new trial period (Chapter Three), longer periods of notice of dismissal Chapter Two) and time off during the notice period to look for work, etc. (Chapter Ten).

[2] The Secretary of State has a responsibility to give an address to which each establishment may send its notification (s. 100 (3)).

include any other particulars, for example, any other subsections of s. 99 (5)' remains to be seen.

CONSULTATION WITH TRADE UNIONS ON REDUNDANCY

[227] The requirement of consultation with trade unions on redundancy, unlike that of notification to the Government, is a comprehensive one. Where an employer proposes to dismiss as redundant *an* employee he has a duty to consult authorised[3] representatives of any trade union recognised by him for that grade of employee "at the earliest opportunity".

[228] The collective nature of this requirement is apparent when one observes that the employee being dismissed for redundancy need not be a member of a trade union as long as he falls within a grade for whom a trade union is recognised by the employer or for whom a trade union has obtained an operative recommendation for recognition from the ACAS.

[229] There are three essential requirements of this stage of the procedure for handling redundancies:

—the timing of consultation
—the disclosure of information
—the procedure for consultation.

THE TIMING OF CONSULTATION

[230] The Act places two types of requirement on the timing of consultation. The first is a general requirement that the employer must consult "at the earliest opportunity". This would appear to apply to an individual redundancy as well as a large-scale redundancy. The second requirement is a specific one that where the dismissals are of scale warranting notification to the Government, that is to say 100 employees or more within a 90-day period, or 10 employees or more within a 30-day period, the consultations must "in any event" begin at least 90 days or 60 days respectively *before the first of those dismissals take effect.*

[231] Where special circumstances render it not reasonably practicable to comply, the employer must take all such steps towards compliance as are reasonably practicable (s. 99 (8)). Otherwise the specific requirements are minima; the employer's obligation is to consult "at the earliest opportunity". Thus even if an employer complies with the specific minima set out for medium- and large-scale redundancies in s. 99 (3), he may nevertheless fail to comply with this general obligation established under that section.

DISCLOSURE OF INFORMATION TO TRADE UNION REPRESENTATIVES

[232] Under s. 99 (3) the employer is required to disclose the following:

—the reasons for his proposals for redundancy
—the numbers and descriptions of employees whom he is proposing to

[3] A trade union representative must be an official or other person *authorised by the trade union* to carry out collective bargaining with the employer (s. 99 (2)).

make redundant, together with the total number of employees in the same grade employed at the establishment

—the proposed method of selecting employees for dismissal for redundancy

—the proposed method of carrying out the dismissal *with due regard to any agreed procedure*, including the period over when the dismissals are to take effect.

[**233**] The Act effectively requires of all employers the "collective notice" often called for in many agreed redundancy procedures. At this stage it is envisaged that the economic basis for the decision to make employees redundant is likely to be questioned. Hence the requirement that the employer set out the reasons for the proposed redundancies. Further discussion of the proposed method of selecting individuals for individual notice of dismissal is also clearly intended. What is perhaps less obvious is that under "the proposed method of carrying out the dismissals" whether or not due regard is paid to any agreed procedure it will be difficult to avoid consideration of the possibilities of resorting to measures to avoid compulsory redundancy, such as reductions of overtime, limits on sub-contracting, temporary short-time working, voluntary redundancies, retirements of over-age employees and early retirements, etc. Certainly in so far as they are not included in the information disclosed to trade union representatives, they are likely to be the subject of representations by trade union representatives in the consultation process.

THE PROCESS OF CONSULTATION

[**234**] The procedural standards an employer must meet in the course of consultation are made quite explicit. Thus the employer must consider any representations made by the trade union representatives and reply to those representations and if he rejects any of those representations state his reasons. (EPA, s. 99 (7)).

[**235**] These procedural standards appear to require the employer to enter a dialogue with the trade union representatives, that is, to engage in reasoned discussion. They do not explicitly require the employer to bargain or to make concessions on any point of substance. Yet of course there is nothing to preclude the possibility that the joint consultations required by the Act may be converted to collective negotiations by the circumstances of the case. The minimum legal duty to consult could provide a platform upon which negotiations commence.

[**236**] The employer's obligation to consult is enforced by a rather novel mixture of collective and individual remedies. The right to complain of non-compliance is limited solely to a trade union[4] which ought to have been consulted in accordance with any of the requirements laid down by s. 99. Where the employer alleges that special circumstances made it not reasonably practicable to comply with *any* of the requirements the onus of proof is laid upon him not only in respect of that test but also to show that he took all steps towards compliance that were reasonably practicable in the circumstances. The remedy for a well-founded complaint of non-compliance consists of a declaration of

[4] The complaint must normally be brought within three months of the date the dismissal takes effect. It may be presented before the dismissal takes effect (EPA, s. 101 (6)).

non-compliance and this may at the tribunal's discretion be combined with a "protective award" stipulating that the employer must pay remuneration to specified employees for a specified protected period. The employees who might be specified for a protective award could include those who the employer proposes to dismiss as well as those who have already been dismissed for redundancy. The protected period may be of a length which the tribunal determines to be just and equitable in all the circumstances taking into account the seriousness of the employer's default in complying with any of the requirements of s. 99 but it is subject to certain maxima, most notably 90 days in a case requiring at least 90 days' notice, 60 days in a case requiring at least 60 days' notice and 28 days in any other case. Again, these maxima apply to each of the specified cases for any of the above requirements. Thus, even where part or the whole of the minimum required notice is given in each of the above cases a tribunal may nevertheless in its discretion make a protective award of up to the specified maximum period for the case (s. 101 (5)).

[**237**] Once a protective award has been made the initiative for enforcement shifts to individual employees in the grades to whom the award relates. If an employer fails to pay remuneration wholly or in part under the award, an employee may present a complaint to an industrial tribunal[5] to be paid remuneration for the period specified in the award. If the tribunal finds the complaint well founded it shall order the employer to pay the complainant the amount due. The obligation of the employer to pay remuneration during the protected period is subject to at least four qualifications that apply to the unexpired portion of the protected period, *viz.*:

(1) Where the employee was fairly dismissed by the employer for reason other than redundancy.
(2) Where the employee unreasonably terminated the employment.
(3) Where the employer makes a timely offer in writing of suitable alternative employment and the employee unreasonably refuses that offer (s. 102 (6) and (7)).
(4) If during a trial period in connection with an offer of alternative or renewed employment, the trial period is unreasonably terminated by the employee or employer (s. 102 (11)).

[**238**] Moreover, any payment made by an employer under the contract of employment or by way of damages for breach of contract goes towards discharging the employer's liability under the protective award (s. 102 (3)).

---

[5] Normally within three months from the last day of failure to pay remuneration (s. 103 (2)).

CHAPTER FIFTEEN

TRADE UNION MEMBERSHIP AND ACTIVITY

[**239**] A statute designed to give legal support for trade unionism and the extension of collective bargaining cannot ignore the need for a complementary protection for individuals who wish to become trade union members, help to organise trade unions and otherwise take part in trade union activities. It is particularly at a stage when employees are beginning to organise or develop a trade union in a particular firm that they are in a vulnerable position. Consequently any legal protection for individuals during the organisational phase can be viewed in essence as support for trade unionism and collective bargaining although the legal support may take the form of safeguards for individual employees. As well, as the trade union representatives develop through various stages of a collective bargaining relationship, the law can be used to provide minimum standards of good industrial relations practice.

[**240**] The specific forms of protection provided by the Act for individual employees as trade unionists may be grouped under five heads:

—a right to belong to an independent trade union
—a right to take part in the activities of an independent trade union at the appropriate time
—a right to interim relief for dismissal in connection with the above rights
—a right of trade union officials to time off with pay for carrying out trade union duties
—a right of trade union members to time off for trade union activities.

"THE RIGHT TO BELONG"

[**241**] The right to belong to an independent trade union is given protection by the EPA in the sense that an employer may not by action short of dismissal prevent or deter an employee or penalise him for joining or seeking to join an independent trade union (s. 53 (1) (*a*)). An employee also has a right not to be compelled to join a trade union if that union is not independent (s. 53 (1) (*c*)).

[**242**] Unlike previous legislation, however, the EPA does not provide a general "right not to join" an independent trade union specified in a union membership arrangement between employer and trade union. Only an employee who genuinely objects to membership of any trade union on grounds of religious belief has a right not to be compelled by action short of dismissal to

[1] See TULRA, Sch. 1, paras. 6 (4) and (5), as amended by the Trade Union and Labour Relations (Amendment) Act 1976, for similar rules in respect of dismissal.

join a trade union (s. 53 (6)).[1] In this sense the Act gives tacit recognition to the legitimacy of union security arrangements which take the form of a closed shop. However, even in a closed shop situation, the EPA does not allow action taken by an employer purely to discourage membership in a *non-specified* independent trade union or membership in a trade union *deemed to be specified* (EPA, s. 53 (5)). Further, an employee may not be discouraged from membership of an independent trade union even where an employer recognises another trade union (EPA, s. 53 (1) (*a*)). In this way, the Act attempts to ensure a balance between the employee's right to join or belong to a trade union of his choice and a recognised and established union's organisational interest in union security.

THE RIGHT TO TAKE PART IN TRADE UNION ACTIVITIES

[243] The Act also entitles trade union members to take part in the activities of an independent trade union in the sense that their employer may not by action short of dismissal[2] prevent or deter them from or penalise them for taking part in such activities. This may be seen as formal recognition of the right to organise and recruit employees as well as the right to engage in activities to maintain existing representation arrangements. The new legal right to take part in trade union activities is circumscribed in two respects. In the first place, the activities must take place at an "appropriate time", that is they must be either outside working hours or at a time when the employee is contractually required to be at work. This would presumably include lunch hours, breaks etc.[3] Alternatively, if they occur within working hours, they must occur with the agreement or consent of the employer (s. 53 (3)).

[244] Secondly where an employee falls within a class, grade or category of employees for whom it is the practice[4] in accordance with a union membership agreement to belong to one or more specified trade unions, the right to take part in trade union activities *on the premises* of the employer is limited only to trade unions which are in fact specified or *deemed to be specified* in the uionn membership agreement (s. 53 (5)). In practice, this means that where a trade union has not made a formal recognition claim the existence of a union membership agreement will operate to preclude any right of employees to take part in the activities of trade unions other than those specified in the closed shop on the employer's premises. However, where a trade union has made a formal recognition claim in the statutory recognition procedure and this clashes with existing closed shop arrangements the employee's "right to organise" allows him to take part in trade union activities on the employer's premises along with the incumbent trade unions. This is true, moreover, whether the trade union has obtained an operative recommendation from the ACAS or has made a reference upon which the ACAS has not declined to proceed (s. 53 (5) (*b*) (ii)).

[245] In the absence of a "union membership agreement", the right to take

---

[2] TULRA, s. 6 (4) offers protection against unfair dismissal for similar reasons.

[3] Cf. *The Post Office* v. *Union of Post Office Workers*, [1974] 1 All E.R. 229; [1974] I.R.L.R. 22.

[4] *Strover* v. *Chrysler* (*U.K.*), *Ltd.*, [1975] I.R.L.R. 66; *Sarvent* v. *Central Electricity Generating Board*, [1976] I.R.L.R. 66.

part in trade union activities would appear to include organisational and recruiting activities on the employer's premises outside working hours[5] even though the employees attempting to exercise such a right may be members of trade unions which are not recognised by the employer. Indeed this right would appear to apply even where the employer has given formal recognition to other trade union organisations within the same grade of employee. It is only a closed shop agreement which places a constraint on trade union activities on the employer's premises.

[**246**] In the event, the Act gives legal support to employees' freedom of organisation even where it might create certain rivalries within the context of recognised and established arrangements for collective bargaining.

[**247**] Where an employee considers that the employer has taken action against him short of dismissal which contravenes his rights to trade union membership and activity, he may present a complaint normally within 3 months to an industrial tribunal. At a tribunal hearing the onus of proof is placed upon the employer to show the purpose of the action taken and that it was not a prohibited purpose under the Act.[6] The tribunal may not take into account any pressure placed on an employer by way of industrial action or threats of industrial action; the employer is treated as solely responsible for his actions (s. 55 (2)).

[**248**] The remedy for a well-founded complaint of action short of dismissal by the employer for trade union membership or activity consists of compensation. The amount shall be such as the tribunal considers just and equitable in all the circumstances taking into account the infringement of the employee's right by the employer (which might include non-pecuniary loss) and the resulting loss sustained by the employee. The loss can include both reasonable expenses actually incurred as well as loss of expected benefits though the employee has a duty as at common law to mitigate his loss. Further, the amount of compensation may be reduced by a proportion if the employee was found to have caused or contributed to the action complained of. The measure of compensation for the infringement of the employee's rights may not take account of any industrial pressure that was exercised on the employer (s. 55).

INTERIM RELIEF FOR DISMISSALS FOR TRADE UNION MEMBERSHIP AND ACTIVITY

[**249**] The third element in the new legal protection for trade union members particularly in the organisational phase is a special form of interim relief given in the case of complaints of unfair dismissal owing to trade union membership or activity (s. 69). Previous legislation had displayed some favour to the complainant in this type of dismissal by removing certain of the disqualifications for making a complaint, such as length of service, age, etc. The EPA retains this feature but gives further favour by increasing the measure and maximum

---

[5] *Cf. Post Office* v. *Union of Post Office Workers*, [1974] 1 All E.R. 229; [1974] I.R.L.R. 22 which held that the right to take part in trade union activities extended to activities on the employer's premises whilst the employees were contractually required to be on the employer's premises but not actually required to be at work.

[6] If the purpose concerned the safeguarding of national security the complaint must be dismissed (s. 55 (3) and (4)).

of the "additional" award for unfair dismissal for this reason (s. 72 (3) (*a*)) and creating a special form of interim relief. The relief takes the form of an order either to revive the employee's contract of employment, if it has been terminated, or to continue it in force until the hearing or settlement of the dismissal complaint. The order would not require the employer specifically to perform the contract by retaining the employee at work; it would revive or continue the contract solely for the purpose of ensuring pay, seniority, pension rights and continuous employment. It thus effectively provides a statutory precautionary suspension with pay, pending the hearing or settlement of the complaint. The tribunal must specify the amount payable by the employer and this may be reduced by any payment by the employer in the form of wages or a lump sum payment which is paid at least in part in lieu of notice. The employee however is under no duty to mitigate the loss (s. 79).

[**250**] To qualify for a revival order, an employee must present an application within seven days after the effective date of termination and during the same period produce a written certificate from an authorised official of the relevant independent trade union stating that there appeared to be reasonable grounds for supposing that the employee's complaint was valid (s. 78 (2)). An authorised official in relation to a trade union means an official of the trade union authorised *by the union* to write a certificate (s. 78 (10)).

After receiving an application the tribunal is required to hold a hearing as soon as practicable, giving the employer at least seven days' notice of the hearing and a copy of the complaint and certificate.[7]

[**251**] If it appears at the hearing that the likely result will be finding that the employee had been unfairly dismissed on grounds of trade union membership and activity the tribunal must ask the employer whether he is willing to reinstate the employee, or re-engage him in another job on not less favourable terms. Where the employer fails to attend the hearing or is unwilling either to reinstate or re-engage the employee or the employee reasonably refuses an offer of re-engagement, the tribunal must make an order for revival or continuation of the employee's contract of employment (s. 79).

[**252**] Once made, the order can be varied or revoked on the grounds of a relevant change of circumstances. However, where an employer refuses to comply with an order the tribunal on application by the employee is empowered to award compensation in respect of the loss suffered by the employee in consequence of the non-compliance (s. 80).

[**253**] If the complaint is determined along with the hearing of the complaint of unfair dismissal, the compensation is to be awarded "separately from" that is in addition to any other sum awarded to the employee (s. 80 (3) (*a*)).

TIME OFF WORK FOR TRADE UNION OFFICIALS

[**254**] The Act gives employees who are trade union officials the right to reasonable time off with pay during working hours for the purpose of carrying out duties concerned with industrial relations, duties or undergoing training in relevant aspects of industrial relations. This right is likely to apply widely to

[7] For the purposes of hearing an application for interim relief, a tribunal may consist solely of a Chairman (s. 80 (4)).

work place representatives, shop stewards, conveners, safety representatives, etc. since the definition of "official" includes "any person who is . . . or person elected or appointed in accordance with the rules of the union to be a representative of its members or of some of them".[8] However, the right to time off for trade union activities applies only to duties which are concerned with industrial relations between an employer or associated employer. The official of a trade union concerned with trade union administration, such as a branch secretary, would be eligible only where they have duties connected with industrial relations.

[255] The right to time off to undergo training for industrial relations purposes could extend to a wide variety of courses from induction to advanced courses. There are essentially three limitations to this right: the training must be relevant to the duties of the official, it must be approved either by the TUC or by his own trade union if it is independent (s. 57 (1) (*b*)), and the amount of time off must be reasonable in the circumstances.

[256] The amount of time off which an employee will be permitted to take as well as the purposes and occasions for which and conditions to which time off are subject will be those that are "reasonable in the circumstances", but regard must be had to the relevant provisions of a Code of Practice to be published by the ACAS.

[257] The amount of pay to which an employee is entitled for time off in accordance with the permission is either his likely actual earnings if they can be readily calculated or average hourly earnings for that work for the period. The latter figure is the "shop average" or average for the group of employees in comparable employment with the same employer, or otherwise a "reasonable" figure. It is to be noted that this measure of earnings will clearly exceed the measure of "normal weekly earnings" that applies to most individual employment protections and excluding most forms of overtime earnings.

[258] Duties for which a trade union official will be entitled to be released with pay during working hours must be duties concerned with industrial relations between his employer or any associated employer and their employees. This would be likely to extend to all forms of representation of individuals in respect of grievance and disciplinary matters with management as well as direct consultations and negotiations with management on collective issues. It would also be likely to include interviews with individual employees and meetings at which the representative reports back to work groups, and it might well include consultation between fellow shop stewards.[9] The extent to which the right to time off with pay will be extended to consultations with outside full-time officials as well as representation of employees before outside bodies such as industrial tribunals, etc. must await clarification in a forthcoming Code of Practice to be issued by the ACAS.[10] Similarly the extent to which there is a

---

[8] According to s. 126 the definition of "official" in the EPA is identical to that in TULRA s. 30, except so far as the context otherwise requires. The Industrial Relations Code of Practice recommends that trade unions should notify management promptly in writing when shop stewards are appointed and should give shop stewards credentials setting out the powers and duties within the union (paras. 109–10). The Code also recommends a union management agreement in respect of the number of shop stewards, senior stewards and deputies needed in the establishment as a whole or for specific work groups (para. 106).

[9] *Cf.* CIR Report 17 *Facilities for Shop Stewards.*

[10] See s. 6.

right to time off with pay for consultations with members and fellow shop stewards in respect of duties connected with industrial action must await the practical guidance of a new Code of Practice.

TIME OFF FOR TRADE UNION ACTIVITIES

[259] The Act provides that employees who are members of trade unions recognised by their employer to any extent for the purposes of collective bargaining have the right to be permitted reasonable time off during working hours to engage in union activities. This is a right to time off without pay. Although the right is limited to the members of trade unions recognised for the purposes of collective bargaining, it extends to time off for any trade union activities as well as any activities in which the employee acts as a representative of the trade union. The only specific exclusion appears to be trade union activities which themselves consist of industrial action whether or not in contemplation of or furtherance of a trade dispute. There is no definition of industrial action contained within the Act or within the 1971 Act, but this could include strikes as well as industrial action short of a strike such as a "go-slow", "work to rule", etc.

[260] A clearer view of the activities for which an employer should permit time off will be obtained from the forthcoming Code of Practice. This Code is required to give some guidance upon the purposes and occasions for which, and any conditions subject to which time off should be permitted (s. 58 (3)). The Code is likely to give some guidance on questions of place and times of trade union meetings, as well as alternative arrangements for employees absent with time off. It may also provide some guidance on the criteria to be taken into account in determining reasonable amounts of time off.

[261] In addition the Code will be required to provide practical guidance on the question whether and the circumstances in which a trade union member is to be permitted to take time off for trade union activities connected with industrial action (s. 58 (4)). Hopefully this guidance will include some indication of how the exclusion of an entitlement to time off for activities which themselves *consist of* industrial action in s. 58 (2) may be applied to activities which are *connected* with industrial action. A line must be drawn between union meetings and activities which are called to consider the possibilities of industrial action in connection with on-going or stalled negotiations which are arguably only connected with industrial action and meetings and other activities which are themselves designed predominantly to stop production and hence constitute a form of industrial action. Similarly some indication might be given whether meetings during working hours must be authorised by the employer in order to be viewed as a permitted activity entitling time off or alternatively whether unauthorised meetings might be permitted activity because of their purpose.

[262] The Code of Practice will not have the force of law. However, its provisions will have to be taken into account when a tribunal determines the reasonableness in the circumstances of an employer's refusal to allow time off (s. 58 (3)).

[263] An employee who is a member of a trade union recognised by his employer may complain to an industrial tribunal if his employer refuses to allow him to take reasonable time off to take part in trade union activities in accordance with s. 58. The complaint must normally be presented within three months of the date when the time off was refused (s. 60 (1)). Where the tribunal finds the complaint well founded it must make a declaration to that effect and it may award compensation to the employee in an amount which the tribunal considers just and equitable taking into account both the employer's default and the loss sustained by the employee in connection with that default (s. 60 (2)). The inclusion of the former element in the measure of compensation would appear to open the door to claims for non-pecuniary loss.

CHAPTER SIXTEEN

WAGES COUNCILS AND STATUTORY JOINT INDUSTRIAL COUNCILS

[**264**] Instead of national minimum wage legislation, Britain has provided statutory machinery to protect the lower paid worker in specific industries. The Wages Council Act 1959 and its counterpart the Agricultural Wages Act 1948 provides statutory machinery for fixing minimum wages in more than fifty specified industries.[1]

[**265**] Although the Wages Council system has been subjected to frequent criticism the Act does not replace it by another. Instead, it attempts to reform and reinforce the existing statutory protections. The changes contained within the Act are of three types:

—Wages Councils are to enjoy greater powers than before to establish minimum terms and conditions of employment in their industries

—the Act makes provision for a new half-way house between Wages Councils and collective bargaining—a statutory joint industrial council—in an attempt to foster collective bargaining arrangements in Wages Councils industries

—the application of s. 8 of the Terms and Conditions of Employment Act 1959 to Wages Council sectors is changed to allow trade unions to extend the lowest rate obtained through collective bargaining to employees in Wages Council industry. This is discussed in Chapter Seventeen.

THE NEW POWERS OF WAGES COUNCILS

[**266**] The Act increases the powers of Wages Councils and allows them more scope to fix terms and conditions of employment in their industries in the following four respects.

[**267**] First, Wages Councils are entitled directly to make their own orders fixing the minimum remuneration to be paid to workers within their sector (Sch. 7, Part I, paras. 1–3A). Under the Wages Councils Act 1959, the Council could only submit "wage regulation proposals" to the Secretary of State and he had the option of either making the order by way of statutory instrument or

[1] Section 8 of the Terms and Conditions of Employment Act 1959 allows trade unions to extend the benefits of recognised terms and conditions established by collective agreements to comparable groups of workers. As well, the Fair Wages Resolution 1946 requires all contractors with the Government to observe terms and conditions not less favourable than those generally established for that industry (see Chapter Seventeen).

referring back the proposals to the Council for reconsideration. The Council could only ensure that the Secretary would give effect to its proposals if it sent them back unchanged.

[**268**] Secondly, the orders which Wages Councils can make are extended to other terms and conditions in addition to pay, holidays and holiday pay (Sch. 7, Part I, para. (1) (*c*)). Under the 1959 Act, Wages Councils could only submit proposals in respect of pay, holidays and holiday pay. They could not include other "conditions of employment" in their formal proposals. They were entitled to widen the scope of their regulations only by making a report or recommendation in respect of "industrial conditions".

[**269**] Thirdly, whereas before a Wages Council award could only become operative after the order had gone through a lengthy procedure, the Wages Councils are given power to specify the dates and indeed backdate the order to the date upon which agreement was reached (Sch. 7, Part I, para. 4).

[**270**] Fourthly, the enforcement provisions of Wages Council machinery have been reinforced. Under the 1959 Act, it is provided that Wages Council orders can be enforced under civil law as well as criminal law. At civil law the orders are incorporated into a worker's contract of employment and allow an action in breach of contract for amounts not paid. Enforcement at criminal law takes the form of an offence by the employer who fails to observe any of the terms of the order and is punishable by a fine on summary conviction. As well, where the employer pays below the statutory minimum he could be ordered to pay to the employee the sums withheld for a period of up to two years. In addition the wages inspectorate have certain powers of enforcement to enter premises, to examine records and to receive complaints from workers. The EPA increases the maximum fine for each and every offence from £20 to £100 (Sch. 10, Part II, para. 5).

STATUTORY JOINT INDUSTRIAL COUNCILS

[**271**] Under the Wages Councils Act 1959, the Secretary of State could abolish a Wages Council on application by a Joint Industrial Council. Under TULRA an application could be made by a trade union representing a substantial proportion of workers or a report of the Commission on Industrial Relations. Yet few Wages Councils have been abolished.

[**272**] The Act attempts to meet this problem by providing a half-way house for Wages Councils, the statutory Joint Industrial Councils. These are essentially Wages Councils without independent members. A Wages Council may be converted into a statutory Joint Industrial Council either by the Secretary of State after consulting both sides, or by an application from one side of the Council, most likely the trade union. Before the order can be made it must be referred to the ACAS.

[**273**] Where there is a dispute between the two sides of a statutory Joint Industrial Council it may be referred initially to the ACAS for conciliation. Failing a conciliated settlement, the dispute may be referred to final and binding arbitration either by an arbitrator or by the CAC. It is thought that the prospect of unilateral arbitration may be more successful in fostering collective negotiation than the order procedure of the Wages Councils.

[**274**] If the half-way house provided by the statutory Joint Industrial Council is successful in providing voluntary machinery to regulate pay and other conditions of employment which would be adequate for the needs of the trade concerned, the Secretary of State may abolish a statutory Joint Industrial Council. In a sense, therefore, the ultimate aim of the new Statutory Joint Industrial Councils, like that of the Wages Council, is to make itself obsolete.

CHAPTER SEVENTEEN

EXTENSION OF TERMS AND CONDITIONS

[**275**] Although the majority of new trade union rights are essentially procedural in nature, the Act contains one provision designed to ensure that the substantive terms of existing collective agreements can be "extended" to groups of workers whose terms and conditions fall below either recognised terms and conditions or, if there are no recognised terms and conditions, as defined, the general level of terms and conditions in the industry in the district.

[**276**] In either case the purpose of the extension process is to ensure that employers who are not party to existing agreements do not "undercut" established collective bargaining agreements. The procedure is designed to provide a floor of protection for employees and at the same time prevent an employer paying lower wages to obtain a competitive advantage over those employers observing collectively agreed terms. That is why employers' organisations as well as trade unions may bring a complaint under either procedure. There is also a special provision for extension of collective negotiated substantive terms with Wages Councils.

THE EXTENSION OF "RECOGNISED TERMS AND CONDITIONS"

[**277**] Where terms and conditions for an industry generally or for a district are settled by a collective agreement award between employers' associations and independent trade unions which represent a substantial proportion of employers and workers, any party to that agreement or award, whether employers' associations or trade unions, may report a claim initially to the ACAS that another employer is observing terms and conditions less favourable than the "recognised terms" for comparable employees. The claim may be brought in respect of any term and condition in which the employer is providing less favourable treatment. However, the CAC in determining the claim must have regard to the whole of the terms and conditions observed by the employer for the employees concerned.

[**278**] This procedure is essentially an amended version of the former s. 8 of the Terms and Conditions of Employer Act 1959. Recognised terms and conditions are likely to be terms and conditions fixed by "national" or industry-wide agreements or Joint Industrial Council awards. Unlike the former extension procedure, recognised terms and conditions can include minimum terms and conditions settled under industry-wide agreements (Sch. 11, para 2 (*b*)).[1]

[1] *Cf. Crittal-Hope, Ltd.* v. *Pay Board* (1974), unreported; *Racal Communications* v. *Pay Board*, [1974] 3 All E.R. 263; [1974] I.R.L.R. 209.

[279] The enforcement process continues to consist of an arbitration award though the award is made by the CAC rather than the Industrial Arbitration Board. Where a claim is well founded, the award continues to have effect as part of the contract of employment of the individual employees concerned in the claim on the date specified by the CAC. However, unlike previous legislation, the statutorily inserted term of the employee's contract cannot be varied by agreement between employer and employee unless the agreement effects an improvement upon the terms specified in the award.[2] It may be changed by a subsequent award or collective agreement.

THE EXTENSION OF "GENERAL TERMS AND CONDITIONS"

[280] Where there are no recognised terms and conditions or recognised terms and conditions do not apply to the particular matter which is the subject of the claim, a claim may be reported initially to the ACAS that an employer is observing terms and conditions less favourable than the general level of terms and conditions for comparable workers in the trade, industry or section in a particular district. The claim may be made in respect of any term and condition which is less favourable, but the CAC in determining the claim must have regard to the whole of the terms and conditions being observed by the employer for the employees concerned. A claim may be reported only by an employers' association with members in the relevant trade, industry or section in the district or a trade union which has a member in the work group concerned. Moreover, if the employer already recognises an independent trade union for the work group in question, only a trade union recognised by the employer for that group may bring the claim.

[281] This extension procedure is essentially a statutory enactment of the substance of the Fair Wages Resolution 1946 which was not legally enforceable as such but was inserted in contracts awarded by Government, local authorities and nationalised industries.[3]

[282] The potential application of this procedure is quite wide, certainly to salaried employment for which recognised terms as defined in the Act are rare, and also to other employees since a claim may be made concerning any term which is not provided in a predominant collective agreement. However, there are likely to be certain evidentiary difficulties in establishing the general level of terms and conditions as defined in the Act.

[283] The onus of proof is placed on the party making the claim to show what the general level of terms and conditions is, and this would include a showing that the general level is observed for comparable workers by employers who are not only in the same trade, industry or section in the district but also whose circumstances are similar. It is only if this initial onus is met that the question of whether the employer in observing less favourable terms can be determined and the onus shifts to the employer.

---

[2] *Cf. Fox* v. *Pianoforte Supplies* (1963), 114 L.Jo. 140.

[3] Enforcement was dependent upon a reference by the Department of Employment to an independent tribunal and award. See *R.* v. *Industrial Court, Ex parte Association of Supervisory Staffs, Executives and Technicians*, [1965] 1 Q.B. 377; [1964] 3 All E.R. 130; *Simpson* v. *Kodak, Ltd.*, [1948] 2 K.B. 184.

[**284**] If the CAC finds a claim well founded in whole or in part, it may make an award which at the date specified in the award takes effect as part of the contract of employment of the employees concerned in the claim on the same basis as an award in respect of recognised terms. It can be varied by subsequent award or collective agreement but only on more favourable terms if by individual agreement between employer and employee.

EXTENSION OF TERMS AND WAGES COUNCILS

[**285**] Although the legal extension procedure in respect of recognised terms and general terms is available to any trade union or employers' association in Wages Council industry, the special difficulties of the low paid employment in those industries have prompted the creation of a special extension procedure. Instead of requiring recognised terms and conditions established in a collective agreement affecting a *substantial* proportion of employees and workers, it is sufficient if the trade union is a party to one or more collective agreements which cover a *significant* number of establishments in the Wages Council sector whether taken nationally or in a particular district. Moreover instead of requiring a claim to be based on recognised terms at a general level, the Schedule allows a claim to be reported to the Service if the employer is paying less than the lowest current rate of remuneration payable to comparable workers in similar circumstances under any of the existing agreements. Otherwise the method of enforcement is the same including a determination by the CAC and an award which has legal effect as part of the contracts of employment of the employees concerned in the claim.

CHAPTER EIGHTEEN

OTHER AMENDMENTS TO EXISTING LEGISLATION

HEALTH AND SAFETY AT WORK ETC. ACT 1974

[**286**] The EPA, s. 116 and Sch. 15, repeals s. 2 (5) of the HSWA 1974. This means that there will be no statutory right for safety representatives to be appointed where there is no recognised trade union. Consultation with safety representatives appointed by trade unions (s. 2 (4)) as well as statutory safety committees (s. 2 (6) and 2 (7)) will be regulated in some detail by regulations soon to be issued by the Health and Safety Commission. The Commission will also issue a Code of Practice applicable to the appointment of safety representatives (see the Health and Safety Commission's Consultative Document, *Safety Representatives and Safety Committees*). The Act also removes the special provisions relating to health and safety at work in agriculture.

[**287**] Finally, the Act amends s. 28 of the HSWA to allow a factory inspector to "furnish to a person who appears to him to be likely to be a party to any civil proceedings arising out of any accident, occurrence, situation or other matter, a written statement of relevant facts observed by him in the course of exercising his powers". Thus factory inspectors will be able to issue statements to potential civil litigants notwithstanding the restrictions on disclosure of information contained in s. 28.

SOCIAL SECURITY ACT 1975 AND SUPPLEMENTARY BENEFITS

[**288**] Where an employee is unemployed owing to a trade dispute at his place of employment he may qualify for unemployment benefit only if he proves that:

(*a*) he is not participating in, financing or directly interested in the trade dispute;

(*b*) he is not in a grade or class of workers, some members of whom were participating in the dispute or financing it or directly interested in it.

[**289**] The EPA removes the possibility of disqualification owing to the "grade or class" provision and by implication rejects the notion that all these employees in the same grade or class automatically have a common interest.

[**290**] The Act also removes the provision from (*a*) which refers to the "finances" of the dispute. This would have the effect of removing the possibility that simply because an employee's trade union is paying strike pay to employees participating in the dispute, the employee is disqualified from unemployment benefit.

TULRA 1974: RESTRICTIONS ON GRANT OF EX PARTE INJUNCTIONS

[**291**] Section 17 of TULRA 1974 is amended to include a positive statement to ensure that

> . . . where an application is made to the Court for an interlocutory injunction and the defendent claims that he acted in contemplation and furtherance of a trade dispute the Court must have regard to the *likelihood* of that party's success in the subsequent trial of the actions in establishing the matters under sections 13, 14 (2) or 15 which would afford a defence (Sch. 16, Part III, para. 6).

[**292**] The amendment's concern "to avoid doubt" on this procedural point was aroused by the recent case of *American Cyanamid Co.* v. *Ethicon, Ltd.*[1] in which the House of Lords reduced the requirement that the plaintiff must establish a *prima facie* case to that of satisfying the Court that there is a "serious question to be tried". It remains to be seen whether the amendments to s. 17 succeed in avoiding the effect of American Cyanamid in trade dispute cases.

---

[1] [1975] A.C. 396; [1975] 1 All E.R. 504, H.L.

CHAPTER NINETEEN

THE NEW INSTITUTIONS

[**293**] The EPA establishes four new institutions:

—the Advisory, Conciliation and Arbitration Service
—the Central Arbitration Committee
—the Certification Officer
—the Employment Appeals Tribunal.

THE ADVISORY, CONCILIATION AND ARBITRATION SERVICE

[**294**] The ACAS is an independent service directed by a ten-man council most of whom are appointed in consultation with employers and trade unions. The Act specifically provides that the Service shall not be subject to directions of any kind from the Minister of the Crown as to the manner of performing its functions. The ACAS is charged with the general duty of promoting the improvement of industrial relations and in particular encouraging the extension of collective bargaining. It is also urged to encourage the reform of collective bargaining machinery where necessary. Its specific functions include the provision of voluntary conciliation, arbitration, advice and inquiry services.

Conciliation

[**295**] The Conciliation function is performed in connection with the resolution of industrial disputes generally as well as with legal claims under the Act. In the case of any trade dispute that has started or is about to develop, the Service may provide conciliation at the request of either party or on its own initiative with a view to obtaining a settlement. In addition, the service is called upon to provide conciliation at the request of either party or on its own initiative if it considers there is a reasonable prospect of success in complaints presented to industrial tribunals under almost all of the individual employment rights, as well as complaints either to industrial tribunals or to the Service under the new collective rights (s. 108).

Arbitration

[**296**] The arbitration function is also to be applied to existing or apprehended trade disputes. The type of arbitration that the Service may provide can consist of a simple arbitrator, or arbitration panel or the CAC. However, before a reference may be made by the Service to arbitration it must obtain the consent of all parties to the dispute. As well, where there are negotiating or dispute procedures these must be exhausted without producing agreement

before the Service can intervene, unless a special reason justifies the provision of arbitration as an alternative to the ordinary procedure.

Advice and inquiry

[**297**] Advice and inquiry are the functions of the Service emphasising the reform of industrial relations. The Service may provide advice without charge on any matter concerned with industrial relations or employment policies directly to employers, employers' associations, trade unions or workers. Moreover, it may publish general advice on any particular matter. Further, it may issue Codes of Practice containing practical guidance for the purpose of promoting the improvement of industrial relations. The Codes of Practice will not themselves contain statutory duties enforceable in any proceedings but they may be admissible in evidence before an industrial tribunal or the CAC, and in so far as they are relevant, they must be taken into account in determining questions presented to such bodies.

[**298**] The inquiry function places the initiative squarely on the Service. It may make a general inquiry or one devoted to a specific industry or firm. It may publish the results of these inquiries if publication is thought to be useful in producing a reform and if the parties have been consulted.

THE CENTRAL ARBITRATION COMMITTEE

[**299**] The Committee consists of a chairman and other members experienced in industrial relations, including representatives of employers and trade unions. It takes over the functions of the Industrial Arbitration Board and assures new functions in respect of recognition, disclosure of information and the extension procedure. If the Committee cannot reach a unanimous decision, the chairman can decide the case, acting with the full powers of an umpire. The Committee must publish its awards although it is required to give its opinion only in certain decisions in respect of the new collective rights.

[**300**] There is no direct appeal from the Committee on a question of law. It is, of course, subject to a prerogative order if it acts outside its authority or fails to perform its duties.

THE CERTIFICATION OFFICER

[**301**] The Certification Officer assumes the functions of the Registrar of Friendly Societies. He maintains the list of trade unions and employers' associations entitled to be listed under TULRA, s. 8, e.g. affiliated to the TUC, registered as a trade union under the Trade Union Acts 1871 to 1964. He also assumes all other functions of the Registrar performed under the Trade Union Act 1913, the Trade Union (Amalgamation etc.) Act 1964 and the 1974 Act.

[**302**] His functions under the EPA include the determination of whether a trade union may be entitled to a certificate of independence (s. 8 discussed in Chapter Eleven.) One feature of the procedure for determining the independence of trade unions which is noteworthy is that appeals against a decision of the Officer are limited to trade unions aggrieved by a decision to refuse to issue a

certificate or to withdraw a certificate. Appeals from the officer's refusal to grant a certificate may be made to the Employment Appeals Tribunal on questions of fact and law. However, where the Certification Officer grants a certificate of independence, no other trade union has a similar right of appeal against that decision.

THE EMPLOYMENT APPEALS TRIBUNAL

[**303**] The Employment Appeals Tribunal is established to hear appeals from industrial tribunals on questions of law arising out of decisions not only under the EPA but also the Redundancy Payments Act 1965, the Equal Pay Act 1970, the Contracts of Employment Act 1972, TULRA 1974 and the Sex Discrimination Act 1975. In addition it must hear appeals on questions of law from decisions of the Certification Officer under ss. 3, 4 and 5 of the Trade Union Act 1913 and s. 4 of the Trade Union (Amalgamation, etc.) Act 1964. Finally, it must hear appeals on questions of both fact and law from decisions of the Certification Officer on certificates of independence EPA s. 8 and on the list of trade unions and employer's associations TULRA, s. 8.

[**304**] The Tribunal shall have the status of a superior court of record. Its president shall be chosen from among the judges appointed to the Tribunal. Each proceeding stage to be chaired by a judge appointed from among the judges of the High Court and the Court of Appeal. Yet it shall also include "appointed members" with special knowledge or experience of industrial relations either as representatives of employers or as representatives of trade unions. Moreover unless both parties to a proceeding consent to an alternative, the tribunal must hear cases sitting with the judge and either two or four appointed members with an equal number chosen from among those with experience as representatives of employers and those with experience as representatives of workers.

THE EMPLOYMENT PROTECTION ACT 1975

(1975 c. 71)

ARRANGEMENT OF SECTIONS

PART I

MACHINERY FOR PROMOTING THE IMPROVEMENT OF INDUSTRIAL RELATIONS

Advisory, Conciliation and Arbitration Service, etc.

Maternity

Trade union membership and activities

Time off work

Insolvency

Written statement of reasons for dismissal

Remedies for unfair dismissal

Itemised pay statement

An Act to establish machinery for promoting the improvement of industrial relations; to amend the law relating to workers' rights and otherwise to amend the law relating to workers, employers, trade unions and employers' associations; to provide for the establishment of a Maternity Pay Fund; to provide for the extension of the jurisdiction of industrial tribunals; to amend the law relating to entitlement to and recoupment of unemployment benefit and supplementary benefit; to amend the Employment Agencies Act 1973 *as respects the exercise of licensing functions under that Act; to amend the Employment and Training Act* 1973 *as respects the status of bodies established, and the powers of the Secretary of State, under that Act; to amend the Health and Safety at Work etc. Act* 1974 *as respects the appointment of safety representatives, health and safety at work in agriculture, the status of bodies established and the disclosure of information obtained under that Act; to provide for the extension of employment legislation to certain parliamentary staff and to certain areas outside Great Britain; and for connected purposes* [12th November 1975]

PART I

MACHINERY FOR PROMOTING THE IMPPROVEMENT OF INDUSTRIAL RELATIONS

Advisory, Conciliation and Arbitration Service, etc.

1. Advisory, Conciliation and Arbitration Service

(1) There shall be a body to be known as the Advisory, Conciliation and Arbitration Service, in this Act referred to as "the Service".

(2) The Service shall be charged with the general duty of promoting the improvement of industrial relations, and in particular of encouraging the extension of collective bargaining and the development and, where necessary, reform of collective bargaining machinery.

(3) The provisions (so far as applicable) of Parts I and III of Schedule 1 to this Act shall have effect with respect to the Service. **[305]**

COMMENCEMENT

This section was brought into force on 1st January 1976 by the Employment Protection Act 1975 (Commencement No. 1) Order 1975, S.I. 1975 No. 1938.

FUNCTIONS

As to the individual functions of the Service under this Act, see s. 2, *post* (conciliation), s. 3, *post* (arbitration), s. 4, *post* (advice), s. 5, *post* (inquiry), s. 6, *post* (codes of practice), and ss. 11 *et seq., post* (recognition issues). The functions of the Service and of its officers and servants are performed on behalf of the Crown but are not subject to directions by any Minister; see sub-s. (3) above and Sch. 1, para. 11 (1), *post.*

COLLECTIVE BARGAINING

For meaning, see s. 126 (1), *post.*

2. Conciliation

(1) Where a trade dispute exists or is apprehended the Service may, at the request of one or more parties to the dispute or otherwise, offer the parties to the dispute its assistance with a view to bringing about a settlement.

(2) The assistance offered by the Service may be by way of conciliation or by other means, and may include the appointment of a person other than an officer or servant of the Service to offer assistance to the parties to the dispute with a view to bringing about a settlement.

(3) In exercising its functions under subsection (1) above, the Service shall have regard to the desirability of encouraging the parties to a dispute to use any appropriate agreed procedures for negotiation or the settlement of disputes.

(4) The Service shall designate officers of the Service to perform the functions of conciliation officers under any enactment (including any provision of this Act or any Act passed after this Act) in respect of matters which are or could be the

subject of proceedings before an industrial tribunal, and accordingly any reference in any such enactment to a conciliation officer is a reference to an officer designated under subsection. [**306**]

COMMENCEMENT
This section was brought into force on 1st January 1976 by the Employment Protection Act 1975 (Commencement No. 1) Order 1975, S.I. 1975 No. 1938.

TRADE DISPUTE
For meaning see, by virtue of s. 126 (1), *post*, the definition in the Trade Union and Labour Relations Act 1974, s. 29.

THE SERVICE
For meaning, see s. 1 (1), *ante*.

OFFICER OR SERVANT
Appointments of officers or servants are made under s. 1 (3), *ante*, and Sch. 1, para. 7, *post*.

OFFICERS . . . TO PERFORM THE FUNCTIONS, ETC.
As, for example, the conciliation function specified in the regulations made under the Trade Union and Labour Relations Act 1974, Sch. 1, para. 21; see sub-para. (3) of that paragraph.

INDUSTRIAL TRIBUNAL
See the note to s. 6, *post*.

TRANSITIONAL PROVISIONS
See s. 125 (2) and Sch. 17, para. 2, *post*.

3. Arbitration

(1) Where a trade dispute exists or is apprehended the Service may, at the request of one or more parties to the dispute and with the consent of all the parties to the dispute, refer all or any of the matters to which the dispute relates for settlement to the arbitration of—

(*a*) one or more persons appointed by the Service for that purpose (not being an officer or servant of the Service); or
(*b*) the Central Arbitration Committee constituted under section 10 below.

(2) In exercising its functions under subsection (1) above, the Service shall consider the likelihood of the dispute being settled by conciliation and, where there exist appropriate agreed procedures for negotiation or the settlement of disputes, shall not refer a matter for settlement to arbitration under that subsection unless those procedures have been used and have failed to result in a settlement or unless, in the opinion of the Service, there is a special reason which justifies arbitration under that subsection as an alternative to those procedures.

(3) Where in any case more than one arbitrator is appointed under subsection (1) (*a*) above the Service shall appoint one of the arbitrators to act as chairman.

(4) An award by an arbitrator appointed under subsection (1) (*a*) above may be published if the Service so decides and all the paties consent.

(5) Part I of the Arbitration Act 1950 shall not apply to an arbitration under this section.

(6) (*Applies to Scotland.*) [**307**]

COMMENCEMENT

This section was brought into force in two stages on 1st January and 1st February 1976 by the Employment Protection Act 1975 (Commencement No. 1) Order 1975, S.I. 1975 No. 1938.

AWARD BY AN ARBITRATOR . . . MAY BE PUBLISHED, ETC.

Awards of the Central Arbitration Committee are required to be published however; see s. 10 (3) and Sch. 1, para. 24, *post*.

DEFINITIONS

For "trade dispute", see, by virtue of s. 126 (1), *post*, the Trade Union and Labour Relations Act 1974, s. 29; for "the Service", see s. 1 (1), *ante*.

TRANSITIONAL PROVISIONS

See s. 125 (2) and Sch. 17, para. 3, *post*.

4. Advice

(1) The Service shall, if it thinks fit, on request or otherwise, provide, without charge, to employers, employers' associations, workers and trade unions such advice as it thinks appropriate on any matter concerned with industrial relations or employment policies, including the following—

(*a*) the organisation of workers or employers for the purpose of collective bargaining;
(*b*) the recognition of trade unions by employers;
(*c*) machinery for the negotiation of terms and conditions of employment, and for joint consultation;
(*d*) procedures for avoiding and settling disputes and workers' grievances;
(*e*) questions relating to communication between employers and workers;
(*f*) facilities for officials of trade unions;
(*g*) procedures relating to the termination of employment;
(*h*) disciplinary matters;
(*i*) manpower planning, labour turnover and absenteeism;
(*j*) recruitment, retention, promotion and vocational training of workers;
(*k*) payment systems, including job evaluation and equal pay.

(2) The Service may publish general advice on any matter concerned with industrial relations or employment policies, including any of the matters referred to in paragraphs (*a*) to (*k*) of subsection (1) above. **[308]**

COMMENCEMENT

This section was brought into force on 1st January 1976 by the Employment Protection Act 1975 (Commencement No. 1) Order 1975, S.I. 1975 No. 1938.

DEFINITIONS

By virtue of s. 126 (1), *post*, for "employer", see the definition inserted in the Trade Union and Labour Relations Act 1974, s. 30 (1), by s. 125 (1) and Sch. 16, Part III, para. 7 (2), *post*, and s. 30 (2) (*b*) of that Act; for "official", see s. 30 (1) of that Act; for "employers' association", see ss. 28 (2) and 30 (1) of that Act, for "trade union", see s. 28 (1)of that Act, and for "worker", see s. 30 (1), (2) (*a*) of that Act; for "collective bargaining", see s. 126 (1), *post*; for "the Service", see s. 1 (1), *ante*.

5. Inquiry

(1) The Service may, if it thinks fit, inquire into any question relating to industrial relations generally or to industrial relations in any particular industry or in any particular undertaking or part of an undertaking.

(2) The findings of any inquiry under this section, together with any advice given by the Service in connection with those findings, may be published by the Service if—

(*a*) it appears to the Service that publication is desirable for the improvement of industrial relations, either generally or in relation to the specific question inquired into; and,

(*b*) after sending a draft of the findings to, and taking into account the views of, all the parties appearing to the Service to be concerned, the Service thinks fit. **[309]**

COMMENCEMENT

This section was brought into force on 1st January 1976 by the Employment Protection Act 1975 (Commencement No. 1) Order 1975, S.I. 1975 No. 1938.

THE SERVICE

I.e., the Advisory, Conciliation and Arbitration Service; see s. 1 (1), *ante*.

6. Codes of Practice

(1) The Service may issue Codes of Practice containing such practical guidance as the Service thinks fit for the purpose of promoting the improvement of industrial relations.

(2) Without prejudice to the generality of subsection (1) above, the Service shall in one or more Codes of Practice, provide practical guidance on the following matters in relation to the application of the following provisions of this Act, that is to say—

(*a*) the disclosure of information, in accordance with sections 17 and 18 below, by employers to trade union representatives for the purpose of collective bargaining;

(*b*) the time off to be permitted by an employer—

(i) to a trade union official in accordance with section 57 below; and

(ii) to a trade union member in accordance with section 58 below.

(3) When the Service proposes to issue a Code of Practice, it shall prepare and publish a draft of that Code, shall consider any representations made to it about the draft and may modify the draft accordingly.

(4) If the Service determines to proceed with the draft, it shall transmit the draft to the Secretary of State who shall—

(*a*) if he approves of it, lay it before both Houses of Parliament; and

(*b*) if he does not approve of it, publish details of his reasons for withholding approval.

(5) In the case of a draft Code of Practice containing practical guidance on the matters referred to in paragraph (*a*) or (*b*) of subsection (2) above, if the draft is approved by resolution of each House of Parliament the Service shall issue the Code in the form of the draft and the Code shall come into effect on such day as the Secretary of State may by order appoint.

(6) In the case of a draft Code of Practice not containing such practical guidance, if, within the period of forty days beginning with the day on which a copy of the draft is laid before each House of Parliament, or, if such copies are laid on different days, with the later of the two days, either House so resolves, no further proceedings shall be taken thereon, but without prejudice to the laying before Parliament of a new draft.

(7) In reckoning the period of forty days referred to in subsection (6) above, no account shall be taken of any period during which Parliament is dissolved or prorogued or during which both Houses are adjourned for more than four days.

(8) If no such resolution is passed as is referred to in subsection (6) above,

the Service shall issue the Code in the form of the draft and the Code shall come into effect on such day as the Secretary of State may by order appoint.

(9) Without prejudice to section 123 (3) below, an order under subsection (5) or subsection (8) above may contain such transitional provisions or savings as appear to the Secretary of State to be necessary or expedient in connection with the Code of Practice thereby brought into operation.

(10) The Service may from time to time revise the whole or any part of a Code of Practice issued under this section and issue that revised Code, and subsections (3) to (9) above shall apply (with appropriate modifications) to such a revised Code as they apply to the first issue of a Code.

(11) A failure on the part of any person to observe any provision of a Code of Practice shall not of itself render him liable to any proceedings; but in any proceedings before an industrial tribunal or the Central Arbitration Committee any Code of Practice issued under this section shall be admissible in evidence, and if any provision of such a Code appears to the tribunal or Committee to be relevant to any question arising in the proceedings it shall be taken into account in determining that question. [**310**]

COMMENCEMENT

This section was brought into force on 1st January 1976 by the Employment Protection Act 1975 (Commencement No. 1) Order 1975, S.I. 1975 No. 1938.

GENERAL NOTE

This section replaces the Trade Union and Labour Relations Act 1974, Sch. 1, Part I, which required the Secretary of State to maintain a code of practice for purposes similar to those outlined in sub-ss. (1) and (2) above, and that Part is repealed by s. 125 (3) and Sch. 18, *post*. The Code of Practice in effect under the provisions so repealed, immediately before such repeal, continues in effect until superseded; see s. 125 (2) and Sch. 17, para. 4, *post*.

LAY IT BEFORE . . . PARLIAMENT

For meaning, see the Laying of Documents before Parliament (Interpretation) Act 1948, s. 1 (1).

FORTY DAYS BEGINNING, ETC.

In calculating this period, the *dies a quo* must be included; see *Hare* v. *Gocher*, [1962] 2 Q.B. 641; [1962] 2 All E.R. 763; *Trow* v. *Ind Coope* (*West Midlands*), *Ltd.*, [1967] 2 Q.B. at p. 909; [1967] 2 All E.R. 900, C.A. Note, however, the provisions at sub-s. (7) above.

INDUSTRIAL TRIBUNAL

I.e., a tribunal established under the Industrial Training Act 1964, s. 12; see the Trade Union and Labour Relations Act 1974, s. 1 (2), Sch. 1, para. 16.

CENTRAL ARBITRATION COMMITTEE

This is established under s. 10 (1), *post*.

DEFINITIONS

By virtue of s. 126 (1), *post*, for "employer", see the definition inserted in the Trade Union and Labour Relations Act 1974, s. 30 (1), by s. 125 (1) and Sch. 16, Part III, para. 7 (2), *post*, and s. 30 (2) (*b*) of that Act; for "official" see s. 30 (1) of that Act, and for "trade union", see s. 28 (1) of that Act; for "collective bargaining", see s. 126 (1), *post*; for "the Service", see s. 1 (1), *ante*.

ORDERS UNDER THIS SECTION

At the time of going to press, no orders had been made under sub-s. (5) or (8) above. As to the making or orders generally, see s. 123, *post*; see, however, s. 125 (2) and Sch. 17, para. 4, *post*.

TRANSITIONAL PROVISIONS

See s. 125 (2) and Sch. 17, para. 4, *post*.

7. Certification Officer

(1) The Secretary of State shall, after consultation with the Service, appoint an officer to be known as the Certification Officer.

(2) The functions under the following Acts which before the commencement of this section were performed by the Chief Registrar of Friendly Societies or any assistant registrar shall become functions of the Certification Officer, that is to say,—

(*a*) the Trade Union Act 1913;
(*b*) the Trade Union (Amalgamations, etc.) Act 1964;
(*c*) the 1974 Act.

(3) The provisions (so far as applicable) of Parts I and III of Schedule 1 to this Act shall have effect with respect to the Certification Officer.

(4) The Certification Officer may appoint one or more assistant certification officers and shall appoint an assistant certification officer for Scotland.

(5) The Certification Officer may delegate to an assistant certification officer such functions as he thinks appropriate and in particular may delegate to the assistant certification officer for Scotland such functions as he thinks appropriate in relation to organisations whose principal office is in Scotland.

(6) References in any enactment (except in subsections (4) and (5) above, this subsection, Part I and paragraph 28 of Schedule 1 to this Act and the House of Commons Disqualification Act 1975) to the Certification Officer shall be construed as including, in relation to such functions as have been delegated in accordance with subsection (5) above, references to an assistant certification officer. [**311**]

COMMENCEMENT
This section was brought into force on 1st February 1976 by the Employment Protection Act 1975 (Commencement No. 1) Order 1975, S.I. 1975 No. 1938.

CONSULTATION
On what constitutes consultation, see, in particular, *Rollo* v. *Minister of Town and Country Planning*, [1948] 1 All E.R. 13; *Re Union of Whippingham and East Cowes Benefices, Derham* v. *Church Comrs. for England*, [1954] A.C. 245, [1954] 2 All E.R. 22, P.C.; and *Agricultural, Horticultural and Forestry Industry Training Board* v. *Aylesbury Mushrooms, Ltd.*, [1972] 1 All E.R. 280.

THE SERVICE
I.e., the Advisory, Conciliation and Arbitration Service; see s. 1 (1), *ante*.

CHIEF REGISTRAR OF FRIENDLY SOCIETIES
As to this officer, see the Friendly Societies Act 1974, s. 1 (1), and the notes to that section.

TRANSITIONAL PROVISIONS
See s. 125 (2) and Sch. 17, para. 5, *post*.

8. Certification as independent trade union

(1) A trade union whose name is entered on the list of trade unions maintained under section 8 of the 1974 Act may apply to the Certification Officer for a certificate that it is independent.

(2) An application under subsection (1) above shall be made in such form and manner as the Certification Officer may require and shall be accompanied by a fee of £21 or such other fee as may be prescribed by regulations made by the Secretary of State.

(3) The Certification Officer shall maintain a record showing details of all applications made under subsection (1) above and shall keep it available for public inspection (free of charge) at all reasonable hours.

(4) If an application is made, or by virtue of subsection (12) below is treated as being made, by a trade union whose name is not entered on the list of trade unions maintained under section 8 of the 1974 Act, the Certification Officer shall refuse a certificate of independence and shall enter that refusal on the record maintained in accordance with subsection (3) above.

(5) In the case of an application not falling within subsection (4) above, the Certification Officer shall—

(*a*) determine whether the applicant trade union is independent;

(*b*) enter his decision and the date of his decision on the record maintained in accordance with subsection (3) above; and

(*c*) if he determines that the trade union is independent, issue a certificate accordingly, or, if he determines that it is not, give reasons for his decision.

(6) The Certification Officer shall not make any determination under subsection (5) above whether a trade union is independent until one month after the application has been entered on the record in accordance with subsection (3) above, and before making such a determination he shall make such inquiries as he thinks fit and shall take into account any relevant information submitted to him by any person.

(7) The Certification Officer may at any time withdraw a certificate, in accordance with subsection (8) below, if he is of the opinion that the trade union in question is no longer independent.

(8) Where the Certification Officer proposes to withdraw a certificate under subsection (7) above—

(*a*) he shall notify the trade union concerned of the proposal;

(*b*) subsections (3), (5) and (6) above shall apply (with appropriate modifications) to such a proposal as they apply to an application under subsection (1) above; and

(*c*) the Certification Officer shall confirm or withdraw the certificate accordingly.

(9) A trade union aggrieved by the refusal of the Certification Officer to issue it with a certificate or by a decision of his to withdraw its certificate may appeal, in accordance with section 88 (3) below, to the Employment Appeal Tribunal; and on any such appeal the Tribunal, if satisfied that the certificate should be issued or as the case may be should not be withdrawn, shall declare that fact and give directions to the Certification Officer accordingly.

(10) Where the name of an organisation is removed from the list of trade unions maintained under section 8 of the 1974 Act, the Certification Officer shall cancel any certificate of independence in force in respect of that organisation by entering on the record the fact that the organisation's name has been removed from the said list and that the certificate is accordingly cancelled.

(11) A certificate of independence which is in force, or, as the case may be, a refusal, withdrawal or cancellation of a certificate entered on the record, shall for all purposes be conclusive evidence that the trade union in question is, or, as the case may be, is not, independent; and a document purporting to be such a certificate or a certified copy of such an entry on the record, and to be signed by the Certification Offcer or by any person authorised to act on his behalf, shall

be taken to be such a certificate or a true copy of such an entry unless the contrary is proved.

(12) If in any proceedings before any court, the Employment Appeal Tribunal, the Central Arbitration Committee, the Service, or an industrial tribunal a question arises as to whether a trade union is independent and there is no certificate of independence in force and no refusal, withdrawal or cancellation of a certificate recorded in relation to that trade union—

(*a*) the question shall not be decided in those proceedings, and those proceedings shall be stayed or, in Scotland, sisted until a certificate has been issued or refused by the Certification Officer; and

(*b*) the body before whom the proceedings are stayed, or sisted, may refer the question as to the independence of the trade union to the Certification Officer who shall proceed in accordance with subsections (3) to (6) above as if the reference were an application by that trade union.

[**312**]

COMMENCEMENT

This section was brought into force on 1st February 1976 by the Employment Protection Act 1975 (Commencement No. 1) Order 1975, S.I. 1975 No. 1938.

GENERAL NOTE

This section makes provision, for the first time, for the certification of a union as an independent trade union, and a certificate issued hereunder is conclusive proof for all purposes that the union in question is independent; see sub-s. (11) above. Proof of the fact of independence is thus facilitated for the purposes, *inter alia*, of the following provisions, namely: the Trade Union and Labour Relations Act 1974, s. 1 (2), Sch. 1, para. 13 (2) (*a*) (exclusion of rights as to unfair dismissal under para. 4 of that Schedule, in respect of a dismissal procedures agreement), and ss. 11, *post* (reference of recognition issue of Service), 17, *post* (general duty of employers to disclose information), 19, *post* (complaint of failure to disclose information), 99, *post* (duty of employer to consult trade union representatives on redundancy) and 101, *post* (compliant by trade union and protective award).

CERTIFICATION OFFICER

This officer is appointed under s. 7, *ante*.

AT ALL REASONABLE HOURS

For a case in point, see *Small* v. *Bickley* (1875) 32 L.T. 726 (Sunday afternoon). For a discussion of this expression, see also 37 Halsbury's Laws (3rd Edn.) 102.

ONE MONTH AFTER

In calculating this period the *dies a quo* is not to be reckoned; see, in particular, *Goldsmiths' Co.* v. *West Metropolitan Rail. Co.*, [1904] 1 K.B. 1; [1900–3] All E.R. Rep. 667, C.A., and *Stewart* v. *Chapman*, [1951] 2 K.B. 792; [1951] 2 All E.R. 613 (and contrast *Hare* v. *Gocher*, [1962] 2. Q.B. 641; [1962] 2 All E.R. 763, and *Trow* v. *Ind Coope* (*West Midlands*), *Ltd.*, [1967] 2 Q.B. at p. 909 [1967] 2 All E.R. 900 C.A.). "Month" means calendar month: see the Interpretation Act 1889, s. 3.

PERSON

Unless the contrary intention appears ,"person" includes a body of persons, corporate or unincorporate; see the Interpretation Act 1889, s. 19.

EMPLOYMENT APPEAL TRIBUNAL

That body is established under s. 87, *post*.

CENTRAL ARBITRATION COMMITTEE

That body is established under s. 10, *post*.

INDUSTRIAL TRIBUNAL

See the note to s. 6, *ante*.

APPEALS

As to appeals to the Employment Appeal Tribunal, and thence to the Court of Appeal, from decisions of the Certification Officer under this section, see s. 88 (3)–(5), *post*.

DEFINITIONS

By virtue of s. 126 (1), *post*, for "trade union", see the Trade Union and Labour Relations Act 1974, s. 28 (1), and for "independent trade union", "independence" and "independent", see s. 30 (1) of that Act, as amended by s. 125 (1) and Sch. 16, Part III, para. 7 (3), *post*; for "the Service", see s. 1 (1), *ante*.

REGULATIONS UNDER THIS SECTION

At the time of going to press, no regulations had been made for the purposes of sub-s. (2) above.

As to the making of regulations generally, see s. 123, *post*.

9. Custody of documents

(1) The Certification Officer shall take custody of all annual returns, accounts, copies of rules and other documents submitted, for the purposes of the Trade Union Acts 1871 to 1964 or the Industrial Relations Act 1971 or the 1974 Act to the Chief Registrar of Friendly Societies or any assistant registrar, or to the Registrar of Trade Unions and Employers' Associations or any assistant registrar, and which are, on the commencement of this section, in the custody of the Chief Registrar of Friendly Societies or any assistant registrar.

(2) The Certification Officer shall keep available for public inspection (either free of charge or on payment of a reasonable charge) at all reasonable hours such of the documents referred to in subsection (1) above as are, or were, available for public inspection in pursuance of any of the Acts referred to in that subsection. [**313**]

COMMENCEMENT

This section was brought into force on 1st February 1976 by the Employment Protection Act 1975 (Commencement No. 1) Order 1975, S.I. 1975 No. 1938.

CERTIFICATION OFFICER

This officer is appointed under s. 7, *ante*.

ANNUAL RETURNS, ACCOUNTS, COPIES OF RULES, ETC.

As to the duty of trade unions and employers' associations to submit annual returns, see the Trade Union and Labour Relations Act 1974, s. 11, Sch. 2, paras. 1–5. Those provisions are appropriately amended by s. 125 (1) and Sch. 16, Part III, para. 1, *post*, by the substitution of "Certification Officer" for "Registrar of Friendly Societies". Copies of certain accounts kept in accordance with the requirements of s. 10 of the 1974 Act, together with a copy of the rules of the trade union or employers' association are required, by para. 2 of Sch. 2 of the 1974 Act, to be contained in every annual return submitted under the afore-mentioned provisions of the said Act.

COMMENCEMENT OF THIS SECTION

See the note above.

CHIEF REGISTRAR OF FRIENDLY SOCIETIES

As to this officer, see the Friendly Societies Act 1974, s. 1 (1), and the notes to that section.

REGISTRAR OF TRADE UNIONS AND EMPLOYERS' ASSOCIATIONS

This officer was appointed under the Industrial Relations Act 1971, s. 63 (repealed), and exercised under that Act the functions subsequently conferred on the Registrar of Friendly Societies by the Trade Union and Labour Relations Act 1974 and by this Act now conferred on the Certification Officer.

AT ALL REASONABLE HOURS

See the note to s. 8, *ante*.

TRADE UNION ACTS 1871 TO 1964

For the Acts which might be cited together by this collective title, see the Introductory Note to the Trade Union Act 1871. Many of those provisions were repealed by the Industrial Relations Act 1971, s. 169, Sch. 9.

10. Central Arbitration Committee

(1) There shall be a body to be known as the Central Arbitration Committee, in this Act referred to as the "Committee".

(2) Any reference in any enactment, statutory instrument or other document to the Industrial Arbitration Board (whether by that or any other name) shall be construed as a reference to the Committee.

(3) The provisions of Part II and (so far as applicable) Parts I and III of Schedule 1 to this Act shall have effect with respect to the Committee. [**314**]

COMMENCEMENT

This section was brought into force on 1st February 1976 by the Employment Protection Act 1975 (Commencement No. 1) Order 1975, S.I. 1975 No. 1938.

INDUSTRIAL ARBITRATION BOARD

The Industrial Courts Act 1919, Part I, as originally enacted, provided, in s. 1, for the establishment of a standing Industrial Court and, in s. 2, for the reference to that Court of trade disputes. The Industrial Relations Act 1971, s. 124 (repealed), renamed the Industrial Court as the Industrial Arbitration Board, and s. 169 of, and Sch. 8 to, that Act (repealed), amended the Act of 1919 by substituting the words "Industrial Arbitration Board" for the words "Industrial Court" wherever they appeared. The Trade Union and Labour Relations Act 1974, s. 25 (1), Sch. 3, para. 3 (now repealed by s. 125 (3) and Sch. 18, *post*) provided that such words were to continue to be so substituted. See also, in this regard, s. 125 (7) and Sch. 16, Part III, para. 35, *post*.

TRANSITIONAL PROVISIONS

See s. 125 (2) and Sch. 17, paras. 3, 6, *post*.

Trade union recognition

11. Reference of recognition issue to Service

(1) A recognition issue may be referred by an independent trade union to the Service by written application in such form as the Service may require.

(2) In this Act, "recognition" in relation to a trade union means the, recognition of the union by an employer, or two or more associated employers, to any extent, for the purpose of collective bargaining.

(3) In this section and sections 12 to 14 below, "recognition issue" means an issue arising from a request by a trade union for recognition by an employer, or two or more associated employers, including, where recognition is already accorded to some extent, a request for further recognition. [**315**]

COMMENCEMENT

This section was brought into force on 1st February 1976 by the Employment Protection Act 1975 (Commencement No. 1) Order 1975, S.I. 1975 No. 1938.

GENERAL NOTE

This section and ss. 12–16, *post*, prescribe for the first time a procedure for securing recognition of a trade union by an employer for the purposes of collective bargaining (see sub-s. 2 (2) above) and the provisions of the following sections of this Act apply only in respect of a trade union which is so recognised: s. 17, *post* (general duty of employers to disclose information); s. 57, *post* (time off for carrying out trade union duties); s. 58, *post* (time off for trade union activities); s. 99, *post* (duty of employer to consult trade union representatives on redundancy); and s. 101, *post* (complaint by trade union (in respect of dismissal as redundant) and protective award).

WRITTEN

Expressions referring to writing are, unless the contrary intention appears, to be construed as including reference to printing, lithography, photography, and other modes of representing or reproducing words in a visible form; see the Interpretation Act 1889, s. 20.

DEFINITIONS

By virtue of s. 126 (1), *post*, for "trade union", see the Trade Union and Labour Relations Act 1974, s. 28 (1); for "employer", see the definition inserted in s. 30 (1) of that Act by s. 125 (1) and Sch. 16, Part III, para. 7 (2), *post*, and s. 30 (2) (*b*) of that Act; for "independent trade union" and "independent", see s. 30 (1) of that Act, as amended by s. 125 (1) and Sch. 16, Part III, para. 7 (3), *post*, and for "associated employer", see s. 30 (5) of that Act; for "the Service", see s. 1 (1), *ante*; for "collective bargaining", see s. 126 (1), *post*. As to "recognition", note sub-s. (2) above and as to "recognition issue", note sub-s. (3) above.

12. Inquiry and report on recognition issue

(1) Subject to subsection (2) below, when a recognition issue is referred to the Service under section 11 above the Service shall examine the issue, shall consult all parties who it considers will be affected by the outcome of the reference and shall make such inquiries as it thinks fit.

(2) The Service may decline to proceed on a reference under section 11 above if it is of the opinion that the issue referred is substantially the same as an issue which has previously been the subject of a reference under that section, or of an application under section 13 below, unless the trade union shows that the circumstances have changed to such an extent as to justify a new reference.

(3) At all times after a recognition issue has been referred to the Service and before the Service has reported on it—

(*a*) the Service shall have regard to the desirability of encouraging the settlement of the issue by agreement and shall, where appropriate, seek to assist such a settlement by conciliation; and

(*b*) the trade union or unions which made the reference may, by notice in writing, withdraw the reference, and one or more such unions may, by notice in writing, withdraw from the reference, and in the latter case only such unions as remain parties to the reference may be recommended for recognition.

(4) If the issue has not been settled and the reference not withdrawn the Service shall prepare a written report setting out its findings, any advice in connection with those findings and any recommendation for recognition and the reasons for it, or, where no such recommendation is made, the reasons for not making any recommendation.

(5) A recommendation for recognition shall specify—

(*a*) the employer or employers and the trade union or unions to which it relates;

(*b*) the description or descriptions of workers in respect of which recognition is recommended;

(*c*) whether the recommendation is for recognition generally or in respect of one or more specified matters;

(*d*) the level or levels at which recognition is recommended.

(6) A recommendation for recognition may be subject to such conditions, to be complied with on the part of the trade union, as the Service thinks fit, and any conditions shall be set out in the report.

(7) The Service shall send a copy of the report to every trade union and employer concerned in the recognition issue and to such other persons as it thinks fit. **[316]**

COMMENCEMENT

This section was brought into force on 1st February 1976 by the Employment Protection Act 1975 (Commencement No. 1) Order 1975, S.I. 1975 No. 1938.

GENERAL NOTE
See the General Note to s. 11, *ante*.

CONSULT
See the note "Consultation" to s. 7, *ante*.

WRITING; WRITTEN
See the note "Written" to s. 11, *ante*.

FURTHER PROVISIONS
See s. 13, *post* (application for variation or revocation of recommendation); s. 14, *post* (ascertaining the opinions of workers); s. 15, *post* (when recommendation becomes operative and complaint of failure to comply with recommendation); and s. 16, *post* (application arising from such failure).

DEFINITIONS
By virtue of s. 126 (1), *post*, for "trade union", see the Trade Union and Labour Relations Act 1974, s. 28 (1); for "employer", see the definition inserted in s. 30 (1) of that Act, by s. 125 (1) and Sch. 16, Part III, para. 7 (2), *post*; and s. 30 (2) (*b*) of that Act, and for "worker", see s. 30 (1), (2) (*a*) of that Act; for "recognition", see s. 11 (2), *ante*; for "recognition issue", see s. 11 (3), *ante*; for "the Service", see s. 1 (1), *ante*.

13. Application for variation or revocation of recommendation

(1) At any time when a recommendation of the Service has been made and has not been—

(*a*) superseded by agreement, whether express of implied, between the employer and the union;
(*b*) superseded by another recommendation under section 12 above; or
(*c*) revoked on an application under this section,

an application may be made under this section for the variation or revocation of that recommendation.

(2) Such an application may be made—

(*a*) jointly by all the trade unions and employers to whom the recommendation relates; or
(*b*) by any trade union or employer to whom the recommendation relates,

and in each case the application shall be in writing and in such form as the Service may require.

(3) Where the Service is of the opinion that the issue raised by an application which is not a joint application such as is referred to in subsection (2) (*a*) above is substantially the same as an issue which has previously been the subject of a reference under section 11 above or of an application under this section, it may decline to proceed with that application unless the applicant shows—

(*a*) that the reconsideration of the recommendation is justified because circumstances have changed or further information has become available; or
(*b*) that a condition to which the recommendation is subject is no longer being sufficiently complied with.

(4) Subject to subsection (3) above, on receipt of an application under this section the Service shall examine the issue raised by the application, shall consult such persons and make such inquiries as it thinks fit and, if the application is not settled or withdrawn, shall report on it stating its conclusions and the reasons for them.

(5) A variation or revocation may be subject to such conditions, to be

complied with on the part of the trade union or the employer, as the Service thinks fit, and any conditions shall be set out in the report.

(6) A variation or revocation shall take effect—

(*a*) in the case of an unconditional variation or revocation, on the date when the Service transmits its report to the parties to whom the recommendation relates; and

(*b*) in the case of a conditional variation or revocation, on the date on which the Service, on the application of the party by whom the condition or conditions were to be complied with, transmits to the other party its opinion that the condition or all the conditions have been sufficiently complied with. [**317**]

COMMENCEMENT

This section was brought into force on 1st February 1976 by the Employment Protection Act 1975 (Commencement No. 1) Order 1975, S.I. 1975 No. 1938.

GENERAL NOTE

See the General Note to s. 11, *ante*.

RECOMMENDATION OF THE SERVICE

I.e., a recommendation made under s. 12 (4), *ante*; see also s. 12 (5) (6), *ante*.

WRITING

See the note "Written" to s. 11, *ante*.

CONSULT

See the note "Consultation" to s. 7, *ante*.

SUPPLEMENTARY PROVISIONS

As to the ascertainment of the opinions of the workers to whom the issue relates, see s. 14, *post*.

DEFINITIONS

By virtue of s. 126 (1), *post*, for "trade union", see the Trade Union and Labour Relations Act 1974, s. 28 (1), and for "employer", see the definition inserted in s. 30 (1) of that Act by s. 125 (1) and Sch. 16, Part III, para. 7 (2), *post*, and s. 30 (2) (*b*) of that Act; for "the Service", see s. 1 (1), *ante*.

14. Inquiries under ss. 12 and 13

(1) In the course of its inquiries into a recognition issue under section 12 or 13 above the Service shall ascertain the opinions of workers to whom the issue relates by any means it thinks fit, but if in any case it determines to take a formal ballot of those workers or any description of such workers, the following provisions of this section shall apply.

(2) In making arrangements for any such ballot the Service shall have regard to the need for securing that every worker invited to take part in the ballot has an equal right and a fair opportunity of voting, and that the vote cast by any individual in the ballot will be kept secret.

(3) Before taking any such ballot the Service shall give notice to every employer and union concerned in the reference or application, including every union known to the Service to have members among the workers proposed to be invited to take part in the ballot, of—

(*a*) the description or descriptions of workers proposed to be invited to take part in the ballot;

(*b*) the question or questions on which the ballot is proposed to be taken; and

(*c*) the manner in which the ballot is proposed to be taken;

and the Service shall consider any representations made by any such employer or union with respect to the proposals.

(4) Subject to subsections (2) and (3) above, any such ballot may be conducted in such manner as the Service thinks fit.

(5) Where a formal ballot has been taken in accordance with this section the Service shall arrange for—

(*a*) the question or questions on which the ballot was taken; and

(*b*) the results of the ballot on that question or on each such question,

to be notified to every employer and union concerned in the reference or application, including every union known to the Service to have members among the workers invited to take part in the ballot.

(6) An employer who is notified in accordance with subsection (5) above of the results of the ballot and who has workers among those invited to take part in the ballot shall arrange for those results to be notified to them. [**318**]

COMMENCEMENT

This section was brought into force on 1st February 1976 by the Employment Protection Act 1975 (Commencement No. 1) Order 1975, S.I. 1975 No. 1938.

GENERAL NOTE

See the General Note to s. 11, *ante*.

DEFINITIONS

By virtue of s. 126 (1), *post*, for "trade union", see the Trade Union and Labour Relations Act 1974, s. 28 (1); for "employer", see the definition of that term inserted in s. 30 (1) of that Act by s. 125 (1) and Sch. 16, Part III, para. 7 (2) *post*, and s. 30 (2) (*b*) of that Act, and for "worker", see s. 30 (1), (2) of that Act; for "recognition issue", see s. 11 (3), *ante*; for "the Service", see s. 1 (1), *ante*.

15. Complaint of failure to comply with recommendation

(1) A recommendation for recognition made by the Service under section 12 above, so far as it relates to employees, but not so far as it relates to workers who are not employees, shall become operative for the purpose of the following provisions of this Act—

(*a*) in the case of an unconditional recommendation, at the end of the period of 14 days beginning with the date on which the Service's report under section 12 above is received by the employer; and

(*b*) in the case of a conditional recommendation, at the end of the period of 14 days beginning with the date on which the Service, on the application of the union, notifies the employer of its opinion that the condition or all the conditions have been sufficiently complied with.

and shall remain operative except in so far as it is—

(i) superseded by agreement, whether express or implied, between the employer and the union;

(ii) superseded by another recommendation under section 12 above; or

(iii) revoked on an application under section 13 above.

(2) Where a recommendation is operative, then at any time after the end of the period of two months beginning with the date on which it became operative, the trade union may refer in writing to the Service a complaint that the employer is at the time of the complaint, wholly or in part, not complying with the recommendation, that is to say, that he is not then taking such action by way of or with a view to carrying on negotiations as might reasonably be expected to

be taken by an employer ready and willing to carry on such negotiations as are envisaged by the recommendation.

(3) When a complaint is referred to the Service under this section the Service shall attempt to settle the matter by conciliation. [**319**]

COMMENCEMENT

This section was brought into force on 1st February 1976 by the Employment Protection Act 1975 (Commencement No. 1) Order 1975, S.I. 1975 No. 1938.

GENERAL NOTE

See the General Note to s. 11, *ante*.

14 DAYS (TWO MONTHS) BEGINNING, ETC.

In calculating the relevant period, the *dies a quo* is to be included; see, in particular, *Hare* v. *Gocher*, [1962] 2 Q.B. 641; [1961] 2 All E.R. 763, and *Trow* v. *Ind Coope* (*West Midlands*), *Ltd.*, [1967] 2 Q.B. at p. 909; [1967] 2 All E.R. 900, C.A. A month is a calendar month; see the Interpretation Act 1889, s. 3.

WRITING

See the note "Written" to s. 11, *ante*.

SERVICE SHALL ATTEMPT TO SETTLE . . . CONCILIATION

If such attempt fails, then the trade union concerned may apply under s. 16, *post*, to the Central Arbitration Committee for an award.

DEFINITIONS

By virtue of s. 126 (1), *post*, for "employer", see the definition inserted in the Trade Union and Labour Relations Act 1974, s. 30 (1), by s. 125 (1) and Sch. 16, Part III, para. 7 (2), *post*, and s. 30 (2) (*b*) of that Act, and for "employer", see s. 30 (1) of that Act; for "the Service", see s. 1 (1), *ante*.

16. Application arising from failure to comply with recommendation

(1) If conciliation under section 15 (3) above does not result in a settlement, the trade union which referred the complaint under that section may apply to the Central Arbitration Committee in accordance with the following provisions of this section.

(2) The application shall be in writing and in such form as the Committee may require and shall consist of—

(*a*) a complaint that the employer is not complying (within the meaning of section 15 (2) above) with a recommendation of the Service; and

(*b*) a claim that in respect of one or more descriptions of employees covered by that recommendation their contracts should include the terms and conditions specified in the claim.

(3) An application under this section comprising a complaint on substantially the same grounds as those of a complaint in a previous application under this section, shall not be entertained by the Committee before the end of the period of 12 months beginning with the date on which the Committee made its award under subsection (6) below, or determined not to make such an award, on that previous application.

(4) Subject to subsection (3) above, the Committee shall proceed to hear and determine the complaint and shall make a declaration stating whether it finds the complaint well founded, wholly or in part, and stating the reasons for its finding.

(5) If the Committee finds the complaint wholly or partly well-founded, the declaration shall specify—

(*a*) the description or descriptions of employees in relation to whom the employer has failed to comply with the recommendation; and (*b*) the matters in relation to which the employer has failed to comply with the recommendation.

(6) If the Committee finds the complaint wholly or partly well-founded, it may, after hearing the parties, make an award that in respect of any description of employees specified in the declaration under subsection (5) (*a*) above the employer shall observe either—

(*a*) the terms and conditions specified in the claim by the trade union in accordance with subsection (2) (*b*) above; or

(*b*) other terms and conditions which the Committee considers appropriate,

being in either case terms and conditions falling within the scope of the matters specified in the declaration under subsection (5) (*b*) above.

(7) Any terms and conditions which by an award under subsection (6) above the employer is required to observe in respect of employees of his shall have effect as part of the contract of employment of any such employee, as from the date specified in the award, except in so far as they are superseded or varied—

(*a*) by a subsequent award under this section;

(*b*) by a collective agreement between the employer and the union for the time being representing that employee; or

(*c*) by express or implied agreement between the employee and the employer so far as that agreement effects an improvement in any terms and conditions having effect by virtue of the award.

(8) Where—

(*a*) by virtue of any enactment, other than one contained in this section, providing for minimum remuneration or terms and conditions, a contract of employment is to have effect as modified by an award, order or other instrument under that enactment, and

(*b*) by virtue of an award under this section any terms and conditions are to have effect as part of that contract,

that contract shall have effect in accordance with that award, order or other instrument or in accordance with the award under this section, whichever is the more favourable, in respect of any terms and conditions of that contract, to the employee.

(9) No award shall be made under this section in respect of any terms and conditions of employment which are fixed by virtue of any enactment. [**320**]

COMMENCEMENT

This section was brought into force on 1st February 1976 by the Employment Protection Act 1975 (Commencement No. 1) Order 1975, S.I. 1975 No. 1938.

GENERAL NOTE

See the General Note to s. 11, *ante*.

CENTRAL ARBITRATION COMMITTEE

That body is established under s. 10, *ante*.

WRITING

See the note "Written" to s. 11, *ante*.

12 MONTHS BEGINNING, ETC.

See the note "14 days (two months) beginning, etc." to s. 15, *ante*.

TERMS ... FIXED BY VIRTUE OF ANY ENACTMENT

As, for example, under s. 98 and Sch. 11, para. 11, *post*; under the Wages Councils Act 1959, s. 11, as substituted by s. 89 (2) and Sch. 7, Part I, *post*; or under the Agricultural Wages Act 1948, s. 3, as substituted by s. 97, and Sch. 9, Part I, *post*.

EXCLUSION OF CROWN EMPLOYMENT

See s. 121, *post.*

DEFINITIONS

By virtue of s. 126 (1), *post,* for "trade union", see the Trade Union and Labour Relations Act 1974, s. 28 (1); for "collective agreement", "employee", see s. 30 (1), (2) of that Act, and for "employer", see the definition inserted in s. 30 (1) of that Act by s. 125 (1) and Sch. 16, Part III, para. 7 (2), *post,* and s. 30 (2) (*b*) of s. 30 of that Act.

Disclosure of information

17. General duty of employers to disclose information

(1) For the purposes of all the stages of such collective bargaining between an employer and representatives of an independent trade union as is referred to in subsection (2) below, it shall be the duty of the employer, subject to section 18 below, to disclose to those representatives on request all such information relating to his undertaking as is in his possession, or that of any associated employer, and is both—

(*a*) information without which the trade union representatives would be to a material extent impeded in carrying on with him such collective bargaining, and

(*b*) information which it would be in accordance with good industrial relations practice that he should disclose to them for the purposes of collective bargaining.

(2) The collective bargaining for the purposes of which an employer must disclose information under subsection (1) above is collective bargaining about matters, and in relation to descriptions of workers,—

(*a*) in respect of which the trade union is recognised by that employer; or

(*b*) falling within the scope of an operative recommendation for recognition (within the meaning of section 15 above) relating to the union,

and in this section and sections 19 to 21 below "representative", in relation to a trade union, means an official or other person authorised by the trade union to carry on such collective bargaining.

(3) Where a request for information is made by trade union representatives under this section, the request shall, if the employer so requests, be in writing or be confirmed in writing.

(4) In determining, for the purposes of subsection (1) (*b*) above, what would be in accordance with good industrial relations practice, regard shall be had to the relevant provisions of any Code of Practice issued by the Service under section 6 above, but not so as to exclude any other evidence of what that practice is.

(5) Where an employer is required by virtue of this section to disclose any information to trade union representatives, the disclosure of it shall, if they so request, be in writing or be confirmed in writing. [**321**]

COMMENCEMENT

See s. 129 (3), *post.*

GOOD INDUSTRIAL RELATIONS PRACTICE

Note sub-s. (4) above.

RECOGNISED BY THAT EMPLOYER

I.e., recognised for the purpose of collective bargaining; see s. 11 (2), *ante*, and s. 126 (1), *post.*

OPERATIVE RECOMMENDATION

S. 15 (1), *ante*, defines when a recommendation for recognition shall become operative.

WRITING

See the note "Written" to s. 11, *ante*.

FURTHER PROVISIONS

See s. 18, *post* (restrictions on general duty under this section); s. 19, *post* (complaint of failure to disclose information); s. 20, *post* (further complaint); and s. 21, *post* (determination of claim and award).

DEFINITIONS

By virtue of s. 126 (1), *post*, for "employer", see the definition inserted in the Trade Union and Labour Relations Act 1974, s. 30 (1), by s. 125 (1) and Sch. 16, Part III, para. 7 (2), *post*; and s. 30 (2) (*b*) of that Act; for "trade union", see s. 28 (1) of that Act; for "independent trade union", and "official", see s. 30 (1) of that Act; for "worker", see s. 30 (1), (2) (*a*) of that Act, and for "associated employer", see s. 30 (5) of that Act; for "collective bargaining", see s. 126 (1), *post* ; for "representative" in relation to a trade union, note sub-s. (2) above.

18. Restrictions on general duty under s. 17

(1) No employer shall, by virtue of section 17 above, be required to disclose—

(*a*) any information the disclosure of which would be against the interests of national security, or

(*b*) any information which he could not disclose without contravening a prohibition imposed by or under an enactment, or

(*c*) any information which has been communicated to the employer in confidence, or which the employer has otherwise obtained in consequence of the confidence reposed in him by another person, or

(*d*) any information relating specifically to an individual, unless he has consented to its being disclosed, or

(*e*) any information the disclosure of which would cause substantial injury to the employer's undertaking for reasons other than its effect on collective bargaining, or

(*f*) any information obtained by the employer for the purpose of bringing, prosecuting or defending any legal proceedings;

and in formulating the provisions of any Code of Practice relating to the disclosure of information, the Service shall have regard to the provisions of this subsection.

(2) In the performance of his duty under section 17 above an employer shall not be required—

(*a*) to produce, or allow inspection of, any document (other than a document prepared for the purpose of conveying or confirming the information) or to make a copy of or extracts from any document, or

(*b*) to compile or assemble any information where the compilation or assembly would involve an amount of work or expenditure out of reasonable proportion to the value of the information in the conduct of collective bargaining. [**322**]

COMMENCEMENT

See s. 129 (3), *post*.

EMPLOYER'S UNDERTAKING

In applying the provisions of this Act to Crown employment, "employer's undertaking" in sub-s. (1) (*e*) above is to be construed as a reference to the national interest, see s. 121 (7) (*e*), *post*.

CODE OF PRACTICE
See s. 6, *ante*.

DEFINITIONS
By virtue of s. 126 (1), *post*, for "employer", see the definition inserted in the Trade Union and Labour Relations Act 1974, s. 30 (1) by s. 125 (1) and Sch. 16, Part III, para. 7 (2), *post*, and s. 30 (2) (*b*) of that Act; for "collective bargaining", see s. 126 (1), *post*; for "the Service", see s. 1 (1), *ante*.

19. Complaint of failure to disclose information

(1) An independent trade union may present to the Central Arbitration Committee, in writing in such form as the Committee may require, a complaint that an employer has failed to disclose to representatives of that trade union information which he was required to disclose to them by section 17 above, or to confirm any such information in writing in accordance with subsection (5) of that section.

(2) If on receipt of such a complaint the Committee is of the opinion that the complaint is reasonably likely to be settled by conciliation, it shall refer the complaint to the Service and shall notify the trade union and employer accordingly, whereupon the Service shall seek to promote a settlement of the matter.

(3) If the complaint is not settled or withdrawn and the Service is of the opinion that further attempts at conciliation are unlikely to result in a settlement it shall inform the Committee of its opinion.

(4) If the complaint is not referred to the Service under subsection (2) above, or, if it is so referred, on the Service informing the Committee of its opinion in accordance with subsection (3) above, the Committee shall proceed to hear and determine the complaint and shall make a declaration stating whether it finds the complaint well-founded, wholly or in part, and stating the reasons for its finding.

(5) On the hearing of a complaint under this section any person who the Committee considers has a proper interest in the complaint shall be entitled to be heard by the Committee, but a failure to accord a hearing to a person other than the trade union and employer directly concerned shall not affect the validity of any decision of the Committee in those proceedings.

(6) If the Committee finds the complaint wholly or partly well-founded, the declaration shall specify—

(*a*) the information in respect of which the Committee finds that the complaint is well founded;

(*b*) the date (or, if more than one, the earliest date) on which the employer refused or failed to disclose, or, as the case may be, to confirm in writing, any of the information specified under paragraph (*a*) above; and

(*c*) a period (not being less than one week from the date of the declaration) within which the employer ought to disclose, or, as the case may be, to confirm in writing, the information specified under paragraph (*a*) above.

(7) On a hearing of a complaint under this section a certificate signed by or on behalf of a Minister of the Crown and certifying that a particular request for information could not be complied with except by disclosing information the disclosure of which would have been against the interests of national security shall be conclusive evidence of that fact; and a document which purports to be

such a certificate shall be taken to be such a certificate unless the contrary is proved. [**323**]

COMMENCEMENT

See s. 129 (3), *post*.

CENTRAL ARBITRATION COMMITTEE

That Committee is established under s. 10 (1), *ante*. As to its constitution and as to proceedings before and awards by it, see s. 10 (3), *ante*, and Sch. 1, Part II, *post*.

WRITING

See the note "Written" to s. 11, *ante*.

ONE WEEK FROM, ETC.

See the note "One month after, etc." to s. 8, *ante*.

DEFINITIONS

By virtue of s. 126 (1), *post*, for "independent trade union", see the Trade Union and Labour Relations Act 1974, s. 30 (1), and for "trade union", see s. 28 (1) of that Act; for "representatives" in relation to a trade union, see s. 17 (2), *ante*; for "the Service", see s. 1 (1), *ante*; for "the Committee", see s. 10 (1), *ante*.

20. Further complaint arising from failure to disclose information

(1) At any time after the expiration of the period specified in a declaration under section 19 (6) (*c*) above the trade union may present to the Committee, in writing in such form as the Committee may require, a complaint (hereafter in this section and section 21 below referred to as a "further complaint") that the employer has failed to disclose, or, as the case may be, to confirm in writing, to representatives of that union information specified in the declaration under section 19 (6) (*a*) above.

(2) On receipt of a further complaint the Committee shall proceed to hear and determine the complaint and shall make a declaration stating whether it finds the complaint well-founded, wholly or in part, and stating the reasons for its finding.

(3) On the hearing of a further complaint under this section any person who the Committee considers has a proper interest in the complaint shall be entitled to be heard by the Committee, but a failure to accord a hearing to a person other than the trade union and employer directly concerned shall not affect the validity of any decision of the Committee in those proceedings.

(4) If the Committee finds the further complaint wholly or partly well-founded the declaration shall specify the information in respect of which the Committee finds that the complaint is well-founded. [**324**]

COMMENCEMENT

See s. 129 (3), *post*.

WRITING

See the note "Written" to s. 11, *ante*.

EXCLUSION OF CROWN EMPLOYMENT

See s. 121, *post*.

DEFINITIONS

By virtue of s. 126 (1), *post*, for "employer", see the definition inserted in the Trade Union and Labour Relations Act 1974, s. 30 (1), by s. 125 (1) and Sch. 16, Part III, para. 7 (2), *post*, and s. 30 (2) (*b*) of that Act, and for "trade union", see s. 28 (1) of that Act; for "the Committee", see s. 10 (1), *ante*; for "representative" in relation to a trade union, see s. 17 (2), *ante*. As to "further complaint", note sub-s. (1) above.

21. Determination of claim and award

(1) On or after presenting a further complaint under section 20 above, the trade union may present to the Committee, in writing, a claim in respect of one or more descriptions of employees (but not workers who are not employees) specified in the claim that their contracts should include the terms and conditions specified in the claim.

(2) The right to present a claim under subsection (1) above shall expire, or, as the case may be, a claim so presented shall be treated as withdrawn, if at any time before the Committee makes an award under this section the employer discloses, or, as the case may be, confirms in writing, to representatives of the trade union the information specified in the declaration under section 19 (6) (*a*) or, as the case may be, section 20 (4) above.

(3) If the Committee finds, or has found, the further complaint wholly or partly well-founded, it may, after hearing the parties, make an award that in respect of any description of employees specified in the claim the employer shall, from a specified date, observe either—

(*a*) the terms and conditions specified in the claim; or
(*b*) other terms and conditions which the Committee considers appropriate.

(4) The date specified in an award under subsection (3) above may be a date earlier than that on which the award is made but shall not be earlier than the date specified in accordance with section 19 (6) (*b*) above in the declaration made by the Committee on the original complaint.

(5) An award under subsection (3) above shall be made only in respect of a description of employees, and shall comprise only terms and conditions relating to matters,—

(*a*) in respect of which the trade union making the claim is recognised by the employer; or
(*b*) which fall within the scope of an operative recommendation for recognition (within the meaning of section 15 above) relating to the trade union making the claim.

(6) Any terms and conditions which by an award under this section the employer is required to observe in respect of employees of his shall have effect as part of the contract of employment of any such employee, as from the date specified in the award, except in so far as they are superseded or varied—

(*a*) by a subsequent award under this section;
(*b*) by a collective agreement between the employer and the union for the time being representing that employee; or
(*c*) by express or implied agreement between the employee and the employer so far as that agreement effects an improvement in any terms and conditions having effect by virtue of the award.

(7) Where—

(*a*) by virtue of any enactment, other than one contained in this section, providing for minimum remuneration or terms and conditions, a contract of employment is to have effect as modified by an award, order or other instrument under that enactment; and
(*b*) by virtue of an award under this section any terms and conditions are to have effect as part of that contract,

that contract shall have effect in accordance with that award, order or other instrument or in accordance with the award under this section, whichever is the more favourable, in respect of any terms and conditions of that contract, to the employee.

(8) No award shall be made under this section in respect of any terms and conditions of employment which are fixed by virtue of any enactment. [325]

COMMENCEMENT

See s. 129 (3), *post*.

WRITING

See the note "Written" to s. 11, *ante*.

OPERATIVE RECOMMENDATION

As to when a recommendation for recognition becomes operative so far as it relates to employees, see s. 15 (1), *ante*.

EXCLUSION OF CROWN EMPLOYMENT

See s. 121, *post*.

DEFINITIONS

By virtue of s. 126 (1), *post*, for "employer", see the definition inserted in the Trade Union and Labour Relations Act 1974, s. 30 (1), by s. 125 (1) and Sch. 16, Part III, para. 7 (2), *post*, and s. 30 (2) (*b*) of that Act; for "trade union", see s. 28 (1) of that Act; for "worker", see s. 30 (1) (2) (*a*) of that Act, and for "collective agreement" and "employee", see s. 30 (1) of that Act; for "further complaint", see s. 20 (1), *ante*; for "the Committee", see s. 1 (1), *ante*; for "representative" in relation to a trade union, see s. 17 (2), *ante*.

Part II

Rights of Employees

Guarantee payments

22. Right to guarantee payment

(1) Where an employee throughout a day during any part of which he would normally be required to work in accordance with his contract of employment is not provided with work by his employer by reason of—

(*a*) a diminution in the requirements of the employer's business for work of the kind which the employee is employed to do, or

(*b*) any other occurrence affecting the normal working of the employer's business in relation to work of the kind which the employee is employed to do,

he shall, subject to the following provisions of this Act, be entitled to be paid by his employer a payment, referred to in this Act as a guarantee payment, in respect of that day and hereafter in this section and sections 23 to 26 below—

(i) such a day is referred to as a "workless day", and

(ii) "workless period" has a corresponding meaning.

(2) In this section and sections 23 to 27 below "day" means the period of 24 hours from midnight to midnight, and where a period of employment begun on any day extends over midnight into the following day, or would normally so extend, then—

(*a*) if the employment before midnight is, or would normally be, of longer duration than that after midnight, that period of employment shall be treated as falling wholly on the first day; and

(*b*) in any other case, that period of employment shall be treated as falling wholly on the second day.

(3) An employee shall not be entitled to a guarantee payment under subsection (1) above in respect of a workless day unless he has been continuously employed for a period of four weeks ending with the last complete week before that day. [**326**]

COMMENCEMENT
See s. 129 (3), *post*.

FURTHER PROVISIONS
See s. 23, *post* (general exclusions from right under this section); s. 24, *post* (calculation of guarantee payment); s. 25, *post*, (limits on amount of and entitlement to guarantee payment); s. 26, *post* (supplementary provisions); s. 27, *post* (complaint of failure to pay guarantee payment), s. 28, *post* (exemption orders); s. 63, *post* (priority of guarantee payments on insolvency), s. 108 (2)–(7), *post* (provision for conciliation), s. 119 (1)–(7), *post* (excluded classes of employment).

MODIFICATIONS AND ADAPTATIONS
Note the power conferred on the Secretary of State by s. 26 (4), *post*, to modify and adapt, by order, the provisions, *inter alia*, of sub-s. (2) above.

DEFINITIONS
By virtue of s. 126 (1), *post*, for "employer", see the definition inserted in the Trade Union and Labour Relations Act 1974, s. 30 (1), by s. 125 (1) and Sch. 16, Part III, para. 7 (2), *post*, and, s. 30 (2) (*b*) of that Act, and for "employee", see s. 30 (1) of that Act. As to "guarantee payment", "workless day" and "workless period", note sub-s. (1) above and as to "day" note sub-s. (2) above.

23. General exclusions from right under s. 22

(1) An employee shall not be entitled to a guarantee payment in respect of a workless day if the failure to provide him with work occurs in consequence of a trade dispute involving any employee of his employer or of an associated employer.

(2) An employee shall not be entitled to a guarantee payment in respect of a workless day if—

(*a*) his employer has offered to provide alternative work for that day which is suitable in all the circumstances, whether or not work which the employee is under his contract employed to perform, and the employee has unreasonably refused that offer; or

(*b*) he does not comply with reasonable requirements imposed by his employer with a view to ensuring that his services are available. [**327**]

COMMENCEMENT
See s. 129 (3), *post*.

DEFINITIONS
By virtue of s. 126 (1), *post*, for "employer", see the definition inserted in the Trade Union and Labour Relations Act 1974, s. 30 (1), by s. 125 (1) and Sch. 16, Part III, para. 7 (2), *post*; and s. 30 (2) (*b*) of that Act; for "associated employer", see s. 30 (5) of that Act; for "employee", see s. 30 (1) of that Act; and for "trade dispute", see s. 29 (1) of that Act; for "guarantee payment" and "workless day", see s. 22 (1), *ante*; for "day", see s. 22 (2), *ante*.

24. Calculation of guarantee payment

(1) Subject to the limits set by section 25 below, the amount of a guarantee payment payable to an employee in respect of any day shall be the sum produced by multiplying the number of normal working hours on that day by the guaran-

teed hourly rate, and accordingly no guarantee payment shall be payable to an employee in whose case there are no normal working hours on the day in question.

(2) Subject to subsection (4) below, the guaranteed hourly rate in relation to an employee shall be the amount of one week's pay divided by—

(*a*) the number of normal working hours in a week for that employee when employed under the contract of employment in force on the day in respect of which the guarantee payment is payable; or

(*b*) where the number of such normal working hours differs from week to week or over a longer period, the average number of such hours calculated by dividing by 12 the total number of the employee's normal working hours during the period of 12 weeks ending with the last complete week before the day in respect of which the guarantee payment is payable; or

(*c*) in a case falling within paragraph (*b*) above but where the employee has not been employed for a sufficient period to enable the calculation to be made under that paragraph, a number which fairly represents the number of normal working hours in a week having regard to such of the following considerations as are appropriate in the circumstances, that is to say,—

(i) the average number of normal working hours in a week which the employee could expect in accordance with the terms of his contract;

(ii) the average number of such hours of other employees engaged in relevant comparable employment with the same employer.

(3) For the purposes of Part II of Schedule 4 to this Act as it applies for the calculation of a week's pay for the purposes of this section, the calculation date is, subject to subsection (4) below, the day in respect of which the guarantee payment is payable.

(4) If in any case an employee's contract has been varied, or a new contract has been entered into, in connection with a period of short-time working, subsections (2) and (3) above shall have effect as if for the references in those subsections to the day in respect of which the guarantee payment is payable there were substituted references to the last day on which the original contract was in force.

(5) In this section and section 25 below "week", in relation to an employee whose remuneration is calculated weekly by a week ending with a day other than Saturday, means a week ending with that other day, and in relation to other employees, means a week ending with Saturday. [**328**]

COMMENCEMENT

See s. 129 (3), *post*.

NORMAL WORKING HOURS

As to the calculation of normal working hours for the purposes of this Act, see s. 85 (1) and Sch. 4, Part I, *post*.

GUARANTEED HOURLY RATE

Note sub-s. (2) above.

WEEK'S PAY

As to the calculation of a week's pay, see s. 85 (1) and Sch. 4, Part, II *post*, in conjunction with sub-s. (3) above.

MODIFICATIONS AND ADAPTATIONS

Note the power conferred on the Secretary of State by s. 26 (4), *post*, to modify and adapt, by order, the provisions, *inter alia*, of this section.

LIMITS ON AMOUNT AND ENTITLEMENT

See s. 25, *post*.

DEFINITIONS

By virtue of s. 126 (1), *post*, for "employer", see the definition inserted in the Trade Union and Labour Relations Act 1974, s. 30 (1), by s. 125 (1) and Sch. 16, Part III, para. 7 (2), *post*, and s. 30 (2) (*b*) of that Act, and for "employee", see s. 30 (1) of that Act; for "day", see s. 22 (2), *ante*; for "guarantee payment", see s. 22 (1), *ante*. As to "week", note sub-s. (5) above.

25. Limits on amount of and entitlement to guarantee payment

(1) The amount of guarantee payment payable to an employee in respect of any day shall not exceed £6.

(2) An employee shall not be entitled to guarantee payments in respect of more than the specified number of days in any one of the relevant periods, that is to say, the periods of three months commencing on 1st February, 1st May, 1st August and 1st November in each year.

(3) The specified number of days for the purposes of subsection (2) above shall be, subject to subsection (4) below,—

(*a*) the number of days, not exceeding five, on which the employee normally works in a week under the contract of employment in force on the day in respect of which the guarantee payment is claimed; or

(*b*) where that number of days varies from week to week or over a longer period, the average number of such days, not exceeding five, calculated by dividing by 12 the total number of such days during the period of 12 weeks ending with the last complete week before the day in respect of which the guarantee payment is claimed and rounding up the resulting figure to the next whole number; or

(*c*) in a case falling within paragraph (*b*) above but where the employee has not been employed for a sufficient period to enable the calculation to be made under that paragraph, a number which fairly represents the number of the employee's normal working days in a week, not exceeding five, having regard to such of the following considerations as are appropriate in the circumstances, that is to say,—

(i) the average number of normal working days in a week which the employee could expect in accordance with the terms of his contract;

(ii) the average number of such days of other employees engaged in relevant comparable employment with the same employer.

(4) If in any case an employee's contract has been varied, or a new contract has been entered into, in connection with a period of short-time working, subsection (3) above shall have effect as if for the references to the day in respect of which the guarantee payment is claimed there were substituted references to the last day on which the original contract was in force.

(5) The Secretary of State may vary any of the limits referred to in this section, and may in particular vary the relevant periods referred to in subsection (2) above, after a review under section 86 below, by order made in accordance with that section. [**329**]

COMMENCEMENT
See s. 129 (3), *post*.

SPECIFIED NUMBER OF DAYS
I.e., specified in sub-s. (3) above.

MONTHS
"Month" means calendar month; see the Interpretation Act 1889, s. 3.

MODIFICATIONS AND ADAPTATIONS
Note the power conferred on the Secretary of State by s. 26 (4), *post*, to modify and adapt, by order, the provisions, *inter alia*, of sub-s. (3) above.

DEFINITIONS
By virtue of s. 126 (1), *post*, for "employer", see the definition inserted in the Trade Union and Labour Relations Act 1974, s. 30 (1), by s. 125 (1) and Sch. 16, Part III, para. 7 (2), and s. 30 (2) (*b*) of that Act, and for "employee", see s. 30 (1) of that Act: for "day", see s. 22 (2), *ante*; for "guarantee payment", see s. 22 (1), *ante*; for "week", see s. 24 (5), *ante*.

26. Supplementary

(1) Subject to subsection (2) below, a right to a guarantee payment shall not affect any right of an employee in relation to remuneration under his contract of employment (hereafter in this section referred to as "contractual remuneration").

(2) Any contractual remuneration paid to an employee in respect of a workless day shall go towards discharging any liability of the employer to pay a guarantee payment in respect of that day, and conversely any guarantee payment paid in respect of a day shall go towards discharging any liability of the employer to pay contractual remuneration in respect of that day.

(3) For the purposes of subsection (2) above, contractual remuneration shall be treated as paid in respect of a workless day—

(*a*) where it is expressed to be calculated or payable by reference to that day or any part of that day, to the extent that it is so expressed; and
(*b*) in any other case, to the extent that it represents guaranteed remuneration, rather than remuneration for work actually done, and is referable to that day when apportioned rateably between that day and any other workless period falling within the period in respect of which the remuneration is paid.

(4) The Secretary of State may by order provide that in relation to any description of employees the provisions of sections 22 (2), 24 and 25 (3) above, as originally enacted or as varied under section 25 (5) above, and of subsections (1) to (3) above, and, so far as they apply for the purposes of those provisions, the provisions of Schedule 4 to this Act, shall have effect subject to such modifications and adaptations as may be prescribed by the order. **[330]**

COMMENCEMENT
See s. 129 (3), *post*.

MODIFICATIONS AND ADAPTATIONS
Note the power conferred on the Secretary of State by sub-s. (4) above to modify and adapt, by order, the provisions, *inter alia*, of sub-ss. (1)–(3) above.

DEFINITIONS
By virtue of s. 126 (1), *post*, for "employer", see the definition inserted in the Trade Union and Labour Relations Act 1974, s. 30 (1), by s. 125 (1) and Sch. 16, Part III, para. 7 (2), *post*, and s. 30 (2) (*b*) of that Act, and for "employee", see s. 30 (1) of that Act;

for "guarantee payment", "workless day" and "workless period", see s. 22 (1), *ante*; for "day", see s. 22 (2), *ante*. Note sub-s. (1) above as to "contractual remuneration".

ORDERS UNDER THIS SECTION

At the time of going to press, no order had been made under sub-s. (4) of this section. As to the making of orders generally, see s. 123, *post*.

27. Complaint to industrial tribunal

(1) An employee may present a complaint to an industrial tribunal that his employer has failed to pay the whole or any part of a guarantee payment to which the employee is entitled.

(2) An industrial tribunal shall not entertain a complaint relating to a guarantee payment in respect of any day unless the complaint is presented to the tribunal before the end of the period of three months beginning with that day or within such further period as the tribunal considers reasonable in a case where it is satisfied that it was not reasonably practicable for the complaint to be presented within the period of three months.

(3) Where an industrial tribunal finds a complaint under subsection (1) above well-founded the tribunal shall order the employer to pay the complainant the amount of guarantee payment which it finds is due to him. [**331**]

COMMENCEMENT

See s. 129 (3), *post*.

COMPLAINT

A complaint under this section is to be made in accordance with regulations under the Trade Union and Labour Relations Act 1974, Sch. 1, para. 21; see s. 108 (1), *post*, and note sub-ss. (2)–(7) of that section as to conciliation.

INDUSTRIAL TRIBUNAL

See the note to s. 6, *ante*.

THREE MONTHS BEGINNING, ETC.

See the note "14 days (two months) beginning, etc." to s. 15, *ante*.

APPEALS

As to appeals to the Employment Appeal Tribunal, and thence to the Court of Appeal, from decisions of an industrial tribunal under this section, see s. 88 (1), (4), (5), *post*.

DEFINITIONS

By virtue of s. 126 (1), *post*, for "employer", see the definition inserted in the Trade Union and Labour Relations Act 1974, s. 30 (1), by s. 125, Sch. 16, Part III, para. 7 (2), *post*, and s. 30 (2) (*b*) of that Act, and for "employee", see s. 30 (1) of that Act; for "day", see s. 22 (2), *ante*; for "guarantee payment", see s. 22 (1), *ante*.

28. Exemption orders

(1) If at any time there is in force a collective agreement or a wages order, whereby employees to whom the agreement or order relates have a right to guaranteed remuneration and on the application of all the parties to the agreement, or as the case may be, of the council or Board making the order, the appropriate Minister, having regard to the provisions of the agreement or order, is satisfied that section 22 above should not apply to those employees, he may make an order under this section excluding those employees from the operation of that section.

(2) In subsection (1) above a wages order means an order made under any of the following provisions, that is to say—

(*a*) section 11 of the Wages Councils Act 1959;
(*b*) section 3 of the Agricultural Wages Act 1948;
(*c*) (*Applies to Scotland.*)

(3) In subsection (1) above the appropriate Minister means—

(*a*) as respects a collective agreement or such an order as is referred to in subsection (2) (*a*) or (*c*) above, the Secretary of State;
(*b*) as respects such an order as is referred to in subsection (2) (*b*) above, the Minister of Agriculture, Fisheries and Food.

(4) The Secretary of State shall not make an order under this section in respect of an agreement unless—

(*a*) the agreement provides for procedures to be followed (whether by arbitration or otherwise) in cases where an employee claims that his employer has failed to pay the whole or any part of any guaranteed remuneration to which the employee is entitled under the agreement, and that those procedures include a right to arbitration or adjudication by an independent referee or body in cases where (by reason of an equality of votes or otherwise) a decision cannot otherwise be reached; or
(*b*) the agreement indicates that an employee to whom the agreement relates may present a complaint to an industrial tribunal that his employer has failed to pay the whole or any part of any guaranteed remuneration to which the employee is entitled under the agreement;

and where an order under this section is in force in respect of such an agreement as is described in paragraph (*b*) above an industrial tribunal shall have jurisdiction over such a complaint as if it were a complaint falling within section 27 above.

(5) Without prejudice to section 123 (4) below, an order under this section may be varied or revoked by a subsequent order thereunder, whether in pursuance of an application made by all or any of the parties to the agreement in question, or, as the case may be, by the council or Board which made the order in question, or without any such application. [**332**]

COMMENCEMENT
See s. 129 (3), *post.*

COUNCIL OR BOARD MAKING THE ORDER
I.e., a wages council established under the Wages Council Act 1959, s. 1 (1), or the Agricultural Wages Board established under the Agricultural Wages Act 1948, s. 1.

COMPLAINT
A complaint within sub-s. (4) (*b*) above is to be made in accordance with regulations under the Trade Union and Labour Relations Act 1974, Sch. 1, para. 21; see s. 108 (1), *post.* As to appeals, see s. 88 (1), (4), (5), *post.*

INDUSTRIAL TRIBUNAL
See the note to s. 6, *ante.*

DEFINITIONS
By virtue of s. 126 (1), *post,* for "employer", see the definition inserted in the Trade Union and Labour Relations Act 1974, s. 30 (1) by s. 125 (1) and Sch. 16, Part III, para. 7 (2), *post,* and s. 30 (2) (*b*) of that Act, and for "collective agreement" and "employee", see s. 30 (1) of that Act. Note sub-s. (2) above as to "wages order" and sub-s. (3) above as to "the appropriate Minister".

ORDERS UNDER THIS SECTION

At the time of going to press, no orders had been made under this section.

As to the making of orders generally, see s. 123, *post*, especially sub-s. (2) thereof, relating to orders under this section. Note also sub-s. (5) above.

Suspension from work on medical grounds

29. Right to remuneration on suspension on medical grounds

(1) An employee who is suspended from work by his employer on medical grounds in consequence of—

(*a*) any requirement imposed by or under any provision of any enactment or of any instrument made under any enactment, or

(*b*) any recommendation in any provision of a code of practice issued or approved under section 16 of the Health and Safety at Work etc. Act 1974,

which is a provision for the time being specified in Schedule 2 to this Act, shall, subject to the following provisions of this Act, be entitled to be paid by his employer remuneration while he is so suspended for a period not exceeding 26 weeks.

(2) For the purposes of this section and sections 30 to 33 below an employee shall be regarded as suspended from work only if, and so long as, he continues to be employed by his employer, but is not provided with work or does not perform the work he normally performed before the suspension.

(3) The Secretary of State may by order add provisions to or remove provisions from the list of specified provisions in Schedule 2 to this Act.

(4) If an employee is dismissed by reason of any such requirement or recommendation as is referred to in subsection (1) above, paragraph 10 (*a*) of Schedule 1 to the 1974 Act (qualifying period for right not to be unfairly dismissed) shall have effect in relation to that dismissal as if for the words "26 weeks" there were substituted the words "4 weeks". [**333**]

COMMENCEMENT

See s. 129 (3), *post*.

SUSPENDED FROM WORK

As to meaning, see sub-s. (2) above.

FURTHER PROVISIONS

See s. 30, *post* (general exclusion from right under this section); s. 31, *post* (calculation of remuneration); s. 32, *post* (complaint to industrial tribunal); s. 33, *post* (dismissal of replacement); s. 63, *post* (priority on insolvency of remuneration on suspension on medical grounds); s. 108 (2)–(7), *post* (provision for conciliation); and s. 119 (1)–(7), *post* (excluded classes of employment).

DEFINITIONS

By virtue of s. 126 (1), *post*, for "employer", see the definition inserted in the Trade Union and Labour Relations Act 1974, s. 30 (1), by s. 125 (1) and Sch. 16, Part III, para. 7 (2), *post*, and s. 30 (2) (*b*) of that Act, and for "employee", see s. 30 (1) of that Act.

TRANSITIONAL PROVISIONS

See s. 125 (2) and Sch. 17, para. 7 (1), *post*.

30. General exclusions from right under s. 29

(1) An employee shall not be entitled to remuneration under section 29 above unless he has been continuously employed for a period of four weeks ending with the last complete week before the day on which the suspension begins.

(2) An employee shall not be entitled to remuneration under section 29 above in respect of any period during which he is incapable of work by reason of disease or bodily or mental disablement.

(3) An employee shall not be entitled to remuneration under section 29 above in respect of any period during which—

(*a*) his employer has offered to provide him with suitable alternative work, whether or not work which the employee is under his contract, or was under the contract in force before the suspension, employed to perform, and the employee has unreasonably refused to perform that work; or

(*b*) he does not comply with reasonable requirements imposed by his employer with a view to ensuring that his services are available.

[334]

COMMENCEMENT
See s. 129 (3), *post*.

CONTINUOUSLY EMPLOYED FOR . . . FOUR WEEKS, ETC.
As to the determination of the period for which an employee has been continuously employed, see s. 126 (5), *post*.

DEFINITIONS
By virtue of s. 126 (1), *post*, for "employer", see the definition inserted in the Trade Union and Labour Relations Act 1974, s. 30 (1), by s. 125 (1) and Sch. 16, Part III, para. 7 (2), *post*, and s. 30 (2) (*b*) of that Act, and for "employee", see s. 30 (1) of that Act; as to "suspension", see s. 29 (2), *ante*.

31. Calculation of remuneration

(1) The amount of remuneration payable by an employer to an employee under section 29 above shall be a week's pay in respect of each week of the period of suspension referred to in subsection (1) of that section, and if in any week remuneration is payable in respect only of part of that week the amount of a week's pay shall be reduced proportionately.

(2) For the purposes of Part II of Schedule 4 to this Act as it applies for the calculation of a week's pay for the purposes of this section the calculation date is the day before that on which the suspension begins.

(3) Subject to subsection (4) below, a right to remuneration under section 29 above shall not affect any right of an employee in relation to remuneration under his contract of employment (hereafter in this section referred to as "contractual remuneration").

(4) Any contractual remuneration paid by an employer to an employee in respect of any period shall go towards discharging the employer's liability under section 29 above in respect of that period, and conversely any payment of remuneration in discharge of an employer's liability under section 29 above in respect of any period shall go towards discharging any obligation of the employer to pay contractual remuneration in respect of that period.

(5) In this section, "week" in relation to an employee whose remuneration is calculated weekly by a week ending with a day other than Saturday means a

week ending with that other day, and in relation to any other employee means a week ending on Saturday. [**335**]

COMMENCEMENT

See s. 129 (3), *post*.

WEEK'S PAY

As to the calculation of a week's pay, see s. 85 (1) and Sch. 4, Part II, *post*, in conjunction with sub-s. (2) above.

DEFINITIONS

By virtue of s. 126 (1), *post*, for "employer", see the definition inserted in the Trade Union and Labour Relations Act 1974, s. 30 (1), by s. 125 (1) and Sch. 16, Part III, para. 7 (2), *post*, and s. 30 (2) (*b*) of that Act, and for "employee", see s. 30 (1) of that Act; as to "suspension", see s. 29 (2), *ante*; for "contractual remuneration", see sub-s. (3) above and for "week", see sub-s. (5) above.

32. Complaint to industrial tribunal

(1) An employee may present a complaint to an industrial tribunal that his employer has failed to pay the whole or any part of remuneration to which the employee is entitled under section 29 above.

(2) An industrial tribunal shall not entertain a complaint relating to remuneration under section 29 above in respect of any day unless the complaint is presented to the tribunal before the end of the period of three months beginning with that day, or within such further period as the tribunal considers reasonable in a case where it is satisfied that it was not reasonably practicable for the complaint to be presented within the period of three months.

(3) Where an industrial tribunal finds a complaint under subsection (1) above well-founded the tribunal shall order the employer to pay the complainant the amount of remuneration which it finds is due to him. [**336**]

COMMENCEMENT

See s. 129 (3), *post*.

COMPLAINT

A complaint under this section is to be made in accordance with regulations under the Trade Union and Labour Relations Act 1974, Sch. 1, para. 21; see s. 108 (1), *post*, and note sub-ss. (2)–(7) of that section as to conciliation.

INDUSTRIAL TRIBUNAL

See the note to s. 6, *ante*.

THREE MONTHS BEGINNING, ETC.

See the note "14 days (two months) beginning, etc." to s. 15, *ante*.

APPEALS

As to appeals from an industrial tribunal to the Employment Appeal Tribunal and thence to the Court of Appeal, from decisions of an industrial tribunal under this section, see s. 88 (1), (4), (5), *post*.

DEFINITIONS

By virtue of s. 126 (1), *post*, for "employer", see the definition inserted in the Trade Union and Labour Relations Act 1974, s. 30 (1), by s. 125 (1) and Sch. 16, Part III, para. 7 (2), *post*, and s. 30 (2) (*b*), and for "employee", see s. 30 (1) of that Act.

33. Dismissal of replacement

Where an employer—

(*a*) on engaging an employee informs the employee in writing that his employment will be terminated on the end of a suspension such as is referred to in section 29 (1) above of another employee; and

(*b*) dismisses the first mentioned employee in order to make it possible to allow the other employee to resume his original work;

then, for the purposes of paragraph 6 (1) (*b*) of Schedule 1 to the 1974 Act (employer to show substantial reason for dismissal), but without prejudice to the application of paragraph 6 (8) of that Schedule (whether dismissal fair or unfair to depend on whether employer acted reasonably), the dismissal shall be regarded as having been for a substantial reason of a kind such as to justify the dismissal of an employee holding the position which that employee held. **[337]**

COMMENCEMENT

See s. 129 (3), *post*. The section applies to a dismissal where the effective date of termination falls on or after the commencement of the section; see s. 125 (2) and Sch. 17, para. 7 (1), *post*.

WRITING

See the note "Written" to s. 11, *ante*.

DEFINITIONS

By virtue of s. 126 (1), *post*, for "employer", see the definition inserted in the Trade Union and Labour Relations Act 1974, s. 30 (1), by s. 125 (1) and Sch. 16, Part III, para. 7 (2), *post*, and s. 30 (2) (*b*) of that Act, and for "employee", see s. 30 (1) of that Act; as to "suspension", see s. 29 (2), *ante*.

TRANSITIONAL PROVISIONS

See s. 125 (2) and Sch. 17, para. 7 (1), *post*.

Maternity

34. Dismissal on grounds of pregnancy

(1) An employee shall be treated for the purposes of Schedule 1 to the 1974 Act as unfairly dismissed if the reason or principal reason for her dismissal is that she is pregnant or is any other reason connected with her pregnancy, except one of the following reasons—

(*a*) that at the effective date of termination she is or will have become, because of her pregnancy, incapable of adequately doing the work which she is employed to do;

(*b*) that, because of her pregnancy, she cannot or will not be able to continue after that date to do that work without contravention (either by her or her employer) of a duty or restriction imposed by or under any enactment.

(2) An employee shall be treated for the purposes of Schedule 1 to the 1974 Act as unfairly dismissed if her employer dismisses her for a reason mentioned in subsection (1) (*a*) or (*b*) above, but neither he nor any successor of his, where there is a suitable available vacancy, makes her an offer before or on the effective date of termination to engage her under a new contract of employment complying with subsection (3) below.

(3) The new contract of employment must—

(*a*) take effect immediately on the ending of employment under the previous contract, or, where that employment ends on a Friday, Saturday or Sunday, on or before the next Monday after that Friday, Saturday or Sunday;

(*b*) be such that the work to be done under the contract is of a kind which is both suitable in relation to the employee and appropriate for her to do in the circumstances; and

(*c*) be such that the provisions of the new contract as to the capacity and place in which she is to be employed and as to the other terms and conditions of her employment are not substantially less favourable to her than the corresponding provisions of the previous contract.

(4) On a complaint of unfair dismissal on the ground of failure to offer to engage an employee as mentioned in subsection (2) above, it shall be for the employer to show that he or a successor made an offer to engage her in compliance with subsections (2) and (3) above or, as the case may be, that there was no suitable available vacancy for her.

(5) Paragraph 5 (3) of Schedule 1 to the 1974 Act (employee treated as dismissed where he gives notice to the employer within the period of the employer's notice) shall not apply in a case where an employer gives notice to an employee to terminate her contract of employment for a reason mentioned in subsection (1) (*a*) or (*b*) above.

(6) In paragraph 12 of Schedule 1 to the 1974 Act (exclusion of certain fixed term contracts) as it applies to an employee treated as unfairly dismissed by virtue of subsection (1) or (2) above, for the reference to 28th February 1972 there shall be substituted a reference to the commencement of this section.

(7) Paragraph 13 (3) of Schedule 1 to the 1974 Act (exlusion of right not to be unfairly dismissed and remedy for breach of that right where a dismissal procedures agreement is in force), shall not apply to the right not to be unfairly dismissed for any reason mentioned in subsection (1) or (2) above. [**338**]

COMMENCEMENT

See s. 129 (3), *post*. The section applies to a dismissal where the effective date of termination falls on or after the commencement of the section; see Sch. 17, para. 7 (1), *post*.

GENERAL NOTE

This section in effect supplements the Trade Union and Labour Relations Act 1974, Sch. 1, para. 6, which relates to the determination for the purposes of that Schedule whether the dismissal of an employee was fair or unfair. Unfair dismissal may form the basis of a complaint to an industrial tribunal under para. 17 of that Schedule, and where the complaint is considered by the tribunal to be well-founded, it may either recommend that the complainant be reinstated or re-engaged, or make an award of compensation. Para. 6 (4)–(7) of the Schedule, specifies the circumstances under which dismissal is to be regarded as fair or unfair, and para. 6 (8) defines, subject to sub-paras. (4)–(7), the general test of fairness. The burden is thereby placed on the employer to show that in the circumstances (having regard to equity and the substantial merits of the case) he acted reasonably in treating the reason for dismissal as a sufficient reason.

SUB-S. (4): COMPLAINT OF UNFAIR DISMISSAL

I.e., a complaint to an industrial tribunal under the Trade Union and Labour Relations Act 1974, Sch. 1, para. 17; see the General Note above.

SUB-S. (6): COMMENCEMENT OF THIS SECTION

See the note "Commencement", above.

RIGHTS UPON DEATH OF EMPLOYEE OR EMPLOYER

See s. 110 and Sch. 12, *post*.

DEFINITIONS

By virtue of s. 126 (1), *post*, for "employer", see the definition inserted in the Trade Union and Labour Relations Act 1974, s. 30 (1), by s. 125 (1) and Sch. 16, Part III, para. 7 (2), *post*, and s. 30 (2) (*b*) of that Act; for "employee", see s. 30 (1) of that Act, and for "successor", see s. 30 (3), (4) of that Act; by virtue of s. 126 (3), *post*, for "dismissal", see Sch. 1, para. 5 (1)–(4), to that Act, and for "effective date of termination", see para. 5 (5) of that Schedule.

TRANSITIONAL PROVISIONS
See s. 125 (2) and Sch. 17, para. 7 (1), (3), *post*.

35. Rights of employee in connection with pregnancy and confinement

(1) An employee who is absent from work wholly or partly because of pregnancy or confinement shall, subject to the following provisions of this Act, be entitled—

(*a*) in accordance with sections 36 to 38 below, to be paid by her employer a sum to be known as maternity pay; and

(*b*) in accordance with sections 48 to 50 below and Schedule 3 to this Act, to return to work.

(2) An employee shall be entitled to the rights referred to in subsection (1) above whether or not a contract of employment subsists during the period of her absence but, subject to subsection (3) below, she shall not be so entitled unless—

(*a*) she continues to be employed by her employer (whether or not she is at work) until immediately before the beginning of the 11th week before the expected week of confinement.

(*b*) she has at the beginning of that 11th week been continuously employed for a period of not less than two years; and

(*c*) she informs her employer (in writing if he so requests) at least three weeks before her absence begins or, if that is not reasonably practicable, as soon as reasonably practicable,—

(i) that she will be (or is) absent from work wholly or partly because of pregnancy or confinement, and

(ii) in the case of the right to return, that she intends to return to work with her employer.

(3) An employee who has been dismissed by her employer for a reason falling within section 34 (1) (*a*) or (*b*) above and has not been re-engaged in accordance with that section, shall be entitled to the rights referred to in subsection (1) above notwithstanding that she has thereby ceased to be employed before the beginning of the 11th week before the expected week of confinement if, but for that dismissal, she would at the beginning of that 11th week have been continuously employed for a period of not less than two years, but she shall not be entitled to the right to return unless she informs her employer (in writing if he so requests), before or as soon as reasonably practicable after the dismissal takes effect, that she intends to return to work with him.

(4) An employee shall not be entitled to either of the rights referred to in subsection (1) above unless, if requested to do so by her employer, she produces for his inspection a certificate from a registered medical practitioner or a certified midwife stating the expected week of her confinement.

(5) The Secretary of State may by order vary the periods of two years referred to in subsections (2) and (3) above, or those periods as varied from time to time under this section, but no such order shall be made unless a draft of the order has been laid before Parliament and approved by resolution of each House of Parliament. [**339**]

COMMENCEMENT
See s. 129 (3), *post*.

SUB-S. (1): MATERNITY PAY

For provisions relating to maternity pay, see (in addition to ss. 36–38, *post*) ss. 39–47, *post*.

SUB-S. (2), (3): CONTINUOUSLY EMPLOYED FOR . . . TWO YEARS

As to the determination of the period for which an employee has been continuously employed, see s. 126 (5), *post*. The periods of two years may be varied by order; see sub-s. (5) above.

WRITING

See the note to s. 11, *ante*.

SUB-S. (4): REGISTERED MEDICAL PRACTITIONER

I.e., a fully registered person as defined by the Medical Act 1956, s. 54 (1); see s. 52 (2) of that Act.

SUB-S. (5): LAID BEFORE PARLIAMENT

For meaning, see the Laying of Documents before Parliament (Interpretation) Act 1948, s. 1 (1).

CONCILIATION

See s. 108 (2)–(7), *post*.

EXCLUDED CLASSES OF EMPLOYMENT

For classes of employment excluded from this section, see s. 119 (1), (2), (4)–(6), *post*.

DEFINITIONS

By virtue of s. 126 (1), *post*, for "employer", see the definition inserted in the Trade Union and Labour Relations Act 1974, s. 30 (1), by s. 125 (1) and Sch. 16, Part III, para. 7 (2), *post*, and s. 30 (2) (*b*) of that Act and for "employee", see s. 30 (1) of that Act; for "to return to work", see s. 48 (2), *post*; for "certified midwife", "confinement", "expected week of confinement" and "week", see s. 52, *post*.

ORDERS UNDER THIS SECTION

At the time of going to press no order had been made under sub-s. (5) above.

As to the making of orders generally, see s. 123, *post*.

36. Maternity pay

(1) Maternity pay shall be paid in respect of a period not exceeding, or periods not exceeding in the aggregate, six weeks during which the employee is absent from work wholly or partly because of pregnancy or confinement (hereafter in this section and sections 37 and 38 below referred to as the payment period or payment periods).

(2) An employee shall not be entitled to maternity pay for any absence before the beginning of the 11th week before the expected week of confinement, and her payment period or payment periods shall be the first six weeks of absence starting on or falling after the beginning of that 11th week.

(3) The Secretary of State may by order vary the periods of six weeks referred to in subsections (1) and (2) above, or those periods as varied from time to time under this section, but no such order shall be made unless a draft of the order has been laid before Parliament and approved by resolution of each House of Parliament.

(4) Where an employee gives her employer the information required by section 35 (2) (*c*) above or produces any certificate requested under section 35 (4) above after the beginning of the payment period or the first of the payment periods, she shall not be entitled to maternity pay for any part of that period until she gives him that information or certificate, but on giving him the information or as the case may be producing the certificate, she shall be entitled

to be paid in respect of that part of the period or periods which fell before the giving of the information or the production of the certificate. [**340**]

COMMENCEMENT

See s. 129 (3), *post*.

MATERNITY PAY

For the right to maternity pay, see s. 35, *ante*, in conjunction with the present section and ss. 37 and 38, *post*; and for further provisions relating to such pay, see ss. 39–47, *post*.

SIX WEEKS

These periods in sub-ss. (1) and (2) above may be varied by order under sub-s. (3) above.

LAID BEFORE PARLIAMENT

See the note to s. 35, *ante*.

DEFINITIONS

By virtue of s. 126 (1), *post*, for "employer", see the definition inserted in the Trade Union and Labour Relations Act 1974, s. 30 (1), by s. 125 (1) and Sch. 16, Part III, para. 7 (2), *post*, and s. 30 (2) (*b*) of that Act; and for "employee", see s. 30 (1) of that Act; for "confinement", "expected week of confinement" and "week", see s. 52, *post*. As to "payment period(s)", note sub-s. (1) above.

ORDERS UNDER THIS SECTION

At the time of going to press no order had been made under sub-s. (3) above.

As to the making of orders generally, see s. 123, *post*.

37. Calculation of maternity pay

(1) The amount of maternity pay to which an employee is entitled as respects any week shall be 9/10ths of a week's pay reduced by the amount of maternity allowance payable for that week under Part I of Schedule 4 to the Social Security Act 1975, whether or not the employee in question is entitled to the whole or any part of that allowance.

(2) Maternity pay shall accrue due to an employee from day to day and in calculating the amount of maternity pay payable for any day—

(*a*) there shall be disregarded Sunday or such other day in each week as may be prescribed in relation to that employee under section 22 (10) of the Social Security Act 1975 for the purpose of calculating the daily rate of maternity allowance under that Act; and

(*b*) the amount payable for any other day shall be taken as 1/6th of the amount of the maternity pay for the week in which the day falls.

(3) Subject to subsection (4) below, a right to maternity pay shall not affect any right of an employee in relation to remuneration under any contract of employment (hereafter in this section referred to as "contractual remuneration").

(4) Any contractual remuneration paid to an employee in respect of a day within a payment period shall go towards discharging any liability of the employer to pay maternity pay in respect of that day, and conversely any maternity pay paid in respect of a day shall go towards discharging any liability of the employer to pay contractual remuneration in respect of that day.

(5) For the purposes of Part II of Schedule 4 to this Act as it applies for the calculation of a week's pay for the purposes of this section, the calculation date is the last day on which the employee worked under the contract of employment in force immediately before the beginning of her absence. [**341**]

COMMENCEMENT
See s. 129 (3), *post*.

MATERNITY PAY
Cf. the note to s. 36, *ante*.

WEEK'S PAY
The amount of a week's pay is to be calculated in accordance with s. 85 (1) and Sch. 4, Part II, *post*, in conjunction with sub-s. (5) above.

DEFINITIONS
By virtue of s. 126 (1), *post*, for "employer", see the definition inserted in the Trade Union and Labour Relations Act 1974, s. 30 (1), by s. 125 (1) and Sch. 16, Part III, para. 7 (2), *post*, and s. 30 (2) (*b*) of that Act, and for "employee", see s. 30 (1) of that Act; for "payment period", see s. 36 (1), *ante*. Note sub-s. (3) above as to "contractual remuneration".

38. Complaint to industrial tribunal of failure to pay maternity pay

(1) A complaint may be presented to an industrial tribunal by an employee against her employer that he has failed to pay her the whole or any part of the maternity pay to which she is entitled.

(2) An industrial tribunal shall not entertain a complaint under subsection (1) above unless it is presented to the tribunal before the end of the period of three months beginning with the last day of the payment period or, as the case may be, the last of the payment periods, or within such further period as the tribunal considers reasonable in a case where it is satisfied that it was not reasonably practicable for the complaint to be presented within the period of three months.

(3) Where an industrial tribunal finds a complaint under subsection (1) above well founded the tribunal shall order the employer to pay the complainant the amount of maternity pay which it finds is due to her. [**342**]

COMMENCEMENT
See s. 129 (3), *post*.

COMPLAINT
A complaint under this section is to be made in accordance with regulations under the Trade Union and Labour Relations Act 1974, Sch. 1, para. 21; see s. 108 (1), *post*.

INDUSTRIAL TRIBUNAL
See the note to s. 6, *ante*.

MATERNITY PAY
Cf. the note to s. 36, *ante*.

THREE MONTHS BEGINNING, ETC.
See the note "14 days (two months) beginning, etc." to s. 15, *ante*.

APPEALS
As to appeals to the Employment Appeal Tribunal, and thence to the Court of Appeal, from decisions of an industrial tribunal under this section, see s. 88 (1), (4), (5), *post*.

DEFINITIONS
By virtue of s. 126 (1), *post*, for "employer", see the definition inserted in the Trade Union and Labour Relations Act 1974, s. 30 (1), by s. 125 (1) and Sch. 16, Part III, para. 7 (2), *post*, and s. 30 (2) (*b*) of that Act, and for "employee", see s. 30 (1) of that Act; for "payment period(s)", see s. 36 (1), *ante*.

39. Maternity Pay Fund

(1) There shall be established under the control and management of the Secretary of State a fund to be called the Maternity Pay Fund out of which payments shall be made in accordance with the following provisions of this Act.

(2) The Secretary of State shall prepare accounts of the Maternity Pay Fund in such form as the Treasury may direct and shall send them to the Comptroller and Auditor General not later than the end of the month of November following the end of the financial year to which the accounts relate; and the Comptroller and Auditor General shall examine and certify every such account and shall lay copies thereof, together with his report thereon, before Parliament.

(3) Any money in the Maternity Pay Fund may from time to time be paid over to the National Debt Commissioners and invested by them, in accordance with such directions as may be given by the Treasury, in any such manner as may be specified by an order of the Treasury for the time being in force under section 22 (1) of the National Savings Bank Act 1971. [**343**]

COMMENCEMENT

See s. 129 (3), *post*.

GENERAL NOTE

The purpose of the Fund established by this section is to provide a vehicle for the financing of the maternity pay to which employees are entitled by virtue of the provisions of ss. 35–38, *ante*, the principal object being to spread the financial burden amongst all employers equally so as to avoid hardship to small employers or to those who employ proportionately large numbers of female employees and so avoid discrimination against the employment of women as a means of evading the duties imposed by such provisions. This object is achieved by linking the financing of the Fund with the system of secondary contributions by employers under the Social Security Act 1975; see the amendments to that Act made by s. 40, *post*. Upon payment of maternity pay the individual employer becomes entitled to a rebate of an equivalent amount payable from the Fund under s. 42, *post*, and under s. 43, *post*, unpaid maternity pay may be recovered by an employer from the Fund. See also ss. 41 and 44–47, *post*.

COMPTROLLER AND AUDITOR GENERAL

The Comptroller and Auditor General is appointed under the Exchequer and Audit Departments Act 1866, s. 6, and hold office in accordance with s. 3 of that Act.

FINANCIAL YEAR

For meaning, see the Interpretation Act 1889, s. 22.

LAY . . . BEFORE PARLIAMENT

For meaning, see the Laying of Documents before Parliament (Interpretation) Act 1948, s. 1 (1).

NATIONAL DEBT COMMISSIONERS

As to these Commissioners, see the National Debt Reduction Act 1786, s. 14, and the notes thereto.

40. Financing of Maternity Pay Fund

(1) In the Social Security Act 1975 for the words "appropriate allocation to the Redundancy Fund", wherever they occur, substitute the words "appropriate employment protection allocation".

(2) In section 1 (1) of that Act (outline of contributory system), after the words "Redundancy Fund" insert the words "and the Maternity Pay Fund".

(3) In section 4 (6) (*b*) of that Act (amount of secondary Class 1 contribution), for the words "8·5 per cent." substitute the words "8·55 per cent.".

(4) In section 122 (4) of that Act (power to alter contributions), after the words "the Redundancy Fund" insert the words "or the Maternity Pay Fund", and for the words "that Fund" substitute the words "either or both those Funds".

(5) In section 134 of that Act (destination of contributions, etc.)—

(*a*) in subsection (4), for the words "0·2 per cent." substitute the words " 0·25 per cent."; and

(*b*) in subsection (5) (*b*), for the words "that Fund" substitute the words "the Redundancy Fund and the Maternity Pay Fund in such shares as the Secretary of State may, with the consent of the Treasury determine."

(6) In Schedule 20 to that Act (glossary of expressions), at the appropriate place in alphabetical order insert in the first column the entry "Appropriate employment protection allocation" and against it in the second column insert the entry "See section 134 (4)". [**344**]

COMMENCEMENT

See s. 129 (3), *post*.

MATERNITY PAY FUND

That fund is established under s. 39, *ante*.

41. Advances out of National Loans Fund

(1) Subject to the provisions of subsections (2) to (4) below, the Treasury may from time to time advance out of the National Loans Fund to the Secretary of State for the purposes of the Maternity Pay Fund, such sums as the Secretary of State may request; and any sums advanced to the Secretary of State under this section shall be paid into that Fund.

(2) The aggregate amount outstanding by way of principal in respect of sums advanced to the Secretary of State under subsection (1) above shall not at any time exceed £4 million, or such larger sum, not exceeding £10 million, as the Secretary of State may by order made with the consent of the Treasury determine.

(3) No order under subsection (2) above shall be made unless a draft of the order has been laid before Parliament and approved by resolution of each House of Parliament.

(4) Any sums advanced to the Secretary of State under subsection (1) above shall be re-paid by the Secretary of State out of the Maternity Pay Fund into the National Loans Fund in such manner and at such times, and with interest thereon at such rate, as the Treasury may direct. [**345**]

COMMENCEMENT

See s. 129 (3), *post*.

NATIONAL LOANS FUND

This is an account kept by the Treasury at the Bank of England under the National Loans Act 1968, s. 1 (1).

MATERNITY PAY FUND

That fund is established under s. 39, *ante*.

LAID BEFORE PARLIAMENT

For meaning, see the Laying of Documents before Parliament (Interpretation) Act 1948, s. 1 (1).

ORDERS UNDER THIS SECTION

At the time of going to press no order had been made under sub-s. (2) above.

As to the making of orders generally, see s. 123, *post*, and note sub-s. (3) above.

42. Maternity pay rebate

(1) Subject to any regulations made under this section, the Secretary of State shall pay out of the Maternity Pay Fund to every employer who makes a claim under this section and who, being liable to pay, has paid maternity pay to an employee, an amount equal to the full amount of maternity pay so paid (in this section and sections 44, 45 and 46 below referred to as a "rebate").

(2) The Secretary of State may if he thinks fit, and if he is satisfied that it would be just and equitable to do so having regard to all the relevant circumstances, pay such a rebate to an employer who makes a claim under this section and who has paid maternity pay to an employee in circumstances in which, by reason of the time limit provided for in section 38 (2) above, a complaint by the employee has been dismissed, or would not be entertained by an industrial tribunal.

(3) For the purposes of subsections (1) and (2) above, a payment of contractual remuneration by an employer shall be treated as a payment of maternity pay to the extent that, by virtue of section 37 (4) above,—

(*a*) it extinguishes the employer's liability to pay maternity pay; or

(*b*) in a case falling within subsection (2) above, it would extinguish that liability if a complaint by the employee were not time-barred as described in that subsection.

(4) The Secretary of State shall make provision by regulations as to the making of claims for rebates under this section and such regulations may in particular—

(*a*) require a claim to be made within such time limit as may be prescribed; and

(*b*) require a claim to be supported by such evidence as may be prescribed. [**346**]

COMMENCEMENT

See s. 129 (3), *post*.

MATERNITY PAY FUND

That fund is established under s. 39, *ante*.

MATERNITY PAY

Cf. the note to s. 36, *ante*.

INDUSTRIAL TRIBUNAL

See the note to s. 6, *ante*.

FURTHER PROVISIONS

See s. 44, *post* (reduction of rebate in certain cases), and s. 45 (2), *post* (supplementary provisions in relation to employer's insolvency).

COMPLAINT AND APPEALS TO INDUSTRIAL TRIBUNAL

See s. 46 (1)–(3), (5), *post*.

OFFENCES

See s. 47 (4), *post*.

DEFINITIONS

By virtue of s. 126 (1), *post*, for "employer", see the definition inserted in the Trade Union and Labour Relations Act 1974, s. 30 (1), by s. 125 (1) and Sch. 16, Part III, para. 7 (2), *post*, and s. 30 (2) (*b*) of that Act and for "employee", see s. 30 (1) of the Act of 1974, Vol. 44, p. 1843. As to "rebate", note sub-s. (1) above.

REGULATIONS UNDER THIS SECTION

At the time of going to press no regulations had been made under this section.

As to the making of regulations generally, see s. 123, *post*.

43. Payments to employees out of Maternity Pay Fund

(1) Where an employee claims that her employer is liable to pay her maternity pay and—

(*a*) that she has taken all reasonable steps (other than proceedings to enforce a tribunal award) to recover payment from the employer; or

(*b*) that her employer is insolvent (as defined in section 69 below for the purposes of sections 64 to 68 below);

and that the whole or part of the maternity pay remains unpaid, the employee may apply to the Secretary of State under this section.

(2) If the Secretary of State is satisfied that the claim is well founded the Secretary of State shall pay the employee out of the Maternity Pay Fund the amount of the maternity pay which appears to the Secretary of State to be unpaid.

(3) A payment made by the Secretary of State to an employee under this section shall be treated for the purpose of discharging any liability of the employer to the employee as if it had been made by the employer. [**347**]

COMMENCEMENT

See s. 129 (3), *post*.

MATERNITY PAY

Cf. the note to s. 36, *ante*.

OTHER THAN PROCEEDINGS TO ENFORCE A TRIBUNAL AWARD

I.e., an award made by virtue of s. 38, *ante*.

MATERNITY PAY FUND

That fund is established by s. 39, *ante*.

FURTHER PROVISIONS

See s. 44, *post* (reduction in rebate), and s. 45 (1), *post* (supplementary provisions in relation to employer's insolvency).

COMPLAINT TO INDUSTRIAL TRIBUNAL

A person who has applied for a payment under this section may present a complaint to an industrial tribunal if no such payment is made or if the amount paid is less than it ought to have been; see s. 46 (1), *post*. See also s. 46 (2), (5), *post*.

OFFENCES

See s. 47, *post*.

DEFINITIONS

By virtue of s. 126 (1), *post*, for "employer", see the definition inserted in the Trade Union and Labour Relations Act 1974, s. 30 (1), by s. 125 (1) and Sch. 16, Part III para. 7 (2), *post*, and s. 30 (2) (*b*) of that Act and for "employee", see s. 30 (1) of the Act of 1974.

44. Unreasonable default by employer

(1) Where the Secretary of State makes a payment to an employee in respect of unpaid maternity pay in a case falling within section 43 (1) (*a*) above and it appears to the Secretary of State that the employer's default in payment was without reasonable excuse, the Secretary of State may recover from the employer such amount as the Secretary of State considers appropriate, not exceeding the amount of maternity pay which the employer failed to pay.

(2) Where a sum is recovered by the Secretary of State by virtue of this section that sum shall be paid into the Maternity Pay Fund. [**348**]

COMMENCEMENT
See s. 129 (3), *post*.

MATERNITY PAY
Cf. the note to s. 36, *ante*.

MATERNITY PAY FUND
That fund is established by s. 39, *ante*.

APPEAL TO INDUSTRIAL TRIBUNAL
As to employer's right of appeal, see s. 46 (4), (5), *post*.

DEFINITIONS
By virtue of s. 126 (1), *post*, for "employer", see the definition inserted in the Trade Union and Labour Relations Act 1974, s. 30 (1), by s. 125 (1) and Sch. 16, Part III, para. 7 (2), *post*, and s. 30 (2) (*b*) of that Act and for "employee", see s. 30 (1) of the Act of 1974.

45. Supplementary provisions in relation to employer's insolvency

(1) Where the Secretary of State makes a payment to an employee under section 64 below (which provides for payments out of the Redundancy Fund in respect of certain debts where an employer is insolvent) and that payment, in whole or in part, represents arrears of pay, then, in ascertaining for the purpose of section 43 above the amount of any unpaid maternity pay, section 37 (4) above shall apply as if the arrears of pay in question had been duly paid by the employer to the employee in accordance with the contract of employment.

(2) Where the Secretary of State makes a payment to an employee out of the Redundancy Fund under section 64 below which, if it had been made by the employer to the employee, would have attracted a rebate from the Maternity Pay Fund in accordance with section 42 above, then, the Secretary of State shall make a payment out of the Maternity Pay Fund into the Redundancy Fund of an amount corresponding to the amount of rebate which would have been so payable. [**349**]

COMMENCEMENT
See s. 129 (3), *post*.

REDUNDANCY FUND
That fund was established under the Redundancy Payments Act 1965, s. 26.

MATERNITY PAY
Cf. the note to s. 36, *ante*.

MATERNITY PAY FUND
That fund is established by s. 39, *ante*.

DEFINITIONS

By virtue of s. 126 (1), *post*, for "employer", see the definition inserted in the Trade Union and Labour Relations Act 1974, s. 30 (1), by s. 125 (1) and Sch. 16, Part III, para. 7 (2), *post*, and s. 30 (2) (*b*) of that Act, and for "employee", see s. 30 (1) of the Act of 1974; for "rebate", see s. 42 (1), *ante*.

46. Complaint and appeals to industrial tribunal

(1) A person who has—

(*a*) made a claim for a rebate under section 42 above, in a case to which subsection (1) of that section applies; or

(*b*) applied for a payment under section 43 above,

may, subject to subsection (5) below, present a complaint to an industrial tribunal that—

(i) the Secretary of State has failed to make any such payment; or

(ii) any such payment made by the Secretary of State is less than the amount which should have been paid.

(2) Where an industrial tribunal finds that the Secretary of State ought to make any such payment or further payment, it shall make a declaration to that effect and shall also declare the amount of any such payment which it finds the Secretary of State ought to make.

(3) An employer who has made a claim for a rebate under section 42 above, in a case to which subsection (2) of that section applies, may, subject to subsection (5) below, appeal to an industrial tribunal on the ground that—

(*a*) the Secretary of State has refused to pay a rebate; or

(*b*) any rebate paid by the Secretary of State is less than the amount which should have been paid,

and if on any such appeal the tribunal is satisfied that it is just and equitable having regard to all the relevant circumstances that a rebate should be paid or, as the case may be, finds that a further payment by way of rebate should be made, the tribunal shall determine accordingly, and the Secretary of State shall comply with the determination.

(4) Where the Secretary of State determines that an amount is recoverable from an employer under section 44 above, the employer may, subject to subsection (5) below, appeal to an industrial tribunal; and if on any such appeal the tribunal is satisfied that no amount should be recovered fro m the employer, or that a lesser or greater amount should be recovered (but in any case not exceeding the amount of maternity pay which the employer failed to pay) the tribunal shall determine accordingly and the amount, if any, so determined shall be the amount recoverable from the employer by the Secretary of State.

(5) An industrial tribunal shall not entertain a complaint or appeal under this section unless it is presented to the tribunal within the period of three months beginning with the date on which the relevant decision of the Secretary of State was communicated to the complainant or appellant or within such further period as the tribunal considers reasonable in a case where it is satisfied that it was not reasonably practicable for the complaint or appeal to be presented within the period of three months. [**350**]

COMMENCEMENT

See s. 129 (3), *post*.

PERSON

Unless the contrary intention appears, "person" includes any body of persons, corporate or unincorporate; see the Interpretation Act 1889, s. 19.

COMPLAINT

Such a complaint is to be made in accordance with regulations under the Trade Union and Labour Relations Act 1974, Sch. 1, para. 21; see s. 108 (1), *post*.

INDUSTRIAL TRIBUNAL

See the note to s. 6, *ante*.

THREE MONTHS BEGINNING, ETC.

See the note "14 days (two months) beginning, etc." to s. 15, *ante*.

APPEALS

As to appeals to the Employment Appeal Tribunal, and thence to the Court of Appeal, from decisions of an industrial tribunal under this section, see s. 88 (1), (4), (5), *post*.

DEFINITIONS

By virtue of s. 126 (1), *post*, for "employer", see the definition inserted in the Trade Union and Labour Relations Act 1974, s. 30 (1), by s. 125 (1) and Sch. 16, Part III, para. 7 (2), *post*, and s. 30 (2) (*b*) of that Act, for "rebate", see s. 42 (1), *ante*.

47. Provisions as to information

(1) Where an application is made to the Secretary of State by an employee under section 43 above, the Secretary of State may require—

(*a*) the employer to provide him with such information as the Secretary of State may reasonably require for the purpose of determining whether the employee's application is well founded; and

(*b*) any person having the custody or control of any relevant records or other documents to produce for examination on behalf of the Secretary of State any such document in that person's custody or under his control which is of such a description as the Secretary of State may require.

(2) Any such requirement shall be made by a notice in writing given to the person on whom the requirement is imposed and may be varied or revoked by a subsequent notice so given.

(3) If a person refuses or wilfully neglects to furnish any information or produce any document which he has been required to furnish or produce by a notice under this section he shall be liable on summary conviction to a fine not exceeding £100.

(4) If any person in making a claim under section 42 above or on application under section 43 above or in purporting to comply with a requirement of a notice under this section knowingly or recklesly makes any false statement he shall be liable on summary conviction to a fine not exceeding £400. [**351**]

COMMENCEMENT

See s. 129 (3), *post*.

PERSON

See the note to s. 46, *ante*; and as to offences by bodies corporate, see also s. 117, *post*.

WRITING

See the note "Written" to s. 11, *ante*.

EXCLUSION OF CROWN EMPLOYMENT

See s. 121, *post*.

KNOWINGLY; RECKLESSLY; FALSE; SUMMARY CONVICTION

See the notes to s. 68, *post*.

DEFINITIONS

By virtue of s. 126 (1), *post*, for "employer", see the definition inserted in the Trade Union and Labour Relations Act 1974, s. 30 (1), by s. 125 (1) and Sch. 16, Part III, para. 7 (2), *post*, and s. 30 (2) (*b*) of that Act and for "employee", see s. 30 (1) of the Act of 1974.

48. Right to return to work

(1) The right to return to work of an employee who has been absent from work wholly or partly because of pregnancy or confinement is, subject to the following provisions of this Act, a right to return to work with her original employer, or, where appropriate, his successor, at any time before the end of the period of 29 weeks beginning with the week in which the date of confinement falls, in the job in which she was employed under the original contract of employment and on terms and conditions not less favourable than those which would have been applicable to her if she had not been so absent.

(2) In subsection (1) above—

(*a*) "job", in relation to an employee, means the nature of the work which she is employed to do in accordance with her contract and the capacity and place in which she is so employed; and

(*b*) "terms and conditions not less favourable than those which would have been applicable to her if she had not been so absent" means, as regards seniority, pension rights and other similar rights, that the period or periods of employment prior to the employee's absence shall be regarded as continuous with her employment following that absence.

(3) In sections 35, and 49 to 51 of, and Schedule 3 to, this Act, except where the context otherwise requires, "to return to work" means to return to work in accordance with subsection (1) above, and cognate expressions shall be construed accordingly.

(4) If an employee is entitled to return to work in accordance with subsection (1) above, but it is not practicable by reason of redundancy for the employer to permit her so to return to work, she shall be entitled, where there is a suitable available vacancy, to be offered alternative employment with her employer (or his successor), or an associated employer, under a new contract of employment complying with subsection (5) below.

(5) The new contract of employment must be such that—

(*a*) the work to be done under the contract is of a kind which is both suitable in relation to the employee and appropriate for her to do in circumstances; and

(*b*) the provisions of the new contract as to the capacity and place in which she is to be employed and as to the other terms and conditions of her employment are not substantially less favourable to her than if she had returned to work in accordance with subsection (1) above.

(6) The remedies of an employee for infringement of either of the rights mentioned in this section are those conferred by or by virtue of the provisions of sections 49 and 50 below and Schedule 3 to this Act. **[352]**

COMMENCEMENT

See s. 129 (3), *post*.

RIGHT TO RETURN TO WORK

For the right to return to work, see s. 35, *ante*, in conjunction with the present section, and ss. 49 and 50 and Sch. 3, *post*. See also s. 51, *post*, as to dismissal of a replacement.

SUBJECT TO THE FOLLOWING PROVISIONS

See, in particular, s. 49, *post* (exercise of right to return), s. 50 (1), *post* (failure to permit to return to work treated as dismissal), and s. 50 (2) and Sch. 3, *post* (supplementary provisions as to right of return.) As to the position where an employee also has a contractual right to return, see Sch. 3, para. 5, *post*.

29 WEEKS BEGINNING, ETC.

See the note "14 days (two months) beginning, etc." to s. 15, *ante*.

REDUNDANCY

See, further, in this connection, s. 50 (2) and Sch. 3, paras. 3, 6, *post*.

ENTITLED . . . TO BE OFFERED ALTERNATIVE EMPLOYMENT

For the position where no such offer is made in the circumstances described in sub-s. (4) above, see s. 50 (2) and Sch. 3, para. 2 (2), *post*.

DEFINITIONS

By virtue of s. 126 (1), *post*, for "employer", see the definition inserted in the Trade Union and Labour Relations Act 1974, s. 30 (1), by s. 125 (1) and Sch. 16, Part III, para. 7 (2), *post*, and s. 30 (2) (*b*) of that Act; for "employee", see s. 30 (1) of that Act; for "successor", see s. 30 (3), (4) of that Act (and see also s. 110 and Sch. 12, para. 4 (2), *post*) and for "associated employer", see s. 30 (5) of that Act; for "confinement", "original contract of employment" and "week", see s. 52, *post*. As to "redundancy" see s. 126 (6), (7), *post*. Note as to "job" and "terms and conditions not less favourable than those which would have been applicable to her if she had not been so absent", see sub-s. (2) above.

49. Exercise of right to return

(1) An employee shall exercise her right to return to work by notifying the employer (who may be her original employer or a successor of that employer) at least one week before the day on which she proposes to return of her proposal to return on that day (hereafter in this section and section 50 below and Schedule 3 to this Act referred to as the "notified day of return").

(2) An employer may postpone an employee's return to work until a date not more than four weeks after the notified day of return if he notifies her before that day that for specified reasons he is postponing her return until that date, and accordingly she will be entitled to return to work with him on that date.

(3) Subject to subsection (4) below, an employee may—

(*a*) postpone her return to work until a date not exceeding four weeks from the notified day of return, notwithstanding that that date falls after the end of the period of 29 weeks mentioned in section 48 (1) above; and

(*b*) where no day of return has been notified to the employer, extend the time during which she may exercise her right to return in accordance with subsection (1) above, so that she returns to work not later than four weeks from the expiration of the said period of 29 weeks;

if before the notified day of return or, as the case may be, the expiration of the period of 29 weeks she gives the employer a certificate from a registered medical practitioner stating that by reason of disease or bodily or mental disablement she will be incapable of work on the notified day of return or the expiration of that period, as the case may be.

(4) Where an employee has once exercised a right of postponement or extension under subsection (3) (*a*) or (*b*) above, she shall not again be entitled to

exercise a right of postponement or extension under that subsection in connection with the same return to work.

(5) If an employee has notified a day of return but there is an interruption of work (whether due to industrial action or some other reason) which renders it unreasonable to expect the employee to return to work on the notified day of return, she may instead return to work when work resumes after the interruption or as soon as reasonably practicable thereafter.

(6) If no day of return has been notified and there is an interruption of work (whether due to industrial action or some other reason) which renders it unreasonable to expect the employee to return to work before the expiration of the period of 29 weeks referred to in section 48 (1) above, or which appears likely to have that effect, and in consequence the employee does not notify a day of return, the employee may exercise her right to return in accordance with subsection (1) above so that she returns to work at any time before the end of the period of 14 days from the end of the interruption notwithstanding that she returns to work outside the said period of 29 weeks.

(7) Where the employee has either—

(*a*) exercised the right under subsection (3) (*b*) above to extend the period during which she may exercise her right to return; or

(*b*) refrained from notifying the day of return in the circumstances described in subsection (6) above,

the other of those subsections shall apply as if for the reference to the expiration of the period of 29 weeks there were substituted a reference to the expiration of the further period of four weeks or, as the case may be, of the period of 14 days from the end of the interruption of work.

(8) Where—

(*a*) an employee's return is postponed under subsection (2) or (3) (*a*) above, or

(*b*) the employee returns to work on a day later than the notified day of return in the circumstances described in subsection (5) above,

then, subject to subsection (4) above, references in those subsections and in section 50 below and Schedule 3 to this Act to the notified day of return shall be construed as references to the day to which the return is postponed, or, as the case may be, that later day. [**353**]

COMMENCEMENT

See s. 129 (3), *post*.

RIGHT TO RETURN TO WORK

Cf. the note to s. 48, *ante*; and as to the position where an employee also has a contracted right to return, see s. 50 (2) and Sch. 3, para. 5, *post*.

FOUR WEEKS AFTER, ETC.; FOUR WEEKS FROM, ETC.

See the note "One month after, etc." to s. 8, *ante*.

DEFINITIONS

By virtue of s. 126 (1), *post*, for "employer", see the definition inserted in the Trade Union and Labour Relations Act 1974, s. 30 (1) by s. 125 (1) and Sch. 16, Part III, para. 7 (2), *post*, and s. 30 (2) (*b*) of that Act; for "employee", see s. 30 (1) of that Act, and for "successor", see s. 30 (3), (4), of that Act (and see also s. 110 and Sch. 12, para. 4 (2), *post*); for "week", see s. 52, *post*; for "to return to work", see s. 48 (3), *ante*. As to "notified day of return", note sub-ss. (1) and (8) above.

50. Failure to permit to return treated as dismissal

(1) Where an employee is entitled to return to work and has exercised her right to return in accordance with section 49 above but is not permitted to return to work, then, she shall be treated for the purposes of—

(*a*) the provisions of this Act and the 1974 Act relating to unfair dismissal; and

(*b*) the Redundancy Payments Act 1965;

as if she had been employed until the notified day of return, and, if she would not otherwise be so treated, as having been continuously employed until that day, and as if she had been dismissed with effect from that day for the reason for which she was not permitted to return.

(2) The provisions of Schedule 3 to this Act shall have effect for the purpose of supplementing the foregoing provisions of this Act relating to an employee's right to return to work. [**354**]

COMMENCEMENT

See s. 129 (3), *post*.

RIGHT TO RETURN TO WORK

Cf. the note to s. 48, *ante*; and as to the position where an employee also has a contractual right to return, see s. 50 (2) and Sch. 3, para. 5, *post*.

PROVISIONS . . . RELATING TO UNFAIR DISMISSAL

The main provisions relating to unfair dismissal are contained in the Trade Union and Labour Relations Act 1974, s. 1 (2), Sch. 1, Parts II, III, as amended by s. 125 (1), (3), Sch. 16, Part III, paras. 8–23, and Sch. 18, *post*, and in ss. 71–80, *post*. See also sub-s. (2) above and Sch. 3, paras. 1, 2, 4, *post*, for adaptations of the unfair dismissal provisions in the Act of 1974 in relation to failure to permit a return to work, and s. 110 and Sch. 12, for modifications applying on the death of an employee or employer.

CONTINUOUSLY EMPLOYED

As to the determination of the period for which an employee has been continuously employed, see s. 126 (5), *post*.

DEFINITIONS

For "employee", see, by virtue of s. 126 (1), *post*, the Trade Union and Labour Relations Act 1974, s. 30 (1); for "to return to work", see s. 48 (3), *ante*; for "notified day of return", see s. 49 (1), (8), *ante*.

51. Dismissal of replacement

Where an employer—

(*a*) on engaging an employee informs the employee in writing that his employment will be terminated on the return to work of another employee who is, or will be, absent wholly or partly because of pregnancy or confinement; and

(*b*) dismisses the first-mentioned employee in order to make it possible to give work to the other employee;

then, for the purposes of paragraph 6 (1) (*b*) of Schedule 1 to the 1974 Act (employer to show substantial reason for dismissal), but without prejudice to the application of paragraph 6 (8) of that Schedule (whether dismissal fair or unfair to depend on whether employer acted reasonably), the dismissal shall be regarded as having been for a substantial reason of a kind such as to justify the dismissal of an employee holding the position which that employee held. [**355**]

COMMENCEMENT
See s. 129 (3), *post*.

WRITING
See the note to "Written" s. 11, *ante*.

DEFINITIONS
By virtue of s. 126 (1), *post*, for "employer", see the definition inserted in the Trade Union and Labour Relations Act 1974, s. 30 (1), by s. 125 (1) and Sch. 16, Part III, para. 7 (2), *post*, and s. 30 (2) (*b*) of that Act, and for "employee", see s. 30 (1) of that Act; for "confinement", see s. 52, *post*; for "to return to work", see s. 48 (3), *ante*.

TRANSITIONAL PROVISIONS
See s. 125 (2) and Sch. 17, para. 7 (1), *post*.

52. Interpretation of ss. 35 to 51

In sections 35 to 51 above, this section and Schedule 3 to this Act, except so far as the context otherwise requires,—

"certified midwife" means a midwife certified under the Midwives Act 1951 or the Midwives (Scotland) Act 1951;

"confinement" means the birth of a living child or the birth of a child whether living or dead after 28 weeks of pregnancy;

"expected week of confinement" means the week in which it is expected that confinement will take place;

"original contract of employment", in relation to an employee who is absent from work wholly or partly because of pregnancy or confinement, means the contract under which she worked immediately before the beginning of her absence or, if she entered into that contract during her pregnancy by virtue of section 34 (2) above or otherwise by reason of her pregnancy, the contract under which she was employed immediately before she entered into the later contract or, if there was more than one later contract, the first of the later contracts;

"week"—

(*a*) in sections 35 (2) (*c*) and 49 (1) above, means a period of seven days;

(*b*) in the expression "expected week of confinement", means a period of seven days beginning with midnight between Saturday and Sunday; and

(*c*) in any other case, means, in relation to an employee whose remuneration is calculated weekly by a week ending with a day other than Saturday, a week ending with that other day, and in relation to any other employee, a week ending with Saturday.

[356]

COMMENCEMENT
See s. 129 (3), *post*.

EMPLOYEE
For meaning, see, by virtue of s. 126 (1), the Trade Union and Labour Relations Act 1974, s. 30 (1), Vol. 44, p. 1843.

MIDWIVES ACT 1951
See Vol. 21, p. 599.

MIDWIVES (SCOTLAND) ACT 1951
14 & 15 Geo. 6 c. 54; not printed in this work.

Trade union membership and activities

53. Trade union membership and activities

(1) Subject to the following provisions of this section every employee shall have the right not to have action (short of dismissal) taken against him as an individual by his employer for the purpose of—

(*a*) preventing or deterring him from being or seeking to become a member of an independent trade union, or penalising him for doing so; or

(*b*) preventing or deterring him from taking part in the activities of an independent trade union at any appropriate time, or penalising him for doing so; or

(*c*) compelling him to be or become a member of a trade union which is not independent.

(2) In this section "appropriate time", in relation to an employee taking part in any activities of a trade union, means time which either—

(*a*) is outside his working hours, or

(*b*) is a time within his working hours at which, in accordance with arrangements agreed with, or consent given by his employer, it is permissible for him to take part in those activities;

and in this subsection "working hours", in relation to an employee, means any time when, in accordance with his contract of employment, he is required to be at work.

(3) The provisions of subsection (4) below shall have effect in relation to an employee—

(*a*) of the same class as employees for whom it is the practice in accordance with a union membership agreement to belong to a specified independent trade union or to one of a number of specified independent trade unions; or

(*b*) not of the same class as described in paragraph (*a*) above but of the same grade or category as such employees as are referred to in that paragraph.

(4) In relation to such an employee the right conferred by subsection (1) (*b*) above in relation to the activities of an independent trade union shall extend to activities on the employer's premises only if that union is a specified union.

(5) For the purposes of this section a trade union—

(*a*) shall be taken to be specified for the purposes of, or in relation to, a union membership agreement if it is specified in the agreement or is accepted by the parties to the agreement as being the equivalent of a union so specified; and

(*b*) shall also be treated as so specified if—

(i) the Service has made a recommendation for recognition of that union covering the employee in question which is operative within the meaning of section 15 above; or

(ii) the union has referred a recognition issue covering that employee to the Service under section 11 above and the Service has not declined to proceed on the reference under section 12 above, the union has not withdrawn the reference, or from the reference, and the issue has not been settled or reported on under that section.

(6) An employee who genuinely objects on grounds of being a member of any trade union whatsoever shall have the right not to have action (short of dismissal) taken against him by his employer for the purpose of compelling him to belong to a trade union.

(7) In this section, unless the context otherwise requires, references to a trade union include references to a branch or section of a trade union. [**357**]

COMMENCEMENT
See s. 129 (3), *post*.

GENERAL NOTE
This section complements the provisions of the Trade Union and Labour Relations Act 1974, Sch. 1, para. 6 (4) whereby dismissal for the reason that the employee was, or proposed to become, a member of an independent trade union, or had taken, or proposed to take, part at any appropriate time in the activities of such a union, is to be regarded as unfair dismissal, entitling the employee to the remedy provided for in paras. 4 and 17 of that Schedule. Similarly sub-s. (7) complements the provisions of para. 6 (5) of Sch. 1 of the Act of 1974 in protecting employees who genuinely object on grounds of religious belief to being a member of any trade union whatsoever.

ACTION (SHORT OF DISMISSAL)
Cf. the General Note above.

FURTHER PROVISIONS
See s. 54, *post* (complaint to industrial tribunal); s. 55, *post* (supplementary provisions as to such complaints); s. 56, *post* (assessment of compensation); s. 108 (2)–(7), *post* (provision for conciliation); and s. 119 (1), (2), (4)–(6), *post* (excluded classes of employment).

DEFINITIONS
By virtue of s. 120 (1), *post*, for "employer", see the definition inserted in the Trade Union and Labour Relations Act 1974, s. 30 (1), by s. 125 (1) and Sch. 16, Part III, para. 7 (2), *post*, and s. 30 (2) (*b*) of that Act, for "employee", "independent trade union" and "union membership agreement", see s. 30 (1) of that Act; for "trade union", see s. 28 (1) of that Act (and note also sub-s. (8) above); for "dismissal", see Sch. 1, para. 5, to the Act of 1974; for "recognition issue", see s. 11 (3), *ante*; for "the Service", see s. 1 (1), *ante*; as to "employees of the same class", see s. 126 (4), *post*. Note as to "appropriate time", sub-s. (2) above and as to "specified trade union", sub-s. (5) above.

54. Complaint to industrial tribunal

(1) An employee may present a complaint to an industrial tribunal on the ground that action has been taken against him by his employer in contravention of section 53 above.

(2) An industrial tribunal shall not entertain a complaint under subsection (1) above unless it is presented to the tribunal before the end of the period of three months beginning with the date on which there occurred the action complained of, or where that action is part of a series of similar actions, the last of those actions, or within such further period as the tribunal considers reasonable in a case where it is satisfied that it was not reasonably practicable for the complaint to be presented within the period of three months.

(3) Where the tribunal finds the complaint well-founded it shall make a declaration to that effect and may make an award of compensation, calculated in accordance with section 56 below, to be paid by the employer to the employee in respect of the action complained of. [**358**]

COMMENCEMENT
See s. 129 (3), *post*.

COMPLAINT
A complaint under this section is to be made in accordance with regulations under the Trade Union and Labour Relations Act 1974, Sch. 1, para. 21; see s. 108 (1), *post*.

INDUSTRIAL TRIBUNAL
See the note to s. 6, *ante*.

THREE MONTHS BEGINNING, ETC.
See the note "14 days (two months) beginning, etc." to s. 15, *ante*.

SUPPLEMENTARY PROVISIONS
See s. 55, *post*.

APPEALS
As to appeals to the Employment Appeal Tribunal, and thence to the Court of Appeal, from decisions of an industrial tribunal under this section, see s. 88 (1), (4), (5), *post*.

DEFINITIONS
By virtue of s. 126 (1), *post*, for "employer", see the definition inserted in the Trade Union and Labour Relations Act 1974, s. 30 (1), by s. 125 (1) and Sch. 16, Part III, para. 7 (2), *post*, and s. 30 (2) (*b*) of that Act, and for "employee", see s. 30 (1) of that Act.

55. Supplementary

(1) On a complaint under section 54 above it shall be for the employer to show—

(*a*) the purpose for which action was taken against the complainant; and

(*b*) that the purpose was not such a purpose as is referred to in section 53 (1) (*a*) to (*c*) or (6) above.

(2) In determining, on a complaint under section 54 above, any question as to whether action was taken by the complainant's employer or the purpose for which it was taken, no account shall be taken of any pressure which, by calling, organising, procuring or financing a strike or other industrial action, or threatening to do so, was exercised on the employer to take the action complained of, and that question shall be determined as if no such pressure had been exercised.

(3) If on a complaint under section 54 above it is shown that the action complained of was taken for the purpose of safe-guarding national security, the industrial tribunal shall dismiss the complaint.

(4) A certificate signed by or on behalf of a Minister of the Crown, and certifying that the action specified in the certificate was taken for the purpose of safeguarding national security, shall for the purposes of this section be conclusive evidence of that fact; and a document purporting to be such a certificate shall be taken to be such a certificate unless the contrary is proved. **[359]**

COMMENCEMENT
See s. 129 (3), *post*.

IT SHALL BE FOR THE EMPLOYER TO SHOW, ETC.
If the employer fails to discharge the burden imposed on him by sub-s. (1) above, the tribunal must find that he has contravened s. 45, *ante*; cf. *Earl* v. *Slater and Wheeler (Airlyne), Ltd.*, [1973] 1 All E.R. 145; [1972] R.L.R. 115; *Green* v. *Southampton Corporation*, [1973] I.C.R. 153.

EMPLOYER
For meaning, see by virtue of s. 126 (1), *post*, the definition inserted in the Trade Union and Labour Relations Act 1974, s. 30 (1) by s. 125 (1) and Sch. 16, Part III, para. 7 (2), *post*, and s. 30 (2) (*b*) of the Act of 1974.

INDUSTRIAL TRIBUNAL
See the note to s. 6, *ante*.

56. Assessment of compensation on a complaint under s. 45

(1) The amount of the compensation awarded by a tribunal on a complaint under section 54 above shall be such amount as the tribunal considers just and equitable in all the circumstances having regard to the infringement of the complainant's right under section 53 above by the employer's action complained of and to any loss sustained by the complainant which is attributable to that action.

(2) The said loss shall be taken to include—

(*a*) any expenses reasonably incurred by the complainant in consequence of the action complained of, and

(*b*) loss of any benefit which he might reasonably be expected to have had but for that action.

(3) In ascertaining the said loss the tribunal shall apply the same rule concerning the duty of a person to mitigate his loss as applies to damages recoverable under the common law of England and Wales or of Scotland, as the case may be.

(4) In determining the amount of compensation to be awarded under subsection (1) above no account shall be taken of any pressure as is referred to in section 55 (2) above, and that question shall be determined as if no such pressure had been exercised.

(5) Where the tribunal finds that the action complained of was to any extent caused or contributed to by any action of the complainant it shall reduce the amount of the compensation by such proportion as it considers just and equitable having regard to that finding. [**360**]

COMMENCEMENT
See s. 129 (3), *post*.

TRIBUNAL
I.e., an industrial tribunal. As to such tribunals, see the note to s. 6, *ante*.

SUCH AMOUNT AS THE TRIBUNAL CONSIDERS JUST AND EQUITABLE, ETC.
Cf. the corresponding note to the Trade Union and Labour Relations Act 1974, Sch. 1, para. 19.

EMPLOYER
For meaning see, by virtue of s. 126 (1), *post*, the definition inserted in the Trade Union and Labour Relations Act 1974, s. 30 (1), by s. 125 and Sch. 16, Part III, para. 7 (2), *post*, and s. 30 (2) (*b*) of that Act.

RULE CONCERNING THE DUTY OF A PERSON TO MITIGATE HIS LOSS
For a judicial statement of this rule, see *British Westinghouse Electric and Manufacturing Co.* v. *Underground Electric Rail. Co. of London*, [1912] A.C. 673, at p. 689, *per* Lord Haldane.

NO ACCOUNT SHALL BE TAKEN OF ANY PRESSURE, ETC.
As to the principles to be applied by tribunals when assessing compensation in cases where pressure of the type referred to in sub-s. (4) above has been exercised on the employer, cf. *Morris* v. *Gestetner, Ltd.*, [1973] 3 All E.R. 1168, at p. 1175.

CAUSED . . . BY ANY ACTION OF THE COMPLAINANT
Cf. the note "Caused . . . by any action of the aggrieved party" to the Trade Union and Labour Relations Act 1974, Sch. 1, para. 19.

Time off work

57. Time off for carrying out trade union duties

(1) An employer shall permit an employee of his who is an official of an independent trade union recognised by him to take time off, subject to and in accordance with subsection (2) below, during the employee's working hours for the purpose of enabling him—

(*a*) to carry out those duties of his as such an official which are concerned with industrial relations between his employer and any associated employer, and their employees; or

(*b*) to undergo training in aspects of industrial relations which is—

(i) relevant to the carrying out of those duties; and

(ii) approved by the Trades Union Congress or by the independent trade union of which he is an official.

(2) The amount of time off which an employee is to be permitted to take under this section and the purposes for which, the occasions on which and any conditions subject to which time off may be so taken are those that are reasonable in all the circumstances having regard to any relevant provisions of a Code of Practice issued by the Service under section 6 above.

(3) In the Code of Practice referred to in section 6 (2) (*b*) (i) above the Service shall in particular provide practical guidance on the circumstances in which a trade union official is to be permitted to take time off under this section in respect of duties connected with industrial action.

(4) An employer who permits an employee to take time off under this section for any purpose shall, subject to the following provisions of this section, pay him for the time taken off for that purpose in accordance with the permission—

(*a*) where the employee's remuneration for the work he would ordinarily have been doing during that time does not vary with the amount of work done, as if he had worked at that work for the whole of that time;

(*b*) where the employee's remuneration for that work varies with the amount of work done, an amount calculated by reference to the average hourly earnings for that work.

(5) The average hourly earnings referred to in subsection (4) (*b*) above shall be the average hourly earnings of the employee concerned or, if no fair estimate can be made of those earnings, the average hourly earnings for work of that description of persons in comparable employment with the same employer or, if there are no such persons, a figure of average hourly earnings which is reasonable in the circumstances.

(6) Subject to subsection (7) below, a right to be paid any amount under subsection (4) above shall not affect any right of an employee in relation to remuneration under his contract of employment (hereafter in this section referred to as "contractual remuneration").

(7) Any contractual remuneration paid to an employee in respect of a period of time off to which subsection (1) above applies shall go towards discharging any liability of the employer under subsection (4) above in respect of that period, and conversely any payment of any amount under subsection (4) above in respect of a period shall go towards discharging any liability of the employer to pay contractual remuneration in respect of that period.

(8) An employee who is an official of an independent trade union recognised

by his employer may present a complaint to an industrial tribunal that his employer has failed to permit him to take time off as required by this section or to pay him the whole or part of any amount so required to be paid. [**361**]

COMMENCEMENT
See s. 29 (3), *post*.

SUB-S. (2)
This subsection should be read in conjunction with s. 59 (4), *post*.

SUB-S. (4): AVERAGE HOURLY EARNINGS
Note sub-s. (5) above.

SUB-S. (8): COMPLAINT
See, further, s. 60, *post*. A complaint under sub-s. (8) above is to be made in accordance with regulations under the Trade Union and Labour Relations Act 1974, Sch. 1, para. 21; see s. 108 (1), *post*, and note sub-ss. (2)–(7) of that section as to conciliation.

INDUSTRIAL TRIBUNAL
See the note to s. 6, *ante*; and as to appeals to the Employment Appeal Tribunal, and thence to the Court of Appeal, from decisions of an industrial tribunal, see s. 88 (1), (4), (5), *post*.

SUPPLEMENTARY PROVISIONS
See s. 63, *post* (priority on insolvency of payment under sub-s. (4) above); and s. 119 (1), (2), (4)–(6), (8)–(11), *post* (excluded classes of employment).

DEFINITIONS
By virtue of s. 126 (1), *post*, for "employer", see the definition inserted in the Trade Union and Labour Relations Act 1974, s. 30 (1), s. 125 (1) and Sch. 16, Part III, para. 7 (2), *post*, and s. 30 (2) (*b*) of that Act; for "employee", "independent trade union" and "official", see s. 30 (1) of that Act, and for "associated employer", see s. 30 (5) of that Act; for "the Service", see s. 1 (1), *ante*; for "working hours", see s. 62 (*b*), *post*; for "recognised", see ss. 62 (*a*) and 126 (1), *post*. As to "contractual remuneration", note sub-s. (6) above.

58. Time off for trade union activities

(1) An employer shall permit an employee of his who is a member of an appropriate trade union to take time off, subject to and in accordance with subsection (3) below, during the employee's working hours for the purpose of taking part in any trade union activity to which this section applies.

(2) In this section "appropriate trade union", in relation to an employee of any description, means an independent trade union which is recognised by his employer in respect of that description of employee, and the trade union activities to which this section applies are—

(*a*) any activities of an appropriate trade union of which the employee is a member; and

(*b*) any activities, whether or not falling within paragraph (*a*) above, in relation to which the employee is acting as a representative of such a union,

excluding activities which themselves consist of industrial action whether or not in contemplation or furtherance of a trade dispute.

(3) The amount of time off which an employee is to be permitted to take under this section and the purposes for which, the occasions on which and any conditions subject to which time off may be so taken are those that are reasonable in all the circumstances having regard to any relevant provisions of a Code of Practice issued by the Service under section 6 above.

(4) In the Code of Practice referred to in section 6 (2) (*b*) (ii) above the Service shall in particular provide practical guidance on the following matters, that is to say, the question whether and the circumstances in which a trade union member is to be permitted to take time off under this section for trade union activities connected with industrial action.

(5) An employee who is a member of an independent trade union recognised by his employer may present a complaint to an industrial tribunal that his employer has failed to permit him to take time off as required by this section. [**362**]

COMMENCEMENT
See s. 129 (3), *post*.

SUB-S. (2): IN CONTEMPLATION OR FURTHERANCE OF A TRADE DISPUTE
See the note to the Trade Union and Labour Relations Act 1974, s. 13.

SUB-S. (3)
This subsection should be read in conjunction with s. 59 (4), *post*.

SUB-S. (5): COMPLAINT
See, further, s. 60 (1), (2), *post*. A complaint under sub-s. (5) above is to be made in accordance with regulations under the Trade Union and Labour Relations Act 1974, Sch. 1, para. 21; see s. 108 (1), *post*, and note sub-ss. (2)–(7) of that section as to conciliation.

INDUSTRIAL TRIBUNAL
See the note to s. 6, *ante*; and as to appeals to the Employment Appeal Tribunal, and thence to the Court of Appeal, from decisions of an industrial tribunal, see s. 88 (1), (4), (5), *post*.

EXCLUDED CLASSES OF EMPLOYMENT
See s. 119 (1), (2), (4)–(6), (8)–(11), *post*.

DEFINITIONS
By virtue of s. 126 (1), *post*, for "employer", see the definition inserted in the Trade Union and Labour Relations Act 1974, s. 30 (1) by s. 125 (1) and Sch. 16, Part III, para. 7 (2), *post*, and s. 30 (2) (*b*) of that Act; for "employee" and "independent trade union", see s. 30 (1) of that Act; for "trade union", see s. 28 (1) of that Act, and for "trade dispute", see s. 29 of that Act; for "the Service", see s. 1 (1), *ante*; for "working hours", see s. 62 (*b*), *post*; for "recognised", see ss. 62 (*a*) and 126 (1), *post*. Note as to "appropriate trade union", sub-s. (2) above.

59. Time off for public duties

(1) An employer shall permit an employee of his who is—

(*a*) a justice of the peace;
(*b*) a member of a local authority;
(*c*) a member of any statutory tribunal;
(*d*) a member of, in England and Wales, a Regional Health Authority or Area Health Authority or, in Scotland, a Health Board;
(*e*) a member of, in England and Wales, the managing or governing body of an educational establishment maintained by a local education authority, or, in Scotland, a school or college council or the governing body of a central institution or a college of education; or
(*f*) a member of, in England and Wales, a water authority or, in Scotland, river purification board,

to take time off, subject to and in accordance with subsection (4) below, during the employee's working hours for the purposes of performing any of the duties of his office or, as the case may be, his duties as such a member.

(2) In subsection (1) above—

(*a*) "local authority" in relation to England and Wales includes the Common Council of the City of London but otherwise has the same meaning as in the Local Government Act 1972, and in relation to Scotland has the same meaning as in the Local Government (Scotland) Act 1973;

(*b*) "Regional Health Authority" and "Area Health Authority" have the same meaning as in the National Health Service Reorganisation Act 1973, and "Health Board" has the same meaning as in the National Health Service (Scotland) Act 1972;

(*c*) "local education authority" means the authority designated by section 192 (1) of the Local Government Act 1972, "school or college council" means a body appointed under section 125 (1) of the Local Government (Scotland) Act 1973, and "central institution" and "college of education" have the meanings assigned to them by section 145 (10) and (14) respectively of the Education (Scotland) Act 1962; and

(*d*) "river purification board" means a board established under section 135 of the Local Government (Scotland) Act 1973.

(3) For the purposes of subsection (1) above the duties of a member of a body referred to in paragraphs (*b*) to (*f*) of that subsection are:—

(*a*) attendance at a meeting of the body or any of its committees or sub-committees;

(*b*) the doing of any other thing approved by the body, or anything of a class so approved, for the purpose of the discharge of the functions of the body or of any of its committees or sub-committees.

(4) The amount of time off which an employee is to be permitted to take under this section and the occasions on which and any conditions subject to which time off may be so taken are those that are reasonable in all the circumstances having regard, in particular, to the following:—

(*a*) how much time off is required for the performance of the duties of the office or as a member of the body in question, and how much time off is required for the performance of the particular duty;

(*b*) how much time off has the employee already been permitted under this section or sections 57 and 58 above;

(*c*) the circumstances of the employer's business and the effect of the employee's absence on the running of that business.

(5) The Secretary of State may by order—

(*a*) modify the provisions of subsection (1) above by adding any office or body to, or removing any office or body from that subsection or by altering the description of any office or body in that subsection; and

(*b*) modify the provisions of subsection (3) above.

(6) An employee may present a complaint to an industrial tribunal that his employer has failed to permit him to take time off as required by this section.

[363]

COMMENCEMENT

See s. 129 (3), *post*.

SUB-S. (1): WATER AUTHORITY

For the establishment of water authorities, see the Water Act 1973, s. 2.

SUB-S. (4)

This subsection should be read in conjunction with ss. 57 (2) and 58 (3), *ante*.

SUB-S. (6): COMPLAINT

See, further, s. 60 (1), (2), *post*. A complaint under sub-s. (6) above is to be made in accordance with regulations under the Trade Union and Labour Relations Act 1974, Sch. 1, para. 21; see s. 108 (1), *post*, and note sub-ss. (2)–(7) of that section as to conciliation.

INDUSTRIAL TRIBUNAL

See the note to s. 6, *ante*; and as to appeals to the Employment Appeal Tribunal, and thence to the Court of Appeal, from decisions of an industrial tribunal, see s. 88 (1), (4), (5), *post*.

EXCLUDED CLASSES OF EMPLOYMENT

See s. 119 (1), (2), (4)–(6), (8)–(13), *post*.

DEFINITIONS

By virtue of s. 126 (1), *post*, for "employer", see the definition inserted in the Trade Union and Labour Relations Act 1974, s. 30 (1), by s. 125 (1) and Sch. 16, Part III, para. 7 (2), *post*, and s. 30 (2) (*b*) of that Act, and for "employee", see s. 30 (1) of that Act; for "working hours", see s. 62 (*b*), *post*. Note also the definitions in sub-s. (2) above.

ORDERS UNDER THIS SECTION

At the time of going to press no order had been made under sub-s. (5) above.

As to the making of orders generally, see s. 123, *post*.

60. Provisions as to industrial tribunals

(1) An industrial tribunal shall not consider—

(*a*) a complaint under section 57, 58 or 59 above that an employer has failed to permit an employee to take time off; or

(*b*) a complaint under section 57 above that an employer has failed to pay an employee the whole or part of any amount required to be paid under that section;

unless it is presented within three months of the date when the failure occurred or within such further period as the tribunal considers reasonable in a case where it is satisfied that it was not reasonably practicable for the complaint to be presented within the period of three months.

(2) Where an industrial tribunal finds any complaint mentioned in subsection (1) (*a*) above well-founded the tribunal shall make a declaration to that effect and may make an award of compensation to be paid by the employer to the employee which shall be of such amount as the tribunal considers just and equitable in all the circumstances having regard to the employer's default in failing to permit time off to be taken by the employee and to any loss sustained by the employee which is attributable to the matters complained of.

(3) Where on a complaint under section 57 above an industrial tribunal finds that the employer has failed to pay the employee the whole or part of the amount required to be paid under that section, the tribunal shall order the employer to pay the employee the amount which it finds due to him. **[364]**

COMMENCEMENT

See s. 129 (3), *post*.

INDUSTRIAL TRIBUNAL

See the note to s. 6, *ante*.

WITHIN THREE MONTHS OF, ETC.
See the note "One month after, etc." to s. 8, *ante*.

SUCH AMOUNT AS THE TRIBUNAL CONSIDERS JUST AND EQUITABLE, ETC.
See the note to s. 56, *ante*.

APPEALS
As to appeals to the Employment Appeal Tribunal, and thence to the Court of Appeal, from decisions of an industrial tribunal under this section, see s. 88 (1), (4), (5), *post*.

DEFINITIONS
By virtue of s. 126 (1), *post*, for "employer", see the definition inserted in the Trade Union and Labour Relations Act 1974, s. 30 (1), by s. 125 (1) and Sch. 16, Part III, para. 7 (2), *post*, and s. 30 (2) (*b*) of that Act, and for "employee", see s. 30 (1) of that Act.

61. Time off to look for work or make arrangements for training

(1) An employee who is given notice of dismissal by reason of redundancy shall, subject to the following provisions of this section, be entitled before the expiration of his notice to be allowed by his employer reasonable time off during the employee's working hours in order to look for new employment or make arrangements for training for future employment.

(2) An employee shall not be entitled to time off under this section unless, on whichever is the later of the following dates, that is to say—

(*a*) the date on which the notice is due to expire; or
(*b*) the date on which it would expire were it the notice required to be given by section 1 (1) of the Contracts of Employment Act 1972 (minimum period of notice),

he will have been or, as the case may be, would have been continuously employed for a period of two years or more.

(3) An employee who is allowed time off during his working hours under subsection (1) above shall, subject to the following provisions of this section, be entitled to be paid remuneration by his employer for the period of absence at the appropriate hourly rate.

(4) The appropriate hourly rate in relation to an employee shall be the amount of one week's pay divided by—

(*a*) the number of normal working hours in a week for that employee when employed under the contract of employment in force on the day when notice was given; or
(*b*) where the number of such normal working hours differs from week to week or over a longer period, the average number of such hours calculated by dividing by 12 the total number of the employee's normal working hours during the period of 12 weeks ending with the last complete week before the day on which notice was given.

(5) For the purposes of Part II of Schedule 4 to this Act as it applies for the calculation of a week's pay for the purposes of this section, the calculation date is the day on which the employer's notice was given.

(6) In this section, "week" in relation to an employee whose remuneration is calculated weekly by a week ending with a day other than Saturday, means a week ending with that other day, and in relation to any other employee means a week ending with Saturday.

(7) If an employer unreasonably refuses to allow an employee time off from

work under this section, the employee shall, subject to subsection (11) below, be entitled to be paid an amount equal to the remuneration to which he would have been entitled under subsection (3) above if he had been allowed the time off.

(8) An employee may present a complaint to an industrial tribunal on the ground that his employer has unreasonably refused to allow him time off under this section or has failed to pay the whole or any part of any amount to which the employee is entitled under subsection (3) or (7) above.

(9) An industrial tribunal shall not entertain a complaint under subsection (8) above unless it is presented to the tribunal within the period of three months beginning with the day on which it is alleged that the time off should have been allowed, or within such further period as the tribunal considers reasonable in a case where it is satisfied that it was not reasonably practicable for the complaint to be presented within the period of three months.

(10) If on a complaint under subsection (8) above the tribunal finds the grounds of the complaint well-founded it shall make a declaration to that effect and shall order the employer to pay to the employee the amount which it finds due to him.

(11) The amount—

(*a*) of an employer's liability to pay remuneration under subsection (3) above; or

(*b*) which may be ordered by a tribunal to be paid by an employer under subsection (7) above,

or, where both paragraphs (*a*) and (*b*) are applicable, the aggregate amount of the liabilities referred to in those paragraphs, shall not exceed, in respect of the notice period of any employee, two-fifths of a week's pay of that employee.

(12) Subject to subsection (13) below, a right to any amount under subsection (3) or (7) above shall not affect any right of an employee in relation to remuneration under the contract of employment (hereafter in this section referred to as "contractual remuneration").

(13) Any contractual remuneration paid to an employee in respect of a period when he takes time off for the purposes referred to in subsection (1) above shall go towards discharging any liability of the employer to pay remuneration under subsection (3) above in respect of that period, and conversely any payment of remuneration under subsection (3) above in respect of a period shall go towards discharging any liability of the employer to pay contractual remuneration in respect of that period. [**365**]

COMMENCEMENT

See s. 129 (3), *post*.

SUB-S. (2): CONTINUOUSLY EMPLOYED FOR . . . TWO YEARS OR MORE

As to the determination of the period for which an employee has been continuously employed, see s. 126 (5), *post*.

SUB-S. (4): WEEK'S PAY

As to the calculation of a week's pay, see s. 85 (1) and Sch. 4, Part II, *post*, in conjunction with sub-s. (5) above.

SUB-S. (8): COMPLAINT

A complaint under sub-s. (8) above is to be made in accordance with regulations under the Trade Union and Labour Relations Act 1974, Sch. 1, para. 21; see s. 108 (1), *post*, and note sub-ss. (2)–(7) of that section as to conciliation.

INDUSTRIAL TRIBUNAL

See the note to s. 6, *ante*; and as to appeals to the Employment Appeal Tribunal, and thence to the Court of Appeal, from decisions of an industrial tribunal under this section, see s. 88 (1), (4), (5), *post*.

SUB-S. (9): THREE MONTHS BEGINNING, ETC.

See the note "14 days (two months) beginning, etc." to s. 15, *ante*.

SUPPLEMENTARY PROVISIONS

See s. 63, *post* (priority on insolvency of payment under sub-s. (3) above); and s. 119 (1)–(6), (12), (13), *post* (excluded classes of employment).

DEFINITIONS

By virtue of s. 126 (1), *post*, for "employer", see the definition inserted in the Trade Union and Labour Relations Act 1974, s. 30 (1) by s. 125 (1) and Sch. 16, Part III, para. 7 (2), *post*, and s. 30 (2) (*b*) of that Act; for "employee", see s. 30 (1) of that Act, and for "dismissal", see Sch. 1, para. 5, to that Act; for "redundancy", see s. 126 (6), *post*; for "working hours", see s. 62 (*b*), *post*; for "normal working hours", see s. 62 (*c*) and Sch. 4, Part I, *post*. Note as "appropriate hourly rate", sub-s. (4) above, as to "week", sub-s. (6) above, and as to "contractual remuneration", sub-s. (12) above.

62. Provisions supplementary to ss. 57 to 61

For the purposes of sections 57 to 61 above—

(*a*) a trade union shall be treated as recognised not only if it is recognised for the purposes of collective bargaining, but also if the Service has made a recommendation for recognition which is operative within the meaning of section 15 above;

(*b*) the working hours of an employee shall be taken to be any time when, in accordance with his contract of employment, he is required to be at work; and

(*c*) "normal working hours" shall be construed in accordance with Part I of Schedule 4 to this Act. [**366**]

COMMENCEMENT

See s. 129 (3), *post*.

DEFINITIONS

By virtue of s. 126 (1), *post*, for "trade union", see the Trade Union and Labour Relations Act 1974, s. 28 (1) and for "employee", see s. 30 (1) of that Act; for "the Service", see s. 1 (1), *ante*.

Insolvency

63. Priority of certain debts on insolvency

(1) An amount to which this section applies shall be treated for the purposes of—

(*a*) section 33 of the Bankruptcy Act 1914;

(*b*) (*applies to Scotland*); and

(*c*) section 319 of the Companies Act 1948;

as if it were wages payable by the employer to the employee in respect of the period for which it is payable.

(2) This section applies to any amount owed by an employer to an employee in respect of:—

(*a*) a guarantee payment;

(*b*) remuneration on suspension on medical grounds under section 29 above;

(*c*) any payment for time off under section 57 (4) or 61 (3) above;
(*d*) remuneration under a protective award made under section 101 below.
[367]

COMMENCEMENT
Section 63 (1) and (2) (*d*) was brought into force on 20th April 1976 by the Employment Protection Act 1975 (Commencement No. 2) Order 1976, S.I. 1976 No. 144.

GUARANTEE PAYMENT
As to the nature of such payment and the right thereto, see s. 22, *ante*, and for ancillary provisions in regard thereto, see ss. 23–28, *ante*.

EXCLUSION OF BUSINESS EMPLOYMENT
See s. 121, *post*.

DEFINITIONS
By virtue of s. 126 (1), *post*, for "employer", see the definition inserted in the Trade Union and Labour Relations Act 1974, s. 30 (1), by s. 125 (1) and Sch. 16, Part III, para. 7 (2), *post*, and s. 30 (2) (*b*) of that Act, and for "employee", see s. 30 (1) of that Act.

64. Employee's rights on insolvency of employer

(1) If on an application made to him in writing by an employee the Secretary of State is satisfied—

(*a*) that the employer of that employee has become insolvent; and
(*b*) that on the relevant date the employee was entitled to be paid the whole or part of any debt to which this section applies,

the Secretary of State shall, subject to the provisions of this section, pay the employee out of the Redundancy Fund the amount to which in the opinion of the Secretary of State the employee is entitled in respect of that debt.

(2) In this section the "relevant date" in relation to a debt means the date on which the employer became insolvent or the date of the termination of the employee's employment, whichever is the later.

(3) This section applies to the following debts:—

(*a*) any arrears of pay in respect of a period or periods not exceeding in the aggregate eight weeks;
(*b*) any amount which the employer is liable to pay the employee for the period of notice required by section 1 (1) or (2) of the Contracts of Employment Act 1972 (minimum period of notice) or for any failure of the employer to give the period of notice required by section 1 (1) of that Act;
(*c*) any holiday pay in respect of a period or periods of holiday, not exceeding six weeks in all, to which the employee became entitled during the 12 months immediately preceding the relevant date;
(*d*) any basic award of compensation for unfair dismissal;
(*e*) any reasonable sum by way of reimbursement of the whole or part of any fee or premium paid by an apprentice or articled clerk.

(4) For the purposes of subsection (3) (*a*) above any such amount as is referred to in section 63 (2) above shall be treated as if it were arrears of pay.

(5) The total amount payable to an employee in respect of any debt mentioned in subsection (3) above, where the amount of that debt is referable to a period of time, shall not exceed £80 in respect of any one week or, in respect of a shorter period, an amount bearing the same proportion to £80 as that shorter period bears to a week.

(6) The Secretary of State may vary the limit referred to in subsection (5) above after a review under section 86 below, by order made in accordance with that section.

(7) A sum shall be taken to be reasonable for the purposes of subsection (3) (*e*) above in a case where a trustee in bankruptcy or liquidator has been or is required to be appointed if it is admitted to be reasonable by the trustee in bankruptcy or liquidator under section 34 of the Bankruptcy Act 1914 (preferential claims of apprentices and articled clerks), whether as originally enacted or as applied to the winding up of a company by section 317 of the Companies Act 1948.

(8) (*Applies to Scotland.*)

(9) The provisions of subsections (10) and (11) below shall apply in a case where one of the following officers (hereafter in this section referred to as the "relevant officer") has been or is required to be appointed in connection with the employer's insolvency, that is to say, a trustee in bankruptcy, a liquidator, a receiver or manager, or a trustee under a composition or arrangement between the employer and his creditors or under a trust deed for his creditors executed by the employer; and in this subsection "liquidator" and "receiver" include the Official Receiver in his capacity as a provisional liquidator or interim receiver.

(10) Subject to subsection (11) below, the Secretary of State shall not in such a case make any payment under this section in respect of any debt until he has received a statement from the relevant officer of the amount of that debt which appears to have been owed to the employee on the relevant date and to remain unpaid; and the relevant officer shall, on request by the Secretary of State, provide him, as soon as reasonably practicable, with such a statement.

(11) Where—

(*a*) a period of six months has elapsed since the application for a payment under this section was received by the Secretary of State, but no such payment has been made;

(*b*) the Secretary of State is satisfied that a payment under this section should be made; and

(*c*) it appears to the Secretary of State that there is likely to be further delay before he receives a statement about the debt in question,

then, the Secretary of State may, if the applicant so requests or, if the Secretary of State thinks fit, without such a request, make a payment under this section, notwithstanding that no such statement has been received. **[368]**

COMMENCEMENT

This section was brought into force on 20th April 1976 by the Employment Protection Act 1975 (Commencement No. 2) Order 1976, S.I. 1976 No. 144, except for para. (*d*) of sub-s. (3) and sub-s. (6).

SUB-S. (1): WRITING

See the note "Written" to s. 11, *ante*.

EMPLOYER . . . HAS BECOME INSOLVENT

As to the circumstances in which for the purposes of this section an employer is to be taken to be insolvent, see s. 69 (1), *post*.

DEBT TO WHICH THIS SECTION APPLIES

See sub-s. (3) above.

REDUNDANCY FUND

That Fund was established under the Redundancy Payments Act 1965, s. 26.

SUB-S. (3): BASIC AWARD OF COMPENSATION FOR UNFAIR DISMISSAL

An award of such compensation is made by an industrial tribunal under ss. 72 *et seq.*, *post*. As to basic awards, see ss. 73–75, *post*.

SUB-S. (3) (e): REASONABLE SUM BY WAY OF REIMBURSEMENT, ETC.

Note sub-s. (7) above.

SUB-S. (9): TRUSTEE IN BANKRUPTCY; RECEIVER; MANAGER; TRUSTEE UNDER A COMPOSITION OR ARRANGEMENT

As to the appointment of a trustee in bankruptcy, see the Bankruptcy Act 1914, s. 19; as to the receiver, see s. 7 of the Act of 1914; as to the appointment of a special manager of a debtor's estate, see s. 10 of the Act of 1914, s. 10; and as to the appointment of a trustee under a composition or arrangement, see s. 16 (17) of the Act of 1914.

LIQUIDATOR

For appointment upon the winding-up of a company, see the Companies Act 1948, s. 237.

OFFICIAL RECEIVER

That officer is appointed under the Bankruptcy Act 1914, s. 70.

FURTHER PROVISIONS

See s. 66 (1), (3), *post* (complaint to industrial tribunal); s. 67 (1), (2), (4), *post* (transfer to the Secretary of State of rights and remedies); s. 68, *post* (power of Secretary of State to obtain information in connection with applications); s. 119 (1)–(6), (12), (13) *post* (excluded classes of employment); and s. 121, *post* (exclusion of Crown employment).

DEFINITIONS

By virtue of s. 126 (1), *post*, for "employer", see the definition inserted in the Trade Union and Labour Relations Act 1974, s. 30 (1), by s. 125 (1) and Sch. 16, Part III, para. 7 (2), *post*, and s. 30 (2) (*b*) of that Act, and for "employee", see s. 30 (1) of that Act; for "holiday pay", see s. 69 (3), *post*. As to "relevant date", note sub-s. (2) above, as to "arrears of pay", note sub-s. (4) above, and as to "relevant officer" note sub-s. (9) above.

TRANSITIONAL PROVISIONS

See s. 125 (2) and Sch. 17, para. 8, *post*.

65. Payment of unpaid contributions to occupational pension scheme

(1) If, on an application made to him in writing by the persons competent to act in respect of an occupational pension scheme, the Secretary of State is satisfied that an employer has become insolvent and that at the time that he did so there remained unpaid relevant contributions falling to be paid by him to the scheme, the Secretary of State shall, subject to the provisions of this section, pay into the resources of the scheme out of the Redundancy Fund the sum which in his opinion is payable in respect of the unpaid relevant contributions.

(2) In this section "relevant contributions" means contributions falling to be paid by an employer in accordance with an occupational pension scheme, either on his own account or on behalf of an employee; and for the purposes of this section a contribution of any amount shall not be treated as falling to be paid on behalf of an employee unless a sum equal to that amount has been deducted from the pay of the employee by way of a contribution from him.

(3) The sum payable under this section in respect of unpaid contributions of an employer on his own account to an occupational pension scheme shall be the least of the following amounts—

(*a*) the balance of relevant contributions remaining unpaid on the date when he became insolvent and payable by the employer on his own account to the scheme in respect of the 12 months immediately preceding that date;

(*b*) the amount certified by an actuary to be necessary for the purpose of meeting the liability of the scheme on dissolution to pay the benefits provided by the scheme to or in respect of the employees of the employer;

(*c*) an amount equal to 10 per cent. of the total amount of remuneration paid or payable to those employees in respect of the 12 months immediately preceding the date on which the employer became insolvent.

(4) For the purposes of subsection (3) (*c*) above, "remuneration" includes holiday pay, maternity pay and any such payment as is referred to in section 63 (2) above.

(5) Any sum payable under this section in respect of unpaid contributions on behalf of an employee shall not exceed the amount deducted from the pay of the employee in respect of the employee's contributions to the occupational pension scheme during the 12 months immediately preceding the date on which the employer became insolvent.

(6) The provisions of subsections (7) to (9) below shall apply in a case where one of the following officers (hereafter in this section referred to as the "relevant officer") has been or is required to be appointed in connection with the employer's insolvency, that is to say, a trustee in bankruptcy, a liquidator, a receiver or manager, or a trustee under a composition or arrangement between the employer and his creditors or under a trust deed for his creditors executed by the employer; and in this subsection "liquidator" and "receiver" include the Official Receiver in his capacity as a provisional liquidator or interim receiver.

(7) Subject to subsection (9) below, the Secretary of State shall not in such a case make any payment under this section in respect of unpaid relevant contributions until he has received a statement from the relevant officer of the amount of relevant contributions which appear to have been unpaid on the date on which the employer became insolvent and to remain unpaid; and the relevant officer shall, on request by the Secretary of State provide him, as soon as reasonably practicable, with such a statement.

(8) Subject to subsection (9) below, an amount shall be taken to be payable, paid or deducted as mentioned in subsection (3) (*a*) or (*c*) or subsection (5) above, only if it is so certified by the relevant officer.

(9) Where—

(*a*) a period of six months has elapsed since the application for a payment under this section was received by the Secretary of State, but no such payment has been made;

(*b*) the Secretary of State is satisfied that a payment under this section should be made; and

(*c*) it appears to the Secretary of State that there is likely to be further delay before he receives a statement or certificate about the contributions in question,

then, the Secretary of State may, if the applicants so request or, if the Secretary of State thinks fit, without such a request, make a payment under this section, notwithstanding that no such statement or certificate has been received. [**369**]

COMMENCEMENT

This section was brought into force on 20th April 1976 by the Employment Protection Act 1975 (Commencement No. 2) Order 1976, S.I. 1976 No. 144.

SUB-S. (1): WRITING
See the note "Written" to s. 11, *ante*.

EMPLOYER HAS BECOME INSOLVENT
As to the circumstances in which for the purposes of this section, an employer is to be taken to be insolvent, see s. 69 (1), *post*.

REDUNDANCY FUND
See the note to s. 64, *ante*.

SUB-S. (4): MATERNITY PAY
This is payable under ss. 35 *et seq.*, *ante*.

SUB-S. (6): TRUSTEE IN BANKRUPTCY; RECEIVER; MANAGER; TRUSTEE UNDER A COMPOSITION OR ARRANGEMENT; LIQUIDATOR; OFFICIAL RECEIVER
See the notes to s. 64, *ante*.

FURTHER PROVISIONS
See s. 66 (2), (3), *post* (complaint to industrial tribunal); s. 67 (3), (4), *post* (transfer to the Secretary of State of rights and remedies); s. 68, *post* (power of Secretary of State to obtain information in connection with applications); s. 119 (1)–(6), (12), (13), *post* (excluded classes of employment); and s. 121, *post* (exclusion of Crown employment).

DEFINITIONS
By virtue of s. 126 (1), *post*, for "employer", see the definition inserted in the Trade Union and Labour Relations Act 1974, s. 30 (1), by s. 125 (1) and Sch. 16, Part III, para. 7 (2), *post*, and s. 30 (2) (*b*) of that Act, and for "employee", see s. 30 (1) of that Act; for "holiday pay" and "occupational pension scheme" and as to the resources of such a scheme, see s. 69 (3), *post*. As to "relevant contributions", note sub-s. (2) above, and as to "relevant officer", note sub-s. (6) above.

TRANSITIONAL PROVISIONS
See s. 125 (2) and Sch. 17, para. 8, *post*.

66. Complaint to industrial tribunal

(1) A person who has applied for a payment under section 64 above may, within the period of three months beginning with the date on which the decision of the Secretary of State on that application was communicated to him or, if that is not reasonably practicable, within such further period as is reasonable, present a complaint to an industrial tribunal that—

(*a*) the Secretary of State has failed to make any such payment; or
(*b*) any such payment made by the Secretary of State is less than the amount which should have been paid.

(2) Any persons who are competent to act in respect of an occupational pension scheme and who have applied for a payment to be made under section 65 above into the resources of the scheme may, within the period of three months beginning with the date on which the decision of the Secretary of State on that application was communicated to them, or, if that is not reasonably practicable, within such further period as is reasonable, present a complaint to an industrial tribunal that—

(*a*) the Secretary of State has failed to make any such payment; or
(*b*) any such payment made by him is less than the amount which should have been paid.

(3) Where an industrial tribunal finds that the Secretary of State ought to make a payment under section 64 or 65 above, it shall make a declaration to that effect and shall also declare the amount of any such payment which it finds the Secretary of State ought to make. **[370]**

COMMENCEMENT

This section was brought into force on 20th April 1976 by the Employment Protection Act 1975 (Commencement No. 2) Order 1976, S.I. 1976 No. 144.

THREE MONTHS BEGINNING, ETC.

See the note "14 days (two months) beginning, etc.", to s. 15, *ante*. .

COMPLAINT

A complaint under this section is to be made in accordance with regulations made under the Trade Union and Labour Relations Act 1974, Sch. 1, para. 21; see s. 108, *post*.

INDUSTRIAL TRIBUNAL

See the note to s. 6, *ante*.

APPEALS

As to appeals to the Employment Appeal Tribunal, and thence to the Court of Appeal, from decisions of an industrial tribunal, see s. 88 (1), (4), (5), *post*.

EXCLUSION OF CROWN EMPLOYMENT

See s. 121, *post*.

DEFINITIONS

For "occupational pension scheme" and as to the resources of such a scheme, see s. 69 (3), *post*.

67. Transfer to the Secretary of State of rights and remedies

(1) Where in pursuance of section 64 above the Secretary of State makes any payment to an employee in respect of any debt to which that section applies—

(*a*) any rights and remedies of the employee in respect of that debt or (if the Secretary of State has paid only part of it) in respect of that part shall, on the making of the payment, become rights and remedies of the Secretary of State; and

(*b*) any decision of an industrial tribunal requiring an employer to pay that debt to the employee shall have the effect that the debt or, as the case may be, that part of it which the Secretary of State has paid, is to be paid to the Secretary of State.

(2) There shall be included among the rights and remedies which become rights and remedies of the Secretary of State in accordance with subsection (1) (*a*) above any right to be paid in priority to other creditors of the employer in accordance with—

(*a*) section 33 of the Bankruptcy Act 1914;
(*b*) (*applies to Scotland*); and
(*c*) section 319 of the Companies Act 1948,

and the Secretary of State shall be entitled to be so paid in priority to any other unsatisfied claim of the employee; and in computing for the purposes of any of those provisions any limit on the amount of sums to be so paid any sums paid to the Secretary of State shall be treated as if they had been paid to the employee.

(3) Where in pursuance of section 65 above the Secretary of State makes any payment into the resources of an occupational pension scheme in respect of any contributions to the scheme, any rights and remedies in respect of those contributions belonging to the persons competent to act in respect of the scheme shall, on the making of the payment, become rights and remedies of the Secretary of State.

(4) Any sum recovered by the Secretary of State in exercising any right or

pursuing any remedy which is his by virtue of this section shall be paid into the Redundancy Fund. [**371**]

COMMENCEMENT

This section was brought into force on 20th April 1976 by the Employment Protection Act 1975 (Commencement No. 2) Order 1976, S.I. 1976 No. 144.

INDUSTRIAL TRIBUNAL

See the note to s. 6, *ante*.

REDUNDANCY FUND

See the note to s. 64, *ante*.

EXCLUSION OF CROWN EMPLOYMENT

See s. 121, *post*.

DEFINITIONS

By virtue of s. 126 (1), *post*, for "employer", see the definition inserted in the Trade Union and Labour Relations Act 1974, s. 30 (1), by s. 125 (1) and Sch. 16, Part III, para. 7 (2), *post*, and s. 30 (2) (*b*) of that Act, and for "employee", see s. 30 (1) of that Act. For "occupational pension scheme" and as to the resources of such a scheme, see s. 69 (3), *post*.

68. Power of Secretary of State to obtain information in connection with applications

(1) Where an application is made to the Secretary of State under section 64 or 65 above in respect of a debt owed, or contributions to an occupational pension scheme falling to be made, by an employer, the Secretary of State may require—

(*a*) the employer to provide him with such information as the Secretary of State may reasonably require for the purposes of determining whether the application is well-founded; and

(*b*) any person having the custody or control of any relevant records or other documents to produce for examination on behalf of the Secretary of State any such document in that person's custody or under his control which is of such a description as the Secretary of State may require.

(2) Any such requirement shall be made by notice in writing given to the person on whom the requirement is imposed and may be varied or revoked by a subsequent notice so given.

(3) If a person refuses or wilfully neglects to furnish any information or produce any document which he has been required to furnish or produce by a notice under this section he shall be liable on summary conviction to a fine not exceeding £100.

(4) If a person, in purporting to comply with a requirement of a notice under this section, knowingly or recklessly makes any false statement he shall be liable on summary conviction to a fine not exceeding £400. [**372**]

COMMENCEMENT

This section was brought into force on 20th April 1976 by the Employment Protection Act 1975 (Commencement No. 2) Order 1976, S.I. 1976 No. 144.

WRITING

See the note "Written" to s. 11, *ante*.

SUMMARY CONVICTION

Summary procedure and jurisdiction in England and Wales are mainly governed by the Magistrates' Courts Act 1952, the Magistrate's Courts Act 1957, and certain provisions of the Criminal Justice Act 1967.

KNOWINGLY

There is authority for saying that, where a person deliberately refrains from making inquiries the result of which he might not care to have, this constitutes in law actual knowledge of the facts in question; see *Knox* v. *Boyd*, 1941 S.C. (J.) 82, at p. 86, and *Taylor's General Garages (Exeter), Ltd.* v. *Roper* (1951), 115 J.P. 445, at pp. 449, 450, *per* Devlin, J.; and see also *Mallon* v. *Allon*, [1964] 1 Q.B. 385; [1963] 3 All E.R. 843, at p. 394, and p. 847, respectively. However, mere neglect to ascertain what would have been found out by making reasonable inquiries is not tantamount to knowledge; see *Taylor's Central Garages (Exeter), Ltd.* v. *Roper*, *ubi supra*, *per* Devlin, J., and cf. *London Computor, Ltd.* v. *Seymour*, [1944] 2 All E.R. 11; but see also *Mallon* v. *Allon*, *ubi supra*.

RECKLESSLY

On the meaning of this expression, see, in particular, *Derry* v. *Peek* [1889), 14 App. Cas. 337; [1886–90] All E.R. Rep. 1; *Williams Bros. Direct Supply Stores, Ltd.* v. *Cloote* (1944), 60 T.L.R. 270; *R.* v. *Bates*, [1952] 2 All E.R. 842; on appeal *sub nom. R.* v. *Russell*, [1953] 1 W.L.R. 77; 97 Sol. Jo. 12; *R.* v. *Mackinnon*, [1959] 1 Q.B. 150; [1958] 3 All E.R. 657; *R.* v. *Grunwald*, [1963] 1 Q.B. 935; [1960] 3 All E.R. 380; *Shawinigan, Ltd.* v. *Vokins & Co., Ltd.*, [1961] 3 All E.R. 396; and *M.F.I. Warehouses, Ltd.* v. *Nattrass*, [1973] 1 All E.R. 762.

FALSE

A statement may be false on account of what it omits even though it is literally true; see *R.* v. *Lord Kylsant*, [1932] 1 K.B. 442; [1931] All E.R. Rep. 179, and *R.* v. *Bishirgian*, [1936] 1 All E.R. 586; and cf. *Curtis* v. *Chemical Cleaning and Dying Co., Ltd.*, [1951] 1 K.B. 805; [1951] 1 All E.R. 631, C.A., at p. 809 and p. 634, respectively, *per* Denning, L.J. Whether or not an advantage accrues from the false statement is immaterial; see *Jones* v. *Meatyard*, [1939] 1 All E.R. 140, and *Stevens and Steeds, Ltd. and Evans* v. *King*, [1943] 1 All E.R. 314.

EXCLUSION OF CROWN EMPLOYMENT

See s. 121, *post*.

DEFINITIONS

By virtue of s. 126 (1), *post*, for "employer", see the definition inserted in the Trade Union and Labour Relations Act 1974, s. 30 (1), by s. 125 (1) and Sch. 16, Part III, para. 7 (2), *post*, and s. 30 (2) (*b*) of that Act; for "occupational pension scheme", see s. 69 (3), *post*.

69. Interpretation of ss. 64 to 68

(1) For the purposes of sections 64 to 68 above an employer shall be taken to be insolvent if, but only if, in England and Wales,—

(*a*) he becomes bankrupt or makes a composition or arrangement with his creditors or a receiving order is made against him;

(*b*) he has died and an order is made under section 130 of the Bankruptcy Act 1914 for the administration of his estate according to the law of bankruptcy, or by virtue of an order of the court his estate is being administered in accordance with rules set out in Part I of Schedule 1 to the Administration of Estates Act 1925; or

(*c*) where the employer is a company, a winding up order is made or a resolution for voluntary winding up is passed with respect to it, or a receiver or manager of its undertaking is duly appointed, or possession is taken, by or on behalf of the holders of any debentures secured by a floating charge, of any property of the company comprised in or subject to the charge.

(2) (*Applies to Scotland.*)

(3) In sections 64 to 68 above—

"holiday pay" means—

(*a*) pay in respect of a holiday actually taken; or

any accrued holiday pay which under the employee's contract of employment would in the ordinary course have become payable to him in respect of the period of a holiday if his employment with the employer had continued until he became entitled to a holiday;

"occupational pension scheme" means any scheme or arrangement which provides or is capable of providing, in relation to employees in any description of employment, benefits (in the form of pensions or otherwise) payable to or in respect of any such employees on the termination of their employment or on their death or retirement;

and any reference in those sections to the resources of such a scheme is a reference to the funds out of which the benefits provided by the scheme are from time to time payable. **[373]**

COMMENCEMENT

This section was brought into force on 20th April 1976 by the Employment Protection Act (Commencement No. 2) Order 1976, S.I. 1976 No. 144.

HE BECOMES BANKRUPT

I.e., upon adjudication of bankruptcy by the court under the Bankruptcy Act 1914, s. 18.

MAKES A COMPOSITION OR ARRANGEMENT WITH HIS CREDITORS

I.e., under the Bankruptcy Act 1914, s. 16.

RECEIVING ORDER

As to such orders, see the Bankruptcy Act 1914, s. 3.

WINDING-UP ORDER

Such an order is made by the court under the Companies Act 1948, ss. 218 *et seq.*

RESOLUTION FOR VOLUNTARY WINDING-UP

I.e., a resolution passed under the Companies Act 1948, s. 278.

EXCLUSION OF CROWN EMPLOYMENT

See s. 121, *post.*

DEFINITIONS

By virtue of s. 126 (1), *post*, for "employer", see the definition inserted in the Trade Union and Labour Relations Act 1974, s. 30 (1), by s. 125 (1) and Sch. 16, Part III, para. 7 (2), *post*, and s. 30 (2) (*b*) of that Act, and for "employee", see s. 30 (1) of that Act.

Written statement of reasons for dismissal

70. Written statement of reasons for dismissal

(1) An employee shall be entitled—

(*a*) if he is given by his employer notice of termination of his contract of employment;

(*b*) if his contract of employment is terminated by his employer without notice; or

(*c*) if, where he is employed under a contract for a fixed term, that term expires without being renewed under the same contract,

to be provided by his employer, on request, within 14 days of that request, with a written statement giving particulars of the reasons for his dismissal.

(2) An employee shall not be entitled to a written statement under subsection (1) above unless on the effective date of termination he has been, or will have been, continously employed for a period of 26 weeks ending with the last complete week before that date.

(3) A written statement provided under this section shall be admissible in evidence in any proceedings.

(4) A complaint may be presented to an industrial tribunal by an employee against his employer on the ground that the employer unreasonably refused to provide a written statement under subsection (1) above or that the particulars of reasons given in purported compliance with that subsection are inadequate or untrue, and if the tribunal finds the complaint well-founded—

(*a*) it may make a declaration as to what it finds the employer's reasons were for dismissing the employee; and

(*b*) it shall make an award that the employer pay to the employee a sum equal to the amount of two weeks' pay.

(5) An industrial tribunal shall not entertain a complaint under this section relating to the reasons for a dismissal unless it is presented to the tribunal at such a time that the tribunal would, in accordance with paragraph 21 (4) or (4A) of Schedule 1 to the 1974 Act, entertain a complaint of unfair dismissal in respect of that dismissal presented at the same time.

(6) For the purposes of Part II of Schedule 4 to this Act as it applies for the calculation of a week's pay for the purposes of this section, the calculation date where the dismissal was with notice is the date on which the employer's notice was given and in any other case is the effective date of termination. **[374]**

COMMENCEMENT
See s. 129 (3), *post*.

SUB-S. (1): WITHIN 14 DAYS OF, ETC.
See the note "One month after, etc." to s. 8, *ante*.

WRITTEN
See the note to s. 11, *ante*.

SUB-S. (2): CONTINUOUSLY EMPLOYED FOR . . . 26 WEEKS, ETC.
As to the determination of the period for which an employee has been continuously employed, see s. 126 (5), *post*.

SUB-S. (4): COMPLAINT
A complaint under this section is to be made in accordance with regulations under the Trade Union and Labour Relations Act 1974, Sch. 1, para. 21; see s. 108 (1), *post*, and note sub-ss. (2)–(7) of that section as to conciliation.

INDUSTRIAL TRIBUNAL
See the note to s. 6, *ante*.

TWO WEEKS' PAY
As to the calculation of a week's pay, see s. 85 (1) and Sch. 4, Part II, *post*, in conjunction with sub-s. (6) above.

APPEALS
As to appeals to the Employment Appeal Tribunal and thence to the Court of Appeal, from decisions of an industrial tribunal, see s. 88 (1), (4), (5), *post*.

EXCLUDED CLASSES OF EMPLOYMENT
See s. 119 (1)–(6), *post*.

DEFINITIONS
By virtue of s. 126 (1), *post*, for "employer", see the definition inserted in the Trade Union and Labour Relations Act 1974, s. 30 (1), by s. 125 (1) and Sch. 16, Part III, para. 7 (2), *post*, and s. 30 (2) (*b*) of that Act, and for "employee", see s. 30 (1) of that Act; for "dismiss", "dismissal" and "effective date of termination", see by virtue of s. 126 (1), *post*, Sch. 1, para. 5 to the Act of 1974.

Remedies for unfair dismissal

71. Order for reinstatement or re-engagement

(1) Where on a complaint under paragraph 17 of Schedule 1 to the 1974 Act (unfair dismissal) an industrial tribunal finds that the grounds of the complaint are well-founded, it shall explain to the complainant what orders for reinstatement or re-engagement may be made under this section and in what circumstances they may be made, and shall ask him whether he wishes the tribunal to make such an order, and if he does express such a wish the tribunal may make an order under this section.

(2) An order under this section may be an order for reinstatement (in accordance with subsections (3) and (4) below) or an order for re-engagement (in accordance with subsection (5) below), as the tribunal may decide, and in the latter case may be on such terms as the tribunal may decide.

(3) An order for reinstatement is an order that the employer shall treat the complainant in all respects as if he had not been dismissed, and on making such an order the tribunal shall specify—

(*a*) any amount payable by the employer in respect of any benefit which the complainant might reasonably be expected to have had but for the dismissal, including arrears of pay, for the period between the date of termination of employment and the date of reinstatement;
(*b*) any rights and privileges, including seniority and pension rights, which must be restored to the employee; and
(*c*) the date by which the order must be complied with.

(4) Without prejudice to the generality of subsection (3) above, if the complainant would have benefited from an improvement in his terms and conditions of employment had he not been dismissed, an order for reinstatement shall require him to be treated as if he had benefited from that improvement from the date on which he would have done so but for being dismissed.

(5) An order for re-engagement is an order that the complainant be engaged by the employer, or by a successor of the employer or by an associated employer, in employment comparable to that from which he was dismissed or other suitable employment, and on making such an order the tribunal shall specify the terms on which re-engagement is to take place including—

(*a*) the identity of the employer;
(*b*) the nature of the employment;
(*c*) the remuneration for the employment;
(*d*) any amount payable by the employer in respect of any benefit which the complainant might reasonably be expected to have had but for the dismissal, including arrears of pay, for the period between the date of termination of employment and the date of re-engagement;
(*e*) any rights and privileges, including seniority and pension rights, which must be restored to the employee; and
(*f*) the date by which the order must be complied with.

(6) In exercising its discretion under this section the tribunal shall first consider whether to make an order for reinstatement and in so doing shall take into account the following considerations, that is to say—

(*a*) whether the complainant wishes to be reinstated;
(*b*) whether it is practicable for the employer to comply with an order for reinstatement;

(*c*) where the complainant caused or contributed to some extent to the dismissal, whether it would be just to order his reinstatement.

(7) If the tribunal decides not to make an order for reinstatement it shall then consider whether to make an order for re-engagement and if so on what terms; and in so doing the tribunal shall take into account the following considerations, that is to say—

(*a*) any wish expressed by the complainant as to the nature of the order to be made;

(*b*) whether it is practicable for the employer or, as the case may be, a successor or associated employer to comply with an order for re-engagement;

(*c*) where the complainant caused or contributed to some extent to the dismissal, whether it would be just to order his re-engagement and if so on what terms;

and except in a case where the tribunal takes into account contributory fault under paragraph (*c*) above it shall, if it orders re-engagement, do so on terms which are, so far as is reasonably practicable, as favourable as an order for reinstatement.

(8) Where in any case an employer has engaged a permanent replacement for a dismissed employee the tribunal shall not take that fact into account in determining, for the purposes of subsection (6) (*b*) or (7) (*b*) above whether it is practicable to comply with an order for reinstatement or re-engagement unless the employer shows—

(*a*) that it was not practicable for him to arrange for the dismissed employee's work to be done without engaging a permanent replacement; or

(*b*) that he engaged the replacement after the lapse of a reasonable period, without having heard from the dismissed employee that he wished to be reinstated or re-engaged, and that when the employer engaged the replacement it was no longer reasonable for him to arrange for the dismissed employee's work to be done except by a permanent replacement.

(9) In calculating for the purpose of subsection (3) (*a*) or (5) (*d*) above any amount payable by the employer the tribunal shall take into account, so as to reduce the employer's liability, any sums received by the complainant in respect of the period between the date of termination of employment and the date of reinstatement or re-engagement by way of—

(*a*) wages in lieu of notice or ex gratia payments paid by the employer;

(*b*) remuneration paid in respect of employment with another employer;

and such other benefits as the tribunal thinks appropriate in the circumstances. [375]

COMMENCEMENT

See s. 129 (3), *post*.

GENERAL NOTE

This section takes the place of the Trade Union and Labour Relations Act 1974, Sch. 1, para. 17 (2) (repealed by s. 125 (3) and Sch. 18, *post*), and makes improved and more detailed provision in respect of orders for reinstatement or re-engagement upon complaints of unfair dismissal.

SUB-S. (1): INDUSTRIAL TRIBUNAL

See the note to s. 6, *ante*.

SUB-SS. (3), (5): AMOUNT PAYABLE BY THE EMPLOYER, ETC.
Note the provisions of sub-s. (9) above.

SUB-SS. (6), (7): WHETHER IT IS PRACTICABLE FOR THE EMPLOYER TO COMPLY, ETC.
Note the provisions of sub-s. (8) above.

FURTHER PROVISIONS
See s. 72, *post* (enforcement of order under this section and compensation); see 73–76, *post* (calculation of compensation); s. 77, *post* (compensation for act which is both sex discrimination and unfair dismissal); ss. 78–80, *post* (interim relief and orders for continuation of contracts of employment), and s. 110 and Sch. 12, *post* (provisions applying on death of employee or employer).

DEFINITIONS
By virtue of s. 126 (1), *post*, for "employer", see the definition inserted in the Trade Union and Labour Relations Act 1974, s. 30 (1), by s. 125 (1) and Sch. 16, Part III, para. 7 (2), *post*, and s. 30 (2) (*b*) of that Act; for "employee", see s. 30 (1) of that Act; for "successor", see s. 30 (3), (4) of that Act; for "associated employer", see s. 30 (5) of that Act, and for "dismiss" and "dismissal", see Sch. 1, para. 5, to that Act; for "the complainant", see, by virtue of s. 126 (3), *post*, Sch. 1, para. 17 (1), to the Act of 1974.

TRANSITIONAL PROVISIONS
See s. 125 (2) and Sch. 17, para. 7, *post*.

72. Enforcement of s. 71 order and compensation

(1) If an order under section 71 above is made and the complainant is reinstated or, as the case may be, re-engaged but the terms of the order are not fully complied with, then, subject to paragraph 20 of Schedule 1 to the 1974 Act (limit on compensation), an industrial tribunal shall make an award of compensation, to be paid by the employer to the employee, of such amount as the tribunal thinks fit having regard to the loss sustained by the complainant in consequence of the failure to comply fully with the terms of the order.

(2) Subject to subsection (1) above, if an order under section 71 above is made but the complainant is not reinstated or, as the case may be, re-engaged in accordance with the order—

(*a*) the tribunal shall make an award of compensation for unfair dismissal, calculated in accordance with sections 73 to 76 below, to be paid by the employer to the employee; and

(*b*) unless the employer satisfies the tribunal that it was not practicable to comply with the order, the tribunal shall make an additional award of compensation to be paid by the employer to the employee of an amount—

(i) where the dismissal is of a description referred to in subsection (3) below, not less than 26 or more than 52 weeks' pay, or

(ii) in any other case, not less than 13 or more than 26 weeks' pay.

(3) The descriptions of dismissal in respect of which an employer may incur a higher additional award in accordance with subsection (2) (*b*) (i) above are the following, that is to say,—

(*a*) a dismissal which is unfair by virtue of paragraph 6 (4) or (5) of Schedule 1 to the 1974 Act (dismissal for membership or non-membership of a trade union, or for taking part in the activities of an independent trade union);

(*b*) a dismissal which is an unlawful act of discrimination by virtue of section 3 (1) of the Race Relations Act 1968;

(*c*) a dismissal which is an act of discrimination (within the meaning of the Sex Discrimination Act 1975) which is unlawful by virtue of that Act.

(4) Where in any case an employer has engaged a permanent replacement for a dismissed employee the tribunal shall not take that fact into account in determining, for the purposes of subsection (2) (*b*) above whether it was practicable to comply with the order for reinstatement or re-engagement unless the employer shows that it was not practicable for him to arrange for the dismissed employee's work to be done without engaging a permanent replacement.

(5) If on a complaint under paragraph 17 of Schedule 1 to the 1974 Act the tribunal finds that the grounds of the complaint are well-founded, and no order is made under section 71 above the tribunal shall make an award of compensation for unfair dismissal, calculated in accordance with sections 73 to 76 below, to be paid by the employer to the employee.

(6) Where in any case the tribunal makes an award of compensation for unfair dismissal, calculated in accordance with section 73 to 76 below, and the tribunal finds that the complainant has unreasonably prevented an order under section 71 above from being complied with, it shall, without prejudice to the generality of section 76 (4) below, take that conduct into account as a failure on the part of the complainant to mitigate his loss.

(7) For the purposes of Part II of Schedule 4 as it applies for the calculation of a week's pay for the purpose of subsection (2) (*b*) above, the calculation date where the dismissal was with notice is the date on which the notice was given and in any other case the effective date of termination.

(8) Notwithstanding anything in the said Part II, the amount of a week's pay for the purpose of calculating an additional award under subsection (2) (*b*) above shall not exceed £80. **[376]**

COMMENCEMENT

See s. 129 (3), *post*.

GENERAL NOTE

This section and ss. 73–76, *post*, take the place of the Trade Union and Labour Relations Act 1974, Sch. 1, paras. 17 (3), 19 (repealed by s. 125 (3) and Sch. 18, *post*), and make new provision in respect of compensation for unfair dismissal.

SUB-S. (1): INDUSTRIAL TRIBUNAL

See the note to s. 6, *ante*.

SUB-S. (2): WEEK'S PAY

As to the calculation of a week's pay, see s. 85 (1) and Sch. 4, Part II, *post*, in conjunction with sub-ss. (7) and (8) above.

SUB-S. (8): £80

As to the review of this limit, see s. 86, *post*.

FURTHER PROVISIONS

See ss. 73–76, *post* (calculation of compensation); s. 77, *post* (compensation for act which is both sex discrimination and unfair dismissal); s. 110 and Sch. 12, *post* (provisions applying on death of employee or employer); s. 113, *post* (treatment as earnings for social security purposes of amounts paid in respect of arrears of pay); and the Trade Union and Labour Relations Act 1974, Sch. 1, para. 20, as substituted by s. 125 (1) and Sch. 16, Part III, para. 17, *post* (limit on compensation).

DEFINITIONS

By virtue of s. 126 (1), *post*, for "employer", see the definition inserted in the Trade Union and Labour Relations Act 1974, s. 30 (1), by s. 125 (1) and Sch. 16, Part III, para. 7 (2), *post*, and s. 30 (2) (*b*) of the Act of 1974; for "dismiss", "dismissal" and "effective date of termination", see Sch. 1, para. 5 to that Act, and for "employee", see s. 30 (1) of the Act of 1974; for "the complainant", see, by virtue of s. 126 (3), *post*, Sch. 1, para. 17 (1), to the Act of 1974.

73. Compensation for unfair dismissal

Where a tribunal makes an award of compensation for unfair dismissal under section 72 (2) (*a*) or (5) above, the award shall consist of a basic award (calculated in accordance with sections 74 and 75 below) and a compensatory award (calculated in accordance with section 76 below). [**377**]

COMMENCEMENT
See s. 129 (3), *post*.

GENERAL NOTE
See the General Note to s. 72, *ante*.

DISMISSAL
For meaning, see, by virtue of s. 126 (1), *post*, the Trade Union and Labour Relations Act 1974, Sch. 1, para. 5, as amended by s. 125 (1), (3), Sch. 16, Part III, paras. 8–10, and Sch. 18, *post*.

EMPLOYEES' RIGHTS ON INSOLVENCY OF EMPLOYER
See s. 64, *post*, and, in particular, sub-s. (3) (*d*) thereof.

74. Calculation of basic award

(1) The amount of the basic award shall be the amount calculated in accordance with subsections (3) to (7) and section 75 (1) to (6) below, subject to the following provisions of this Act, namely,—

(*a*) subsection (2) below (which provides for an award of two weeks' pay in certain cases);
(*b*) section 75 (7) below (which provides for the amount of the award to be reduced where the employee contributed to the dismissal);
(*c*) section 75 (8) below (which provides for the amount of the award to be reduced where the employee received a payment in respect of redundancy); and
(*d*) section 77 (which prohibits double compensation where compensation in respect of the same matter is also awarded under the Sex Discrimination Act 1975).

(2) In the following cases the amount of the basic award shall be two weeks' pay:—

(*a*) where the tribunal finds that the reason or principal reason for the dismissal of the employee was that he was redundant and the employee—
(i) by virtue of section 2 (5) or (6) of the Redundancy Payments Act 1965 (unreasonable refusal or relinquishment of suitable alternative employment) is not, or if he were otherwise entitled would not be, entitled to a redundancy payment; or
(ii) by virtue of the operation of section 3 (3) of that Act (renewal of employment or re-engagement) is not treated as dismissed for the purposes of Part I of that Act;
(*b*) where the amount calculated in accordance with subsections (3) to (7) and section 75 (1) to (7) below is less than the amount of two weeks' pay.

(3) The amount of the basic award shall be calculated by reference to the period, ending with the effective date of termination, during which the employee has been continuously employed, by starting at the end of that period and reckoning backwards the numbers of years of employment falling within that period, and allowing—

(*a*) one and a half weeks' pay for each such year of employment which consists wholly of weeks in which the employee was not below the age of 41;

(*b*) one weeks' pay for each such year of employment which consists wholly of weeks in which the employee was below the age of 41 and was not below the age of 22; and

(*c*) half a week's pay for each such year of employment which consists wholly of weeks in which the employee was below the age of 22 and was not below the age of 18.

(4) In ascertaining for the purpose of subsection (3) above the period for which an employee has been continuously employed, where the effective date of termination falls to be determined in accordance with paragraph 5 (6) of Schedule 1 to the 1974 Act, a period falling within such an interval as is referred to in paragraph 30 (1A) of that Schedule (period of continuous employment) shall count as a period of employment notwithstanding that it does not count under Schedule 1 to the Contracts of Employment Act 1972 (computation of period of employment).

(5) Where in reckoning the number of years of employment in accordance with subsection (3) above 20 years of employment have been reckoned no account shall be taken of any year of employment earlier than those 20 years.

(6) Where in the case of an employee the effective date of termination is after the specified anniversary the amount of the basic award calculated in accordance with subsections (3) to (5) above shall be reduced by the appropriate fraction.

(7) In subsection (6) above "the specified anniversary" in relation to a man means the 64th anniversary of the day of his birth, and in relation to a woman means the 59th anniversary of the day of her birth, and "the appropriate fraction" means the fraction of which—

(*a*) the numerator is the number of whole months reckoned from the specified anniversary in the period beginning with that anniversary and ending with the effective date of termination; and

(*b*) the denominator is 12. **[378]**

COMMENCEMENT

See s. 129 (3), *post*.

GENERAL NOTE

See the General Note to s. 72, *ante*.

SUB-S. (1): BASIC AWARD

I.e., the basic award mentioned in s. 73, *ante*.

SUB-S. (2): TWO WEEKS' PAY

As to the calculation of a week's pay, see s. 85 (1) and Sch. 4, Part II, *post*, in conjunction with s. 75 (1)–(6), *post*.

THE TRIBUNAL

I.e., the industrial tribunal.

SUB-S. (3): CONTINUOUSLY EMPLOYED

As to the determination of the period for which an employee has been continuously employed, see s. 126 (5), *post*. Note also sub-ss. (4) and (5) above.

SUB-S. (7): MONTHS

I.e., calendar months; see the Interpretation Act 1889, s. 3.

DEFINITIONS

By virtue of s. 126 (1), *post*, for "employer", see the definition inserted in the Trade Union and Labour Relations Act 1974, s. 30 (1), by s. 125 (1) and Sch. 16, Part III, para. 7 (2), *post*, and s. 30 (2) (*b*) of that Act, and for "employee", see s. 30 (1) of that Act, and for "dismissal" and "effective date of termination", see Sch. 1, para. 5, to that Act; for "redundant", see s. 126 (6), *post*. As to "the appropriate fraction", and "the specified anniversary", note sub-s. (7) above.

75. Provisions supplementary to s. 74

(1) For the purposes of Part II of Schedule 4 to this Act as it applies for the calculation of a week's pay for the purposes of section 74 above, the calculation date is, subject to subsection (3) below, the date on which notice would have been given by the employer had the conditions referred to in subsection (2) below been fulfilled (whether those conditions were in fact fulfilled or not).

(2) Those conditions are that the contract was terminable by notice and was terminated by the employer giving such notice as is required to terminate that contract by section 1 (1) of the Contracts of Employment Act 1972 (minimum period of notice), and that the notice expired on the effective date of termination.

Where by virtue of paragraph 5 (6) of Schedule 1 to the 1974 Act a date is to be treated as the effective date of termination for the purposes of section 74 (3) above which is later than the effective date of termination as defined by paragraph 5 (5) of that Schedule, then, for the purposes of Part II of Schedule 4 to this Act as it applies for the calculation of a week's pay for the purpose of section 74 above, the calculation date is the effective date of termination as defined by the said paragraph 5 (5).

(4) Notwithstanding anything in the said Part II, the amount of a week's pay for the purpose of calculating a basic award shall not exceed £80.

(5) The Secretary of State may, after a review under section 86 below, vary the limit referred to in subsection (4) above by order made in accordance with that section.

(6) Without prejudice to the generality of the power to make transitional provision in an order under subsection (5) above, such an order may provide that it shall apply in the case of a dismissal in relation to which the effective date of termination for the purposes of this subsection (as defined by paragraph 5 (6) of Schedule 1 to the 1974 Act) falls after the order comes into operation, notwithstanding that the effective date of termination for the purposes of other provisions of this Act or the 1974 Act (as defined by paragraph 5 (5) of Schedule 1 to the 1974 Act) falls before the order comes into operation.

(7) Where the tribunal finds that the dismissal was to any extent caused or contributed to by any action of the complainant it shall, except in a case where the dismissal was by reason of redundancy, reduce the amount of the basic award by such proportion as it considers just and equitable having regard to that finding.

(8) The amount of the basic award shall be reduced or, as the case may be, be further reduced, by the amount of any redundancy payment awarded by the

tribunal under the Redundancy Payments Act 1965 in respect of the same dismissal or of any payment made by the employer to the employee on the ground that the dismissal was by reason of redundancy, whether in pursuance of the said Act of 1965 or otherwise. [**379**]

COMMENCEMENT
See s. 129 (3), *post*.

GENERAL NOTE
See the General Note to s. 72, *ante*.

SUB-S. (4): BASIC AWARD
I.e., the basic award mentioned in ss. 73 and 74, *ante*.

SUB-S. (6): POWER TO MAKE TRANSITIONAL PROVISION
See s. 123 (3), *post*.

SUB-S. (7): THE TRIBUNAL
I.e., the industrial tribunal.

CAUSED . . . BY ANY ACTION OF THE COMPLAINANT
See the note "Caused . . . by any action of the aggrieved party" to the Trade Union and Labour Relations Act 1974, Sch. 1, para. 19.

DEFINITIONS
By virtue of s. 126 (1), *post*, for "employer", see the definition inserted in the Trade Union and Labour Relations Act 1974, s. 30 (1), by s. 125 (1) and Sch. 16, Part III, para. 7 (2), *post*, and s. 30 (2) (*b*) of that Act, for "dismissal" and "effective date of termination", see Sch. 1, para. 5 to that Act, and for "employee", see s. 30 (1) of the Act of 1974; for "complainant", see by virtue of s. 126 (3), *post*, Sch. 1, para. 17 (1), to the Act of 1974; for "redundancy", see s. 126 (6), *post*.

76. Calculation of compensatory award

(1) Subject to paragraph 20 of Schedule 1 to the 1974 Act (limit on compensation) and to section 77 below, the amount of the compensatory award shall be such amount as the tribunal considers just and equitable in all the circumstances having regard to the loss sustained by the complainant in consequence of the dismissal in so far as that loss is attributable to action taken by the employer.

(2) The said loss shall be taken to include—

(*a*) any expenses reasonably incurred by the complainant in consequence of the dismissal, and
(*b*) subject to subsection (3) below, loss of any benefit which he might reasonably be expected to have had but for the dismissal.

(3) The said loss, in respect of any loss of any entitlement or potential entitlement to, or expectation of, a payment on account of dismissal by reason of redundancy, whether in pursuance of the Redundancy Payments Act 1965 or otherwise, shall include only the loss referable to the amount, if any, by which the amount of that payment would have exceeded the amount of a basic award (apart from any reduction under section 75 (7) or (8) above) in respect of the same dismissal.

(4) In ascertaining the said loss the tribunal shall apply the same rule concerning the duty of a person to mitigate his loss as applies to damages recoverable under the common law of England and Wales or of Scotland, as the case may be.

(5) In determining for the purposes of subsection (1) above how far any loss sustained by the complainant was attributable to action taken by the employer

no account shall be taken of any pressure which, by calling, organising, procuring or financing a strike or other industrial action, or threatening to do so, was exercised on the employer to dismiss the employee, and that question shall be determined as if no such pressure had been exercised.

(6) Where the tribunal finds that the dismissal was to any extent caused or contributed to by any action of the complainant it shall reduce the amount of the compensatory award by such proportion as it considers just and equitable having regard to that finding.

(7) If the amount of any payment made by the employer to the employee on the ground that the dismissal was by reason of redundancy, whether in pursuance of the Redundancy Payments Act 1965 or otherwise, exceeds the amount of the basic award which would be payable but for section 75 (8) above that excess shall go to reduce the amount of the compensatory award. [**380**]

COMMENCEMENT
See s. 129 (3), *post*.

GENERAL NOTE
See the General Note to s. 72; *ante*.

SUB-S. (1): COMPENSATORY AWARD
I.e., the compensatory award mentioned in s. 73, *ante*.

SUCH AMOUNT AS THE TRIBUNAL CONSIDERS JUST AND EQUITABLE . . . HAVING REGARD TO THE LOSS SUSTAINED
See the note to the Trade Union and Labour Relations Act 1974, Sch. 1, para. 19.

THE TRIBUNAL
I.e., the industrial tribunal.

SUB-S. (3): BASIC AWARD
See ss. 73–75, *ante*.

SUB-S. (4): RULE CONCERNING THE DUTY OF A PERSON TO MITIGATE HIS LOSS
See the note to s. 56, *ante*.

SUB-S. (5): NO ACCOUNT SHALL BE TAKEN OF ANY PRESSURE, ETC.
Cf. the note to s. 56, *ante*.

SUB-S. (6): CAUSED . . . BY ANY ACTION OF THE COMPLAINANT
See the note "Caused by any action of the aggrieved party" to the Trade Union and Labour Relations Act 1974, Sch. 1, para. 19.

DEFINITIONS
By virtue of s. 126 (1), *post*, for "employer", see the definition inserted in the Trade Union and Labour Relations Act 1974, s. 30 (1), by s. 126 (1) and Sch. 16, Part III, para. 7 (2), *post*, and s. 30 (2) (*b*) of that Act; "dismiss", "dismissal" and "effective date of termination", see Sch. 1, para. 5, to that Act, and for "employee", see s. 30 (1) of the Act of 1974; for "complainant", see, by virtue of s. 126 (3), *post*, Sch. 1, para. 17 (1), to the Act of 1974; for "redundancy", see s. 126 (6), *post*.

77. Compensation for act which is both sex discrimination and unfair dismissal

(1) Where compensation falls to be awarded in respect of any act both under the Sex Discrimination Act 1975 and under the provisions of this Act relating to unfair dismissal, an industrial tribunal shall not award compensation under that Act or this Act in respect of any loss or other matter which is or has been taken

into account under the other Act by the tribunal or another industrial tribunal in awarding compensation on the same or another complaint in respect of that act.

(2) Without prejudice to paragraph 20 of Schedule 1 to the 1974 Act (limit on compensation), whether as set out in Part III of Schedule 16 to this Act or as applied by section 65 of the Sex Discrimination Act 1975, in a case to which subsection (1) above applies the aggregate of the following amounts of compensation awarded by an industrial tribunal, that is to say—

(*a*) any compensation awarded under the said Act of 1975; and

(*b*) any compensation awarded under section 72 (1) above or, as the case may be, which is calculated in accordance with section 76 above,

shall not exceed the limit for the time being imposed by the said paragraph 20.

[381]

COMMENCEMENT

See s. 129 (3), *post*.

INDUSTRIAL TRIBUNAL

See the note to s. 6, *ante*.

78. Interim relief pending determination of complaint of unfair dismissal

(1) An employee who presents a complaint to an industrial tribunal that he has been unfairly dismissed by his employer and that the reason for the dismissal (or, if more than one, the principal reason) was that the employee—

(*a*) was, or proposed to become, a member of a particular independent trade union, or

(*b*) had taken, or proposed to take, part at any appropriate time in the activities of a particular independent trade union of which he was or proposed to become a member;

may, subject to the following provisions of this section, apply to the tribunal for an order under the following provisions of this section.

(2) An industrial tribunal shall not entertain an application under this section unless—

(*a*) it is presented to the tribunal before the end of the period of seven days immediately following the effective date of termination (whether before, on or after that date); and

(*b*) before the end of that period there is also so presented a certificate in writing signed by an authorised official of the independent trade union of which the employee was or had proposed to become a member stating that on the date of the dismissal the employee was or had proposed to become a member of the union and that there appear to be reasonable grounds for supposing that the reason for his dismissal (or, if more than one, the principal reason) was one alleged in the complaint.

(3) An industrial tribunal shall determine an application under this section as soon as practicable after receiving the application and the relevant certificate, but shall, at least seven days before the date of the hearing, give the employer a copy of the application and certificate, together with notice of the date, time and place of the hearing.

(4) An industrial tribunal shall not exercise any power it has of postponing the hearing in the case of an application under this section except where the tribunal is satisfied that special circumstances exist which justify it in doing so.

(5) If on hearing an application under this section it appears to an industrial tribunal that it is likely that on determining the complaint to which the application relates the tribunal will find that the complainant was unfairly dismissed and that the reason for the dismissal or (if more than one, the principal reason) was a reason mentioned in subsection (1) above, the tribunal shall announce its findings and explain to both parties (if present) what powers the tribunal may exercise on an application under this section and in what circumstances it may exercise them, and shall ask the employer (if present) whether he is willing, pending the determination or settlement of the complaint—

(*a*) to reinstate the employee, that is to say, to treat the employee in all respects as if he had not been dismissed; or,

(*b*) if not, to re-engage him in another job on terms and conditions not less favourable than those which would have been applicable to him if he had not been dismissed.

(6) In subsection (5) above "terms and conditions not less favourable than those which would have been applicable to him if he had not been dismissed" means, as regards seniority, pension rights and other similar rights, that the period prior to the dismissal shall be regarded as continuous with his employment following the dismissal.

(7) If the employer states that he is willing to reinstate the employee, the tribunal shall make an order to that effect.

(8) If the employer states that he is willing to re-engage the employee in another job and specifies the terms and conditions on which he is willing to do so, the tribunal shall ask the employee whether he is willing to accept the job on those terms and conditions, and—

(*a*) if the employee is willing to accept the job on those terms and conditions, the tribunal shall make an order to that effect; and

(*b*) if the employee is unwilling to accept the job on those terms and contions, then, if the tribunal is of the opinion that the refusal is reasonable, the tribunal shall make an order for the continuation of his contract of employment, but otherwise the tribunal shall make no order under this section.

(9) If on the hearing of an application under this section the employer fails to attend before the tribunal or he states that he is unwilling either to reinstate the employee or re-engage him as mentioned in subsection (5) above, the tribunal shall make an order for the continuation of the employee's contract of employment.

(10) In this section—

"appropriate time" has the same meaning as in section 53 above;

"authorised official", in relation to a trade union, means an official of the union authorised by the union to act for the purposes of this section;

and any reference to the date of dismissal is a reference—

(*a*) where the employee's contract of employment was terminated by notice (whether given by his employer or by him), to the date on which the employer's notice was given; and

(*b*) in any other case, to the effective date of termination.

(11) A document purporting to be an authorisation of an official by a trade union to act for the purposes of this section and to be signed on behalf of the union shall be taken to be such an authorisation unless the contrary is proved,

and a document purporting to be a certificate signed by such an official shall be taken to be signed by him unless the contrary is proved. [**382**]

COMMENCEMENT

See s. 129 (3), *post*.

SUB-S. (1): COMPLAINT . . . THAT HE HAS BEEN UNFAIRLY DISMISSED

The remedy of an employee who has been unfairly dismissed is by way of a complaint to an industrial tribunal under the Trade Union and Labour Relations Act 1974, Sch. 1, Part III and not otherwise; see para. 4 (1) of that Schedule.

INDUSTRIAL TRIBUNAL

See the note to s. 6, *ante*.

SUB-S. (2): CERTIFICATE . . . SIGNED BY AN AUTHORISED OFFICIAL

As to the burden of proof in regard to such a certificate and a document evidencing such authority, see sub-s. (11) above.

WRITING

See the note "Written" to s. 11, *ante*.

SUB-S. (4): POWER . . . OF POSTPONING THE HEARING

Such a power is conferred upon tribunals by the Industrial Tribunals (Labour Relations) Regulations 1974, S.I. 1974 No. 1386, r. 11 (2) (*b*) (made under the Trade Union and Labour Relations Act 1974, Sch. 1, para. 21.

SUB-SS. (8), (9): ORDER FOR THE CONTINUATION OF . . . CONTRACT OF EMPLOYMENT

See, further, as to such orders, s. 79, *post*.

FURTHER PROVISIONS

See s. 79, *post* (order for continuation of contract of employment); s. 80 *post* (supplementary provisions as to interim relief): s. 110 and Sch. 12 *post* (provisions applying on death of employee or employer); and s. 113, *post* (treatment as earnings for social security purposes of amounts paid in respect of arrears of pay).

DEFINITIONS

By virtue of s. 126 (1), *post*, for "employer", see the definition inserted in the Trade Union and Labour Relations Act 1974, s. 30 (1), by s. 125 (1) and Sch. 16, Part III, para. 7 (2), *post*, and s. 30 (2) (*b*) of that Act; for "dismiss", "dismissal" and "effective date of termination", see Sch. 1, para. 5, to that Act, and for "employee" "independent trade union" and "official" see s. 30 (1) of the Act of 1974.

As to "appropriate time", "authorised official" and "the date of dismissal', note sub-s. (10) above, and as to "terms and conditions not less favourable than those which would have been applicable to him if he had not been dismissed" (in sub-s. (5) above), note sub-s. (6) above.

79. Orders for continuation of contract of employment

(1) An order for the continuation of a contract of employment under section 78 above shall be an order that the contract of employment, if it has been terminated, shall continue in force as if it had not been terminated, and if not shall on its termination continue in force, in either case until the determination or settlement of the complaint and only for the purposes of pay or any other benefit derived from the employment, seniority, pension rights and other similar matters and for the purpose of determining for any purpose the period for which the employee has been continuously employed.

(2) Where the tribunal makes any such order it shall specify in the order the amount which is to be paid by the employer to the employee by way of pay in respect of each normal pay period or part of any such period falling between the date of the dismissal and the determination or settlement of the complaint and, subject to subsection (5) below, the amount so specified shall be that which the

employee could reasonably have been expected to earn during that period or part, and shall be paid, in the case of a payment for any such period falling wholly or partly after the order, on the normal pay day for that period and, in the case of a payment for any past period, within a time so specified.

(3) If an amount is payable by way of pay in pursuance of any such order in respect only of part of a normal pay period the amount shall be calculated by reference to the whole period and be reduced proportionately.

(4) Any payment made to an employee by an employer under his contract of employment, or by way of damages for breach of that contract, in respect of any normal pay period or part of any such period shall go towards discharging the employer's liability in respect of that period under subsection (2) above, and conversely any payment under subsection (2) above in respect of any period shall go towards discharging any liability of the employer under, or in respect of breach of, the contract of employment in respect of that period.

(5) If an employee, on or after being dismissed by his employer, receives a lump sum which, or part of which, is in lieu of wages but is not referable to any normal pay period, the tribunal shall take the payment into account in determining the amount of pay to be payable in pursuance of any such order.

(6) For the purposes of this section the amount which an employee could reasonably have been expected to earn, his normal pay period and the normal pay day for each such period shall be determined as if he had not been dismissed. [**383**]

COMMENCEMENT

See s. 129 (3), *post*.

CONTINUOUSLY EMPLOYED

As to the determination of the period for which an employee has been continuously employed, see s. 126 (5), *post*.

TRIBUNAL

I.e., the industrial tribunal.

DEATH OF EMPLOYEE OR EMPLOYER

As to the effect of death upon the accrual of rights and the institution or continuance of tribunal proceedings, see s. 110 and Sch. 12, *post*.

DEFINITIONS

By virtue of s. 126 (1), *post*, for "employer", see the definition inserted in the Trade Union and Labour Relations Act 1974, s. 30 (1), by s. 125 (1) and Sch. 16, Part III, para. 7 (2), *post*, and s. 30 (2) (*b*) of that Act, for "employee", see s. 30 (1) of that Act, and for "dismiss", see Sch. 1, para. 5, to that Act.

80. Supplementary provisions as to interim relief

(1) At any time between the making of an order by an industrial tribunal under section 78 above and the determination or settlement of the complaint to which it relates, the employer or the employee may apply to the tribunal for the revocation or variation of the order on the ground of a relevant change of circumstances since the making of the order, and that section shall apply to the application as it applies to an application for an order under that section except that—

(*a*) no certificate need be presented to the tribunal under subsection (2) (*b*), and no copy of the certificate need be given to the employer under subsection (3), of that section; and (*b*) in the case of an application by an employer, for the reference in the said subsection (3) to the employer there shall be substituted a reference to the employee.

(2) If on the application of an employee an industrial tribunal is satisfied that the employer has not complied with the terms of an order for the reinstatement or re-engagement of the employee under section 78 (7) or (8) above,—

(*a*) the tribunal shall make an order for the continuation of the employee's contract of employment and section 79 above shall apply to an order under this subsection as it applies to an order for the continuation of a contract of employment under section 78 above; and

(*b*) the tribunal shall also order the employer to pay the employee such compensation as the tribunal considers just and equitable in all the circumstances having regard to the infringement of the employee's right to be reinstated or re-engaged in pursuance of the order under section 78 (7) or (8) above and to any loss suffered by the employee in consequence of the non-compliance.

(3) If on the application of an employee an industrial tribunal is satisfied that the employer has not complied with the terms of an order for the continuation of a contract of employment, then—

(*a*) if the non-compliance consists of a failure to pay an amount by way of pay specified in the order, the tribunal shall determine the amount of pay owed by the employer to the employee on the date of the determination, and, if on that date the tribunal also determines the employee's complaint that he has been unfairly dismissed by his employer, the tribunal shall specify that amount separately from any other sum awarded to the employee; and

(*b*) in any other case, the tribunal shall order the employer to pay the employee such compensation as the tribunal considers just and equitable in all the circumstances having regard to any loss suffered by the employee in consequence of the non-compliance.

(4) An industrial tribunal hearing an application under section 78 above or this section may consist of a President of Industrial Tribunals, the chairman of the tribunal or a member of a panel of chairmen of such tribunals for the time being nominated by a President to hear such applications. [**384**]

COMMENCEMENT

See s. 129 (3), *post*.

INDUSTRIAL TRIBUNAL

See the note to s. 6, *ante*.

PRESIDENT OF INDUSTRIAL TRIBUNALS; CHAIRMAN; MEMBER OF A PANEL OF CHAIRMEN

As to these officers see the Industrial Tribunals (England and Wales) Regulations 1965, S.I. 1965 No. 1101, as amended (made under the Industrial Training Act 1964, s. 12.

DEATH OF EMPLOYEE OR EMPLOYER

As to the effect of death upon the institution or continuance of tribunal proccedings, the doing of anything by the employee or employer and the accrual of rights, see s. 110 and Sch. 12, *post*.

DEFINITIONS

By virtue of s. 126 (1), *post*, for "employer", see the definition inserted in the Trade Union and Labour Relations Act 1974, s. 30 (1), by s. 125 (1) and Sch. 16, Part III, para. 7 (2), *post*, and s. 30 (2) (*b*) of that Act, and for "employee", see s. 30 (1) of that Act.

Itemised pay statement

81. Right to itemised pay statement

Every employee shall have the right to be given by his employer at or before the time at which any payment of wages or salary is made to him an itemised pay statement, in writing, containing the following particulars, that is to say,—

(*a*) the gross amount of the wages or salary;

(*b*) the amounts of any variable and, subject to section 82 below, any fixed deductions from that gross amount and the purposes for which they are made;

(*c*) the net amount of wages or salary payable; and

(*d*) where different parts of the net amount are paid in different ways, the amount and method of payment of each part-payment. [**385**]

COMMENCEMENT

See s. 129 (3), *post*.

WRITING

See the note "Written" to s. 11, *post*.

SUPPLEMENTARY PROVISIONS

See, in particular, s. 82, *post* (standing statement of fixed deductions); s. 83, *post*, (variation of this section by order); s. 84, *post* (reference to industrial tribunal); s. 108 (2)–(7), *post* (provision for conciliation); and s. 119 (1), (2), (4)–(6), (8)–(13), *post* (excluded classes of employment).

DEFINITIONS

By virtue of s. 126 (1), *post*, for "employer", see the definition inserted in the Trade Union and Labour Relations Act 1974, s. 30 (1), by s. 125 (1) and Sch. 16, Part III, para. 7 (2), *post*, and s. 30 (2) (*b*) of that Act, and for "employee", see s. 30 (1) of that Act.

82. Standing statement of fixed deductions

(1) A pay statement given in accordance with section 81 above need not contain separate particulars of a fixed deduction if it contains instead an aggregate amount of fixed deductions, including that deduction, and the employer has given to the employee, at or before the time at which that pay statement is given, a standing statement of fixed deductions, in writing, which contains the following particulars of each deduction comprised in that aggregate amount, that is to say,—

(*a*) the amount of the deduction;

(*b*) the intervals at which the deduction is to be made; and

(*c*) the purpose for which it is made.

and which, in accordance with subsection (4) below, is effective at the date on which the pay statement is given.

(2) A standing statement of fixed deductions may be amended, whether by addition of a new deduction or by a change in the particulars or cancellation of an existing deduction by notice in writing, containing particulars of the amendment, given by the employer to the employee.

(3) An employer who has given to an employee a standing statement of fixed deductions shall, within the period of 12 months beginning with the date on which the first standing statement was given and at intervals of not more than 12 months thereafter, re-issue it in a consolidated form incorporating any amendments notified in accordance with subsection (2) above.

(4) A standing statement of fixed deductions shall become effective, for the purposes of subsection (1) above, on the date on which it is given to the employee and shall cease to have effect on the expiration of the period of 12 months beginning with that date, or, where it is re-issued in accordance with subsection (3) above, the expiration of the period of 12 months beginning with the date on which it was last re-issued. [**386**]

COMMENCEMENT
See s. 129 (3), *post*.

12 MONTHS BEGINNING ETC.
See the note "14 days (two months) beginning, etc.", to s. 15, *ante*.

SUPPLEMENTARY PROVISIONS
See s. 83, *post* (variation of this section by order), and s. 84, *post* (reference to industrial tribunal).

DEFINITIONS
By virtue of s. 126 (1), *post*, for "employer", see the definition inserted in the Trade Union and Labour Relations Act 1974, s. 30 (1), by s. 125 (1) and Sch. 16, Part III, para. 7 (2), *post*, and s. 30 (2) (*b*) of that Act, and for "employee", see s. 30 (1) of that Act.

83. Supplementary

The Secretary of State may by order—

(*a*) vary the provisions of sections 81 and 82 above as to the particulars which must be included in a pay statement or a standing statement of fixed deductions by adding items to or removing items from the particulars listed in those sections or by amending any such particulars; and

(*b*) vary the provisions of section 82 (3) and (4) above so as to shorten or extend the periods of 12 months referred to in those subsections, or those periods as varied from time to time under this section. [**387**]

COMMENCEMENT
s. 129 (3), *post*.

ORDERS UNDER THIS SECTION
At the time of going to press no orders had been made under this section.
As to the making of orders generally, see s. 123, *post*.

84. Reference to industrial tribunal

(1) Where an employer is required by section 81 above to give any employee a pay statement and he does not do so, the employee may require a reference to be made to an industrial tribunal to determine what particulars ought to have been included in a statement so as to comply with the requirements of that section.

(2) Where a pay statement, or a standing statement of fixed deductions, purporting to comply with section 81 or 82 (1) above, has been given to an employee and a question arises as to the particulars which ought to have been included in that statement so as to comply with the requirements of section 81, or, as the case may be, section 82 (1), either the employer or the employee may require that question to be referred to and determined by an industrial tribunal.

(3) In this section a question as to the particulars which ought to have been included in a statement does not include a question solely as to the accuracy of an amount stated in any such particulars.

(4) An industrial tribunal shall not entertain a reference under this section in a case where the employment to which the reference relates has ceased unless an application requiring the reference to be made is made before the end of the period of three months beginning with the date on which the employment ceased.

(5) Where on a reference under this section an industrial tribunal finds that an employer has failed to give an employee any pay statement in accordance with section 81 above or that a pay statement or standing statement of fixed deductions does not, in relation to a deduction, contain the particulars required to be included in that statement by that section or section 82 (1) above—

(*a*) the tribunal shall make a declaration to that effect; and

(*b*) where the tribunal further finds that any unnotified deductions have been made from the pay of the employee during the period of 13 weeks immediately preceding the date of the application for the reference (whether or not the deductions were made in breach of the contract of employment), the tribunal may order the employer to pay the employee a sum not exceeding the aggregate of the unnotified deductions so made.

In this subsection "unnotified deduction" means a deduction made without the employer giving the employee, in any pay statement or standing statement of fixed deductions, the particulars of that deduction required by section 81 or 82 (1) above. [**388**]

COMMENCEMENT

See s. 129 (3), *post*.

REFERENCE

A reference to an industrial tribunal is to be made in accordance with regulations under the Trade Union and Labour Relations Act 1974, Sch. 1, para. 21; see s. 108 (1), *post*; and note sub-ss. (2)–(7) of that section as to conciliation.

INDUSTRIAL TRIBUNAL

See the note to s. 6, *ante*.

THREE MONTHS BEGINNING ETC.

See the note "14 days (two months) beginning, etc." to s. 15, *ante*.

APPEALS

As to appeals to the Employment Appeal Tribunal, and thence to the Court of Appeal, from decisions of an industrial tribunal, see s. 88 (1), (4), (5), *post*.

DEFINITIONS

By virtue of s. 126 (1), *post*, for "employer", see the definition inserted in the Trade Union and Labour Relations Act 1974, s. 30 (1), by s. 125 (1) and Sch. 16, Part III, para. 7 (2), *post*, and s. 30 (2) (*b*) of that Act, and for "employee", see s. 30 (1) of that Act.

Normal working hours and a week's pay

85. Calculation of normal working hours and a week's pay

(1) Schedule 4 to this Act shall have effect for calculating for the purposes of this Act, the Redundancy Payments Act 1965, the Contracts of Employment Act 1972, and the 1974 Act the normal working hours and the amount of a week's pay of any employee and, in the case of the said Acts of 1965 and 1972, shall have effect instead of the relevant provisions of paragraph 5 of Schedule 1 and of Schedule 2 to the said Act of 1965 and of Schedule 2 to the said Act of 1972.

(2) In consequence of subsection (1) above, Schedule 2 to the said Act of 1972 shall have effect (as respects the liability of an employer to an employee for the period of notice required by section 1 (1) or (2) of that Act), as set out in Schedule 5 to this Act. [**389**]

COMMENCEMENT

Section 85 (1) was brought into force on 8th March 1976 by the Employment Protection Act 1975 (Commencement No. 2) Order 1976, S.I. 1976 No. 144, in so far as it relates to the purposes of s. 102.

DEFINITIONS

By virtue of s. 126 (1), *post*, for "employer", see the definition inserted in the Trade Union and Labour Relations Act 1974, s. 30 (1), by s. 125 (1) and Sch. 16, Part III, para. 7 (2), *post*, and s. 30 (2) (*b*) of the Act of 1974, and for "employee", see s. 30 (1) of the Act of 1974.

86. Review of limits

(1) The Secretary of State shall in each calendar year beginning with the first year after that in which this section first comes into force, review—

(*a*) the limits referred to in section 25 above;
(*b*) the limit referred to in section 64 (5) above; and
(*c*) the limits imposed by paragraph 5 (4) of Schedule 1 to the Redundancy Payments Act 1965 and by section 72 (8) or 75 (4) above on the amount of a week's pay for the purposes of those provisions;

and shall determine whether any of those limits should be varied.

(2) In making a review under this section the Secretary of State shall consider—

(*a*) the general level of earnings obtaining in Great Britain at the time of the review;
(*b*) the national economic situation as a whole; and
(*c*) such other matters as he thinks relevant.

(3) If on a review under this section the Secretary of State determines that, having regard to the considerations mentioned in subsection (2) above, any of those limits should be varied, he shall prepare and lay before each House of Parliament the draft of an order giving effect to his decision.

(4) Where a draft of an order under this section is approved by resolution of each House of Parliament the Secretary of State shall make an order in the form of the draft.

(5) If, following the completion of an annual review under this section, the Secretary of State determines that any of the limits referred to in subsection (1) above should not be varied, he shall lay before each House of Parliament a report containing a statement of his reasons for that determination.

(6) The Secretary of State may at any time, in addition to the annual review provided for in subsection (1) above, conduct a further review of the limits mentioned in subsection (1) above, so as to determine whether any of those limits should be varied, and subsections (2) to (4) above shall apply to such a review as if it were a review under subsection (1) above. [**390**]

COMMENCEMENT

See s. 129 (3), *post*.

GREAT BRITAIN

I.e., England, Scotland and Wales; see the Union with Scotland Act 1706, preamble, art. I, Vol. 6, p. 502, and the Wales and Berwick Act 1746, s. 3.

LAY BEFORE . . . PARLIAMENT
For meaning, see the Laying of Documents before Parliament (Interpretation) Act 1948, s. 1 (1).

ORDERS UNDER THIS SECTION
At the time of going to press, no orders had been made under this section.
As to the making of orders generally, see s. 123, *post*.

Employment Appeal Tribunal

87. Establishment and membership of Employment Appeal Tribunal

(1) For the purpose of hearing appeals under section 88 below there shall be a tribunal to be known as the Employment Appeal Tribunal (hereafter in this Act referred to as "the Appeal Tribunal").

(2) The Appeal Tribunal shall consist of—

(*a*) such number of judges as may be nominated from time to time by the Lord Chancellor from among the judges (other than the Lord Chancellor) of the High Court and the Court of Appeal;
(*b*) at least one judge of the Court of Session nominated from time to time by the Lord President of that Court; and
(*c*) such number of other members as may be appointed from time to time by Her Majesty on the joint recommendation of the Lord Chancellor and the Secretary of State.

(3) The members of the Appeal Tribunal appointed under subsection (2) (*c*) above shall be persons who appear to the Lord Chancellor and the Secretary of State to have special knowledge or experience of industrial relations, either as representatives of employers or as representatives of workers.

(4) The Lord Chancellor shall, after consultation with the Lord President of the Court of Session, appoint one of the judges nominated under subsection (2) above to be President of the Appeal Tribunal.

(5) No judge shall be nominated a member of the Appeal Tribunal except with his consent.

(6) The provisions of Schedule 6 to this Act shall have effect with respect to the Appeal Tribunal and proceedings before the Tribunal. **[391]**

COMMENCEMENT
This section was brought into force on 30th March 1976 by the Employment Protection Act 1975 (Commencement No. 3) Order 1976, S.I. 1976 No. 321.

CONSULTATION
See the note to s. 7, *ante*.

DEFINITIONS
By virtue of s. 126 (1), *post*, for "employer", see the definition inserted in the Trade Union and Labour Relations Act 1974, s. 30 (1), by s. 125 (1) and Sch. 16, Part III, para. 7 (2), *post*, and s. 30 (2) (*b*) of the Act of 1974, and for "worker", see s. 30 (1) (2) (*a*) of the Act of 1974.

88. Appeals from industrial tribunals and Certification Officer

(1) An appeal shall lie to the Appeal Tribunal on a question of law arising from any decision of, or arising in any proceedings before, an industrial tribunal under, or by virtue of, the following Acts—

(*a*) the Redundancy Payments Act 1965;
(*b*) the Equal Pay Act 1970;
(*c*) the Contracts of Employment Act 1972;

(*d*) the 1974 Act;
(*e*) the Sex Discrimination Act 1975;
(*f*) this Act.

(2) The Appeal Tribunal shall hear appeals on questions of law arising in any proceedings before, or arising from any decision of, the Certification Officer under the following enactments—

(*a*) sections 3, 4 and 5 of the Trade Union Act 1913;
(*b*) section 4 of the Trade Union (Amalgamations, etc.) Act 1964.

(3) The Appeal Tribunal shall hear appeals on questions of fact or law arising in any proceedings before, or arising from any decision of, the Certification Officer under the following enactments—

(*a*) section 8 of the 1974 Act;
(*b*) section 8 above.

(4) Without prejudice to section 13 of the Administration of Justice Act 1960 (appeal in case of contempt of court), an appeal shall lie on any question of law from any decision or order of the Appeal Tribunal with the leave of the Tribunal or of the Court of Appeal, or as the case may be, the Court of Session,—

(*a*) in the case of proceedings in England and Wales, to the Court of Appeal;
(*b*) in the case of proceedings in Scotland, to the Court of Session.

(5) No appeal shall lie except to the Appeal Tribunal from any decision of an industrial tribunal under the Acts listed in subsection (1) above or from any decision of the Certification Officer under the enactments listed in subsections (2) and (3) above. [**392**]

COMMENCEMENT
This section was brought into force on 30th March 1976 by the Employment Protection Act 1975 (Commencement No. 3) Order 1976, S.I. 1976 No. 321.

APPEAL TRIBUNAL
For meaning, see s. 87 (1), *ante*.

INDUSTRIAL TRIBUNAL
See the note to s. 6, *ante*.

CERTIFICATION OFFICER
This officer is appointed under s. 7 (1), *ante*, to perform certain statutory functions formerly performed by the Chief Registrar of Friendly Societies.

TRANSITIONAL PROVISIONS
See s. 125 (2) and Sch. 17, paras. 9, 10, *post*.

Part III

Regulations of Terms and Conditions of Employment

Wages councils and statutory joint industrial councils

89. Amendments of Wages Councils Act 1959

(1) The Service shall perform those functions under the Wages Councils Act 1959 which immediately before the commencement of this section were performed by a commission of inquiry, and accordingly for any reference in that Act to a commission of inquiry there shall be substituted a reference to the Service.

(2) For the following provisions of that Act, that is to say—

(*a*) section 11 (power to fix remuneration and holidays);

(*b*) section 12 (effect and enforcement of wages regulation orders);

(*c*) Schedule 2 (constitution, etc. of wages councils and central co-ordinating committees);

there shall be respectively substituted the sections and Schedule set out in Parts I, II and III of Schedule 7 to this Act (which reproduce those provisions with the amendments broadly described in the note at the beginning of each Part).

(3) The other provisions of that Act shall have effect subject to the amendments set out in Part IV of that Schedule, being minor amendments and amendments consequential on subsections (1) and (2) above. [**393**]

COMMENCEMENT

This section was brought into force on 1st January 1976 by the Employment Protection Act 1975 (Commencement No. 1) Order 1975, S.I. 1975 No. 1938.

THE SERVICE

I.e., the Advisory, Conciliation and Arbitration Service; see s. 1 (1), *ante*.

COMMISSION OF INQUIRY

Such commissions were constituted under the Wages Councils Act 1959 (repealed by s. 125 (3) and Sch. 18, *post*). S. 6 of that Act, provided for the Secretary of State to refer to commissions of inquiry matters relating to the variation or revocation of wages council orders.

90. Conversion of wages councils to statutory joint industrial councils

(1) The Secretary of State may by order made in accordance with the following provisions of this section provide that a wages council shall become a statutory joint industrial council having the functions conferred by section 91 below.

(2) The Secretary of State may make an order under this section with respect to a wages council—

(*a*) on an application made to him by the employers' association or trade union nominated in relation to the council or by that association and union jointly; or

(*b*) without an application under paragraph (*a*) above, but after consultation with the employers' association and trade union so nominated.

(3) An order under this section shall not be made on an application by an employers' association or trade union alone unless the Secretary of State has consulted every employers' association and trade union nominated in relation to the wages council in question and (whether so nominated or not) all organisations of employers and workers which in his opinion represent a substantial proportion of employers and workers respectively in relation to whom that council operates.

(4) The Secretary of State shall before making an order under this section refer the question whether he should do so to the Service, and the Service shall inquire into it and report on that question.

(5) Part I of Schedule 8 to this Act shall have effect with respect to the constitution, officers and proceedings of statutory joint industrial councils and Part II of that Schedule shall have effect with respect to the transition of a wages council to a statutory joint industrial council. [**394**]

COMMENCEMENT

This section was brought into force on 1st January 1975 by the Employment Protection Act (Commencement No. 1) Order 1975, S.I. 1975 No. 1398.

GENERAL NOTE

This section allows for the substitution for wages councils under the Wages Councils Act 1959 of "statutory joint industrial councils". The latter bodies, by virtue of their constitution under Sch. 8, *post*, consist of an equal number of members appointed by the nominated employers' associations and trade unions respectively, whereas the members of wage councils were appointed by the Secretary of State. In addition to the degree of representation and self-regulation so provided, the councils themselves have a greater degree of autonomy than their predecessors by virtue of having wider powers of regulating their procedure.

WAGES COUNCILS

Such councils are established under the Wages Councils Act 1959, s. 1, to perform in relation to the workers described in the order establishing them and their employers the functions specified in the Act (particularly in relation to the fixing of the workers' remuneration and holidays), see s. 11 of the Act of 1959.

CONSULTATION

See the note to s. 7, *ante*.

THE SERVICE

I.e., the Advisory, Conciliation and Arbitration Service; see s. 1 (1), *ante*.

FURTHER PROVISIONS

See, in particular, s. 91, *post* (functions of statutory joint industrial councils); s. 92, *post* (disputes between employers' and workers' representatives); s. 93, *post* (abolition of statutory joint industrial councils); s. 94, *post* (supplementary provisions); s. 95, *post* (power to obtain information); s. 96, *post* (duty of the Service to report on machinery for regulating remuneration, etc.) and s. 121, *post* (exclusion of Crown employment).

DEFINITIONS

By virtue of s. 126 (1), *post*, for "employer", see the definition inserted in the Trade Union and Labour Relations Act 1974, s. 30 (1), by s. 125 (1) and Sch. 16, Part III, para. 7 (2), *post*, and s. 30 (2) (*b*) of that Act, for "trade union", see s. 28 of that Act, and for "worker" see s. 30 (1) (2) (*a*) of that Act; for "nominated", see s. 94 (1), *post*; for "employers' association" see s. 126 (2), *post*.

ORDERS UNDER THIS SECTION

At the time of going to press no orders had been made under this section.

As to the making of orders generally, see s. 123, *post*.

91. Functions of statutory joint industrial councils.

A statutory joint industrial council shall have in relation to the workers and employers within its field of operation the functions which a wages council has under Part II of the Wages Councils Act 1959 in relation to the workers and employers within its field of operation, and that Part shall apply to a statutory joint industrial council and the workers and employers within its field of operation as it applies to a wages council and the workers and employers within its field of operation. **[395]**

COMMENCEMENT

This section was brought into force on 1st January 1976 by the Employment Protection Act 1975 (Commencement No. 1) Order 1975, S.I. 1975 No. 1938.

STATUTORY JOINT INDUSTRIAL COUNCIL

I.e., a wages council which is the subject of an order under s. 90, *ante*.

WAGES COUNCIL

See the note to s. 90, *ante*.

EXCLUSION OF CROWN EMPLOYMENT

See s. 121, *post*.

DEFINITIONS

By virtue of s. 126 (1), *post*, for "employer", see the definition inserted in the Trade Union and Labour Relations Act 1974, s. 30 (1), by s. 125 (1) and Sch. 16, Part III, para. 7 (2), *post*, and s. 30 (2) (*b*) of that Act, and for "worker", see s. 30 (1) of that Act, Vol. 44, p. 1843.

92. Disputes between employers' and workers' representatives

(1) If in the opinion of either the persons appointed to represent employers or the persons appointed to represent workers on a statutory joint industrial council, a dispute has arisen on any question and cannot be settled by the members of the council, those persons may request the Service to attempt to bring about a settlement of the dispute and the Service shall attempt to do so accordingly.

(2) If the Service are unable to bring about a settlement of any such dispute, the Service shall refer the dispute for settlement to the arbitration of—

(*a*) one or more persons appointed by the Service for that purpose (not being an officer or servant of the Service);

(*b*) the Committee.

(3) Where more than one arbitrator is appointed under subsection (2) (*a*) above, the Service shall appoint one of the arbitrators to act as chairman.

(4) Any determination of the arbitrator, arbitrators or Committee on a dispute referred to him, them or it under this section shall be final and binding on the statutory joint industrial council and its members, and the council shall make an order under section 11 of the Wages Councils Act 1959 or take any other steps which may be necessary to give effect to the determination.

(5) Part I of the Arbitration Act 1950 shall not apply to an arbitration under this section.

(6) (*Applies to Scotland.*) **[396]**

COMMENCEMENT

This section was brought into force in two stages on 1st January and 1st February 1976 by the Employment Protection Act 1975 (Commencement No. 1) Order 1975, S.I. 1975 No. 1938.

PERSONS APPOINTED TO REPRESENT EMPLOYERS, ETC.

Such appointments are made under s. 90 (5), *ante*, and Sch. 8, para. 1 (1), *post*.

STATUTORY JOINT INDUSTRIAL COUNCIL

I. e., a wages council which is the subject of an order under s. 90, *ante*.

EXCLUSION OF CROWN EMPLOYMENT

See s. 121, *post*.

DEFINITIONS

By virtue of s. 126 (1), *post*, for "employer", see the definition inserted in the Trade Union and Labour Relations Act 1974, s. 30 (1), by s. 125 (1) and Sch. 16, Part III, para. 7 (2), *post*, and s. 30 (2) (*b*) of that Act, and for "worker", see s. 30 (1) (2) (*a*) of that Act; for "the Service", see s. 1 (1), *ante*; for "the Committee", see s. 10 (1), *ante*.

93. Abolition of statutory joint industrial councils

(1) If the Secretary of State is of the opinion that, in the event of the abolition of a statutory joint industrial council, adequate machinery would be established for the effective regulation of the remuneration and other terms and conditions of employment of the workers within the council's field of operation and is likely thereafter to be maintained, he may by order abolish the council.

(2) An order under this section may be made on the application of the statutory joint industrial council concerned or without such an application, but shall not be made without such an application unless the Secretary of State has consulted the council.

(3) The Secretary of State shall before making an order under this section

refer the question whether he should do so to the Service, and the Service shall inquire into it and report on that question.

(4) Where an order under this section abolishes a statutory joint industrial council, then, save as is otherwise provided by the order, anything done by the council shall, except as respects things previously done or omitted to be done, cease to have effect. [**397**]

COMMENCEMENT

This section was brought into force on 1st January 1976 by the Employment Protection Act 1975 (Commencement No. 1) Order 1975, S.I. 1975 No. 1938.

GENERAL NOTE

This section is the equivalent of the Wages Councils Act 1959, s. 4 which provides for the abolition of wages councils.

STATUTORY JOINT INDUSTRIAL COUNCIL

I.e., a wages council which is the subject of an order under s. 90, *ante*.

WORKERS

By virtue of s. 126 (1), *post*, for meaning see the Trade Union and Labour Relations Act 1974, s. 30 (1) (2) (*a*).

THE SERVICE

I.e., the Advisory, Conciliation and Arbitration Service; see s. 1 (1), *ante*.

EXCLUSION OF CROWN EMPLOYMENT

See s. 121, *post*.

ORDERS UNDER THIS SECTION

At the time of going to press, no orders had been made under this section.

As to the making of orders generally, see s. 123, *post*. See also s. 94 (2), *post*, which applies the provisions of the Wages Councils Act 1959, Sch. 1, to orders under this section.

94. Supplementary

(1) In sections 90 to 93 above "nominated", in relation to an employers' association or trade union, means, an association or union for the time being nominated under paragraph 1 (2) of Schedule 2 to the Wages Councils Act 1959 to appoint persons to represent employers or workers on the wages council in question.

(2) Schedule 1 to the Wages Councils Act 1959 (as amended by this Act) shall apply in relation to an order under section 90 above providing that a wages council shall become a statutory joint industrial council and in relation to an order under section 93 above abolishing a statutory joint industrial council as it applies in relation to an order establishing or abolishing a wages council. [**398**]

COMMENCEMENT

This section was brought into force on 1st January 1976 by the Employment Protection Act 1975 (Commencement No. 1) Order 1975, S.I. 1975 No. 1938.

WAGES COUNCIL

See the note to s. 90, *ante*.

EXCLUSION OF CROWN EMPLOYMENT

See s. 121, *post*.

DEFINITIONS

By virtue of s. 126 (1), *post*, for "employer", see the definition inserted in the Trade Union and Labour Relations Act 1974, s. 30 (1), by s. 125 (1) and Sch. 16, Part III, para. 7 (2), *post*, and s. 30 (2) (*b*) of that Act; for "trade union", see s. 28 of that Act, and for "worker", see s. 30 (1) (2) (*a*), of that Act; for "employers' association", see s. 126 (2), *post*.

95. Power to obtain information

(1) The Secretary of State may, for the purpose of, or in connection with the enforcement of, an order under section 11 of the Wages Councils Act 1959, by notice in writing require an employer within the field of operation of a council making such an order to furnish such information as may be specified or described in the notice.

(2) A notice under this section may specifiy the way in which, and the time within which, it is to be complied with.

(3) A notice given under this section may be varied or revoked by a subsequent notice so given.

(4) If a person refuses or wilfully neglects to furnish any information which he has been required to furnish by a notice under subsection (1) above, he shall be liable on summary conviction to a fine not exceeding £100.

(5) If a person, in purporting to comply with a requirement of a notice under subsection (1) above, knowingly or recklessly makes any false statement he shall be liable on summary conviction to a fine not exceeding £400. [**399**]

COMMENCEMENT

This section was brought into force on 1st January 1976 by the Employment Protection Act 1975 (Commencement No. 1) Order 1975, S.I. 1975 No. 1938.

WRITING

See the note "Written" to s. 11, *ante*.

EMPLOYER

For meaning see, by virtue of s. 126 (1), *post*, the definition inserted in the Trade Union and Labour Relations Act 1974, s. 30 (1), by s. 125 (1) and Sch. 16, Part III, para. 7 (2), *post*, and s. 30 (2) (*b*) of that Act.

SUMMARY CONVICTION; KNOWINGLY; RECKLESSLY; FALSE

See the notes to s. 68, *ante*.

EXCLUSION OF CROWN EMPLOYMENT

See s. 121, *post*.

96. Duty of the Service to report on machinery for regulating remuneration and terms and conditions of employment

The Service shall, if requested to do so by the Secretary of State—

(*a*) inquire into and report on the development by agreement of machinery for the regulation of the remuneration and terms and conditions of employment of workers within the field of operation of a wages council or statutory joint industrial council and the question whether, in order to maintain a reasonable standard of remuneration and terms and conditions of employment of those workers, it is necessary to regulate their remuneration and other terms and conditions of employment by means of orders under section 11 of the Wages Councils Act 1959;

(*b*) inquire into and report on the operation generally of that Act and the provisions of this Act relating to wages councils and statutory joint industrial councils;

(*c*) publish a report made under paragraph (*a*) or (*b*) above. [**400**]

COMMENCEMENT

This section was brought into force on 1st January 1976 by the Employment Protection Act 1975 (Commencement No. 1) Order 1975, S.I. 1975 No. 1938.

THE SERVICE

I.e., the Advisory, Conciliation and Arbitration Service established under s. 1 (1), *ante*.

WAGES COUNCIL

See the note to s. 90, *ante*.

STATUTORY JOINT INDUSTRIAL COUNCIL

I.e., a wages council which is the subject of an order under s. 90, *ante*.

PROVISIONS OF THIS ACT RELATING TO WAGES COUNCILS AND STATUTORY JOINT INDUSTRIAL COUNCILS

I.e., ss. 89–95, *ante*, and Schs. 7 and 8, *post*.

WORKERS

For meaning see, by virtue of s. 126 (1), *post*, the Trade Union and Labour Relations Act 1974, s. 30 (1), (2) (*a*).

EXCLUSION OF CROWN EMPLOYMENT

See s. 121, *post*.

Powers of Agricultural Wages Boards

97. Amendments of Agricultural Wages Acts

(1) For section 3 of the Agricultural Wages Act 1948 (power to fix remuneration and holidays) there shall be substituted the section set out in Part I of Schedule 9 to this Act (which reproduces section 3 with amendments enabling the Agricultural Wages Board to fix other terms and conditions of employment as well as remuneration and holidays and to specify the date from which remuneration fixed by them is to be payable).

(2) The other provisions of that Act shall have effect subject to the amendments set out in Part II of Schedule 9 to this Act, being minor and consequential amendments.

(3), (4) (*Apply to Scotland.*) **[401]**

COMMENCEMENT

This section was brought into force on 1st January 1976 by the Employment Protection Act 1975 (Commencement No. 1) Order 1975, S.I. 1975 No. 1938.

Extension of terms and conditions

98. Extension of terms and conditions

The provisions of Schedule 11 to this Act shall have effect in place of section 8 of the Terms and Conditions of Employment Act 1959 and that Act is hereby repealed. **[402]**

COMMENCEMENT

See s. 129 (3), *post*.

GENERAL NOTE

This section and Sch. 11, *post*, replace the provisions for the maintenance of standards in terms and conditions of employment embodied in the Terms and Conditions of Employment Act 1959, s. 8, with modified provisions designed to bring the subject under the control of the Advisory, Conciliation and Arbitration Service established under s. 1, *ante*, and the Central Arbitration Committee established under s. 10, *ante*.

EXCLUSION OF CROWN EMPLOYMENT

See s. 121, *post*.

PART IV

PROCEDURE FOR HANDLING REDUNDANCIES

99. Duty of employer to consult trade union representatives on redundancy

(1) An employer proposing to dismiss as redundant an employee of a description in respect of which an independent trade union is recognised by him shall consult representatives of that trade union about the dismissal in accordance with the following provisions of this section.

(2) In this section and sections 100 and 101 below, "trade union representative" in relation to a trade union means an official or other person authorised to carry on collective bargaining with the employer in question by that trade union.

(3) The consultation required by this section shall begin at the earliest opportunity, and shall in any event begin—

(*a*) where the employer is proposing to dismiss as redundant 100 or more employees at one establishment within a period of 90 days or less, at least 90 days before the first of those dismissals takes effect: or

(*b*) where the employer is proposing to dismiss as redundant 10 or more employees at one establishment within a period of 30 days or less, at least 60 days before the first of those dismissals takes effect.

(4) In determining for the purpose of subsection (3) above whether an employer is proposing to dismiss as redundant 100 or more, or, as the case may be, 10 or more, employees within the periods mentioned in that subsection, no account shall be taken of employees whom he proposes to dismiss as redundant in respect of whose proposed dismissals consultation has already begun.

(5) For the purposes of the consultation required by this section the employer shall disclose in writing to trade union representatives—

(*a*) the reasons for his proposals;

(*b*) the numbers and descriptions of employees whom it is proposed to dismiss as redundant;

(*c*) the total number of employees of any such description employed by the employer at the establishment in question;

(*d*) the proposed method of selecting the employees who may be dismissed; and

(*e*) the proposed method of carrying out the dismissals, with due regard to any agreed procedure, including the period over which the dismissals are to take effect.

(6) The information which is to be given to trade union representatives under this section shall be delivered to them, or sent by post to an address notified by them to the employer, or sent by post to the union at the address of its head or main office.

(7) In the course of the consultation required by this section the employer shall—

(*a*) consider any representations made by the trade union representatives; and

(*b*) reply to those representations and, if he rejects any of those representations, state his reasons.

(8) If in any case there are special circumstances which render it not reasonably practicable for the employer to comply with any of the requirements

of subsections (3), (5) or (7) above, the employer shall take all such steps towards compliance with that requirement as are reasonably practicable in those circumstances.

(9) This section shall not be construed as conferring any rights on a trade union or an employee except as provided by sections 101 to 103 below. **[403]**

COMMENCEMENT

This section was brought into force on 8th March 1976 by the Employment Protection Act 1975 (Commencement No. 2) Order 1976, S.I. 1976 No. 144.

GENERAL NOTE

This Part (ss. 99–107) of this Act complements the provisions of the Redundancy Payments Act 1965, by requiring an employer to follow a consultation procedure before implementing proposed redundancies in certain cases, and enacting other provisions relating to the procedure for handling redundancies.

SUB-S (1): CONSULT

See the note "Consultation" to s. 7, *ante*.

SUB-S (3)

This subsection may be varied by order made in accordance with s. 106 (4), (5), *post*.

SUB-S (5): WRITING

See the note "Written" to s. 11, *ante*.

SUB-S (6): SENT BY POST

For meaning, see the Intrepretation Act 1889, s. 26.

FURTHER PROVISIONS

See s. 100, *post* (duty of employer to notify Secretary of State of certain redundancies); s. 101, *post* (complaint by trade union and protective award); s. 102, *post* (entitlement under protective award); s. 103 (complaint by employee to industrial tribunal); s. 104, *post* (reduction of rebate on failure to notify redundancies); s. 106, *post* (supplementary provisions); s. 107, *post* (power to adopt this Part in case of collective agreements on redundancies); s. 108 (2)–(7), *post* (provisions as to conciliation); s. 119 (1), (3)–(7), (12)–(14), *post* (excluded classes of employment); and s. 121, *post* (exclusion of Crown employment).

DEFINITIONS

By virtue of s. 126 (1), *post*, for "employer", see the definition inserted in the Trade Union and Labour Relations Act 1974, s. 30 (1), by s. 125 (1) and Sch. 16, Part III, para. 7 (2), *post*, and s. 30 (2) (*b*) of that Act; for "employee", "independent trade union" and "official", see s. 30 (1) of that Act; for "trade union" see s. 28 (1) of that Act; and for "dismiss" and "dismissal", see Sch. 1, para. 5 to that Act; for "recognised", see ss. 106 (1) and 126 (1), *post*, for "redundancy" and "redundant", see s. 126 (6), *post*. As to "trade union representative", note sub-s. (2) above.

100. Duty of employer to notify Secretary of State of certain redundancies

(1) An employer proposing to dismiss as redundant—

(*a*) 100 or more employees at one establishment within a period of 90 days or less; or

(*b*) 10 or more employees at one establishment within a period of 30 days or less,

shall notify the Secretary of State, in writing, of his proposal—

(i) in a case falling within paragraph (*a*) above, at least 90 days before the first of those dismissals takes effect; and

(ii) in a case falling within paragraph (*b*) above, at least 60 days before the first of those dismissals takes effect,

and where the notice relates to employees of any description in respect of which an independent trade union is recognised by him, he shall give a copy of the notice to representatives of that union.

(2) In determining for the purpose of subsection (1) above whether an employer is proposing to dismiss as redundant 100 or more, or, as the case may be, 10 or more, employees within the periods mentioned in that subsection, no account shall be taken of employees whom he proposes to dismiss as redundant in respect of whose proposed dismissals notice has already been given to the Secretary of State.

(3) A notice under this section shall—

(*a*) be given to the Secretary of State by delivery to him or by sending it by post to him, at such address as the Secretary of State may direct in relation to the establishment where the employees proposed to be dismissed are employed;

(*b*) in a case where consultation with trade union representatives is required by section 90 above, identify the trade union concerned and state the date when consultation began; and

(*c*) be in such form and contain such particulars, in addition to those required by paragraph (*b*) above, as the Secretary of State may direct.

(4) The copy of the notice under this section which is to be given to trade union representatives shall be delivered to them, or sent by post to an address notified by them to the employer, or sent by post to the union at the address of its head or main office.

(5) At any time after receiving a notice under this section from an employer the Secretary of State may by written notice require the employer to give him such further information as may be specified in the requirement.

(6) If in any case there are special circumstances rendering it not reasonably practicable for the employer to comply with any of the requirements of subsections (1) to (5) above, he shall take all such steps towards compliance with that requirement as are reasonably practicable in those circumstances. [**404**]

COMMENCEMENT

This section was brought into force on 8th March 1976 by the Employment Protection Act 1975 (Commencement No. 2) Order 1976, S.I. 1976 No. 144.

SUB-S (1)

This subsection may be varied by order made in accordance with s. 106 (4), (5), *post*.

WRITING

See the note "Written" to s. 11, *ante*.

SUB-S (3): SENDING IT BY POST

For meaning, see the Interpretation Act 1889, s. 26.

CONSULTATION

See the note to s. 7, *ante*.

FURTHER PROVISIONS

See s. 104, *post* (reduction of rebate on failure to notify redundancies); s. 105, *post* (offences and proceedings); s. 106, *post* (supplementary provisions); s. 107, *post* (power to adapt this Part in case of collective agreements on redundancies); s. 119 (1), (3)–(7), (12)–(14), *post* (excluded classes of employment); and s. 121, *post* (exclusive of Crown employment).

DEFINITIONS

By virtue of s. 126 (1), *post*, for "employer", see the definition inserted in the Trade Union and Labour Relations Act 1974, s. 30 (1), by s. 125 (1) and Sch. 16, Part III, para.

7 (2), *post*, and s. 30 (2) (*b*) of that Act, for "employee" and "independent trade union", see s. 30 (1) of that Act, for "trade union" see s. 28 (1) of that Act, and for "dismiss" and "dismissal", see Sch. 1, para. 5, to that Act; for "recognised", see ss. 106 (1) and 126 (1), *post*; for "trade union representative", see s. 99 (2), *ante*; for "redundancy" and "redundant", see s. 126 (6), *post*.

101. Complaint by trade union and protective award

(1) An appropriate trade union may present a complaint to an industrial tribunal on the ground that an employer has dismissed as redundant or is proposing to dismiss as redundant one or more employees and has not complied with any of the requirements of section 99 above.

(2) If on a complaint under this section a question arises as to the matters referred to in section 99 (8) above, it shall be for the employer to show—

(*a*) that there were special circumstances which rendered it not reasonably practicable for him to comply with any requirement of section 99 above; and

(*b*) that he took all such steps towards compliance with that requirement as were reasonably practicable in those circumstances.

(3) Where the tribunal finds a complaint under subsection (1) above well-founded it shall make a declaration to that effect and may also make a protective award in accordance with sub-section (4) below.

(4) A protective award is an award that in respect of such descriptions of employees as may be specified in the award, being employees who have been dismissed, or whom it is proposed to dismiss, as redundant, and in respect of whose dismissal or proposed dismissal the employer has failed to comply with any requirement of section 99 above, the employer shall pay remuneration for a protected period.

(5) The protected period under an award under subsection (4) above shall be a period beginning with the date on which the first of the dismissals to which the complaint relates takes effect, or the date of the award, whichever is the earlier, of such length as the tribunal shall determine to be just and equitable in all the circumstances having regard to the seriousness of the employer's default in complying with any requirement of section 99 above, not exceeding—

(*a*) in a case falling within section 99 (3) (*a*) above, 90 days;

(*b*) in a case falling within section 99 (3) (*b*) above, 60 days; or

(*c*) in any other case, 28 days.

(6) An industrial tribunal shall not consider a complaint under subsection (1) above in respect of an employer's default in relation to a dismissal or proposed dismissal unless it is presented to the tribunal before the proposed dismissal takes effect or before the end of the period of three months beginning with the date on which the dismissal takes effect or within such further period as the tribunal considers reasonable in a case where it is satisfied that it was not reasonably practicable for the complaint to be presented within the period of three months.

(7) "Appropriate trade union", in relation to an employee of any description, means an independent trade union recognised by his employer in respect of that description of employee. [**405**]

COMMENCEMENT

This section was brought into force on 8th March 1976 by the Employment Protection Act 1975 (Commencement No. 2) Order 1976, S.I. 1976 No. 144.

SUB-S (1): COMPLAINT

A complaint is to be made in accordance with regulations under the Trade Union and Labour Relations Act 1974, Sch. 1, para. 21; see s. 108 (1), *post*, and note sub-ss. (2)–(7) of that section as to conciliation.

INDUSTRIAL TRIBUNAL

See the note to s. 6, *ante*.

SUB-S (4): SHALL PAY REMUNERATION

See, further, s. 102, *post*.

SUB-S (5): 90 DAYS; 60 DAYS; 28 DAYS

These periods may be varied by order made in accordance with s. 106 (4), (5), *post*.

FURTHER PROVISIONS

See s. 63, *ante* (priority of remuneration under protective award on insolvency); s. 102, *post* (entitlement under protective award); s. 103, *post* (complaint by employee to industrial tribunal); s. 106, *post* (supplementary provisions); s. 107, *post* (power to adapt this Part in case of collective agreements on redundancies); s. 110 and Sch. 12, para. 7, *post* (death during protected period); s. 113, *post* (treatment as earnings for social security purposes of remuneration under protective award), and s. 121, *post*, (exclusion of Crown employment).

APPEALS

As to appeals to the Employment Appeal Tribunal, and thence to the Court of Appeal, from decisions of an industrial tribunal, see s. 88 (1), (4), (5), *ante*.

DEFINITIONS

By virtue of s. 126 (1), *post*, for "employer", see the definition inserted in the Trade Union and Labour Relations Act 1974, s. 30 (1), by s. 125 (1) and Sch. 16, Part III, para. 7 (2), *post*, and s. 30 (2) (*b*) of that Act; for "employee" and "independent trade union", see s. 30 (1) of that Act; for "trade union", see s. 28 (1) of that Act, and for "dismiss" and "dismissal", see Sch. 1, para. 5, to that Act; for "recognised", see ss. 106 (1) and 126 (1), *post*, for "redundant", see s. 126 (6), *post*. As to "appropriate trade union", note sub-s. (7) above.

102. Entitlement under protective award

(1) Where an industrial tribunal has made a protective award under section 101 above, every employee of a description to which the award relates shall be entitled, subject to the following provisions of this section, to be paid remuneration by his employer for the protected period specified in the award.

(2) The rate of remuneration payable under a protective award shall be a week's pay for each week of the protected period, and if remuneration falls to be calculated for a period less than one week the amount of a week's pay shall be reduced proportionately.

(3) Any payment made to an employee by an employer under his contract of employment, or by way of damages for breach of that contract, in respect of a period falling within a protected period, shall go towards discharging the employer's liability to pay remuneration under the protective award in respect of that first mentioned period, and conversely any payment of remuneration under a protective award in respect of any period shall go towards discharging any liability of the employer under, or in respect of breach of, the contract of employment in respect of that period.

(4) In respect of a period during which he is employed by the employer an employee shall not be entitled to remuneration under a protective award unless he would be entitled to be paid by the employer in respect of that period, either by virtue of his contract of employment or by virtue of Schedule 2 to the Contracts of Employment Act 1972 (rights of employee in period of notice), if that period fell within the period of notice required to be given by section 1 (1) of that Act.

(5) Where the employee is employed by the employer during the protected period and—

(*a*) he is fairly dismissed by his employer for a reason other than redundancy; or

(*b*) he unreasonably terminates the contract of employment,

then, subject to the following provisions of this section, he shall not be entitled to remuneration under the protective award in respect of any period during which but for that dismissal or termination he would have been employed.

(6) If an employer makes an employee an offer (whether in writing or not and whether before or after the ending of his employment under the previous contract) to renew his contract of employment, or to re-engage him under a new contract, so that the renewal or re-engagement would take effect before or during the protected period and either—

(*a*) the provisions of the contract as renewed, or of the new contract, as to the capacity and place in which he would be employed, and as to the other terms and conditions of his employment, would not differ from the corresponding provisions of the previous contract; or

(*b*) the first mentioned provisions would differ from those corresponding provisions, but the offer constitutes an offer of suitable employment in relation to the employee;

the provisions of subsections (7) to (11) below shall effect.

(7) If, in a case to which subsection (6) above applies, the employee unreasonably refuses that offer, then, he shall not be entitled to any remuneration under a protective award in respect of any period during which but for that refusal he would have been employed.

(8) If an employee's contract of employment is renewed, or he is re-engaged under a new contract of employment, in pursuance of such an offer as is referred to in subsection (6) (*b*) above, there shall be trial period in relation to the contract as renewed, or the new contract (whether or not there has been a previous trial period under this section).

(9) The trial period shall begin with the ending of the employee's employment under the previous contract and end with the expiration of the period of four weeks beginning with the date on which the employee starts work under the contract as renewed, or the new contract, or such longer period as may be agreed in accordance with subsection (10) below for the purpose of retraining the employee for employment under that contract.

(10) Any such agreement shall—

(*a*) be made between the employer and the employee or his representative before the employee starts work under the contract as renewed or, as the case may be, the new contract;

(*b*) be in writing;

(*c*) specify the date of the end of the trial period; and

(*d*) specify the terms and conditions of employment which will apply in the employee's case after the end of that period.

(11) If during the trial period—

(*a*) the employee, for whatever reason, terminates the contract, or gives notice to terminate it and the contract is thereafter, in consequence, terminated; or

(*b*) the employer, for a reason connected with or arising out of the change to the renewed, or new, employment, terminates the contract, or gives notice to terminate it and the contract is thereafter, in consequence, terminated,

then, the employee shall remain entitled under the protective award unless, in a case falling within paragraph (*a*) above, he acted unreasonably in terminating or giving notice to terminate the contract. **[406]**

COMMENCEMENT

This section was brought into force on 8th March 1976 by the Employment Protection Act 1975 (Commencement No. 2) Order 1976, S.I. 1976 No. 144.

SUB-S. (1): INDUSTRIAL TRIBUNAL

See the note to s. 6, *ante*.

PROTECTED PERIOD

See s. 101 (5), *ante*.

SUB-S. (2): WEEK'S PAY

As to the calculation of a week's pay, see s. 85 (1), *ante*, and Sch. 4, Part II, *post*, in conjunction with s. 106 (3), *post*.

SUB-S. (5): FAIRLY DISMISSED

As to what is fair dismissal, cf. the Trade Union and Labour Relations Act 1974, Sch. 1, para. 6, as amended by s. 125 (1) and Sch. 16, Part III, paras. 11, 12, *post*.

SUB-S. (9): FOUR WEEKS BEGINNING, ETC.

See the note "14 days (two months) beginning, etc." to s. 15, *ante*.

SUB-S. (10): WRITING

See the note "Written" to s. 11, *ante*.

FURTHER PROVISIONS

See s. 103, *post* (complaint by employee to industrial tribunal); s. 106, *post* (supplementary provisions); s. 107, *post* (power to adapt this Part in case of collective agreements on redundancies); s. 108 (2)–(7), *post* (provisions as to conciliation); and s. 121, *post* (exclusion of Crown employment).

DEFINITIONS

By virtue of s. 126 (1), *post*, for "employer", see the definition inserted in the Trade Union and Labour Relations Act 1974, s. 30 (1), by s. 125 (1) and Sch. 16, Part III, para. 7 (2), *post*, and s. 30 (2) (*b*) of that Act; for "employee", see s. 30 (1) of that Act, and for "dismissal", see Sch. 1, para. 5, to that Act; for "protective award", see s. 101 (4), *ante*; for "redundancy", see s. 126 (6), *post*.

103. Complaint by employee to industrial tribunal

(1) An employee may present a complaint to an industrial tribunal on the ground that he is an employee of a description to which a protective award relates and that his employer has failed, wholly or in part, to pay him remuneration under that award.

(2) An industrial tribunal shall not entertain a complaint under subsection (1) above unless it is presented to the tribunal before the end of the period of three months beginning with the day (or, if the complaint relates to more than one day, the last of the days) in respect of which the complaint is made of failure to pay remuneration, or within such further period as the tribunal considers reasonable in a case where it is satisfied that it was not reasonably practicable for the complaint to be presented within the period of three months.

(3) Where the tribunal finds a complaint under subsection (1) above well-founded it shall order the employer to pay the complainant the amount of remuneration which it finds is due to him. **[407]**

COMMENCEMENT

This section was brought into force on 8th March 1976 by the Employment Protection Act 1975 (Commencement No. 2) Order 1976, S.I. 1976 No. 144.

COMPLAINT

A complaint to an industrial tribunal is to be made in accordance with regulations under the Trade Union and Labour Relations Act 1974, Sch. 1, para. 21, see s. 108 (1), *post*, and note sub-ss. (2)–(7) of that section as to conciliation.

REMUNERATION UNDER THE AWARD

See s. 102, *ante*.

INDUSTRIAL TRIBUNAL

See the note to s. 6, *ante*.

PROTECTIVE AWARD

Such an award is made under s. 101 (3), (4), *ante*.

THREE MONTHS BEGINNING, ETC.

See the note "14 days (two months) beginning, etc." to s. 15, *ante*.

FURTHER PROVISIONS

See s. 107, *post* (power to adapt this Part in case of collective agreements on redundancies); and s. 121, *post* (exclusion of Crown employment).

APPEALS

As to appeals to the Employment Appeal Tribunal and thence to the Court of Appeal, from decisions of an industrial tribunal, see s. 88 (1), (4), (5), *ante*.

DEFINITIONS

By virtue of s. 126 (1), *post*, for "employer", see the definition inserted in the Trade Union and Labour Relations Act 1974, s. 30 (1), by s. 125 (1) and Sch. 16, Part III, para. 7 (2), *post*, and s. 30 (2) (*b*) of that Act, and for "employee", see s. 30 (1) of that Act.

104. Reduction of rebate on failure to notify redundancies

(1) Where an employer—

(*a*) is under section 30 (1) of the Redundancy Payments Act 1965 (rebates in respect of redundancy, etc., payments) entitled to any rebate in respect of a payment made to an employee dismissed by reason of redundancy; and

(*b*) fails to give notice to the Secretary of State in accordance with section 100 above of his proposal to dismiss that employee,

the Secretary of State may, subject to subsection (2) below, reduce the amount of that rebate by such proportion (not exceeding one-tenth) as appears to the Secretary of State to be appropriate in the circumstances.

(2) No reduction of a rebate shall be made in respect of a failure to comply with section 100 above if proceedings have been instituted for an offence under section 105 below arising out of the same failure by the employer.

(3) Where the Secretary of State reduces a rebate in pursuance of this section, the employer may appeal to an industrial tribunal within the period of three months beginning with the date on which the decision of the Secretary of State is communicated to him or within such further period as the tribunal considers reasonable in a case where it is satisfied that it was not reasonably practicable for the appeal to be presented within the period of three months.

(4) Where on an appeal under this section an industrial tribunal is satisfied that a rebate which was reduced to any extent should not have been reduced, or should have been reduced by a greater or lesser proportion, the tribunal shall

determine accordingly, and the Secretary of State shall comply with the determination. [408]

COMMENCEMENT

This section was brought into force on 8th March 1976 by the Employment Protection Act 1975 (Commencement No. 2) Order 1976, S.I. 1976 No. 144.

INDUSTRIAL TRIBUNAL

See the note to s. 6, *ante*.

THREE MONTHS BEGINNING, ETC.

See the note "14 days (two months) beginning, etc." to s. 15, *ante*.

FURTHER PROVISIONS

See s. 107, *post* (power to adapt this Part in case of collective agreements on redundancies); and s. 121, *post* (exclusion of Crown employment).

APPEALS

As to appeals to the Employment Appeal Tribunal and thence to the Court of Appeal, from decisions of an industrial tribunal, see s. 88 (1), (4), (5), *ante*.

DEFINITIONS

By virtue of s. 126 (1), *post*, for "employer", see the definition inserted in the Trade Union and Labour Relations Act 1974, s. 30 (1), by s. 125 (1) and Sch. 16, Part III, para. 7 (2), *post*, and s. 30 (2) (*b*) of that Act, and for "employee", see s. 30 (1) of that Act, and for "dismiss", see Sch. 1, para. 5, to that Act; for "redundancy", see s. 126 (6), *post*.

105. Offence and proceedings

(1) If an employer fails to give notice to the Secretary of State in accordance with section 100 above, he shall be liable on summary conviction to a fine not exceeding £400.

(2) Proceedings in England or Wales for an offence under subsection (1) above shall be instituted only by or with the consent of the Secretary of State or by an officer authorised for that purpose by special or general directions of the Secretary of State.

(3) An officer so authorised may, although not of counsel or a solicitor, prosecute or conduct before a magistrates' court any proceedings for such an offence.

(4) No proceedings for an offence under subsection (1) above shall be instituted in respect of a failure to comply with section 100 above if the Secretary of State has, by reason of the same failure by the employer, reduced to any extent, in accordance with section 104 above, the amount payable to the employer of any rebate.

(5) For the purposes of subsection (4) above, a certificate signed by or on behalf of the Secretary of State stating that no such reduction of a rebate has been made shall be conclusive evidence of that fact; and a document which purports to be such a certificate shall be taken to be such a certificate unless the contrary is proved. [409]

COMMENCEMENT

This section was brought into force on 8th March 1976 by the Employment Protection Act 1975 (Commencement No. 2) Order 1976, S.I. 1976 No. 144.

EMPLOYER

By virtue of s. 126 (1), *post*, see the definition inserted in the Trade Union and Labour Relations Act 1974, s. 30 (1), by s. 125 (1) and Sch. 16, Part III, para. 7 (2), *post*, and s. 30 (2) (*b*) of that Act.

SUMMARY CONVICTION

See the note to s. 68, *ante*.

OFFENCES BY BODIES CORPORATE

See s. 117, *post*.

FURTHER PROVISIONS

See s. 107, *post* (power to adapt this Part in case of collective agreements on redundancies); and s. 121, *post* (exclusion of Crown employment).

106. Supplementary

(1) For the purposes of this Part of this Act a trade union shall be treated as recognised not only if it is recognised for the purposes of collective bargaining, but also if the Service has made a recommendation for recognition which is operative within the meaning of section 15 above.

(2) For the purposes of any proceedings under this Part of this Act, the dismissal or proposed dismissal of an employee shall be presumed, unless the contrary is proved, to be by reason of redundancy.

(3) For the purposes of Part II of Schedule 4 to this Act as it applies for the calculation of a week's pay for the purposes of section 102 above, the calculation date is—

(*a*) in the case of an employee who was dismissed before the date on which the protective award was made, the date which by virtue of paragraph 5 of Schedule 1 to the Redundancy Payments Act 1965 is the calculation date for the purpose of computing the amount of a redundancy payment in relation to that dismissal (whether or not the employee concerned is entitled to any such payment); and

(*b*) in any other case, the date on which the protective award was made.

(4) The Secretary of State may by order vary the provisions of sections 99 (3) and 100 (1) above and the periods referred to in section 101 (5) (*a*) to (*c*) above and may vary those provisions or periods either generally or in their application to any description of employees, but no such order shall be made which has the effect of reducing to less than 30 days the periods referred to in sections 99 (3) and 100 (1) as the periods which must elapse before the first of the dismissals takes effect.

(5) No order shall be made under subsection (4) above unless a draft of the order has been laid before Parliament and approved by a resolution of each House of Parliament. [**410**]

COMMENCEMENT

This section was brought into force on 8th March 1976 by the Employment Protection Act 1975 (Commencement No. 2) Order 1976, S.I. 1976 No. 144.

THIS PART OF THIS ACT

I.e., Part IV (ss. 99–107).

RECOGNISED FOR THE PURPOSES OF COLLECTIVE BARGAINING

I.e., under ss. 11 *et seq.*, *ante*.

PROTECTIVE AWARD

Such an award is made under s. 101 (3), (4), *ante*.

LAID BEFORE PARLIAMENT

For the meaning of these words, see the Laying of Documents before Parliament (Interpretation) Act 1948, s. 1 (1).

EXCLUSION OF PERSONS IN CROWN EMPLOYMENT

See s. 121, *post*.

DEFINITIONS

By virtue of s. 126 (1), *post*, for "employee", see the Trade Union and Labour Relations Act 1974, s. 30 (1), and for "dismissal", see Sch. 1, para. 5 to that Act; for "the Service", see s. 1 (1), *ante*; for "collective bargaining", see s. 126 (1), *post*; for "redundancy", see s. 126 (6), *post*.

ORDERS UNDER THIS SECTION

At the time of going to press no orders had been made under sub-s. (4) above.

As to the making of orders generally, see s. 123, *post*. Note also sub-s. (5) above.

107. Power to adapt foregoing provisions in case of collective agreements on redundancies

(1) If at any time there is in force a collective agreement which establishes—

(*a*) arrangements for providing alternative employment for employees to whom the agreement relates if they are dismissed as redundant by an employer to whom it relates; or

(*b*) arrangements for the handling of redundancies;

and on the application of all the parties to the agreement the Secretary of State, having regard to the provisions of the agreement, is satisfied that the arrangements are on the whole at least as favourable to those employees as the foregoing provisions of this Part of this Act, he may make an order under this section adapting, modifying or excluding any of those provisions both in their application to all or any of those employees and in their application to any other employees of any such employer.

(2) The Secretary of State shall not make an order under this section in respect of an agreement unless—

(*a*) the agreement provides for procedures to be followed (whether by arbitration or otherwise) in cases where an employee to whom the agreement relates claims that any employer or other person to whom it relates has not complied with the provisions of the agreement, and that those procedures include a right to arbitration or adjudication by an independent referee or body in cases where (by reason of an equality of votes or otherwise) a decision cannot otherwise be reached; or

(*b*) the agreement indicates that any such employee may present a complaint to an industrial tribunal that any such employer or other person has not complied with those provisions.

(3) An order under this section may confer on an industrial tribunal to whom a complaint is presented as mentioned in subsection (2) (*b*) above such powers and duties as the Secretary of State considers appropriate.

(4) Without prejudice to section 123 below, an order under this section may be varied or revoked by a subsequent order thereunder, whether in pursuance of an application made by all or any of the parties to the agreement in question or without any such application. [**411**]

COMMENCEMENT

This section was brought into force on 8th March 1976 by the Employment Protection Act 1975 (Commencement No. 2) Order 1976, S.I. 1976 No. 144.

GENERAL NOTE

This section provides that the Secretary of State may, by order, modify, adapt or exclude the provisions of this Part of this Act where satisfactory arrangements have already been made by collective agreement between the relative trade unions and employers or their associations as to the handling of redundancies and the provision of alternative employment.

THIS PART OF THIS ACT
I.e., Part IV (ss. 99–107).

INDUSTRIAL TRIBUNAL
See the note to s. 6, *ante*.

DEFINITIONS
By virtue of s. 126 (1), *post*, for "employer", see the definition inserted in the Trade Union and Labour Relations Act 1974, s. 30 (1), by s. 125 (1) and Sch. 16, Part III, para. 7 (2), *post*, and s. 30 (2) (*b*) of that Act, and for "collective agreement" and "employee", see s. 30 (1) of that Act; for "redundancy" and "redundant", see s. 126 (6), *post*.

ORDERS UNDER THIS SECTION
At the time of going to press no orders had been made under this section.
As to the making of orders generally, see s. 123, *post*. Note also sub-s. (4) above.

PART V

MISCELLANEOUS AND SUPPLEMENTARY PROVISIONS

108. General provisions as to industrial tribunals and conciliation officers

(1) The remedy of an employee for infringement of any of the rights conferred on him by any provision of this Act shall, if provision is made for a complaint or for the reference of a question to an industrial tribunal, be by way of such complaint or reference in accordance with the relevant provisions of this Act and with tribunal regulations made under paragraph 21 of Schedule 1 to the 1974 Act, and not otherwise.

(2) The provisions of subsections (3) to (7) below shall have effect in relation to industrial tribunal proceedings, or claims which could be the subject of tribunal proceedings,—

(*a*) arising out of a contravention, or alleged contravention, of the following provisions of this Act, that is to say, sections 22, 29, 35, 53, 57, 58, 59, 61, 70, 81, 99 and 102; or
(*b*) arising out of a contravention, or alleged contravention, of a provision of any other Act specified by an order under subsection (8) below; or
(*c*) which are proceedings or claims in respect of which an industrial tribunal has jurisdiction by virtue of an order under section 109 below.

(3) Where a complaint has been presented to an industrial tribunal, and a copy of it has been sent to a conciliation officer, it shall be the duty of the conciliation officer—

(*a*) if he is requested to do so by the complainant and by the person against whom the complaint is presented, or
(*b*) if, in the absence of any such request, the conciliation officer considers that he could act under this subsection with a reasonable prospect of success,

to endeavour to promote a settlement of the complaint without its being determined by an industrial tribunal.

(4) Where at any time—

(*a*) a person claims that action has been taken in respect of which a complaint could be presented by him to an industrial tribunal, but
(*b*) before any complaint relating to that action has been presented by him,

a request is made to a conciliation officer (whether by that person or by the person against whom the complaint could be made) to make his services available to them, the conciliation officer shall act in accordance with subsection (3) above as if a complaint has been presented to an industrial tribunal.

(5) Subsections (3) and (4) above shall apply, with appropriate modifications, to the presentation of a claim and the reference of a question to an industrial tribunal as they apply to the presentation of a complaint.

(6) In proceeding under subsection (3) or (4) above a conciliation officer shall where appropriate have regard to the desirability of encouraging the use of other procedures available for the settlement of grievances.

(7) Anything communicated to a conciliation officer in connection with the performance of his functions under this section shall not be admissible in evidence in any proceedings before an industrial tribunal, except with the consent of the person who communicated it to that officer.

(8) The Secretary of State may by order—

(*a*) direct that further provisions of this Act be added to the list in subsection (2) (*a*) above;

(*b*) specify a provision of any other Act as one to which subsection (2) (*b*) above applies. [**412**]

COMMENCEMENT

This section was brought into force on 8th March 1976 by the Employment Protection Act 1975 (Commencement No. 2) Order 1976, S.I. 1976 No. 144.

EMPLOYEE

For meaning, see, by virtue of s. 126 (1), *post*, the Trade Union and Labour Relations Act 1974, s. 30 (1).

INDUSTRIAL TRIBUNAL

See the note to s. 6, *ante*.

CONCILIATION OFFICER

I.e., an officer designated by the Service under s. 2 (4), *ante*, to perform the functions there referred to.

ORDERS UNDER THIS SECTION

At the time of going to press no order had been made under sub-s. (8) above.

As to the making of orders generally, see s. 123, *post*.

109. Power to confer jurisdiction on industrial tribunals in respect of damages, etc., for breach of contract of employment

(1) The appropriate Minister may by order provide that on any claim to which this section applies or any such claim of a description specified in the order, being in either case a claim satisfying the relevant condition or conditions mentioned in subsection (3) below, proceedings for the recovery of damages or any other sum, except damages or a sum due in respect of personal injuries, may be brought before an industrial tribunal.

(2) Subject to subsection (3) below, this section applies to any of the following claims, that is to say—

(*a*) a claim for damages for breach of a contract of employment or any other contract connected with employment;

(*b*) a claim for a sum due under such a contract;

(*c*) a claim for the recovery of a sum in pursuance of any enactment relating to the terms or performance of such a contract;

being in each case a claim such that a court in England and Wales or Scotland, as the case may be, would under the law for the time being in force have jurisdiction to hear and determine an action in respect of the claim.

(3) An order under this section may make provision with respect to any such claim only if it satisfies either of the following conditions, that is to say—

(*a*) it arises or is outstanding on the termination of the employee's employment; or

(*b*) it arises in circumstances which also give rise to proceedings already or simultaneously brought before an industrial tribunal otherwise than by virtue of this section;

or, if the order so provides, it satisfies both those conditions.

(4) Where on proceedings under this section an industrial tribunal finds that the whole or part of a sum claimed in the proceedings is due, the tribunal shall order the respondent to the proceedings to pay the amount which it finds due.

(5) Without prejudice to the generality of the power to make supplementary, incidental or transitional provision in an order under this section, such an order may include provisions—

(*a*) as to the manner in which and time within which proceedings are to be brought by virtue of this section; and

(*b*) modifying any other enactment.

(6) Regulations under paragraph 21 of Schedule 1 to the 1974 Act may include provision for enabling an industrial tribunal to hear and determine proceedings brought by virtue of this section concurrently with proceedings brought before the tribunal otherwise than by virtue of this section.

(7) Any jurisdiction conferred on an industrial tribunal by virtue of this section in respect of any claim shall be exercisable concurrently with any court in England and Wales or in Scotland, as the case may be, which has jurisdiction to hear and determine an action in respect of the claim.

(8) In this section—

"appropriate Minister", as respects a claim in respect of which an action could be heard and determined in England and Wales, means the Lord Chancellor and, as respects a claim in respect of which an action could be heard and determined by a court in Scotland, means the Secretary of State;

"personal injuries" includes any disease and any impairment of a person's physical or mental condition;

and any reference to breach of a contract includes a reference to breach of—

(*a*) a term implied in a contract by or under any enactment or otherwise;

(*b*) a term of a contract as modified by or under any enactment or otherwise; and

(*c*) a term which, although not contained in a contract, is incorporated in the contract by another term of the contract.

(9) No order shall be made under this section unless a draft of the order has been laid before Parliament and approved by resolution of each House of Parliament. [**413**]

COMMENCEMENT

This section was brought into force on 1st January 1976 by the Employment Protection Act 1975 (Commencement No. 1) Order 1975, S.I. 1975 No. 1938.

INDUSTRIAL TRIBUNAL
See the note to s. 6, *ante*.

LAID BEFORE . . . PARLIAMENT
For the meaning of these words, see the Laying of Documents before Parliament (Interpretation) Act 1948, s. 1 (1).

DEFINITIONS
For "employee", see, by virtue of s. 126 (1), *post*, the Trade Union and Labour Relations Act 1974, s. 30 (1). As to "appropriate Minister", "personal injuries" and "breach of a contract", note sub-s. (8) above.

ORDERS UNDER THIS SECTION
At the time of going to press no order had been made under this section.
As to the making of orders generally, see s. 123, *post*.

REGULATIONS
At the time of going to press no regulations had been made by virtue of sub-s. (6) above.

110. Death of employee or employer

The provisions of Schedule 12 to this Act shall have effect in relation to the death of an employee or employer. [**414**]

COMMENCEMENT
This section was brought into force in two stages on 8th March and 20th April 1976 by the Employment Protection Act (Commencement No. 2) Order 1976, S.I. 1976 No. 144, so far as it relates to ss. 99–107 and 63–69.

DEFINITIONS
By virtue of s. 126 (1), *post*, for "employer", see the definition inserted in the Trade Union and Labour Relations Act 1974, s. 30 (1), by s. 125 (1) and Sch. 16, Part III, para. 7 (2), *post*, and s. 30 (2) (*b*) of that Act; for "employee", see s. 30 (1) of that Act.

111. Disentitlement to unemployment benefit and supplementary benefit during trade dispute

(1) In section 19 (1) of the Social Security Act 1975 (disqualification for unemployment benefit where stoppage of work due to trade dispute)—

(*a*) in paragraph (*a*) the words "or financing" and the word "and", and
(*b*) paragraph (*b*),

are hereby repealed.

(2) In section 10 (2) of the Supplementary Benefit Act 1966 (persons affected by trade disputes)—

(*a*) in paragraph (*a*) the words "or financing" and the word "and", and
(*b*) paragraph (*b*),

are hereby repealed. [**415**]

COMMENCEMENT
See s. 129 (3), *post*.

GENERAL NOTE
This section limits the scope of the provisions of the Social Security Act 1975 and the Supplementary Benefit Act 1966 disentitling employees to unemployment benefit and supplementary benefit during a trade dispute by modifying the exemption provisions of the relevant section. To obtain such exemption a worker need, as a result, prove only that he is not participating in or directly interested in the dispute.

TRANSITIONAL PROVISIONS
See s. 125 (2) and Sch. 17, para. 15, *post*.

112. Entitlement to unemployment benefit and recoupment of that benefit and supplementary benefit

(1) Section 139 (1) of the Social Security Act 1975 (submission of regulations in draft to the National Insurance Advisory Committee) shall not apply to regulations made under that Act and contained in a statutory instrument which states that the regulations provide only that a day in respect of which there is payable a particular description of any payment to which this section applies shall not be treated as a day of unemployment for the purposes of entitlement to unemployment benefit.

(2) The Secretary of State may by regulations make provision for all or any of the purposes mentioned in this subsection with respect to payments to which this section applies and which are subject of proceedings before an industrial tribunal, that is to say—

(*a*) enabling the Secretary of State to recover from an employer, by way of total or partial recoupment of unemployment benefit or supplementary benefit, a sum not exceeding the amount of the prescribed element of the monetary award;

(*b*) requiring or authorising the tribunal to order the payment of such a sum, by way of total or partial recoupment of either benefit, to the Secretary of State instead of to the employee;

(*c*) requiring the tribunal to order the payment to the employee of only the excess of the prescribed element of the monetary award over the amount of any unemployment benefit or supplementary benefit shown to the tribunal to have been paid to the employee, and enabling the Secretary of State to recover from the employer, by way of total or partial recoupment of the benefit, a sum not exceeding that amount.

(3) Without prejudice to subsection (2) above, regulations under that subsection may—

(*a*) be so framed as to apply to all payments to which this section applies or one or more classes of those payments and so as to apply both to unemployment benefit and supplementary benefit or only to one of those benefits;

(*b*) confer powers and impose duties on industrial tribunals, on the Supplementary Benefits Commission and on insurance officers and other persons;

(*c*) confer on an employee who is aggrieved by any decision of the Commission as to the total or partial recoupment of supplementary benefit in pursuance of the regulations (including any decisions as to the amount of benefit) a right to appeal against the decision to an Appeal Tribunal constituted under the Supplementary Benefit Act 1966 and for that purpose apply section 18 (2) and (3) of that Act (appeals) with or without modifications;

(*d*) provide for the proof in proceedings before industrial tribunals (whether by certificate or in any other manner) of any amount of unemployment benefit or supplementary benefit paid to an employee; and

(*e*) make different provision for different cases.

(4) It is hereby declared for the avoidance of doubt that the power to make regulations under section 114 of the Social Security Act 1975 for the determination of questions arising in connection with that Act includes power to make regulations for the determination of any question arising as to the total or

partial recoupment of unemployment benefit in pursuance of regulations under subsection (2) above (including any decision as to the amount of benefit).

(5) Where in pursuance of any regulations under that subsection a sum has been recovered by or paid to the Secretary of State by way of total or partial recoupment of unemployment benefit or supplementary benefit—

(*a*) section 119 (1) and (2) of the Social Security Act 1975 (repayment of benefit revised on review) shall not apply to the unemployment benefit recouped; and

(*b*) the following provisions of the Supplementary Benefit Act 1966, that is to say, section 23 (recovery of cost of supplementary benefit from persons liable for maintenance) and section 26 (recovery of benefit and other sums in cases of misrepresentation and non-disclosure), shall not apply to the supplementary benefit recouped.

(6) Any amount found to have been duly recovered by or paid to the Secretary of State in pursuance of regulations under subsection (2) above by way of total or partial recoupment of unemployment benefit shall be paid into the National Insurance Fund.

(7) This section applies—

(*a*) to a payment of wages or compensation for loss of wages;

(*b*) to any payment under this Act by an employer to an employee or a payment by an employer to an employee of a nature similar to, or for a purpose corresponding to the purpose of, any payment under this Act.

(8) In this section—

"monetary award", in relation to an industrial tribunal, means the amount which is awarded, or ordered to be paid, to the employee by the tribunal or would be so awarded or ordered apart from any provision of regulations under this section;

"the prescribed element", in relation to any monetary award, means so much of that award as is attributable to such matters as may be prescribed by regulations under subsection (2) above;

"supplementary benefit" means benefit under the Supplementary Benefit Act 1966; and

"unemployment benefit" means unemployment benefit under the Social Security Act 1975. [**416**]

COMMENCEMENT

This section was brought into force on 1st January 1976 by the Employment Protection Act 1975 (Commencement No. 1) Order 1975, S.I. 1975 No. 1938.

SUB-S. (1): STATUTORY INSTRUMENT

For provisions as to statutory instruments, see the Statutory Instruments Act 1946.

SUB-S. (2): PAYMENT TO WHICH THIS SECTION APPLIES

See sub-s. (7) above.

DAY OF UNEMPLOYMENT

As to such days for the purposes of entitlement to unemployment benefit, see the Social Security Act 1975, s. 17.

SUB-S. (2): INDUSTRIAL TRIBUNAL

See the note to s. 6, *ante*.

SUB-S. (3): SUPPLEMENTARY BENEFITS COMMISSION

That body is established under the Supplementary Benefits Act 1966 (the Ministry of Social Security Act 1966), s. 3.

INSURANCE OFFICERS

Such officers are appointed under the Social Security Act 1975, s. 97; see p. 434, *ante*.

SUB-S. (6): NATIONAL INSURANCE FUND

This fund is established under the Social Security Act 1975, s. 133.

DEFINITIONS

By virtue of s. 126 (1), *post*, for "employer", see the definition of that expression inserted in the Trade Union and Labour Relations Act 1974, s. 30 (1), by s. 125 (1) and Sch. 16, Part III, para. 7 (2), *post*, and s. 30 (2) (*b*) of that Act, and for "employee", see s. 30 (1) of that Act. As to "monetary award", "the prescribed element", "supplementary benefit" and "unemployment benefit", note sub-s. (8) above.

REGULATIONS UNDER THIS SECTION

At the time of going to press no regulations had been made under sub-s. (2) above or by virtue of sub-s. (4) above.

As to the making of regulations generally, see s. 123, *post*.

113. Payments which are to be treated as earnings for social security purposes

(1) Where a payment to which this section applies is made by an employer to an employee, the payment and the period for which it is made shall, notwithstanding that the payment is made in respect of a period during which no contract of employment subsists, be respectively treated for the purposes of the Supplementary Benefit Act 1966 and the Social Security Act 1975 as earnings of that employee and a period of his employment by that employer.

(2) This section applies to the following payments—

(*a*) any amount paid in respect of arrears of pay in pursuance of an order for reinstatement or re-engagement under section 71 or 78 above;

(*b*) any amount paid by way of pay in pursuance of an order for the continuation of a contract of employment under section 78 or 80 above;

(*c*) any remuneration paid under a protective award under section 101 above. **[417]**

COMMENCEMENT

This section was brought into force on 8th March 1976 by the Employment Protection Act 1975 (Commencement No. 2) Order 1976, S.I. 1976 No. 144, so far as it relates to remuneration paid under a protective award under s. 101.

DEFINITIONS

By virtue of s. 125 (1), *post*, for "employer", see the definition inserted in the Trade Union and Labour Relations Act 1974, s. 30 (1), by s. 125 (1), and Sch. 16, Part III, para. 7 (2), *post*, and s. 30 (2) (*b*) of that Act, and for "employee", see s. 30 (1) of that Act.

114. Amendments of the Employment Agencies Act 1973

The Employment Agencies Act 1973 shall have effect subject to the amendments specified in Schedule 13 to this Act, being amendments which transfer the licensing functions under that Act from local authorities to the Secretary of State. **[418]**

COMMENCEMENT

This section was brought into force on 1st January 1976 by the Employment Protection Act (Commencement No. 1) Order 1975, S.I. 1975 No. 1938.

LOCAL AUTHORITIES

For meaning in the Employment Agencies Act 1973, see s. 13 (1) of that Act.

115. Amendments of the Employment and Training Act 1973

The Employment and Training Act 1973 shall have effect subject to the amendments specified in Schedule 14 to this Act, being amendments which provide for the status of the bodies established under section 1 (1) of that Act and enlarge the powers of the Secretary of State to make arrangments for the purpose of providing or obtaining employment. [**419**]

COMMENCEMENT

This section was brought into force on 1st January 1976 by the Employment Protection Act 1975 (Commencement No. 1) Order 1975, S.I. 1975, No. 1938.

116. Amendments of the Health and Safety at Work, etc. Act 1974

The Health and Safety at Work, etc. Act 1974 shall have effect subject to the amendments specified in Schedule 15 to this Act, being amendments which restrict the appointment of safety representatives to those appointed by recognised trade unions, remove the special provisions relating to health and safety at work in agriculture and enable certain statements to be given notwithstanding the restrictions on disclosure of information obtained under that Act. [**420**]

COMMENCEMENT

This section was brought into force in two stages on 1st January and 1st March 1976 by the Employment Protection Act 1975 (Commencement No. 1) Order 1975, S.I. 1975 No. 1938.

SAFETY REPRESENTATIVES

These are appointed by recognised trade unions by virtue of regulations made under the Health and Safety at Work, etc. Act 1974, s. 2 (4). The provision of that Act providing an alternative method of appointment is s. 2 (5), which is repealed by Sch. 15, para. 2, *post*, and by s. 125 (3) and Sch. 18, *post*.

RECOGNISED TRADE UNION

As to the recognition of trade unions, see ss. 11 *et seq*., *ante*.

ENABLE CERTAIN STATEMENTS TO BE GIVEN, ETC.

See the amendment effected by Sch. 15, para. 9, *post*.

117. Offences by bodies corporate

(1) Where an offence under this Act committed by a body corporate is proved to have been committed with the consent or connivance of, or to be attributable to any neglect on the part of, any director, manager, secretary or other similar officer of the body corporate, or any person who was purporting to act in any such capacity, he as well as the body corporate shall be guilty of that offence and shall be liable to be proceeded against and punished accordingly.

(2) Where the affairs of a body corporate are managed by its members, subsection (1) above shall apply in relation to the acts and defaults of a member in connection with his functions of management as if he were a director of the body corporate. [**421**]

COMMENCEMENT

This section was brought into force in two stages on 8th March and 20th April 1976 by the Employment Protection Act 1975 (Commencement No. 2) Order 1976, S.I. 1976 No. 144, so far as it relates to any offence under ss. 105 and 68.

OFFENCE ... COMMITTED BY A BODY CORPORATE

Where an offence is committed by an agent of a corporation under such circumstances that his act and his knowledge or intent can be said to be those of the corporation, the offence is committed by the corporation; see *Director of Public Prosecutions* v. *Kent and Sussex Contractors, Ltd.*, [1944] K.B. 146; [1944] 1 All E.R. 119; *R.* v. *I.C.R. Haulage, Ltd.*, [1944] K.B. 551; [1944] 1 All E.R. 691; and *Tesco Supermarkets, Ltd.* v. *Nattrass*, [1972] A.C. 153; [1971] 2 All E.R. 127, H.L.

CONSENT

There is authority for saying that this presupposes knowledge; see *Re Caughey, Ex parte Ford* (1876), 1 Ch. D. 521, C.A. at p. 528, *per* Jessel, M.R., and *Lamb* v. *Wright & Co.*, [1924] 1 K.B. 857; [1924] All E.R. Rep. 220, at p. 864 and p. 223, respectively. It is thought, however, that actual knowledge is not necessary; cf. *Knox* v. *Boyd*, [1941] S.C. (J.) 82, at p. 86, and *Taylor's Central Garages (Exeter), Ltd.* v. *Roper* (1951), 115 J.P. 445, at pp. 449, 450, *per* Devlin, J.; and see also, in particular, *Mallon* v. *Allon*, [1964] 1 Q.B. 385; [1963] 3 All E.R. 843, at p. 394 and p. 847, respectively.

CONNIVANCE

There are many decisions on the meaning of this word in matrimonial law; see *Godfrey* v. *Godfrey*, [1965] A.C. 444; [1964] 3 All E.R. 154, H.L., especially the speech of Lord Guest, in which earlier decisions are reviewed. It would seem that an element of encouragement is essential. The word has been used in a number of statutes in the same context as in this section, but there is little authority as to its meaning in this context. See Glanville Williams *Criminal Law: The General Part*, para. 222, and *Gregory* v. *Walker* (1912), 77 J.P. 55; 29 T.L.R. 51.

NEGLECT

This term, in the words of Simonds, J. (as he then was) in *Re Hughes, Rea* v. *Black*, [1943] Ch. 296; [1943] 2 All E.R. 269, at p. 298 and p. 271, respectively, "in its legal connotation implies failure to perform a duty of which the person knows or ought to know". This it, is thought, is also the meaning that the expression has in the present context.

118. Restrictions on contracting out

(1) Except as provided by subsection (2) below, any provision in an agreement (whether a contract of employment or not) shall be void in so far as it purports—

(*a*) to exclude or limit the operation of any provision of this Act; or

(*b*) to preclude any person from presenting a complaint to, or bringing any proceedings under this Act before, an industrial tribunal, or for making any reference, claim, complaint or application under this Act to the Service or the Committee.

(2) Subsection (1) above shall not apply—

(*a*) to any provision in a collective agreement excluding rights under section 22 above or Part IV of this Act, if an order under section 28 or, as the case may be, section 107 above is for the time being in force in respect of it;

(*b*) to any union membership agreement so far as it affects the rights of an employee under section 53 above in accordance with subsection (4) of that section;

(*c*) to any agreement to refrain from instituting or continuing any proceedings before an industrial tribunal where a conciliation officer has taken action in accordance with section 108 (3) or (4) above;

(*d*) to any agreement such as is referred to in section 16 (7) (*b*) or (*c*), or 21 (6) (*b*) or (*c*) above, or paragraph 11 (*b*) or (*c*) of Schedule 11 to this Act, to the extent that it varies or supersedes an award under section 16 or 21 above, or, as the case may be, paragraph 10 of the said Schedule 11. [**422**]

COMMENCEMENT

This section was brought into force on 1st January 1976 by the Employment Protection Act 1975 (Commencement No. 1) Order 1975, S.I. 1975 No. 1938.

INDUSTRIAL TRIBUNAL

See the note to s. 6, *ante*.

CONCILIATION OFFICER

I.e., an officer designated by the Service under s. 2 (4), *ante*, to perform the functions there referred to.

DEFINITIONS

For "collective agreement", "employee" and "union membership agreement", see, by virtue of s. 126 (1), *post*, the Trade Union and Labour Relations Act 1974, s. 30 (1); for "the Service", see s. 1 (1), *ante*; for "the Committee", see s. 10 (1), *ante*.

119. Excluded classes of employment

(1) Subject to the following provisions of this section, Parts II and IV of this Act apply to every employment.

(2) The following provisions of this Act do not apply to employment where the employer is the husband or wife of the employee, that is to say, sections 22, 29, 35, 53, 57, 58, 59, 61, 64, 65, 70, and 81.

(3) The following provisions of this Act do not apply to employment as a registered dock worker, as defined by any scheme for the time being in force under the Dock Workers (Regulation of Employment) Act 1946, not being employment by virtue of which the employee is wholly or mainly engaged in work which is not dock work as defined by the scheme, that is to say, sections 22, 29, 61, 64, 65, 70, 99 and 100.

(4) The following provisions of this Act do not apply to employment as master or as a member of the crew of a fishing vessel, where the employee is not remunerated otherwise than by a share in the profits or gross earnings of the vessel, that is to say sections 22, 29, 35, 53, 57, 58, 59, 61, 64, 65, 70, 81, 99 and 100.

(5) The following provisions of this Act do not apply to employment where under his contract of employment the employee ordinarily works outside Great Britain, that is to say, sections 22, 29, 35, 53, 57, 58, 59, 61, 64, 65, 70, 81, 99 and 100.

(6) For the purposes of subsection (5) above, a person employed to work on board a ship registered in the United Kingdom (not being a ship registered at a port outside Great Britain) shall, unless—

(*a*) the employment is wholly outside Great Britain or
(*b*) he is not ordinarily resident in Great Britain,

be regarded as a person who under his contract ordinarily works in Great Britain.

(7) The following provisions of this Act do not apply to employment under a contract for a fixed term of 12 weeks or less or to employment under a contract made in contemplation of the performance of a specific task which is not expected to last for more than 12 weeks, unless in either case the employee has been continuously employed for a period of more than 12 weeks, that is to say, sections 22, 29, 99 and 100.

(8) Subject to subsections (9), (10) and (11) below, the following provisions of this Act (which confer rights which do not depend upon an employee having a qualifying period of continuous employment) do not apply to employment under a contract which normally involves employment for less than 16 hours weekly, that is to say, sections 57, 58, 59 and 81.

(9) If the employee's relations with his employer cease to be governed by a contract which normally involves work for 16 hours or more weekly and become governed by a contract which normally involves employment for 8 hours or more, but less than 16 hours, weekly, the employee shall nevertheless for a period of

26 weeks computed in accordance with subsection (10) below be treated for the purposes of subsection (8) above as if his contract normally involved employment for 16 hours or more weekly.

(10) In computing the said period of 26 weeks no account shall be taken of any week—

(*a*) during which the employee is in fact employed for 16 hours or more;
(*b*) during which the employee takes part in a strike, or is absent from work because of a lock-out by his employer; or
(*c*) during which there is no contract of employment but which, by virtue of paragraph 5 (1) of Schedule 1 to the Contracts of Employment Act 1972, counts in computing a period of continuous employment.

(11) An employee whose relations with his employer are governed by a contract of employment which normally involves employment for 8 hours or more, but less than 16 hours, weekly shall nevertheless, if he has been continuously employed for a period of five years or more be treated for the purposes of subsection (8) above as if his contract normally involved employment for 16 hours or more weekly.

(12) The following provisions of this Act do not apply to employment as a merchant seaman, that is to say, sections 59, 61, 64, 65, 81, 99 and 100.

(13) Subject to subsection (14) below, employment as a merchant seaman does not include employment in the fishing industry or employment on board a ship otherwise than by the owner, manager or charterer of that ship except employment as a radio officer but save as aforesaid includes employment as master or a member of the crew of any ship, as an apprentice to the sea service, and as a trainee undergoing training for the sea service, and employment in or about a ship in port by the owner, manager or charterer of the ship to do work of the kind ordinarily done by a merchant seaman on such a ship while it is in port.

(14) For the purposes of subsection (12) above as it applies in relation to sections 99 and 100, employment as a merchant seaman means employment as master or as a member of the crew of a sea-going ship, including an apprentice or trainee employed on any such ship and employment as a radio officer on such a ship.

(15) The Secretary of State may by order—

(*a*) provide that any enactment contained in this Act which is specified in the order shall not apply to persons or to employments of such classes as may be prescribed by the order, or shall apply to persons or employments of such classes as may be prescribed by the order subject to such exceptions and modifications as may be so prescribed;
(*b*) vary or revoke any of the provisions of subsections (1) to (14) of this section.

(16) No order under subsection (15) above shall be made unless a draft of the order has been laid before Parliament and approved by a resolution of each House of Parliament. **[423]**

COMMENCEMENT

This section was brought into force in two stages on 8th March and 20th April 1976 by the Employment Protection Act 1975 (Commencement No. 2) Order 1976, S.I. 1976 No. 144, so far as it relates to ss. 99 and 100, and ss. 64 and 65.

SUB-S. (1): PARTS II AND IV OF THIS ACT

I.e., ss. 22–88, *ante*, and ss. 99–107, *ante*, respectively.

SUB-S. (3): DOCK WORKER
This expression is defined in the Dock Workers (Regulation of Employment) Act 1946, s. 6.

ANY SCHEME . . . IN FORCE, ETC.
The Dock Workers (Regulation of Employment) Act 1946, s. 1, provides for schemes for ensuring greater regularity of employment for dock workers and for ensuring an adequate supply of such workers. Such schemes are made under s. 2 of the Act.

SUB-S. (5): ORDINARILY WORKS
Cf. the note "Ordinarily resident" below.

GREAT BRITAIN
See the note to s. 86, *ante*.

SUB-S. (6): UNITED KINGDOM
I.e., Great Britain and Northern Ireland; see the Royal and Parliamentary Titles Act 1927, s. 2 (2).

ORDINARILY RESIDENT
"Ordinarily" means here according to the way in which one's life is usually ordered; see *Levene* v. *Inland Revenue Comrs.*, [1928] A.C. 271; [1928] All E.R. Rep. 746, at p. 232 and p. 754, respectively, *per* Lord Warrington of Clyffe. "I think the converse of 'ordinarily' is 'extraordinarily' and that part of the regular order of a man's life, adopted voluntarily and for settled purposes, is not 'extraordinary',"; see *Inland Revenue Comrs.* v. *Lysaght*, [1928] A.C. 234; [1928] All E.R. Rep. 575, at p. 243 and p. 580, respectively, *per* Viscount Sumner.

A temporary sojourn may become ordinary residence owing to circumstances beyond the control of the person concerned; see *Re Mackenzie*, [1941] Ch. 69; [1940] 4 All E.R. 310; and cf. *Re Bright Ex parte Bright* (1903), 51 W.R. 342, C.A.; *R.* v. *Denman, Ex parte Staal* (1917), 86 L.J.K.B. 1328; and *Pittar* v. *Richardson* (1918), 87 L.J.K.B. 59. However, ordinary residence can be changed in a day; see, in particular, *Macrae* v. *Macrae*, [1949] P. 397; [1949] 2 All E.R. 34, C.A. See also *Hopkins* v. *Hopkins*, [1951] P. 116; [1950] 2 All E.R. 1035; *Stransky* v. *Stranksy*, [1954] P. 428; [1954] 2 All E.R. 536; and *Lewis* v. *Lewis*, [1956] 1 All E.R. 375; and cf. *Lowry* v. *Lowry*, [1952] P. 252; [1952] 2 All E.R. 61.

A person resides where in common parlance he lives, and a temporary absence is immaterial providing there is an intention to return and a house or lodging to which to return; see *R.* v. *St Leonard's, Shoreditch (Inhabitants)* (1865), L.R. 1 Q.B. 21; *R.* v. *Glossop Union* (1866), L.R. 1 Q.B. 227. There is authority for saying that a person may be resident in more than one place at the same time; see *Levene* v. *Inland Revenue Comrs.*, [1928] A.C. 217; [1928] All E.R. Rep. 746, H.L., *per* Viscount Cave, L.C. at pp. 223 and 749, respectively, and *Langford Property Co., Ltd.* v. *Tureman*, [1949] 1 K.B. 29; *sub nom. Langford Property Co., Ltd.* v. *Athanassoglou*, [1948] 2 All E.R. 722, C.A. See also *Fox* v. *Stirk*, [1970] 2 Q.B. 463; [1970] 3 All E.R. 7, C.A.

SUB-S. (11): CONTINUOUSLY EMPLOYED FOR . . . FIVE YEARS, ETC.
As to the determination of the period for which an employee has been continuously employed, see s. 126 (5), *post*.

SUB-S. (12): EMPLOYMENT AS A MERCHANT SEAMAN
Note the provisions of sub-ss. (13) and (14) above.

SUB-S. (16): LAID BEFORE PARLIAMENT
For meaning, see the Laying of Documents before Parliament (Interpretation) Act 1948, s. 1 (1).

DEFINITIONS
By virtue of s. 126 (1), *post*, for "employer", see the definition inserted in the Trade Union and Labour Relations Act 1974, s. 30 (1), by s. 125 (1) and Sch. 16, Part III, para. 7 (2), *post*, and s. 30 (2) (*b*) of that Act, and for "employee", see s. 30 (1) of that Act.

ORDERS UNDER THIS SECTION
At the time of going to press no orders had been made under sub-s. (15) of this section.

As to the making of orders generally, see s. 123, *post*. Note also sub-s. (16) above.

120. Transfers to and from Crown employment

(1) In Schedule 1 to the Contracts of Employment Act 1972 (computation of period of employment) after paragraph 10 there shall be inserted the following paragraph:—

"10A.—(1) Subject to the following provisions of this paragraph, the provisions of this Schedule shall have effect (for the purpose of computing an employee's period of employment, but not for any other purpose) in relation to Crown employment and to persons in Crown employment as they have effect in relation to other employment and to other employees, and accordingly, except where the context otherwise requires, references to an employer shall be construed as including a reference to the Crown.

(2) In this paragraph, subject to the next following sub-paragraph, "Crown employment" means employment under or for the purposes of a government department or any officer or body exercising on behalf of the Crown functions conferred by any enactment.

(3) This paragraph does not apply to service as a member of the naval, military or air forces of the Crown, or of any women's service administered by the Defence Council, but does apply to employment by any association established for the purposes of the Auxiliary Forces Act 1953.

(4) In so far as a person in Crown employment is employed otherwise than under a contract of employment, references in this Schedule to an employee's relations with his employer being governed by a contract of employment which normally involves employment for a certain number of hours weekly shall be modified accordingly.

(5) The reference in paragraph 9 (2) of this Schedule to an undertaking shall be construed as including a reference to any function of (as the case may require) a Minister of the Crown, a government department, or any other officer or body performing functions on behalf of the Crown.".

(2) After section 13 of the Redundancy Payments Act 1965 (change of ownership of business) there shall be inserted the following section—

13A. Transfer to Crown employment

(1) Section 13 of this Act shall apply to a transfer of functions from a person not acting on behalf of the Crown (in this section referred to as the transferor) to a Minister of the Crown, a government department or any other officer or body exercising functions on behalf of the Crown (in this section referred to as the transferee) as that section applies to transfer of a business, but with the substitution for references to the previous owner and new owner of references to the transferor and transferee respectively.

(2) In so far as the renewal or re-engagement of the employee by the transferee is in employment otherwise than under a contract of employment—

(*a*) references in section 13 of this Act (and in sections 2 (4) to (6) and 3 (3) to (10) of this Act as they apply by virtue of that section) to a contract of employment or to the terms of such a contract shall be construed as references to employment otherwise than under such a contract and to the terms of such employment; and

(*b*) references in subsection (4) of that section, as modified by subsection (1) of this section, to the substitution of the transferee for the transferor shall be construed as references to the substitution of employment by the transferee otherwise than under a contract of employment for employment by the transferor under such a contract."

(3) After section 24 of the said Act of 1965 (modification of right to redundancy payment where previous redundancy payment has been paid) there shall be inserted the following section—

"24A. Modification of right to redundancy payment where payment equivalent to redundancy payment has previously been paid

(1) The provisions of this section shall have effect where—

(*a*) a payment has been made, whether in respect of the termination of any person's employment or in respect of lay-off or short-time,—

(i) in accordance with any provisions of a scheme under section 1 of the Superannuation Act 1972; or

(ii) in accordance with any such arrangements as are mentioned in section 41 (3) of this Act;

(*b*) he commences new, or renewed, employment; and

(*c*) the circumstances of the commencement of the new, or renewed, employment are such that, in determining for the purposes of section 1 (1) of, or Schedule 1 to, this Act whether at any subsequent time he has been continuously employed for the requisite period, or for what period he has been continuously employed, the continuity of his period of employment would, apart from this section, be treated as not having been broken by the termination of the previous employment and the commencement of the new, or renewed, employment.

(2) Where the conditions mentioned in the preceding subsection are fulfilled, then in determining, for the purposes of section 1 (1) of, or Schedule 1 to, this Act, whether at any subsequent time he has been continuously employed for the requisite period, or for what period he has been continuously employed, the continuity of the period of employment shall be treated as having been broken—

(*a*) in so far as the employment was under a contract of employment, at the date which was the relevant date in relation to the payment mentioned in paragraph (*a*) of the preceding subsection; or

(*b*) in so far as the employment was otherwise than under a contract of employment, at the date which would have been the relevant date in relation to that payment had the employment been under a contract of employment,

and accordingly no account shall be taken of any time before that date.". [**424**]

COMMENCEMENT

See s. 129 (3), *post*.

EMPLOYEE

As to the meaning of "employee" in the Contracts of Employment Act 1972, see s. 11 (1) of that Act.

CROWN EMPLOYMENT

For meaning in para. 10A of Sch. 1 to the Contracts of Employment Act 1972, as inserted by sub-s. (1) above, see sub-para. (2) of that paragraph.

BUSINESS; NEW OWNER; PREVIOUS OWNER

For the meaning of "business" in the Redundancy Payments Act 1965, Part I, see s. 25 (1) of that Act and for the meaning of "new owner" and "previous owner" in s. 13 of that Act, see sub-ss. (1), (2) of that section.

121. Application to Crown

(1) Subject to the following provisions of this section, the provisions of this Act (except sections 16, 20, 21, 47, 63 to 69, 90 to 96 and 98 to 107) shall have effect in relation to Crown employment and to persons in Crown employment as they have effect in relation to other employment and to other employees.

(2) In this section, subject to subsections (3) to (5) below, "Crown employment" means employment under or for the purposes of a government department or any officer or body exercising on behalf of the Crown functions conferred by any enactment.

(3) This section does not apply to service as a member of the naval, military or air forces of the Crown, or of any women's service administered by the Defence Council, but does apply to employment by any association established for the purposes of the Auxiliary Forces Act 1953.

(4) For the purposes of this section, Crown employment does not include any employment in respect of which there is in force a certificate issued by or on behalf of a Minister of the Crown certifying that employment of a description specified in the certificate, or the employment of a particular person so specified, is (or, at a time specified in the certificate, was) required to be excepted from this section for the purpose of safeguarding national security; and any document purporting to be a certificate so issued shall be received in evidence and shall, unless the contrary is proved, be deemed to be such a certificate.

(5) For the purposes of this Act (except sections 47 (3) and (4), 68 (3) and (4), 90 to 96 and 105), none of the bodies referred to in Schedule 3 to the Redundancy Payments Act 1965 (national health service employers) shall be regarded as performing functions on behalf of the Crown, and accordingly employment by any such body shall not be Crown employment within the meaning of this section.

(6) For the purposes of the application of the provisions of this Act in relation to employment by any such body as is referred to in subsection (5) above, any reference to redundancy shall be construed as a reference to the existence of such circumstances as, in accordance with any arrangements for the time being in force as mentioned in section 41 (3) of the Redundancy Payments Act 1965, are treated as equivalent to redundancy in relation to such employment.

(7) For the purposes of the application of the provisions of this Act in relation to Crown employment in accordance with subsection (1) above—

(*a*) any reference to an employee shall be construed as a reference to a person in Crown employment;

(*b*) any reference to a contract of employment shall be construed as a reference to the terms of employment of a person in Crown employment;

(*c*) any reference to dismissal shall be construed as a reference to the termination of Crown employment;

(*d*) any reference to redundancy shall be construed as a reference to the existence of such circumstances as, in accordance with any arrangements for the time being in force as mentioned in section 41 (3) of the

Redundancy Payments Act 1965, are treated as equivalent to redundancy in relation to Crown employment;

(*e*) the reference in section 18 (1) (*e*) above to the employer's undertaking shall be construed as a reference to the national interest; and

(*f*) any other reference to an undertaking shall be construed, in relation to a Minister of the Crown, as a reference to his functions or (as the context may require) to the department of which he is in charge and, in relation to a government department, officer or body, shall be construed as a reference to the functions of the department, officer or body or (as the context may require) to the department, officer or body.

(8) Where the terms of employment of a person in Crown employment restrict his right to take part in—

(*a*) certain political activities; or

(*b*) activities which may conflict with his official functions,

nothing in section 59 above shall require him to be allowed time off work for public duties connected with any such activities. [**425**]

COMMENCEMENT

This section was brought into force on 1st January 1976 by the Employment Protection Act 1975 (Commencement No. 1) Order 1975, S.I. 1975 No. 1938.

DEFINITIONS

By virtue of s. 126 (1), *post*, for "dismissal", see the Trade Union and Labour Relations Act 1974, Sch. 1, para. 5, and for "employee", see s. 30 (1) of that Act and note sub-s. (7) (*a*) above; for "redundancy", see s. 126 (6), *post*. As to "Crown employment", note sub-s. (2), together with sub-ss. (3)–(5), above.

122. Application of employment legislation to House of Commons staff

(1) The provisions of this Act, Schedule 1 to the Contracts of Employment Act 1972 and Parts I and II of Schedule 1 to the 1974 Act shall apply to relevant members of House of Commons staff as they apply to persons in Crown employment within the meaning of section 121 above, and accordingly for the purposes of the application of those provisions in relation to any such members—

(*a*) any reference to an employee shall be construed as a reference to any such member;

(*b*) any reference to a contract of employment shall be construed as a reference to the terms of employment of any such member;

(*c*) any reference to dismissal shall be construed as a reference to the termination of any such member's employment;

(*d*) the references in paragraph 21 (5) (*c*) of Schedule 1 to the 1974 Act and section 18 (1) (*e*) above to any person's undertaking or any undertaking in which he works shall be construed as a reference to the national interest or, if the case so requires, the interests of the House of Commons; and

(*e*) any other reference to an undertaking shall be construed as a reference to the House of Commons.

(2) The provisions of section 1 of the Equal Pay Act 1970 and Parts II and IV of the Sex Discrimination Act 1975 shall apply to an act done by an employer of a relevant member of House of Commons staff and to service as such a member as they apply to an act done by, and to service for the purposes of, a Minister of the Crown or Government department, and accordingly shall so apply as if references in those provisions to a contract of employment included references to the terms of service of such a member.

(3) Nothing in any rule of law or the law or practice of Parliament shall prevent proceedings under any enactment applied by subsection (1) or (2) above being instituted before an industrial tribunal.

(4) In this section "relevant member of House of Commons staff" means any person employed in or for the purposes of the House of Commons as follows:—

(*a*) in the Department of the Clerk of that House;
(*b*) in Mr. Speaker's Department;
(*c*) in the Department of the Serjeant at Arms;
(*d*) in the Department of the Library;
(*e*) in the administration department;
(*f*) in the refreshment department.

(5) It is hereby declared that in this section "relevant member of House of Commons staff" does not include the Clerk of that House or any Clerk Assistant or the Serjeant at Arms of that House.

(6) For the purposes of the enactments applied by subsection (1) and (2) above, Mr. Speaker shall be deemed to be the employer of House of Commons staff, except that in relation to any description of members of the staff for the time being designated by Mr. Speaker a person so designated shall be deemed to be the employer of members of that description for those purposes or, if it is so stated in the designation, such of those purposes as are so designated.

(7) Where any proceedings are brought by virtue of this section against Mr. Speaker or any person designated under subsection (6) above, the person against whom the proceedings are brought may apply to the industrial tribunal to have some other person against whom the proceedings could have been properly brought so substituted for him as a party to those proceedings.

(8) If the House of Commons resolves at any time that any provision of subsections (4) to (6) above should be amended in its application to any member of the staff of that House, Her Majesty may by Order in Council amend that provision accordingly.

(9) It is hereby declared that the powers of nominating or appointing and suspending or removing members of House of Commons staff conferred by sections 14 and 15 of the House of Commons (Offices) Act 1812 (clerks, attendants and messengers) and the power of Mr. Speaker to require the suspension or removal of any such member conferred by section 16 of that Act are exercisable subject to the provisions of the enactments applied by subsections (1) and (2) above to such members. [**426**]

COMMENCEMENT

This section was brought into force on 1st January 1976 by the Employment Protection Act 1975 (Commencement No. 1) Order 1975, S.I. 1975 No. 1938.

INDUSTRIAL TRIBUNAL

See the note to s. 6, *ante*.

FINANCIAL PROVISIONS

See s. 124 (1) (*b*), *post*.

DEFINITIONS

By virtue of s. 126 (1), *post*, for "employer", see the definition inserted in the Trade Union and Labour Relations Act 1974, s. 30 (1), by s. 125 (1) and Sch. 16, Part III, para. 7 (2), *post*, and s. 30 (2) (*b*) of that Act, and for "employee", see s. 30 (1) of that Act. As to "relevant member of the House of Commons Staff", note sub-ss. (4) and (5) above.

ORDERS IN COUNCIL UNDER THIS SECTION

At the time of going to press no Order in Council had been made under sub-s. (8) above. Such an order is a statutory instrument and is governed by the Statutory Instruments Act 1946; see s. 1 (1) of that Act.

123. Orders, rules and regulations

(1) Any power conferred by any provision of this Act to make an order (other than an Order in Council) or to make rules or regulations shall be exercisable by statutory instrument.

(2) Any statutory instrument made under any power conferred by this Act to make an Order in Council or other order or to make rules or regulations, except—

(*a*) an instrument required to be laid before Parliament in draft; and
(*b*) an order under section 28 or 107 above or section 129 below,

shall be subject to annulment in pursuance of a resolution of either House of Parliament.

(3) Any such power shall include power to make such incidental, supplementary or transitional provisions as appear to the authority exercising the power to be necessary or expedient.

(4) Any such power to make an order shall, except in the case of an order made under Part III of this Act, include power to revoke or vary the order by a subsequent order made under that provision. **[427]**

COMMENCEMENT

This section was brought into force on 1st January 1976 by the Employment Protection Act 1975 (Commencement No. 1) Order 1975, S.I. 1975 No. 1938.

STATUTORY INSTRUMENT; SUBJECT TO ANNULMENT

For provisions as to statutory instruments generally, see the Statutory Instruments Act 1946; and for provisions as to instruments subject to annulment, see ss. 5 (1) and 7 (1) of that Act.

LAID BEFORE PARLIAMENT

For meaning, see the Laying of Documents before Parliament (Interpretation) Act 1948, s. 1 (1).

PART III OF THIS ACT

I.e., ss. 89–98, *ante*.

124. Financial provisions

(1) Subject to the following provisions of this section, there shall be defrayed out of moneys provided by Parliament—

(*a*) all expenses incurred by the Secretary of State or any other Minister of the Crown or any government department in consequence of the provisions of this Act;
(*b*) any expenses incurred by Mr. Speaker or by any person designated by him under section 122 above, in consequence of any enactment which is applied by that section; and
(*c*) any increase attributable to the provisions of this Act in the sums payable out of moneys so provided under any other enactment.

(2) The expenses to be so defrayed shall not include—

(*a*) any sums payable out of the National Loans Funds under section 41 above;
(*b*) any increase in the sums payable out of that Fund under section 35 of

the Redundancy Payments Act 1965 which is attributable to paragraph 17 of Part I of Schedule 16 to this Act, and any sums or increase shall be payable out of that Fund.

(3) There shall be paid out of the Maternity Pay Fund into the Consolidated Fund sums equal to the amount of any expenses incurred by the Secretary of State in exercising his functions under the provisions of this Act relating to maternity pay.

(4) There shall be paid out of the Redundancy Fund into the Consolidated Fund sums equal to the amount of—

(*a*) any expenses incurred by the Secretary of State (including expenses incurred by persons acting on his behalf) in exercising his functions under sections 64 to 68 above;

(*b*) any increase attributable to provisions of this Act in the sums falling to be so paid under section 55 (5) of the Redundancy Payments Act 1965.

(5) There shall be paid into the Consolidated Fund any sums received by a Minister of the Crown by virtue of this Act except sums which are expressly required to be paid into the Maternity Pay Fund, the Redundancy Fund or the National Insurance Fund.

(6) As respect any increase attributable to the provisions of this Act in the expenses which under section 135 (3) (*a*) of the Social Security Act 1975 are to be paid out of moneys provided by Parliament, subsection (1) (*c*) above is without prejudice to the provision made by subsection (5) of that section for reimbursement out of the National Insurance Fund. [**428**]

COMMENCEMENT

Section 124 (1), 2 (*b*), 5 and 6 was brought into force on 1st January 1976 by the Employment Protection Act 1975 (Commencement No. 1) Order 1975, S.I. 1975 No. 1938.

NATIONAL LOANS FUND

This fund is established under the National Loans Act 1968, s. 1 (1).

MATERNITY PAY FUND

See s. 39, *ante*.

MATERNITY PAY

This is payable under ss. 35 *et seq.*, *ante*.

REDUNDANCY FUND

This fund is established under the Redundancy Payments Act 1965, s. 26.

NATIONAL INSURANCE FUND

This fund is established under the Social Security Act 1975 s. 133.

125. Minor and consequential amendments, transitional provisions and repeals

(1) The provisions of the Redundancy Payments Act 1965 specified in Part I of Schedule 16 to this Act, the provisions of the Contracts of Employment Act 1972 specified in Part II of that Schedule, the provisions of the 1974 Act specified in Part III of that Schedule and the enactments specified in Part IV of that Schedule, shall have effect subject to the amendments so specified respectively, being minor amendments and amendments consequential on any provisions of this Act.

(2) The transitional provisions in Schedule 17 to this Act shall have effect.

(3) The enactments specified in Schedule 18 to this Act are hereby repealed to the extent specified in column 3 of that Schedule. [**429**]

COMMENCEMENT

This section was brought into force on 1st January, 1st February, 1st March and 20th April 1976 by the Employment Protection Act 1975 (Commencement No. 1) Order 1975, S.I. 1975 No. 1938 and the Employment Protection Act 1975 (Commencement No. 2) Order 1976, S.I. 1976 No. 144, in so far as it relates to certain parts of Schedules 16, 17 and 18; see the notes to these Schedules.

TRANSITIONAL PROVISIONS

See s. 125 (3) and Sch. 17, para. 15, *post.*

126. Interpretation

(1) In this Act, except so far as the context otherwise requires—

"associated employer", "collective agreement", "employee", "employer", "independent trade union" and "independence" and "independent" (in relation to a trade union), "official", "successor", "trade dispute", "trade union", "union membership agreement" and "worker" have the same meanings respectively as in the 1974 Act;

"business" includes a trade or profession and includes any activity carried on by a body of persons, whether corporate or unincorporate;

"collective bargaining" means negotiations relating to or connected with one or more of the matters specified in section 29 (1) of the 1974 Act;

"Committee" has the meaning assigned to it by section 10 above;

"dismiss", "dismissal" and "effective date of termination" shall be construed in accordance with paragraph 5 of Schedule 1 to the 1974 Act;

"guarantee payment" has the meaning assigned to it by section 22 above;

"maternity pay" has the meaning assigned to it by section 35 above;

"the 1974 Act" means the Trade Union and Labour Relations Act 1974;

"recognition" has the meaning assigned to it by section 11 above and cognate expressions shall be construed accordingly;

"Service" has the meaning assigned to it by section 1 above.

(2) "Employers' associations", except in Part III of this Act, has the same meaning as in the 1974 Act and in the said Part III and in any enactment thereby amended means any organisation representing employers and any association of such organisations or of employers and such organisations.

(3) Without prejudice to subsection (1) above, expressions used in the provisions of this Act relating to unfair dismissal and in provisions of the 1974 Act relating to unfair dismissal have the same meaning in this Act as in that Act.

(4) For the purposes of this Act employees are to be treated, in relation to a union membership agreement, as belonging to the same class if they have been identified as such by the parties to the agreement, and employees may be so identified by reference to any characteristics or circumstances whatsoever.

(5) The provisions of Schedule 1 to the Contracts of Employment Act 1972 (computation of period of employment) and, so far as they modify that Schedule, the provisions of any order under section 10 of that Act and any regulations under paragraph 30 (3) of Schedule 1 to the 1974 Act shall have effect for the purposes of this Act in determining for what period an employee has been continuously employed; and, for the purposes of any proceedings brought under or by virtue of this Act, a person's employment during any period shall, unless the contrary is shown, be presumed to have been continuous.

(6) In this Act references to redundancy or to being redundant, in relation to an employee, are references to—

(*a*) the fact that the employer has ceased, or intends to cease to carry on the business for the purposes of which the employee is or was employed by him, or has ceased, or intends to cease, to carry on that business in the place where the employee is or was so employed, or

(*b*) the fact that the requirements of that business for employees to carry out work of a particular kind, or for employees to carry out work of a particular kind in the place where he is or was so employed, have ceased or diminished or are expected to cease or diminish.

(7) In subsection (6) above, "cease" means cease either permanently or temporarily and from whatsoever cause, and "diminish" has a corresponding meaning.

(8) For the purposes of this Act it is immaterial whether the law which (apart from this Act) governs any person's employment is the law of the United Kingdom, or a part of the United Kingdom, or not.

(9) Except so far as the context otherwise requires, any reference in this Act to any enactment shall be construed as a reference to that enactment as amended or extended by or under any other enactment, including this Act. **[430]**

COMMENCEMENT

This section was partly brought into force in three stages on 1st January, 1st February and 8th March 1976 by the Employment Protection Act 1975 (Commencement No. 1) Order 1975, S.I. 1975 No. 1938 and the Employment Protection Act 1975 (Commencement No. 2) Order 1976, S.I. 1976 No. 144, except for s. 126 (1) so far as it relates to the definition of "guarantee payment" and "maternity pay" and s. 126 (3).

SUB-S. (2): PART III OF THIS ACT

I.e., ss. 89–98, *ante*.

SUB-S. (6): CEASE

Note the definition in sub-s. (7) above.

UNITED KINGDOM

See the note to s. 119, *ante*.

TRADE UNION AND LABOUR RELATIONS ACT 1974

Para. 5 of Sch. 1 is amended by s. 125 (1), *ante*, and Sch. 16, Part III, paras. 8–10, *post*, and para. 30 (3) is amended by Sch. 16, Part III, para. 30, *post*. "Trade union" and "employers' association" are defined in s. 28 of that Act, and "trade dispute" in s. 29 of that Act. The remaining expressions defined in sub-s. (1) above by reference to the Act of 1974 are defined in s. 30 of that Act.

127. Power to extend employment legislation

(1) Her Majesty may by Order in Council provide that the provisions of—

(*a*) the Wages Councils Act 1959;
(*b*) the Industrial Training Act 1964;
(*c*) the Redundancy Payments Act 1965;
(*d*) the Contracts of Employment Act 1972;
(*e*) the 1974 Act;
(*f*) this Act; and
(*g*) any legislation (that is to say any enactment of the Parliament of Northern Ireland and any provision made by or under a Measure of the Northern Ireland Assembly) for the time being in force in Northern Ireland which makes provision for purposes corresponding to any of the purposes of any of the Acts mentioned in paragraphs (*a*) to (*f*) above,

shall, to such extent and for such purposes as may be specified in the Order, apply (with or without modification) to or in relation to any person in employment to which this section applies.

(2) This section applies to employment for the purposes of any activities—

(*a*) in the territorial waters of the United Kingdom; or

(*b*) connected with the exploration of the sea bed or subsoil or the exploitation of their natural resources in any area designated by order under section 1 (7) of the Continental Shelf Act 1964.

(3) An Order in Council under subsection (1) above—

(*a*) may make different provision for different cases;

(*b*) may provide that all or any of the provisions of any Act mentioned in that subsection, as applied by such an Order, shall apply to individuals whether or not they are British subjects and to bodies corporate whether or not they are incorporated under the law of any part of the United Kingdom (notwithstanding that the application may affect their activities outside the United Kingdom);

(*c*) may make provision for conferring jurisdiction on any court or class of court specified in the Order, or on industrial tribunals, in respect of offences, causes of action or of matters arising in connection with employment to which this section applies;

(*d*) without prejudice to the generality of subsection (1) above or of paragraph (*a*) above, may provide that the enactments referred to in that subsection shall apply in relation to any person in employment for the purposes of such activities as are referred to in subsection (2) above in any part of the areas specified in paragraphs (*a*) and (*b*) of that subsection;

(*e*) may exclude from the operation of section 3 of the Territorial Waters Jurisdiction Act 1878 (consents required for prosecutions) proceedings for offences under the enactments referred to in subsection (1) above in connection with employment to which this section applies;

(*f*) may provide that such proceedings shall not be brought without such consent as may be required by the Order;

(*g*) may, without prejudice to the generality of the power under subsection (1) above to modify the enactments referred to in that subsection in their application for the purposes of this section, modify or exclude the operation of the following provisions (which relate to mariners and to employment wholly or partly outside Great Britain)—

(i) sections 17 and 20 of the Redundancy Payments Act 1965;

(ii) sections 9 (2) and 12 of the Contracts of Employment Act 1972;

(iii) sub-paragraphs (2) and (3) of paragraph 9 of Schedule 1 to the 1974 Act;

and also of section 119 above and of any corresponding provision in any such Northern Irish legislation as is referred to in subsection (1) (*g*) above.

(4) Any jurisdiction conferred on any court or tribunal under this section shall be without prejudice to jurisdiction exercisable apart from this section by that or any other court or tribunal. [**431**]

COMMENCEMENT

This section was brought into force on 1st January 1976 by the Employment Protection Act 1975 (Commencement No. 1) Order 1975, S.I. 1975 No. 1938.

UNITED KINGDOM

See the note to s. 119, *ante*.

INDUSTRIAL TRIBUNALS

See the note to s. 6, *ante*.

GREAT BRITAIN

See the note to s. 86, *ante*.

ORDERS IN COUNCIL UNDER THIS SECTION

At the time of going to press no Order in Council had been made under this section. The power to make Orders in Council is exercisable by statutory instrument; see the Statutory Instruments Act 1946, s. 1 (1).

128. Northern Ireland

(1) If provision is made by Northern Irish legislation (that it to say by or under a Measure of the Northern Ireland Assembly) for purposes corresponding to any of the purposes of this Act, or of the 1974 Act so far as it relates to unfair dismissal, the Secretary of State may, with the consent of the Treasury make reciprocal arrangements with the appropriate Northern Irish authority for co-ordinating the relevant provisions of this Act and the 1974 Act with the corresponding provisions of the Northern Irish legislation, so as to secure that they operate, to such extent as may be provided by the arrangements, as a single system.

(2) For the purpose of giving effect to any such arrangements the Secretary of State shall have power, in conjunction with the appropriate Northern Irish authority—

(*a*) where the arrangements relate to the provisions of this Act relating to maternity pay, to make any necessary financial adjustments between the Maternity Pay Fund and any fund established under Northern Irish legislation; and

(*b*) where the arrangements relate to the provisions of sections 64 to 68 above, to make any necessary financial adjustments between the Redundancy Fund and the Northern Ireland Redundancy Fund.

(3) The Secretary of State may make regulations for giving effect in Great Britain to any such arrangements, and any such regulations may make different provision for different cases, and may provide that this Act and the relevant provisions of the 1974 Act shall have effect in relation to persons affected by the arrangements subject to such modifications and adaptations as may be specified in the regulations, including provision—

(*a*) for securing that acts, omissions and events having any effect for the purposes of the Northern Irish legislation shall have a corresponding effect for the purposes of this Act and the relevant provisions of the 1974 Act (but not so as to confer a right to double payment in respect of the same act, omission or event); and

(*b*) for determining, in cases where rights accrue both under this Act or the relevant provisions of the 1974 Act and under the Northern Irish legislation, which of those rights shall be available to the person concerned.

(4) In this section "the appropriate Northern Irish authority" means such authority as may be specified in that behalf in the Northern Irish legislation.

[432]

COMMENCEMENT

This section was brought into force on 1st February 1976 by the Employment Protection Act 1975 (Commencement No. 1) Order 1975, S.I. 1975 No. 1938.

UNFAIR DISMISSAL

For meaning of "dismissal", see, by virtue of s. 126 (1), *ante*, the Trade Union and Labour Relations Act 1974, Sch. 1, para. 5. As to fair and unfair dismissal, see para. 6 of that Schedule.

APPROPRIATE NORTHERN IRISH AUTHORITY
For meaning, see sub-s. (4) above.

MATERNITY PAY
This is payable under ss. 35 *et seq*.

MATERNITY PAY FUND
That Fund is established under s. 39, *ante*.

REDUNDANCY FUND
The Fund is established under the Redundancy Payments Act 1965, s. 26

GREAT BRITAIN
See the note to s. 86, *ante*.

REGULATIONS UNDER THIS SECTION
At the time of going to press no regulations had been made under sub-s. (3) above. As to the making of regulations generally, see s. 123, *ante*.

129. Short title, commencement and extent

(1) This Act may be cited as the Employment Protection Act 1975.

(2) Sections 87 and 88 above and Schedule 6 to this Act shall come into operation on such day as the Lord Chancellor may by order appoint, and different days may be so appointed for different purposes.

(3) The other provisions of this Act shall come into operation on such day as the Secretary of State may by order appoint, and different days may be so appointed for different purposes.

(4) Any reference in this Act to the commencement of any provision of this Act shall be construed as a reference to the day appointed under this section for the coming into operation of that provision.

(5) Without prejudice to the generality of section 123 (3) above, an order under this section may contain such transitional provision or savings as appear to the Lord Chancellor or, as the case may be, the Secretary of State to be necessary or expedient in connection with the provisions of this Act which are thereby brought (wholly or in part) into operation, including such adaptations of those provisions then in force as appear to the Lord Chancellor or, as the case may be, the Secretary of State to be necessary or expedient in consequence of their partial operation (whether before, on or after the day appointed by the order).

(6) Sections 127 and 128 above and any provision of this Act which amends or repeals any provision of the House of Commons Disqualification Act 1975 or the Northern Ireland Assembly Disqualification Act 1975 shall extend to Northern Ireland, but except as aforesaid this Act shall not extend there.

[**433**]

ORDERS UNDER THIS SECTION
The Employment Protection Act 1975 (Commencement No. 1) Order 1975, S.I. 1975 No. 1938, the Employment Protection Act 1975 (Commencement No. 2) Order 1976, S.I. 1976 No. 144 and the Employment Protection Act 1975 (Commencement No. 3) Order 1976, S.I. 1976 No. 321, bringing parts of the Act into force as detailed in the notes to the sections and Schedules affected. As to the making of orders generally, see s. 123, *ante*.

SCHEDULES

SCHEDULE 1

Sections 1, 7 and 10

Advisory, Conciliation and Arbitration Service, etc.

Part I

Constitution, Etc. of Advisory, Conciliation and Arbitration Service and its Council

The Council

1. The Service shall be directed by a Council constituted in accordance with paragraphs 2 to 4 below and shall be a body corporate of which the corporators are the members of that Council. [**434**]

2.—(1) The Council shall consist of a full-time chairman appointed by the Secretary of State and, subject to sub-paragraphs (3) (*b*) and (4) below, nine other members appointed by the Secretary of State in accordance with sub-paragraph (2) below.

(2) Before appointing the members of the Council (other than the chairman and any deputy chairman appointed as mentioned in sub-paragraph (3) (*b*) below) the Secretary of State shall—

(*a*) as to three of them, consult such organisations representing employers as he considers appropriate; and

(*b*) as to three of them, consult such organisations representing workers as he considers appropriate.

(3) The Secretary of State may appoint up to three full-time or part-time deputy chairmen of the Council who may be appointed—

(*a*) from the members appointed in accordance with sub-paragraph (2) above or sub-paragraph (4) below; or

(*b*) in addition to those members.

(4) The Secretary of State may, if he thinks fit, appoint a further two members of the Council (who shall be appointed so as to take office at the same time) and before making those appointments he shall—

(*a*) as to one of them, consult such organisations representing employers as he considers appropriate; and

(*b*) as to one of them, consult such organisations representing workers as he considers appropriate. [**435**]

3.—(1) Subject to the following provisions of this paragraph, the members, chairman and any deputy chairman of the Council shall hold and vacate office in accordance with their terms of appointment.

(2) A person shall not be appointed to the Council for a term exceeding five years; but previous membership shall not affect eligibility for re-appointment.

(3) The Secretary of State may appoint persons to the Council either as full-time members or as part-time members.

(4) The Secretary of State may, with the consent of the member concerned, vary the terms of appointment of any member of the Council so as to provide for him to serve as a full-time member instead of a part-time member or, as the case may be, as a part-time member instead of as a full-time member.

(5) A member may at any time resign his membership, and the chairman and any deputy chairman may at any time resign his office as such, by, in each case, notice in writing addressed to the Secretary of State.

(6) A deputy chairman appointed as mentioned in paragraph 2 (3) (*b*) above shall on resigning his office as deputy chairman cease to be a member of the council.

(7) If the Secretary of State is satisfied that a member—

(*a*) has been absent from meetings of the Council for a period longer than six consecutive months without the permission of the Council; or

(*b*) has become bankrupt or made an arrangement with his creditors; or (*c*) is incapacitated by physical or mental illness; or

(*d*) is otherwise unable or unfit to discharge the functions of a member,

the Secretary of State may declare his office as a member to be vacant and shall notify the declaration in such manner as the Secretary of State thinks fit; and thereupon the office shall become vacant.

(8) (*Applies to Scotland.*)

(9) If the chairman ceases to be a member of the Council, or if a deputy chairman ceases to be a member of the Council, he shall cease to be chairman or, as the case may be, a deputy chairman. [**436**]

4.—(1) The Council shall determine its own procedure, including the quorum necessary for its meetings.

(2) If the Secretary of State has not appointed a deputy chairman the Council may choose a member to act as chairman in the absence or incapacity of the chairman. [**437**]

5. The validity of any proceedings of the Council shall not be affected by any vacancy among the members of the Council or by any defect in the appointment of any member of the Council. [**438**]

Staff

6. The Service may, with the approval of the Secretary of State, appoint a secretary, such an appointment shall not be made without the consent as to terms and conditions of service of the Secretary of State, and such consent shall not be given without the approval of the Minister for the Civil Service. [**439**]

7. The Service may appoint such other officers and servants as it may determine with the consent as to numbers, manner of appointment and terms and conditions of service of the Secretary of State; and such consent shall not be given without the approval of the Minister for the Civil Service. [**440**]

8. The Service shall provide for the Certification Officer and the Committee the requisite staff (from among the Service's officers and servants) and the requisite accommodation, equipment and other facilities. [**441**]

Supplemental

9. The Service shall maintain offices in such of the major centres of employment in Great Britain as it thinks fit for the purpose of discharging its functions under any enactment. [**442**]

10.—(1) The fixing of the common seal of the Service shall be authenticated by the signature of the secretary of the Service or some other person authorised by the Service to act for that purpose.

(2) A document purporting to be duly executed under the seal of the Service shall be received in evidence and shall, unless the contrary is proved, be deemed to be so executed. [**443**]

11.—(1) The functions of the Service and of its officers and servants shall be performed on behalf of the Crown, but, subject to paragraph 35 below, the Service shall not be subject to directions of any kind from any Minister of the Crown as to the manner in which it is to exercise any of its functions under any enactment.

(2) For the purposes of any civil proceedings arising out of those functions, the Crown Proceedings Act 1947 and the Crown Suits (Scotland) Act 1857 shall apply to the Service as if it were a government department within the meaning of the said Act of 1947 or, as the case may be, a public department within the meaning of the said Act of 1857. [**444**]

12. Nothing in section 9 of the Statistics of Trade Act 1947 (restriction on the disclosure of information obtained under that Act) shall prevent or penalise the disclosure to the Service, for the purpose of the exercise of any of its functions, of information obtained under that Act by any government department. [**445**]

13.—(1) The Service shall, as soon as practicable after the end of each calendar year, make a report to the Secretary of State on its activities and the activities of the Central Arbitration Committee during that year.

(2) The Certification Officer shall, as soon as practicable after the end of each calendar year, make a report of his activities during that year to the Service and to the Secretary of State.

(3) The Secretary of State shall lay before each House of Parliament a copy of every report received by him under sub-paragraph (1) or sub-paragraph (2) above and shall arrange for it to be published. [**446**]

COMMENCEMENT

Sch. 1, Part I was brought into force in two stages on 1st January and 1st February 1976 by the Employment Protection Act 1975 (Commencement No. 1) Order 1975, S.I. 1975 No. 1938.

CONSULT

See the note "Consultation" to s. 7, *ante*.

CERTIFICATION OFFICER

That officer is appointed under s. 7, *ante*. The expression "Certification Officer" does not, in this Part of this Schedule, include an assistant certification officer; see s. 7 (6), *ante*.

CENTRAL ARBITRATION COMMITTEE

This committee is established by s. 10, *ante*, and Part II of this Schedule, *post*.

GREAT BRITAIN

See the note to s. 86, *ante*.

DEFINITIONS

By virtue of s. 126 (1), *ante*, for "employer", see the definition inserted in the Trade Union and Labour Relations Act 1974, s. 30 (1) by s. 125 (1) *ante*, and Sch. 16, Part III, para. 7 (2), *post*, and s. 30 (2) (*b*) of that Act, and for "worker", see s. 30 (1), (2) (*a*) of that Act, for "the Service", see s. 1 (1), *ante;* for "the Committee", see s. 10 (1), *ante*.

PART II

CENTRAL ARBITRATION COMMITTEE

Constitution

14.—(1) The Committee shall consist of a chairman appointed by the Secretary of State after consultation with the Service and other members appointed by the Secretary of State in accordance with sub-paragraph (2) below.

(2) The members of the Committee (apart from the chairman) shall be appointed by the Secretary of State from persons nominated by the Service as experienced in industrial relations and shall include some persons whose experience is as representatives of employers and some persons whose experience is as representatives of workers.

(3) The Secretary of State may, after consultation with the Service, appoint one or more deputy chairmen of the Committee in addition to the existing members of the Committee. [**447**]

15.—(1) Subject to the following provisions of this paragraph, the members, chairman and any deputy chairman of the Committee shall hold and vacate office in accordance with their terms of appointment.

(2) A person shall not be appointed to the Committee for a term exceeding five years; but previous membership shall not affect eligibility for re-appointment.

(3) The Secretary of State may, with the consent of the member concerned, vary the terms of appointment of any member of the Committee so as to provide for him to serve as a full-time member instead of a part-time member or, as the case may be, as a part-time member instead of as a full-time member.

(4) A member may at any time resign his membership, and the chairman and any deputy chairman may at any time resign his office as such, by, in each case, notice in writing addressed to the Secretary of State.

(5) If the Secretary of State is satisfied that a member—

(*a*) has become bankrupt or made an arrangement with his creditors; or
(*b*) is incapacitated by physical or mental illness; or
(*c*) is otherwise unable or unfit to discharge the functions of a member,

the Secretary of State may declare his office as a member to be vacant and shall notify the declaration in such manner as the Secretary of State thinks fit; and thereupon the office shall become vacant.

(6) (*Applies to Scotland.*)

(7) If the chairman ceases to be a member of the Committee, or if a deputy chairman ceases to be a member of the Committee, he shall cease to be chairman or, as the case may be, a deputy chairman. [**448**]

16.—(1) At any time when the chairman of the Committee is absent or otherwise incapable of acting, or there is a vacancy in the office of chairman, and the Committee has a deputy chairman or deputy chairmen—

(*a*) the deputy chairman, if there is only one; or
(*b*) if there is more than one deputy chairman, such one of them as they may agree or, in default of agreement, as the Secretary of State may direct,

may perform any of the functions of the chairman of the Committee.

(2) At any time when every person who is chairman or deputy chairman of the Committee is absent or otherwise incapable of acting, or there is no such person, such member of the Committee as the Secretary of State may direct, may perform any of the functions of the chairman of the Committee. [**449**]

Proceedings

17.—(1) For the purpose of discharging any of its functions under this or any other enactment, the Committee shall, subject to sub-paragraph (2) below, consist of the chairman and such other members as the chairman may direct.

(2) The Committee may sit in two or more divisions constituted of such members as the chairman may direct, and in a division in which the chairman does not sit the functions of the chairman shall be performed by a deputy chairman.

(3) The Committee may, at the discretion of the chairman, where it appears expedient to do so, call in the aid of one or more assessors, and may settle the matter wholly or partly with their assistance. [**450**]

18. The Committee may at the discretion of the chairman sit in private where it appears expedient to do so. [**451**]

19. If in any case the Committee cannot reach a unanimous decision on its award the chairman shall decide the matter acting with the full powers of an umpire, or, in Scotland, an oversman. [**452**]

20. Subject to paragraphs 17 to 19 above, the Committee shall determine its own procedure. [**453**]

21. The validity of any proceedings of the Committee shall not be affected by any vacancy among the members of the Committee or by any defect in the appointment of any member of the Committee. [**454**]

Awards

22. The Committee may correct in any award any clerical mistake or error arising from an accidental slip or omission. [**455**]

23.—(1) If any question arises as to the interpretation of an award of the Committee, any party to the award may apply to the Committee for a decision on that question.

(2) The Committee shall decide the question after hearing the parties or, if the parties consent, without a hearing, and shall notify the parties of the decision. [**456**]

24. Decisions of the Committee in the exercise of any of its functions conferred by any enactment shall be published. [**457**]

Supplemental

25. For the purpose of assisting the Service in the discharge of its duty under paragraph 13 (1) above, the Committee shall, as soon as practicable after the end of each calendar year, transmit to the Service an account of its activities during that year. [**458**]

26. Part I of the Arbitration Act 1950 shall not apply to any proceedings of the Committee. [**459**]

27. The functions of the Committee shall be performed on behalf of the Crown, but the Committee shall not be subject to directions of any kind from any Minister of the Crown as to the manner in which it is to exercise any of its functions under any enactment. [**460**]

COMMENCEMENT

Sch. 1, Part II, was brought into force on 1st February 1976 by the Employment Protection Act (Commencement No. 1) Order 1975, S.I. 1975 No. 1938.

CONSULTATION

See the note to s. 7, *ante*.

WRITING

See the note "Written" to s. 11, *ante*.

DEFINITIONS

By virtue of s. 126 (1), *post*, for "employer", see the definition inserted in the Trade Union and Labour Relations Act 1974, s. 30 (1), by s. 125 (1), *ante*, and Sch. 16, Part III, para. 7 (2), *post*, and s. 30 (2) (*b*) of that Act, and for "worker", see s. 30 (1), (2) (*a*) of that Act, for "the Service", see s. 1 (1), *ante*; for "the Committee", see s. 10 (1), *ante*.

Part III

Supplementary Provisions

Remuneration and allowances

28. The Service shall pay to—

(*a*) members of the Council of the Service;
(*b*) members of the Central Arbitration Committee; and
(*c*) the Certification Officer and any assistant certification officer,

such remuneration and travelling and other allowances as may be determined by the Secretary of State with the approval of the Minister for the Civil Service. [**461**]

29. The Service may pay to—

(*a*) persons appointed under section 2 (2) above who are not officers or servants of the Service; and
(*b*) arbitrators or arbiters appointed by the Service under any provision of this Act or any other enactment,

such fees and travelling and other allowances as may be determined by the Secretary of State with the approval of the Minister for the Civil Service. [**462**]

Sums payable on retirement

30. The Secretary of State may pay, or make provision for paying, to, or in respect of, any holder of an office mentioned in paragraph 28 above, such pension, allowance or gratuity on the death or retirement of that office-holder as he may, with the approval of the Minister for the Civil Service, determine. [**463**]

31. Where a person ceases to be the holder of an office mentioned in paragraph 28 above otherwise than on the expiry of his term of office, and it appears to the Secretary of State that there are special circumstances which make it right for him to receive compensation, the Secretary of State may make him a payment of such amount as the Secretary of State may, with the approval of the Minister for the Civil Service, determine. [**464**]

32. The Service shall pay to the Minister for the Civil Service, at such times in each accounting year as may be determined by that Minister subject to any directions of the Treasury, sums of such amounts as he may so determine for the purpose of this paragraph as being equivalent to the increase during that year of such liabilities of his as are attributable to the provision of pensions, allowances or gratuities to or in respect of persons who are or have been in the service of the Service in so far as that increase results from the service of those persons during that accounting year and to the expense to be incurred in administering those pensions, allowances or gratuities. [**465**]

Expenses

33. The Secretary of State shall pay to the Service such sums as are approved by the Treasury and as he considers appropriate for the purpose of enabling the Service to perform its functions. [**466**]

Accounts

34. It shall be the duty of the Service to keep proper accounts and proper records in relation to the accounts. [**467**]

35.—(1) The Service shall prepare in respect of each accounting year a statement of accounts, in particular showing separately any sums disbursed to or on behalf of the Committee or the Certification Officer in consequence of the foregoing provisions of this Schedule, in such form as the Secretary of State may direct with the approval of the Treasury.

(2) The Service shall, not later than 30th November following the end of the accounting year to which the statement relates, send copies of the statement to the Secretary of State and to the Comptroller and Auditor General, and the Comptroller and Auditor General shall examine, certify and report on each such statement and shall lay copies of each statement and of his report before each House of Parliament.

(3) In this paragraph "accounting year" means the period of 12 months ending with 31st March in any year except that the first accounting year of the Service shall, if the Secretary of State so directs, be such period shorter or longer than 12 months (but not longer than two years) as is specified in the direction. [**468**]

COMMENCEMENT

Sch. 1, Part III, was partly brought into force on 1st January 1976 and brought completely into force on 1st February 1976 by the Employment Protection Act 1975 (Commencement No. 1) Order 1975, S.I. 1975 No. 1938.

COUNCIL OF THE SERVICE

This is constituted under paras. 1–4 in Part I of this Schedule, *ante*.

CENTRAL ARBITRATION COMMITTEE

This committee is established by s. 10 and Part II of this Schedule, *ante*.

CERTIFICATION OFFICER

That officer is appointed under s. 7, *ante*. This expression does not, in para. 28 above, include an assistant certification officer; see s. 7 (6), *ante*.

ASSISTANT CERTIFICATION OFFICER
See s. 7 (4), *ante*, as to the appointment of such officers.

ARBITRATORS . . . APPOINTED BY THE SERVICE
As, for example, under s. 3, *ante*.

LAY . . . BEFORE . . . PARLIAMENT
As to meaning, see the Laying of Documents before Parliament (Interpretation) Act 1948, s. 1 (1).

DEFINITIONS
For "the Service", see s. 1 (1), *ante*; for "the Committee", see s. 10 (1), *ante*. Note as to "accounting year", para. 35 (3) above.

SCHEDULE 2

Section 29

PROVISIONS LEADING TO SUSPENSION ON MEDICAL GROUNDS

1. The Paints and Colours Manufacture Regulations 1907	S.R. & O. 1907 No. 17	Reg. 5.
2. The Yarn (Dyed by Lead Compounds) Heading Regulations 1907	S.R. & O. 1907 No. 616	Reg. 4.
3. The Vitreous Enamelling Regulations 1908	S.R. & O. 1908 No. 1258	Reg. 10.
4. The Tinning of Metal Hollow-ware, Iron Drums and Harness Furniture Regulations 1909	S.R. & O. 1909 No. 720	Reg. 6.
5. The Lead Smelting and Manufacture Regulations 1911	S.R. & O. 1911 No. 752	Reg. 13.
6. The Lead Compounds Manufacture Regulations 1921	S.R. & O. 1921 No. 1443	Reg. 11.
7. The India Rubber Regulations 1922	S.R. & O. 1922 No. 329	Reg. 12.
8. The Chemical Works Regulations 1922	S.R. & O. 1922 No. 731	Reg. 30.
9. The Electric Accumulator Regulations 1925	S.R. & O. 1925 No. 28	Reg. 13.
10. The Lead Paint Regulations 1927	S.R. & O. 1927 No. 847	Reg. 6.
11. The Pottery (Health and Welfare) Special Regulations 1950	S.I. 1950 No. 65	Reg. 7.
12. The Factories Act 1961	1961 c. 34	Section 75 (2) (including that section as extended by section 128).
13. The Ionising Radiations (Unsealed Radioactive Substances) Regulations 1968	S.I. 1968 No. 780	Regs. 12 and 33.
14. The Ionising Radiations (Sealed Sources) Regulations 1969	S.I. 1969 No. 808	Regs. 11 and 30.
15. The Radioactive Substances (Road Transport Workers) (Great Britain) Regulations 1970 **[469]**	S.I. 1970 No. 1827	Reg. 14.

COMMENCEMENT
See s. 129 (3), *ante*.

AMENDMENT OF SCHEDULE
By virtue of s. 29 (3), *ante*, the Secretary of State may by order add provisions to or remove provisions from this Schedule.

Section 50

SCHEDULE 3

Supplementary Provisions as to Maternity

Introductory

1. References in this Schedule to provisions of this Act and the 1974 Act relating to unfair dismissal and to provisions of the Redundancy Payments Act 1965 are references to those provisions as they apply by virtue of section 50 above. [**470**]

Adaptation of unfair dismissal provisions

2.—(1) Paragraph 6 of Schedule 1 to the 1974 Act (fair and unfair dismissal) shall have effect as if for sub-paragraph (8) there were substituted the following sub-paragraph—

"(8) Subject to sub-paragraphs (4), (6) and (7) above, the determination of the question whether the dismissal was fair or unfair, having regard to the reason shown by the employer, shall depend on whether the employer can satisfy the tribunal that in the circumstances (having regard to equity and the substantial merits of the case) he would have been acting reasonably in treating it as a sufficient reason for dismissing the employee if she had not been absent from work.".

(2) If in the circumstances described in section 48 (4) above no offer is made of such alternative employment as is referred to in that subsection, then the dismissal which by virtue of section 50 above is treated as taking place shall, notwithstanding anything in paragraph 6 of that Schedule, be treated as an unfair dismissal for the purposes of that Schedule.

(3) The following references shall be construed as references to the notified day of return, that is to say—

(*a*) references in that Schedule and in section 74 above to the effective date of termination;

(*b*) references in section 71 above to the date of termination of employment.

(4) The following provisions of that Schedule shall not apply, that is to say, paragraphs 5, 6 (5), 9 to 14, and 30 (1A).

(5) The following provisions of this Act shall not apply, that is to say, sections 72 (7), 74 (4), (6) and (7) and 75 (1) to (3) and (6).

(6) For the purposes of Part II of Schedule 4 to this Act as it applies for the calculation of a week's pay for the purposes of section 72 or 74 above, the calculation date is the last day on which the employee worked under the original contract of employment. [**471**]

Adaptation of redundancy payments provisions

3.—(1) References in the Redundancy Payments Act 1965 shall be adapted as follows, that is to say—

(*a*) references to the relevant date, wherever they occur, shall be construed, except where the context otherwise requires, as references to the notified day of return;

(*b*) references in sections 2 (4) and 3 (3) of that Act (offer of alternative employment) to a renewal or re-engagement taking effect immediately on the ending of employment under the previous contract or after an interval of not more than four weeks thereafter, shall be construed as references to a renewal or re-engagement taking effect on the notified day of return or not more than four weeks after that day; and

(*c*) references in section 3 (5) of that Act (trial period) to the provisions of the previous contract shall be construed as references to the provisions of the original contract of employment.

(2) Nothing in section 50 above shall prevent an employee from being treated by reason of the operation of section 3 (3) of the said Act of 1965, as not having been dismissed for the purposes of that Act.

(3) The following provisions of the said Act of 1965 shall not apply, that is to say, sections 1 (1) (*b*), 2 (1) and (2), 3 (1), (2) and (10), 4 to 7, 10, 11, 16 (2) and (3), 22, 23 and 40, paragraphs 4 and 5 (3) and (7) of Schedule 1 and Schedule 4.

(4) For the purposes of Part II of Schedule 4 to this Act as it applies for the calculation of a week's pay for the purposes of Schedule 1 to the said Act of 1965 (computation of redundancy payments), the calculation date is the last day on which the employee worked under the original contract of employment. [**472**]

Dismissal during period of absence

4.—(1) This paragraph applies to the dismissal of an employee who is under the foregoing provisions of this Act entitled to return to work and whose contract of employment continues to subsist during the period of her absence but who is dismissed by her employer during that period after the beginning of the 11th week before the expected week of confinement.

(2) For the purposes of sub-paragraph (1) above an employee shall not be taken to be dismissed during the period of her absence if the dismissal occurs in the course of the employee's attempting to return to work in accordance with her contract in circumstances in which paragraph 5 below applies.

(3) In the application of Schedule 1 to the 1974 Act to a dismissal to which this paragraph applies, the following provisions shall not apply, that is to say, paragraphs 6 (5), 9, 10, 11, 13 and 14.

(4) Any such dismissal shall not affect the employee's right to return to work, but—

(*a*) compensation in any unfair dismissal proceedings arising out of that dismissal shall be assessed without regard to the employee's right to return; and

(*b*) that right shall be exercisable only on her repaying any redundancy payment or compensation for unfair dismissal paid in respect of that dismissal, if the employer requests such repayment. [**473**]

Contractual right to return

5.—(1) An employee who has a right both under this Act and under a contract of employment, or otherwise, to return to work, may not exercise the two rights separately but may in returning to work take advantage of whichever right is, in any particular respect, the more favourable.

(2) The provisions of sections 48 to 50 and paragraphs 1 to 4 above, shall apply, subject to any modifications necessary to give effect to any more favourable contractual terms, to the exercise of the composite right described in sub-paragraph (1) above as they apply to the exercise of the right to return conferred solely by this Act. [**474**]

Prior redundancy

6. If in proceedings arising out of a failure to permit an employee to return to work, the employer shows—

(*a*) that the reason for the failure is that the employee is redundant; and

(*b*) that the employee was dismissed or, had she continued to be employed by him, would have been dismissed, by reason of redundancy during her absence on a day earlier than the notified day of return and falling after the beginning of the 11th week before the expected week of confinement, then, for the purposes of the Redundancy Payments Act 1965 the employee—

(i) shall not be treated as having been dismissed with effect from the notified day of return; but

(ii) shall, if she would not otherwise be so treated, be treated as having been continuously employed until that earlier day and as having been dismissed by reason of redundancy with effect from that day. [**475**]

Power to amend or modify

7.—(1) The Secretary of State may by order amend the provisions of this Schedule or modify the application of those provisions to any description of case.

(2) No order under this paragraph shall be made unless a draft of the order has been laid before Parliament and approved by a resolution of each House of Parliament. [**476**]

COMMENCEMENT

See s. 129 (3), *ante*.

PARA. 1: PROVISIONS . . . RELATING TO UNFAIR DISMISSAL

See the note to s. 50, *ante*.

PARA. 2: TRIBUNAL

I.e., the industrial tribunal.

PARA. 4: COMPENSATION IN ANY UNFAIR DISMISSAL PROCEEDINGS

As to the award and calculation of such compensation, see ss. 72 *et seq.*, *ante*.

RIGHT TO RETURN

As to this right, see ss. 35 and 48–50, *ante*.

REDUNDANCY PAYMENT

Such payments may be made under the Redundancy Payments Act 1965, Part I, as amended by s. 125 (1), *ante*, and Sch. 16, Part I, *post*. Note also para. 3 above.

PARA. 5: RIGHT . . . TO RETURN TO WORK

See ss. 35 and 48–50, *ante*.

PARA. 6: PROCEEDINGS ARISING OUT OF A FAILURE TO PERMIT . . . RETURN TO WORK

I.e., proceedings taken by virute of s. 50 (1), *ante*.

PARA. 7: LAID BEFORE PARLIAMENT

For meaning, see the Laying of Documents before Parliament (Interpretation) Act 1948, s. 1 (1)

DEATH OF EMPLOYER OR EMPLOYEE

As to the effect of the death of an employee or employer, see s. 110, *ante*, and Sch. 12, *post*.

DEFINITIONS

By virtue, where required, of s. 126 (1), *post*, for "employer", see the definition inserted in the Trade Union and Labour Relations Act 1974, s. 30 (1), by s. 125 (1), *ante*, and Sch. 16, Part III, para. 7 (2), *post*, and s. 30 (2) (*b*), of that Act, for "employee" see s. 30 (1) of that Act, and for "dismiss" and "dismissal", see Sch. 1, para. 5, to that Act; for "to return to work", see s. 48 (3), *ante*; for "notified day of return", see s. 49 (1), *ante*; for "confinement", "expected week of confinement", "original contract of employment", and "week", see s. 52, *ante*; for "redundancy" and "redundant", see s. 126 (6), *ante*.

ORDERS UNDER THIS SCHEDULE

At the time of going to press no order had been made under para. 7 above.

As to the making of orders generally, see s. 123, *ante*.

SCHEDULE 4

Section 85

CALCULATION OF NORMAL WORKING HOURS AND A WEEK'S PAY

PART I

NORMAL WORKING HOURS

1. For the purposes of this Schedule the cases where there are normal working hours include cases where the employee is entitled to overtime pay when employed for more than a fixed number of hours in a week or other period, and, subject to paragraph 2 below, in those cases that fixed number of hours shall be the normal working hours. [**477**]

2. If in such a case—

(*a*) the contract of employment fixes the number, or the minimum number, of hours of employment in the said week or other period (whether or not it also provides for the reduction of that number or minimum in certain circumstances), and

(*b*) that number or minimum number of hours exceeds the number of hours without overtime,

that number or minimum number of hours (and not the number of hours without overtime) shall be the normal working hours. [**478**]

PART II

A WEEK'S PAY

Employments for which there are normal working hours

3.—(1) This paragraph and paragraph 4 below shall apply if there are normal working hours for an employee when employed under the contract of employment in force on the calculation date.

(2) Subject to paragraph 4 below, if an employee's remuneration for employment in normal working hours, whether by the hour or week or other period, does not vary with the amount of work done in the period, the amount of a week's pay shall be the amount which is payable by the employer under the contract of employment in force on the calculation date if the employee works throughout his normal working hours in a week.

(3) Subject to paragraph 4 below, if sub-paragraph (2) above does not apply, the amount of a week's pay shall be the amount of remuneration for the number of normal working hours in a week calculated at the average hourly rate of remuneration payable by the employer to the employee in respect of the period of 12 weeks—

(*a*) where the calculation date is the last day of a week, ending with that week;

(*b*) in any other case, ending with the last complete week before the calculation date.

(4) References in this paragraph to remuneration varying with the amount of work done include references to remuneration which may include any commission or similar payment which varies in amount. [**479**]

4.—(1) This paragraph shall apply if there are normal working hours for an employee when employed under the contract of employment in force on the calculation date, and he is required under that contract to work during those hours on days of the week or at times of the day which differ from week to week or over a longer period so that the remuneration payable for, or apportionable to, any week varies according to the incidence of the said days or times.

(2) The amount of a week's pay shall be the amount of remuneration for the average weekly number of normal working hours (calculated in accordance with sub-paragraph (3) below) at the average hourly rate of remuneration (calculated in accordance with sub-paragraph (4) below).

(3) The average number of weekly hours shall be calculated by dividing by 12 the total number of the employee's normal working hours during the period of 12 weeks—

(*a*) where the calculation date is the last day of a week, ending with that week;

(*b*) in any other case, ending with the last complete week before the calculation date.

(4) The average hourly rate of remuneration shall be the average hourly rate of remuneration payable by the employer to the employee in respect of the period of 12 weeks—

(*a*) where the calculation date is the last day of a week, ending with that week;

(*b*) in any other case, ending with the last complete week before the calculation date. [**480**]

5.—(1) For the purpose of paragraphs 3 and 4 above, in arriving at the average hourly rate of remuneration only the hours when the employee was working, and only the remuneration payable for, or, apportionable to, those hours of work, shall be brought in; and if for any of the 12 weeks mentioned in either of those paragraphs no such remuneration was payable by the employer to the employee, account shall be taken of remuneration in earlier weeks so as to bring the number of weeks of which account is taken up to 12.

(2) Where, in arriving at the said hourly rate of remuneration, account has to be taken of remuneration payable for, or apportionable to, work done in hours other than normal working hours, and the amount of that remuneration was greater than it would have been if the work had been done in normal working hours, account shall be taken of that remuneration as if—

(*a*) the work had been done in normal working hours; and

(*b*) the amount of that remuneration had been reduced accordingly.

(3) For the purpose of the application of sub-paragraph (2) above to a case falling within paragraph 2 above, sub-paragraph (2) shall be construed as if for the words "had been done in normal working hours", in each place where those words occur, there were substituted the words "had been done in normal working hours falling within the number of hours without overtime". [**481**]

Employments for which there are no normal working hours

6.—(1) This paragraph shall apply if there are no normal working hours for an employee when employed under the contract of employment in force on the calculation date.

(2) The amount of a week's pay shall be the amount of the employee's average weekly remuneration in the period of 12 weeks—

(*a*) where the calculation date is the last day of a week, ending with that week;

(*b*) in any other case, ending with the last complete week before the calculation date.

(3) In arriving at the said average weekly rate of remuneration no account shall be taken of a week in which no remuneration was payable by the employer to the employee and remuneration in earlier weeks shall be brought in so as to bring the number of weeks of which account is taken up to 12. [**482**]

Supplemental

7. In any case in which an employee has not been employed for a sufficient period to enable a calculation to be made under any of the foregoing provisions of this Part of this Schedule, the amount of a week's pay shall be an amount which fairly represents a week's pay; and in determining that amount the tribunal shall apply as nearly as may be such of the foregoing provisions of this Part as it con-

siders appropriate, and may have regard to such of the following considerations as it thinks fit, that is to say—

(*a*) any remuneration received by the employee in respect of the employment in question;

(*b*) the amount offered to the employee as remuneration in respect of the employment in question;

(*c*) the remuneration received by other persons engaged in relevant comparable employment with the same employer;

(*d*) the remuneration received by other persons engaged in relevant comparable employment with other employers. [**483**]

8. In arriving at an average hourly rate or average weekly rate of remuneration under this Part of this Schedule—

(*a*) account shall be taken of work for a former employer within the period for which the average is to be taken if, by virtue of Schedule 1 to the Contracts of Employment Act 1972 (computation of period of employment) a period of employment with the former employer counts as part of the employee's continuous period of employment with the later employer, and

(*b*) "week" means, for an employee whose remuneration is calculated weekly by a week ending with a day other than Saturday, a week ending with that other day, and, for other employees, means a week ending with Saturday. [**484**]

9. Where under this Part of this Schedule account is to be taken of remuneration or other payments for a period which does not coincide with the periods for which the remuneration or other payments are calculated, then the remuneration or other payments shall be apportioned in such manner as may be just. [**485**]

10. The Secretary of State may by regulations provide that in prescribed cases the amount of a week's pay shall be calculated in such manner as the regulations may prescribe. [**486**]

COMMENCEMENT

This Schedule was brought into force on 8th March 1975 by the Employment Protection Act 1975 (Commencement No. 2) Order 1976, S.I. 1976 No. 144, to the extent that s. 85 (1) came into effect, i.e. so far as it relates to the purposes of s. 102.

GENERAL NOTE

This Schedule has, by virtue of s. 85, *ante*, effect for calculating normal working hours and the amount of a week's wages of an employee for the purposes of this Act and the other enactments referred to in s. 85, *ante*.

CALCULATION DATE

This date is specified in each provision of the Act to which Part II of this Schedule applies for the purposes of calculating a week's pay; see, for example, s. 24 (3), *ante* (calculation of guarantee payment), s. 37 (5), *ante* (calculation of maternity pay), s. 61 (5), *ante* (time off to look for work), s. 70 (6), *ante* (written statement of reasons for dismissal) s. 72 (7), *ante* (enforcement of re-instatement or re-engagement order after unfair dismissal, and compensation) and s. 75 (1), *ante* (provisions supplementary to s. 74 *ante* (calculation of basic award)).

TRIBUNAL

I.e., the industrial tribunal.

DEFINITIONS

By virtue of s. 126 (1), *post*, for "employer", see the definition inserted in the Trade Union and Labour Relations Act 1974, s. 30 (1), by s. 125 (1), *ante*, and Sch. 16, Part III, para. 7 (2), *post*, and s. 30 (2) (*b*) of that Act, and for "employee", see s. 30 (1) of that Act. As to "week" in Part II, note para. 8 (*b*) above.

REGULATIONS UNDER THIS SCHEDULE

At the time of going to press no regulations had been made under para. 10 above.

As to the making of regulations generally, see s. 123, *ante*.

SCHEDULE 5

Section 85

SCHEDULE 2 TO THE CONTRACTS OF EMPLOYMENT ACT 1972, AS SUBSTITUTED

RIGHTS OF EMPLOYEE IN PERIOD OF NOTICE

Preliminary

1.—(1) In this Schedule—

(*a*) the "period of notice" means the period of notice required by section 1 (1) or, as the case may be, section 1 (2) of this Act; and

(*b*) "normal working hours" shall be construed in accordance with Part I of Schedule 4 to the Employment Protection Act 1975.

(2) For the purposes of Part II of Schedule 4 to the Employment Protection Act 1975 as it applies for the calculation of a week's pay for the purposes of this Schedule, the calculation date is the day immediately preceding the first day of the period of notice. [**487**]

Employments for which there are normal working hours

2.—(1) If an employee has normal working hours under the contract of employment in force during the period of notice, and if during any part of those normal working hours—

(*a*) the employee is ready and willing to work but no work is provided for him by his employer; or

(*b*) the employee is incapable of work because of sickness or injury; or

(*c*) the employee is absent from work in accordance with the terms of his employment relating to holidays,

then the employer shall be liable to pay the employee for the part of normal working hours covered by paragraphs (*a*), (*b*) and (*c*) above a sum not less than the amount of remuneration for that part of normal working hours calculated at the average hourly rate of remuneration produced by dividing a week's pay by the number of normal working hours.

(2) Any payments made to the employee by his employer in respect of the relevant part of the period of notice whether by way of sick pay, holiday pay or otherwise, shall go towards meeting the employer's liability under this paragraph.

(3) Where notice was given by the employee, the employer's liability under this paragraph shall not arise unless and until the employee leaves the service of the employer in pursuance of the notice. [**488**]

Employments for which there are no normal working hours

3.—(1) If an employer does not have normal working hours under the contract of employment in force in the period of notice the employer shall be liable to pay the employee for each week of the period of notice a sum not less than a week's pay.

(2) Subject to the next following sub-paragraph, the employer's obligation under this paragraph shall be conditional on the employee being ready and willing to do work of a reasonable nature and amount to earn a week's pay.

(3) Sub-paragraph (2) shall not apply—

(*a*) in respect of any period during which the employee is incapable of work because of sickness or injury, or

(*b*) in respect of any period during which the employee is absent from work in accordance with the terms of his employment relating to holidays,

and any payment made to an employee by his employer in respect of such a period, whether by way of sick pay, holiday pay or otherwise, shall be taken into account for the purposes of this paragraph as if it were remuneration paid by the employer in respect of that period.

(4) Where the notice was given by the employee, the employer's liability under

this paragraph shall not arise unless and until the employee leaves the service of the employer in pursuance of the notice. [**489**]

Sickness or industrial injury benefit

4.—(1) The following provisions of this paragraph shall have effect where the arrangements in force relating to the employment are such that—

(*a*) payments by way of sick pay are made by the employer to employees to whom the arrangements apply, in cases where any such employees are incapable of work because of sickness or injury and

(*b*) in calculating any payment so made to any such employee an amount representing, or treated as representing, sickness benefit or industrial injury benefit is taken into account, whether by way of deduction or by way of calculating the payment as a supplement to that amount.

(2) If during any part of the period of notice the employee is incapable of work because of sickness or injury, and—

(*a*) one or more payments, by way of sick pay are made to him by the employer in respect of that part of the period of notice, and

(*b*) in calculating any such payment such an amount as is referred to in sub-paragraph (1) (*b*) of this paragraph is taken into account as therein mentioned,

then for the purposes of this Schedule the amount so taken into account shall be treated as having been paid by the employer to the employee by way of sick pay in respect of that part of that period, and shall go towards meeting the liability of the employer under paragraph 2 or paragraph 3 of this Schedule accordingly. [**490**]

Absence on leave granted at request of employee

5. The employer shall not be liable under the foregoing provisions of this Schedule to make any payment in respect of a period during which the employee is absent from work with the leave of the employer granted at the request of the employee (including any period of time off taken in accordance with section 57, 58, 59 or 61 of the Employment Protection Act 1975). [**491**]

Notice given before a strike

6. No payment shall be due under this Schedule in consequence of a notice to terminate a contract given by an employee if, after the notice is given and on or before the termination of the contract, the employee takes part in a strike of employees of the employer.

In this paragraph "strike" has the same meaning as in Schedule 1 to this Act. [**492**]

Termination of employment during period of notice

7.—(1) If, during the period of notice, the employer breaks the contract of employment, payments received under this Schedule in respect of the part of the period after the breach shall go towards mitigating the damages recoverable by the employee for loss of earnings in that part of the period of notice.

(2) If, during the period of notice, the employee breaks the contract and the employer rightfully treats the breach as terminating the contract, no payment shall be due to the employee under this Schedule in respect of the part of the period of notice falling after the termination of the contract. [**493**]

COMMENCEMENT

See s. 129 (3), *ante*.

WEEK'S PAY

As to the calculation of a week's pay, see s. 85 (1) and Sch. 4, Part II, *ante*.

DEFINITIONS

For "employee" and cognate expressions, see the Contracts of Employment Act 1972, s. 11 (1). As to "normal working hours" and "period of notice", note para. 1 above.

SCHEDULE 6

Section 87

EMPLOYMENT APPEAL TRIBUNAL

PART I

PROVISIONS AS TO MEMBERSHIP, SITTINGS, PROCEEDINGS AND POWERS

Tenure of office of appointed members of Appeal Tribunal

1. Subject to paragraphs 2 and 3 below, a member of the Appeal Tribunal appointed by Her Majesty under section 87 (2) (*c*) above (in this Schedule referred to as an "appointed member") shall hold and vacate office as such a member in accordance with the terms of his appointment. [**494**]

2. An appointed member may at any time resign his membership by notice in writing addressed to the Lord Chancellor and the Secretary of State. [**495**]

3.—(1) If the Lord Chancellor, after consultation with the Secretary of State, is satisfied that an appointed member—

(*a*) has been absent from sittings of the Appeal Tribunal for a period longer than six consecutive months without the permission of the President of the Tribunal; or
(*b*) has become bankrupt or made an arrangement with his creditors; or
(*c*) is incapacitated by physical or mental illness; or
(*d*) is otherwise unable or unfit to discharge the functions of a member;

the Lord Chancellor may declare his office as a member to be vacant and shall notify the declaration in such manner as the Lord Chancellor thinks fit; and thereupon the office shall become vacant. [**496**]

(2) (*Applies to Scotland.*)

Temporary membership of Appeal Tribunal

4. At any time when the office of President of the Appeal Tribunal is vacant, or the person holding that office is temporarily absent or otherwise unable to act as president of the Tribunal, the Lord Chancellor may nominate another judge nominated under section 87 (2) (*a*) above to act temporarily in his place. [**497**]

5. At any time when a judge of the Appeal Tribunal nominated by the Lord Chancellor is temporarily absent or otherwise unable to act as a judge of that Tribunal, the Lord Chancellor may nominate another person who is qualified to be nominated under section 87 (2) (*a*) above to act temporarily in his place. [**498**]

6. At any time when a judge of the Appeal Tribunal nominated by the Lord President of the Court of Session is temporarily absent or otherwise unable to act as a judge of the Appeal Tribunal, the Lord President may nominate another judge of the Court of Session to act temporarily in his place. [**499**]

7. At any time when an appointed member is temporarily absent or otherwise unable to act as a member of the Appeal Tribunal, the Lord Chancellor and the Secretary of State may jointly appoint a person appearing to them to have the qualifications for appointment as such a member to act temporarily in his place. [**500**]

8. A person appointed to act temporarily in place of the President or any other member of the Appeal Tribunal shall, when so acting, have all the functions of the person in whose place he acts. [**501**]

9. No judge shall be nominated under paragraph 5 or 6 above except with his consent. [**502**]

Organisation and sittings of Appeal Tribunal

10. The Appeal Tribunal shall be a superior court of record and shall have an official seal which shall be judicially noticed. [**503**]

11. The Appeal Tribunal shall have a central office in London. [**504**]

12. The Appeal Tribunal may sit at any time and in any place in Great Britain. [**505**]

13. The Appeal Tribunal may sit, in accordance with directions given by the President of the Tribunal, either as a single tribunal or in two or more divisions concurrently. [**506**]

14. With the consent of the parties to any proceedings before the Appeal Tribunal, the proceedings may be heard by a judge and one appointed member, but, in default of such consent, any proceedings before the Tribunal shall be heard by a judge and either two or four appointed members, so that in either case there are equal numbers of persons whose experience is as representatives of employers and whose experience is as representatives of workers. [**507**]

Rules

15.—(1) The Lord Chancellor, after consultation with the Lord President of the Court of Session, shall make rules with respect to proceedings before the Appeal Tribunal.

(2) Subject to those rules, the Tribunal shall have power to regulate its own procedure. [**508**]

16.—(1) Without prejudice to the generality of paragraph 15 above, the rules may include provision—

(*a*) with respect to the manner in which an appeal may be brought and the time within which it may be brought;
(*b*) for requiring persons to attend to give evidence and produce documents, and for authorising the administration of oaths to witnesses;
(*c*) enabling the Appeal Tribunal to sit in private for the purpose of hearing evidence to hear which an industrial tribunal may sit in private by virtue of paragraph 21 (5) of Schedule 1 to the 1974 Act. [**509**]

17.—(1) Without prejudice to the generality of paragraph 15 above, the rules may empower the Appeal Tribunal to order a party to any proceedings before the Tribunal to pay to any other party to the proceedings the whole or part of the costs or expenses incurred by that other party in connection with the proceedings, where in the opinion of the Tribunal—

(*a*) the proceedings were unnecessary, improper or vexatious, or
(*b*) there has been unreasonable delay or other unreasonable conduct in bringing or conducting the proceedings.

(2) Except as provided by sub-paragraph (1) above, the rules shall not enable the Appeal Tribunal to order the payment of costs or expenses by any party to proceedings before the Tribunal. [**510**]

18. Any person may appear before the Appeal Tribunal in person or be represented by counsel or by a solicitor or by a representative of a trade union or an employers' association or by any other person whom he desires to represent him. [**511**]

Powers of Tribunal

19.—(1) For the purpose of disposing of an appeal the Appeal Tribunal may exercise any powers of the body or officer from whom the appeal was brought or may remit the case to that body or officer. [**512**]

(2) Any decision or award of the Appeal Tribunal on an appeal shall have the same effect and may be enforced in the same manner as a decision or award of a body or officer from whom the appeal was brought. [**513**]

20.—(1) The Appeal Tribunal shall, in relation to the attendance and examination of witnesses, the production and inspection of documents and all other matters incidental to its jurisdiction, have the like powers, rights, privileges and authority—

(*a*) in England and Wales, as the High Court,
(*b*) (*applies to Scotland*).

(2) No person shall be punished for contempt of the Tribunal except by, or with the consent of, a judge. [**514**]

21.—(1) In relation to any fine imposed by the Appeal Tribunal for contempt of the Tribunal, section 14 of the Criminal Justice Act 1948 and section 47 of the Criminal Justice Act 1967 (which relate to fines imposed and recognizances forfeited at certain courts) shall have effect as if in those provisions any reference to the Crown Court included a reference to the Tribunal.

(2) A magistrates' court shall not remit the whole or any part of a fine imposed by the Appeal Tribunal except with the consent of a judge who is a member of the Tribunal.

(3) This paragraph does not extend to Scotland. [**515**]

Staff

22. The Secretary of State may appoint such officers and servants of the Appeal Tribunal as he may determine, subject to the approval of the Minister for the Civil Service as to numbers and as to terms and conditions of service. [**516**]

Part II

Supplementary

Remuneration and allowances

23. The Secretary of State shall pay the appointed members of the Appeal Tribunal, the persons appointed to act temporarily as appointed members, and the officers and servants of the Tribunal such remuneration and such travelling and other allowances as he may with the approval of the Minister for the Civil Service determine. [**517**]

Pensions, etc.

24. If the Secretary of State determines, with the approval of the Minister for the Civil Service, that this paragraph shall apply in the case of an appointed member, the Secretary of State shall pay such pension, allowance or gratuity to or in respect of that member on his retirement or death or make that member such payments towards the provision of such a pension, allowance or gratuity as the Secretary of State may with the like approval determine. [**518**]

25. Where a person ceases to be an appointed member otherwise than on his retirement or death and it appears to the Secretary of State that there are special circumstances which make it right for him to receive compensation, the Secretary of State may make him a payment of such amount as the Secretary of State may, with the approval of the Minister for the Civil Service, determine. [**519**]

COMMENCEMENT

This Schedule was brought into force on 30th March 1976 by the Employment Protection Act 1975 (Commencement No. 3) Order 1976, S.I. 1976 No. 321.

CONSULTATION

See the note to s. 7, *ante*.

PRESIDENT

The President is appointed under s. 87 (4), *ante*.

GREAT BRITAIN

See the note to s. 86, *ante*.

DEFINITIONS

By virtue of s. 126 (1), *post*, for "employer", see the definition inserted in the Trade Union and Labour Relations Act 1974, s. 30 (1) by s. 125, *ante*, and Sch. 16, Part III, para. 7 (2), *post*, and s. 30 (2) (*b*) of that Act, for "worker", see s. 30 (1), (2) (*a*) of that Act, for "trade union", see s. 28 of that Act, Vol. 44, p. 1842; for "employer's associations", see s. 126 (2), *ante*.; As to "appointed member", note para. 1 above.

RULES UNDER THIS SCHEDULE

The Employment Appeal Tribunal Rules 1976, S.I. 1976 No. 322, made under para. 15 above.

As to the making of rules generally, see s. 123, *ante*.

SCHEDULE 7

Section 89

Amendments of Wages Councils Act 1959

Part I

Section 11, as Substituted

Note: This Part of the Schedule reproduces section 11 with amendments enabling wages councils, instead of the Secretary of State, to make orders under that section and enabling wages councils to fix other terms and conditions of employment as well as remuneration and holidays and to specify the date from which remuneration fixed by them is to be payable.

11. Power to fix terms and conditions of employment

(1) A wages council may make an order, subject to and in accordance with the provisions of this section,—

(*a*) fixing the remuneration,
(*b*) requiring holidays to be allowed,
(*c*) fixing any other terms and conditions,

for all or any of the workers in relation to whom the council operates.

(2) An order under this section requiring a holiday to be allowed for a worker—

(*a*) shall not be made unless both holiday remuneration in respect of the period of the holiday and remuneration other than holiday remuneration have been or are being fixed under this Part of this Act for that worker;
(*b*) shall provide for the duration of the holiday being related to the duration of the period for which the worker has been employed or engaged to be employed by the employer who is to allow the holiday; and
(*c*) subject as aforesaid, may make provision as to the times at which or the periods within which, and the circumstances in which, the holiday shall be allowed.

(2A) Any order under this section fixing holiday remuneration may contain provisions—

(*a*) as to the times at which, and the conditions subject to which, that remuneration shall accrue and shall become payable, and
(*b*) for securing that any such remuneration which has accrued due to a worker during his employment by any employer shall, in the event of his ceasing to be employed by that employer before he becomes entitled to be allowed a holiday by him, nevertheless become payable by the employer to the worker.

(3) Before making an order under this section, a wages council shall make such investigations as it thinks fit and shall—

(*a*) publish in the prescribed manner notice of the council's proposals with respect to any new terms and conditions of employment (that is to say, any terms and conditions of employment differing from any then in force by virtue of an order made under this section); and (*b*) give the prescribed notice for the purpose of informing, so far as practicable, all persons affected by the proposals, stating the place where copies of the proposals may be obtained and the period (which shall not be less than fourteen days from the date of publication of the notice) within which written representations with respect to the proposals may be sent to the council.

(3A) After considering any written representations made with respect to any such proposals within the said period and making such further inquiries as the council considers necessary, or if no such representations are made within that period, after the expiration of that period, the wages council may make an order—

(*a*) giving effect to the proposals; or

(*b*) giving effect to them with such modifications as the council thinks fit having regard to any such representations;

but if it appears to the council that, having regard to the nature of any proposed modifications, an opportunity should be given to persons concerned to consider the modifications, the council shall again publish the proposals and give notice under subsection (3) of this section, and that subsection and this subsection shall apply accordingly.

(4) An order under this section shall have effect as regards any terms as to remuneration as from a date specified in the order, which may be a date earlier than the date of the order but not earlier than the date on which the council agreed on those terms prior to publishing the original proposals to which effect is given, with or without modifications, by the order; but where any such order fixing workers' remuneration applies to any worker who is paid wages at intervals not exceeding seven days and the date so specified does not correspond with the beginning of the period for which the wages are paid (hereafter in this section referred to as a wages period), the order shall, as respects that worker, have effect as from the beginning of the next wages period following the date specified in the order.

(4A) Any increase in remuneration payable by virtue of an order under this section in respect of any time before the date of the order shall be paid by the employer within a period specified in the order, being—

(*a*) in the case of a worker who is in the employment of the employer on the date of the order, a period beginning with that date;

(*b*) in the case of a worker who is no longer in the employment of the employer on that date, a period beginning with the date on which the employer receives from the worker or a person acting on his behalf a request in writing for the remuneration;

but if, in the case of a worker falling within paragraph (*a*) of this subsection who is paid wages at intervals not exceeding seven days, pay day (the day on which wages are normally paid to him) for any wages period falling wholly or partly within the period so specified occurs within seven days from the end of that specified period, any such remuneration shall be paid not later than pay day.

(5) As soon as a wages council has made an order under this section it shall give the prescribed notice of the making and contents of the order and shall then and subsequently give such notice of other prescribed matters affecting its operation for the purpose of informing, so far as practicable, all persons who will be affected by it.

(6) An order under this section may make different provision for different cases and may amend or revoke previous orders under this section.

(7) A document purporting to be a copy of an order made by a wages council under this section and to be signed by the secretary of the council shall be taken to be a true copy of the order unless the contrary is proved.

(8) An order under this section shall not prejudice any rights conferred on any worker by or under any other enactment. [**520**]

COMMENCEMENT

This Schedule was brought into force on 1st January 1976 by the Employment Protection Act (Commencement No. 1) Order 1975, S.I. 1975 No. 1938.

WAGES COUNCIL

Those councils are established under the Wages Councils Act 1959, s. 1.

THIS PART OF THIS ACT

I.e., the Wages Councils Act 1959, Part II (ss. 11–21).

WRITTEN

See the note to s. 11, *ante*.

PERIOD BEGINNING, ETC.

See the note "Period of 14 days (two months) beginning, etc". to s. 15, *ante*.

WITHIN SEVEN DAYS FROM

See the note "One month after, etc." to s. 8, *ante*.

DEFINITIONS

For "prescribed", "wages council" and "worker", see the Wages Councils Act 1959, s. 24, as amended by para. 9 in Part IV of this Schedule, *post*. As to "wages period", note sub-s. (4) of the new s. 11, above.

WAGES COUNCILS ACT 1959, S. 11

See Vol. 12, p. 167.

PART II

SECTION 12, AS SUBSTITUTED

NOTE: This Part of this Schedule reproduces section 12 with amendments substituting any terms and conditions of employment fixed by an order under section 11 (as well as remuneration so fixed) for those contained in a worker's contract of employment, making it an offence to fail to pay arrears of remuneration related to a period before the making of any such order and increasing the powers of a convicting court to order an employer to pay the remuneration or arrears.

12. Effect and enforcement of orders under section 11

(1) If a contract between a worker to whom an order under section 11 of this Act applies and his employer provides for the payment of less remuneration than the statutory minimum remuneration, it shall have effect as if the statutory minimum remuneration were substituted for the remuneration provided for in the contract, and if any such contract provides for the payment of any holiday remuneration at times or subject to conditions other than those specified in the order, it shall have effect as if the times or conditions specified in the order were substituted for those provided for in the contract.

(1A) If any such contract fixes terms and conditions other than those relating to remuneration or wages which are less favourable than the corresponding terms and conditions specified in an order under section 11 of this Act it shall have effect as if the corresponding terms and conditions were substituted for those fixed by the contract.

(2) If an employer fails—

(*a*) to pay a worker to whom an order under section 11 of this Act applies remuneration not less than the statutory minimum remuneration; or

(*b*) to pay him arrears of remuneration before the expiration of the period specified in the order; or

(*c*) to pay him holiday remuneration at the times and subject to the conditions specified in the order, or

(*d*) to allow to any such worker the holidays fixed by the order;

he shall for each offence be liable on summary conviction to a fine not exceeding £100.

(3) Where proceedings are brought under the foregoing subsection in respect of an offence consisting of a failure to pay remuneration not less than the statutory minimum remuneration, or to pay arrears of remuneration, and the employer or any other person charged as a person to whose act or default the offence was due is found guilty of the offence, then, subject to subsection (3A) below—

(*a*) evidence may be given of any failure on the part of the employer to pay any such remuneration or arrears during the two years ending with the date of the offence to any worker employed by him; and

(*b*) on proof of the failure, the court may order the employer to pay such sum as is found by the court to represent the difference between the amount of any such remuneration or arrears which ought to have been paid during that period to any such worker, if the provisions of this Part of this Act had been complied with, and the amount actually so paid.

(3A) Evidence of any failure to pay any such remuneration or arrears may be given under subsection (3) of this section only if—

(*a*) the employer or any other person charged as aforesaid has been convicted of the offence consisting of the failure; and

(*b*) notice of intention to adduce such evidence has been served with the summons or warrant.

(4) The powers given by this section for the recovery of sums due from an employer to a worker shall not be in derogation of any right to recover such sums by civil proceedings.

(5) (*Applies to Scotland.*) [**521**]

COMMENCEMENT
This Schedule was brought into force on 1st January 1976 by the Employment Protection Act 1975 (Commencement No. 1) Order 1975, S.I. 1975 No. 1938.

OFFENCE
As to the defences available to an employer when charged with an offence under the Wages Councils Act 1959, Part II, see s. 18 of that Act.

SUMMARY CONVICTION
See the note to s. 68, *ante*.

THIS PART OF THIS ACT
I.e., Part II of the Wages Councils Act 1959, Part II (ss. 11–21).

DEFINITIONS
For "statutory minimum remuneration" and "worker", see the Wages Councils Act 1959, s. 24, as amended by paras. 1 and 9 in Part IV of this Schedule, *post*.

Part III

Schedule 2, as Substituted

Note: This Part of this Schedule reproduces Schedule 2 with amendments as to the method and terms of appointment of members of wages councils.

Constitution, Officers and Proceedings of Wages Councils and Co-ordinating Committees

1.—(1) A wages council or, subject to paragraph 2 of this Schedule, central coordinating committee shall consist of—

(*a*) not more than three persons appointed by the Secretary of State as being independent persons;

(*b*) such number of persons appointed to represent employers and workers on the council or committee as falls within the limits for the time being specified for the purposes of this paragraph by the Secretary of State.

(2) Subject to sub-paragraphs (4) and (5) of this paragraph, the persons ap-

pointed under the foregoing sub-paragraph to represent employers shall be appointed by one or more employers' associations for the time being nominated for that purpose by the Secretary of State and those so appointed to represent workers shall be appointed by one or more trade unions so nominated.

(3) A nominated employers' association or trade union shall on making such an appointment inform the secretary of the wages council or central co-ordinating committee, in writing, of that appointment.

(4) If the nominated employers' association or the nominated trade union are unable to agree on such an appointment, they shall consult the Secretary of State who may make the appointment on their behalf.

(5) If it appears to the Secretary of State that an insufficient number of persons has been appointed to represent either employers or workers on a wages council or central co-ordinating committee he may, after consultation with such persons or organisations as he thinks fit, himself appoint such number of persons for the purpose as will secure a sufficiency of representatives of employers or workers, as the case may be, on the council or committee.

(6) Of the independent persons appointed under sub-paragraph (1) (*a*) above, one shall be appointed by the Secretary of State to act as chairman, and another may be appointed by the Secretary of State to act as chairman in the absence of the chairman. **[522]**

2.—(1) A central co-ordinating committee operating in relation only to two or more statutory joint industrial councils shall consist of equal numbers of persons appointed by one or more employers' associations to represent employers on the committee and of persons appointed by one or more trade unions to represent workers on the committee.

(2) Any such committee shall elect a chairman and deputy chairman from among its members. **[523]**

3. The Secretary of State may on the application of a wages council or central co-ordinating committee make such changes in the number of members or the machinery for appointing them as is necessary or expedient in the circumstances. **[524]**

4. The Secretary of State may appoint a secretary and such other officers as he thinks fit of a wages council or central co-ordinating committee. **[525]**

5. The proceedings of a wages council or central co-ordinating committee shall not be invalidated by reason of any vacancy therein or by any defect in the appointment of a member. **[526]**

6.—(1) A wages council or central co-ordinating committee may delegate any of its functions, other than the power to make orders under section 11 of this Act, to a committee or sub-committee consisting of such number of members of the council as the council or committee thinks fit.

(2) The number of members representing employers and the number of members representing workers on a committee of a council or any such sub-committee shall be equal. **[527]**

7. The Secretary of State may make regulations as to the meetings and procedure of a wages council or central co-ordinating committee and of any committee or, as the case may be, sub-committee thereof, including regulations as to the quorum and the method of voting, but, subject to the provisions of this Act and to any regulations so made, a wages council or central co-ordinating committee and any committee or, as the case may be, sub-committee thereof may regulate its procedure in such manner as it thinks fit. **[528]**

8.—(1) A member of a wages council or central co-ordinating committee shall hold and vacate office in accordance with the terms of his appointment, but the period for which he is to hold office, shall, without prejudice to his re-appointment, not exceed five years.

(2) Where the term for which the members of a wages council or central co-ordinating committee were appointed comes to an end before their successors are appointed, those members shall, except so far as the Secretary of State or, as the case may be, the appointing body otherwise directs, continue in office until the new appointments take effect. [**529**]

9. There may be paid to the members of a wages council or central co-ordinating committee appointed under sub-paragraph (*a*) of paragraph 1 of this Schedule such remuneration, and to any member of any such council or committee such travelling and other allowances, as the Secretary of State may, with the consent of the Minister for the Civil Service, determine, and all such remuneration and allowances shall be defrayed as part of the expenses of the Secretary of State in carrying this Act into effect. [**530**]

COMMENCEMENT

This Schedule was brought into force on 1st January 1976 by the Employment Protection Act 1975 (Commencement No. 1) Order 1975, S.I. 1975 No. 1938.

WAGES COUNCIL

See the note to Part I of this Schedule, *ante*.

CENTRAL CO-ORDINATING COMMITTEE

Such committees are established under the Wages Councils Act 1959, s. 7 (1), as substituted by para. 3 (1) in Part IV of this Schedule, *post*.

WRITING

See the note "Written" to s. 11, *ante*.

CONSULT: CONSULTATION

See the note to s. 7, *ante*.

DEFINITIONS

For "employers' association", "statutory joint industrial council", "trade union". "wages council" and "worker", see the Wages Council Act 1959, s. 24, as amended by para. 9 in Part IV of this Schedule, *post*.

REGULATIONS

No regulations had been made under para. 7 above up to the time of going to press, but by virtue of s. 125 (2), *ante*, and Sch. 17, para. 1, *post*, the Wages Councils (Meetings and Procedure) Regulations 1945, S.R. & O. 1945 No. 438 (which had effect under the Wages Councils Act 1959, Sch. 3, para. 7, as originally enacted) will, if in force at the commencement of this Part of this Schedule, continue in force under the substituted paragraph.

Part IV

Minor and Consequential Amendments

1. For the words "a wages regulation order", wherever they occur, substitute the words "an order under section 11 of this Act". [**531**]

2.—(1) In section 4, after subsection (2) (power by order to vary the field of operation of a wages council) insert the following subsections—

"(2A) The power of the Secretary of State to make an order under this section varying the field of operation of a wages council shall include power to vary that field by excluding from it any employers to whom there for the time being applies, as members of an organisation named in the order, an agreement, to which the organisation or any other organisation of which it is a member or on which it is represented, is a party, regulating remuneration or other terms or conditions of employment of their employees.

(2B) Any organisation so named shall if it has not already done so furnish the Secretary of State with a list of its members and shall from time to time, and also if so required by the Secretary of State, furnish him with particulars of any changes in their membership which have occurred since the list was furnished or, as the case may be, when particulars were last furnished to him." [**532**]

3.—(1) In section 7 (central co-ordinating committees), for subsection (1) substitute the following subsection:—

"(1) The Secretary of State may, if he thinks fit to do so, by order establish a central co-ordinating committee in relation to any two or more wages councils or statutory joint industrial councils, or wages councils and statutory joint industrial councils, or abolish, or vary the field of operation of, any central co-ordinating committee so established:

Provided that, except where either of the two following subsections applies, the Secretary of State shall, before making any such order, consult the wages councils or statutory joint industrial councils, or, as the case may be, the wages councils and the statutory joint industrial councils, concerned."

(2) In section 7 (2) after the words "wages council" in the first place where they occur, insert the words "or statutory joint industrial council", and for the words "wages council" wherever else they occur substitute the word "council".

(3) In section 7 (3) after the words "wages council" in the first place where they occur, insert the words "or statutory joint industrial council", and for the words "wages council" wherever else they occur substitute the word "council".

(4) In section 7 (5), in paragraph (*a*) for the words "wages councils" substitute the word "councils". [**533**]

4.—(1) Section 13 (permits to infirm and incapacitated persons) shall be amended in accordance with the following provisions of this paragraph.

(2) In subsection (1) for the words from "it may, if it thinks fit" to the end there shall be substituted the words "or makes it inappropriate for other terms and conditions fixed by the order to apply to him, it may, if it thinks fit, grant, subject to any conditions it may determine, a permit authorising his employment at less than the statutory minimum remuneration or dispensing with a term or condition specified in the permit; and while the permit is in force the remuneration authorised by the permit shall, if the conditions specified in the permit are complied with, be deemed to be the statutory minimum remuneration or, as the case may be, the terms and conditions fixed by the order shall be deemed to be observed.".

(3) In subsection (2) after the words "statutory minimum remuneration" insert the words "or dispensing with a term or condition specified in the permit" and after the words "specified remuneration" insert the words "or without compliance with any such term or condition". [**534**]

5. In section 14 (2) (power to authorise benefits to be reckoned as wages) for the words "wages regulation proposals and wages regulation orders" substitute the words "orders under section 11 of this Act". [**535**]

6. The provisions specified in column 1 of the following Table (which create offences) shall each have effect as if the maximum fine which may be imposed on summary conviction of any offence specified in that provision were a fine not exceeding the amount specified in column 3 of that Table instead of a fine not exceeding the amount specified in column 2 of that Table. [**536**]

TABLE

Provision	*Old maximum fine*	*New maximum fine*
Section 16 (2) (employers not to receive premiums) ..	£20	£100
Section 17 (3) (failure to keep records or post or give notices)	£20	£100
Section 19 (6) (obstruction, etc.)	£20	£100
Section 20 (false records and false information) ..	£100	£400

7. In section 17 (2) (notices to be displayed) for the words "wages regulation proposals or wages regulation order" substitute the words "proposals or orders under section 11 of this Act". [**537**]

8. In section 19 (3) (power of officers to obtain information, etc.) for the words

"outworkers" and "outworker", wherever occurring, substitute respectively the words "homeworkers" and "homeworker". [**538**]

9.—(1) In section 24 (definitions), before the definition of "homeworker" insert the following definition:—

" "employers' association" has the same meaning as in Part III of the Employment Protection Act 1975;".

(2) In the said section, for the definition of "organisation" substitute the following definition:—

" "organisation", in relation to workers means a trade union and in relation to employers means an employers' association;".

(3) In the said section, after the definition of "prescribed" insert the following definition:—

" "statutory joint industrial council" means a council established under section 90 of the Employment Protection Act 1975;".

(4) In the said section, for the definition of "trade union" substitute the following definition:—

" "trade union" has the same meaning as in the Trade Union and Labour Relations Act 1974".

(5) In the said section, for the provision defining "wages council" and "commission of inquiry", substitute the following definition:—

" "wages council" means a wages council established under this Act;".

(6) In the said section, for the definition of "worker" substitute the following definition:—

" "worker" means any person—

(*a*) who has entered into or works under a contract with an employer (whether express or implied, and, if express, whether oral or in writing) whether it be a contract of service or of apprenticeship or any other contract whereby he undertakes to do or perform personally any work or services for another party to the contract who is not a professional client of his; or

(*b*) whether or not he falls within the foregoing provision, who is a homeworker;

but does not include any person who is employed casually and otherwise than for the purposes of the business of the employer or other party to the contract.". [**539**]

10. For paragraph 4 of Schedule 1 to the Wages Councils Act 1959 (cases where the Secretary of State may make an order establishing, abolishing or varying the field of operation of a wages council without further proceedings) there shall be substituted the following paragraph:—

"4.—(1) If there is no objection which the Secretary of State is required by the foregoing paragraph to consider or if, after considering any such objection, he is of the opinion that it satisfies one of the following conditions, that is to say—

(*a*) in the case of an order to be made in pursuance of a recommendation of the Advisory, Conciliation and Arbitration Service, the objection was made to the Service and was expressly dealt with in the report embodying the recommendations; or

(*b*) in the case of such an order as is referred to in paragraph (*a*) above, the objection is one the subject-matter of which was considered by the Service and was expressly dealt with in that report or is such that a further inquiry into that subject-matter would serve no useful purpose; or

(*c*) in any case, the objection will be met by a modification which he proposes to make under this paragraph, or is frivolous, he may make the order either in the terms of the draft or subject to such modifications, if any, as he thinks fit, being modifications which, in his opinion, do not effect important alterations in the character of the draft order as published.

(2) The Secretary of State shall not form an opinion as to any matter mentioned in paragraph (*b*) of the foregoing sub-paragraph without consulting the Service.". [**540**]

COMMENCEMENT

This Schedule was brought into force on 1st January 1976 by the Employment Protection Act 1975 (Commencement No. 1) Order 1975, S.I. 1975 No. 1938.

SCHEDULE 8

Section 90

STATUTORY JOINT INDUSTRIAL COUNCILS

PART I

CONSTITUTION, ETC.

1.—(1) A statutory joint industrial council (hereafter in this Part of this Schedule referred to as a council) shall consist of equal numbers (being numbers within the limits specified by the Secretary of State) of persons appointed by a nominated employers' association to represent employers on the council and of persons appointed by a nominated trade union to represent workers on the council.

(2) A nominated employers' association or trade union shall on making such an appointment inform the secretary of the council, in writing, of that appointment. [**541**]

2.—(1) On the conversion of a wages council to a statutory joint industrial council—

(*a*) the limits as to the number of persons to be appointed to represent employers and workers on that wages council which are immediately before the date on which that council becomes a statutory joint industrial council for the time being specified by the Secretary of State, shall continue, subject to sub-paragraph (2) below, to be the limits in relation to that statutory joint industrial council; and

(*b*) an employers' association or trade union which immediately before the date on which that wages council becomes a statutory joint industrial council is for the time being nominated by the Secretary of State for the purpose of appointing persons to represent employers or workers on that wages council, shall continue, subject to sub-paragraph (2) below, to be so nominated in relation to that statutory joint industrial council.

(2) The Secretary of State may, on the application of a statutory joint industrial council, make such changes in the number of members of the council or in the machinery for appointing them as are necessary or expedient in the circumstances. [**542**]

3. A council shall elect a chairman and deputy chairman from among its members. [**543**]

4. The proceedings of a council shall not be invalidated by reason of any vacancy among its members or by any defect in the appointment of a member. [**544**]

5.—(1) A council may delegate any of its functions, other than the power to make orders under section 11 of the Wages Councils Act 1959, to a committee consisting of such number of members of the council as the council thinks fit.

(2) The number of members representing employers and the number of members representing workers on a committee of a council shall be equal. [**545**]

6. A council may regulate its own procedure. [**546**]

7.—(1) A member of a council shall hold and vacate office in accordance with the terms of his appointment, but the period for which he is to hold office shall, without prejudice to his re-appointment, not exceed five years.

(2) Where the term for which the members of a council were appointed comes to an end before their successors are appointed, those members shall, except so far as the appointing body otherwise directs, continue in office until the new appointments take effect. [**547**]

8. The Secretary of State may pay to the members of a council such travelling and other allowances, including allowances for loss of remunerative time, as the Secretary of State may, with the consent of the Minister for the Civil Service, determine. [**548**]

9. The expenses of a statutory joint industrial council, to such an extent as may be approved by the Secretary of State with the consent of the Treasury, shall be paid by the Secretary of State. [**549**]

10. The Secretary of State may appoint a secretary and such other officers of a council as he thinks fit. [**550**]

COMMENCEMENT

This Schedule was brought into force on 1st January 1976 by the Employment Protection Act 1975 (Commencement No. 1) Order 1975, S.I. 1975 No. 1938.

PARA. 1: NOMINATED EMPLOYERS' ASSOCIATION; NOMINATED TRADE UNION

For the meaning of "nominated" in this context, see s. 94 (1), *ante*.

WRITING

See the note "Written" to s. 11, *ante*.

PARA. 2: CONVERSION OF A WAGES COUNCIL TO A STATUTORY JOINT INDUSTRIAL COUNCIL

Such conversion is effected under s. 90, *ante*.

EMPLOYERS' ASSOCIATION OR TRADE UNION . . . NOMINATED . . . FOR THE PURPOSE OF APPOINTING, ETC.

Such nomination takes place in terms of the Wages Councils Act 1959, Sch. 2, para. 1 (2), as substituted by s. 89 (2) and Sch. 7, Part III, *ante*.

DEFINITIONS

By virtue of s. 126 (1), *ante*, for "employer", see the definition inserted in the Trade Union and Labour Relations Act 1974, s. 30 (1) by s. 125 (1), *ante*, and Sch. 16, Part III, para. 7 (2), *post*, and s. 30 (2) of that Act; for "trade union", see s. 28 (1) of that Act, Vol. 44, p. 1842, and for "worker", see s. 30 (1) of that Act for "employers' association", see s. 126 (2), *ante*.

PART II

TRANSITIONAL PROVISIONS

11. Any of the following things done by, to or in relation to a wages council, that is to say—

any order made under section 11 of the Wages Councils Act 1959 (power to fix terms and conditions of employment);

any proposals published in relation to making of such an order, and any notice published and representations made with respect thereto;

any permit issued under section 13 of that Act (permits to infirm and incapacitated persons);

any approval given under the proviso to section 16 (1) of that Act (approval of payments by apprentices);

shall as from the date when that council becomes a statutory joint industrial council be treated as having been done by, to or in relation to the latter council. [**551**]

12. The persons who immediately before the date on which a wages council

becomes a statutory joint industrial council are the members of the wages council appointed by an employers' association or trade union shall, subject to paragraph 2 (2) above, become and continue to be members of the statutory joint industrial council as if they had been appointed under paragraph 1 above. **[552]**

13. The persons who immediately before the date on which a wages council becomes a statutory joint industrial council are the secretary and officers of the wages council shall on that date become the secretary and officers of the statutory joint industrial council. **[553]**

COMMENCEMENT

This Schedule was brought into force on 1st January 1976 by the Employment Protection Act 1975 (Commencement No. 1) Order 1975, S.I. 1975 No. 1938.

DEFINITIONS

For "trade union" see, by virtue of s. 126 (1), *ante*, the Trade Union and Labour Relations Act 1974, s. 28 (1); for "employers' association", see s. 126 (2), *ante*.

SCHEDULE 9

Section 97

Amendments of Agricultural Wages Act 1948

Part I

Section 3, as Substituted

3. Power of Agricultural Wages Board to fix wages, holidays and other terms and conditions

(1) Subject to and in accordance with the provisions of this section, the Board shall have power, for each county for which an agricultural wages committee is established under this Act, to make an order in accordance with the provisions of Schedule 4 to this Act—

(*a*) fixing minimum rates of wages;
(*b*) directing holidays to be allowed;
(*c*) fixing any other terms and conditions of employment;

for workers employed in agriculture.

(2) The power of the Board to make an order under subsection (1) (*a*) of this section fixing minimum rates of wages is a power to make an order—

(*a*) fixing minimum rates for time work;
(*b*) fixing minimum rates for piece work;
(*c*) fixing minimum rates for time work, to apply in the case of workers employed on piece work, for the purpose of securing to such workers a minimum rate of remuneration on a time work basis; or
(*d*) fixing separate minimum rates by way of pay in respect of holidays:

Provided that the minimum time rate for piece work shall not in any case be higher than the minimum rate which, if the work were time work, would be applicable thereto by virtue of paragraph (*a*) of this subsection.

(2A) It shall be the duty of the Board to make an order under this section fixing such minimum rates of wages for time work as are referred to in paragraph (*a*) of the last preceding subsection.

(3) An order under paragraph (*b*) of subsection (1) of this section directing that a worker shall be allowed a holiday—

(*a*) shall not be made unless both minimum rates of wages in respect of the period of the holiday and minimum rates of wages otherwise than in respect of the holiday have been or are being fixed under this section for that worker;

(*b*) shall provide for the duration of the holiday being related to the duration of the period for which the worker has been employed or engaged to be employed by the employer who is to allow the holiday; and

(*c*) subject as aforesaid, may make provision as to the times at which or the periods within which, and the circumstances in which, the holiday shall be allowed.

(3A) An order under this section fixing separate minimum rates of wages in respect of holidays may make provision—

(*a*) with respect to the times at which, and the conditions subject to which, those wages shall accrue and shall become payable, and

(*b*) for securing that any such wages which have accrued to a worker during his employment by any employer shall, in the event of his ceasing to be employed by that employer before he becomes entitled to be allowed a holiday by him, nevertheless become payable by the employer to the worker.

(4) Any such minimum rates of wages as are mentioned in subsection (2) of this section may be fixed so as to vary according as the employment is for a day, week, month or other period, or according to the number of working hours, or the conditions of the employment, or so as to provide for a differential rate in the case of employment defined by the Board as being overtime employment, whether that employment is remunerated on a time work or a piece work basis.

In the exercise of their powers under this subsection, the Board shall, so far as is reasonably practicable, secure a weekly half-holiday for workers.

(5) An order under this section shall have effect as regards any terms as to remuneration from a date specified in the order, which may be a date earlier than the date of the order but not earlier than the date on which the Board agreed on those terms prior to publishing (in accordance with Schedule 4 to this Act) the original proposals to which effect is given, with or without modifications, by the order.

(6) Any increase of wages payable by virtue of an order under this section in respect of any time before the date of the order (hereafter in this Act referred to as arrears of wages) shall be paid by the employer within a period specified in the order being—

(*a*) in the case of a worker who is in the employment of the employer on that date, a period beginning with that date;

(*b*) in the case of a worker who is no longer in the employment of the employer on that date a period beginning with that date or the date on which the employer receives from the worker or a person acting on his behalf a request in writing for those wages, whichever is the later.

(7) Nothing in this section shall be construed as preventing the Board fixing a minimum rate of wages so as to secure that workers employed in agriculture receive remuneration calculated by reference to periods during the currency of their employment. **[554]**

Part II

Minor and Consequential Amendments

1. In section 4 (1) (enforcement) after paragraph (*c*) there shall be inserted the words "or

(*d*) to pay to any such worker arrears of wages within the period specified in the order";

and accordingly references in the provisions of that section following that paragraph and in any other provisions of the Agricultural Wages Act 1948 to wages or to the payment of wages at a rate not less than the minimum rate or the minimum rate applicable shall include references to arrears of wages or their payment, as the case may require. **[555]**

2.—(1) In section 5 (permits to incapacitated persons) after subsection (2) insert the following subsection:—

"(2A) If on an application in that behalf an agricultural wages committee are satisfied that a worker employed or desiring to be employed in their county is so affected by any physical injury or mental deficiency, or any infirmity due to age or any other cause, as to make it inappropriate for any terms and conditions of employment (other than those with respect to wages and holidays) fixed by an order under this Act to apply to him, the committee shall grant him, subject to any conditions they may determine, a permit dispensing, as from the date of the application or a later date specified in the permit, with a term or condition specified in the order, and while the permit is in force and any conditions to which the permit is subject are complied with, the terms and conditions fixed by the order shall be deemed to be observed.".

(2) In section 5 (3) (revocation of permit) after the words "subsection (1)" in both places where they occur insert the words "or (2A)".

(3) In section 5 (4) (variation of condition of permit) at the end insert the words "and, in the case of a variation caused by a change made by an order under this Act in the minimum rates of wages, that variation shall take effect from a date specified in the direction, not being earlier than the date of the change.".

(4) After section 5 (4) insert the following subsection—

"(4A) Any increase of wages payable by virtue of a variation of a permit under subsection (4) of this section in respect of any time before the date of the variation shall be paid by the employer within a period specified in the order being—

(*a*) in the case of a worker who is in the employment of the employer on the date on which notice of the variation is given in accordance with subsection (5) of this section, a period beginning with that date;

(*b*) in the case of a worker who is no longer in the employment of the employer on the date referred to in the last preceding paragraph, a period beginning with that date or the date on which the employer receives from the worker or a person acting on his behalf a request in writing for those wages, whichever is the later.". [**556**]

3.—(1) In section 11 (1) (void agreements) at the end add the following paragraph:—

"(*c*) any term or condition of a contract of employment that is inconsistent with a term or condition of employment fixed by an order of the Board under this Act or any agreement for abstaining from enforcing a term or condition so fixed.".

(2) In section 11 (2) (saving for more favourable agreements), at end add the words "or a term or condition of a contract of employment that is not inconsistent with a term or condition so fixed". [**557**]

4.—(1) In section 12 (3) (*a*) (inspection of records), at the end add the words "and records of terms and conditions of employment of such workers".

(2) In section 12 (5) omit the words from "and in any such civil proceedings" onwards, and at the end of that subsection insert the following subsections:—

"(5A) Where it appears to an officer so appointed that a term or condition of employment fixed by order of the Board is not being complied with by an employer, the officer (if he is authorised as aforesaid) may institute, on behalf or in the name of the worker, civil proceedings in respect of the failure to comply with the term or condition.

(5B) In any civil proceedings instituted by an officer by virtue of this section the court shall, if the officer is not a party to the proceedings, have the same power to make an order for the payment of costs by the officer as if he were a party to the proceedings."

(3) In section 12, for subsection (6) (saving for ordinary right to bring proceedings) substitute the following subsection:—

"(6) Nothing in subsection (5) or (5A) of this section shall be taken to exclude the bringing otherwise than in accordance with either of those subsections of proceedings of any description mentioned in those subsections. **[558]**

5. The provisions specified in column 1 of the following Table (which create offences) shall each have effect as if the maximum fine which may be imposed on summary conviction of any offence specified in that provision were a fine not exceeding the amount specified in column 3 of that Table instead of a fine not exceeding the amount specified in column 2 of that Table.

TABLE

Provision	*Old maximum fine*	*New maximum fine*
Section 4 (1) (failure to pay wages, or arrears, or allow holidays).	£20 and in addition £1 for each day on which the offence is continued after conviction.	£100 and an additional £5 for each day on which the offence is continued after conviction.
Section 6 (6) (payment of unlawful premiums).	£20.	£100.
Section 12 (7) (hindering officers (paragraph (*a*)), failure to produce documents or information (paragraph (*b*)), producing false documents (paragraph (*c*)) and furnishing false information (paragraph (*d*))).	£20.	£100 in the case of an offence under paragraph (*a*) or (*b*) and £400 in the case of an offence under paragraph (*c*) or (*d*). **[559]**

6. In paragraph 6 of Schedule 4 (power to vary and revoke orders) omit the words from the beginning to "holidays". **[560]**

COMMENCEMENT

This Schedule was brought into force on 1st January 1976 by the Employment Protection Act 1975 (Commencement No. 1) Order 1975, S.I. 1975 No. 1938.

AGRICULTURAL WAGES COMMITTEE

Such committees are established under the Agricultural Wages Act 1948, s. 2.

MONTH

This means a calendar month; see the Interpretation Act 1889, s. 3.

PERIOD BEGINNING, ETC.

See the note "14 days (two months) beginning, etc." to s. 15, *ante*.

SICK PAY

The minimum rates which the Board has power to fix under s. 3 (1) (*a*) above may include minimum rates for periods when a worker is absent through sickness or injury and this notwithstanding that under the contract of employment no remuneration is payable in respect of any such period; see the Agriculture Act 1967, s. 67.

REMUNERATION CALCULATED BY REFERENCE TO PERIODS DURING CURRENCY OF EMPLOYMENT

See the Agricultural Wages Act 1948, Sch. 4, para. 5 and the Agriculture Act 1967, s. 67 (2).

DEFINITIONS

For "the Board", see the Agricultural Wages Act 1948, s. 1 (1); for "agriculture", "county", "employment", "employed", "employer", "worker", see s. 17 of that Act. As to "areas of wages", note s. 3 (6) above.

ORDERS OF THE BOARD

These are not statutory instruments, but are published in the *London Gazette* and copies may be obtained from the Secretary to the Board.

(*Sch.* 10 *applies to Scotland.*)

SCHEDULE 11

Section 98

Extension of Terms and Conditions

Part I

Recognised Terms and Conditions and General Level of Terms and Conditions

1. A claim may be reported to the Service, in accordance with and subject to the following provisions of this Part of this Schedule, that as respects any worker an employer is, in respect of any matter, observing terms and conditions of employment less favourable than the recognised terms and conditions or, where, or so far as, there are no recognised terms and conditions the general level of terms and conditions. **[561]**

2. In this Part of this Schedule—

(*a*) the "recognised terms and conditions" means terms and conditions of workers in comparable employment in the trade or industry, or section of a trade or industry, in which the employer in question is engaged, either generally or in the district in which he is so engaged, which have been settled by an agreement or award, to which the parties are employers' associations and independent trade unions which represent (generally or in the district in question, as the case may be) a substantial proportion of the employers and of the workers in the trade, industry or section, being workers of the description to which the agreement or award relates; and

(*b*) the "general level of terms and conditions" means the general level of terms and conditions observed for comparable workers by employers—

(i) in the trade, industry or section in which the employer in question is engaged in the district in which he is so engaged; and

(ii) whose circumstances are similar to those of the employer in question,

and for the purposes of sub-paragraph (*a*) above the reference to terms and conditions, in a case where minimum terms and conditions have been settled as mentioned in that sub-paragraph, is a reference to those minimum terms and conditions. **[562]**

3. No claim shall be reported under paragraph 1 above as respects workers whose remuneration or terms and conditions, or minimum remuneration or terms and conditions is or are fixed (otherwise than by the employer, with or without the approval of any other person) in pursuance of any enactment other than—

(*a*) the Agricultural Wages Act 1948 or the Agricultural Wages (Scotland) Act 1949;

(*b*) the Wages Councils Act 1959;

(*c*) sections 90 to 94 above; or

(*d*) this Schedule;

or in the case of whom provision is made by or under any such enactment for the settlement of questions as to remuneration or terms and conditions or minimum remuneration or terms and conditions. **[563]**

4. A claim may be reported under paragraph 1 above, where, or so far as, the claim is founded upon recognised terms and conditions, by an employers' association or an independent trade union being one of the parties mentioned in paragraph 2 (*a*) above. **[564]**

5.—(1) A claim may be reported under paragraph 1 above, where, or so far as the claim is founded upon the general level of terms and conditions, by—

(*a*) an employers' association having members engaged in the trade, industry or section, in the district to which the claim relates; or (*b*) subject to sub-paragraph (2) below, a trade union of which any worker concerned is a member.

(2) Where any such worker is of a description in respect of which an employer recognises one or more independent trade unions, such a claim may be reported by a trade union only if it is that recognised union or, as the case may be, one of those recognised unions. [**565**]

6. A claim under paragraph 1 above shall be in writing and shall contain such particulars as the Service may require. [**566**]

7. When a claim is reported to the Service under paragraph 1 above the Service shall take any steps which seem to it expedient to settle the claim or to secure the use of appropriate machinery to settle the claim and shall if the claim is not otherwise settled refer it to the Committee. [**567**]

8. The Committee shall hear and determine the claim and it shall be for—

(*a*) the party making the claim to show that there are recognised terms and conditions and what those terms and conditions are, or, as the case may be, what the general level of terms and conditions is; and

(*b*) the employer to satisfy the Committee that he is observing terms and conditions of employment not less favourable than the recognised terms and conditions or, as the case may be, the general level of terms and conditions. [**568**]

9. In ascertaining whether, in respect of any matter which is the subject of a claim under paragraph 1 above, the employer is observing terms and conditions less favourable than the recognised terms and conditions, or as the case may be, the general level of terms and conditions regard shall be had to the whole of the terms and conditions observed by the employer as respects the worker to whom the claim relates. [**569**]

10. If the Committee finds the claim wholly or partly well-founded it shall make an award that the employer shall observe the recognised terms and conditions or, as the case may be, terms and conditions conforming to the general level of terms and conditions and shall identify or specify—

(*a*) the recognised terms and conditions or, as the case may be, terms and conditions conforming to the general level of terms and conditions;

(*b*) the description or descriptions of employees in respect of which they are to be observed; and

(*c*) the date from which they are to be observed, being a date not earlier than the date on which the employer was first informed of the claim giving rise to the award by the union or association which reported the claim to the Service. [**570**]

11. Any terms and conditions which by an award under paragraph 10 above the employer is required to observe in respect of employees of his shall have effect as part of the contract of employment of any such employee as from the date specified in the award, except in so far as they are superseded or varied—

(*a*) by a subsequent award under that paragraph;

(*b*) by a collective agreement between the employer and the trade union for the time being representing that employee; or

(*c*) by express or implied agreement between the employee and the employer so far as that agreement effects an improvement in any terms and conditions having effect by virtue of the award. [**571**]

12. Where—

(*a*) by virtue of any enactment, other than one contained in this Part of this Schedule, providing for minimum remuneration or terms and conditions a contract of employment is to have effect as modified by an award, order or other instrument under that enactment, and

(*b*) by virtue of an award under paragraph 10 above any terms and conditions are to have effect as part of that contract, that contract shall have effect in accordance with that award, order or other instrument or in accordance with the award under paragraph 10 above, whichever is the more favourable, in respect of any terms and conditions of that contract, to the employee. **[572]**

13. If in the course of determining a claim under this Schedule after the commencement of section 3 of the Equal Pay Act 1970, it appears to the Committee that a collective agreement or pay structure within the meaning of that section contains any provision applying specifically to men only or to women only so that it would, had it been referred to the Committee by the Secretary of State under that section, have required amendment in accordance with subsection (4) of that section so as to remove that discrimination between men and women—

(*a*) that provision shall not be regarded as part of the recognised terms and conditions or, as the case may be, shall not be taken into account in assessing the general level of terms and conditions; and

(*b*) the Committee shall report its opinion to the Secretary of State and, in the case of a collective agreement, to the parties to that agreement or, in the case of a pay structure, to the employer concerned. **[573]**

14. For the purposes of this Schedule the carrying on of the activities of public or local authorities shall be treated as the carrying on of a trade or industry. **[574]**

COMMENCEMENT

See s. 129 (3), *ante*.

GENERAL NOTE

See the General Note to s. 98, *ante*.

PARA. 2: TRADE OR INDUSTRY . . . IN WHICH THE EMPLOYER . . . IS ENGAGED

See para. 14 above as to the carrying on of the activities of public or local authorities.

WRITING

See the note "Written" to s. 11, *ante*.

PARA. 3: PROVISION IS MADE . . . FOR THE SETTLEMENT OF QUESTIONS AS TO REMUNERATION, ETC.

See, *e.g.*, the Civil Aviation Act 1949, s. 15 as amended by s. 125 (1), *ante*, and Sch. 16. Part IV, para. 5, *post*.

DEFINITIONS

By virtue of s. 126 (1), *ante*, for "employer", see the definition inserted in the Trade Union and Labour Relations Act 1974, s. 30 (1) by s. 125 (1), *ante*, and Sch. 16, Part III, para. 7 (2), *post*, and s. 30 (2) (*b*) of that Act; for "trade union", see s. 28 (1) of that Act; for "independent trade union", see s. 30 (1) of that Act; and for "worker", see s. 30 (1), (2) (*a*) of that Act; for "the Service", see s. 1 (1), *ante*; for "the Committee", see s. 10 (1), *ante*; for "recognised", see s. 126 (1), *ante*; for "employers' association", see s. 126 (2), *ante*. As to "recognised terms and conditions" and "general level of terms and conditions", note para. 2 above.

TRANSITIONAL PROVISIONS

See s. 125 (2), *ante*, and Sch. 17, para. 13, *post*.

PART II

COLLECTIVELY NEGOTIATED TERMS AND CONDITIONS IN CERTAIN INDUSTRIES

15. A claim may be reported to the Service under this paragraph by an independent trade union as respects any worker who is a member of that trade union and who falls within the field of operation of a wages council, a statutory joint industrial council, the Agricultural Wages Board or the Scottish Agricultural Wages Board—

(*a*) that the union is a party to one or more collective agreements and that those agreements cover a significant number of establishments within the field of operation of that council or Board either generally or in the district in which the worker is employed; and

(*b*) that in those establishments the circumstances of the employer are similar to those of the employer of the worker in question; and

(*c*) that the employer is paying him less than the lowest current rate of remuneration (disregarding any rate agreed to more than 12 months before the date on which the claim was reported) payable to workers of his description under any of those agreements. **[575]**

16. The provisions of paragraphs 7, 8 and 10 to 14 above shall apply to a claim under paragraph 15 above—

(*a*) as if for any reference to the recognised terms and conditions there were substituted a reference to the rate of remuneration referred to in paragraph 15 (*c*) above;

(*b*) as if references to the general level of terms and conditions were omitted; and

(*c*) as if the reference in paragraph 12 (*a*) to Part I of this Schedule were a reference to Part II of this Schedule and so much of Part I as is thereby applied. **[576]**

COMMENCEMENT
See s. 129 (3), *ante*.

WAGES COUNCIL
Those councils are established under the Wages Councils Act 1959, s. 1.

STATUTORY JOINT INDUSTRIAL COUNCIL
As to these councils, see ss. 90 *et seq*. and Sch. 8, *ante*.

AGRICULTURAL WAGES BOARD
That Board was established under the Agricultural Wages Act 1948, s. 1 (1).

DEFINITIONS
By virtue of s. 126 (1), *ante*, for "employer", see the definition inserted in the Trade Union and Labour Relations Act 1974, s. 30 (1) by s. 125 (1), *ante*, and Sch. 16, Part III, para. 7 (2), *post*, and s. 30 (2) (*b*) of that Act; for "trade union", see s. 28 (1) of that Act, for "collective agreement" and "independent trade union" see s. 30 (1), of that Act, and for "worker", see s. 30 (1), (2) (*a*) of that Act; for "the Service", see s. 1 (1), *ante*.

SCHEDULE 12

Section 110

Death of Employee or Employer

Part I

General

Introductory

1. In this Schedule "the relevant provisions" means the provisions of this Act (including this Schedule) conferring rights on employees, or connected therewith, and so much of the 1974 Act as relates to unfair dismissal. **[577]**

Institution or continuance of tribunal proceedings

2. Where an employee or employer has died tribunal proceedings arising under any of the relevant provisions may be instituted or continued by a personal representative of the deceased employee or, as the case may be, defended by a personal representative of the deceased employer. **[578]**

3.—(1) If there is no personal representative of a deceased employee, tribunal proceedings arising under any of the relevant provisions or proceedings to enforce a tribunal award made in any such proceedings may be instituted or continued on behalf of the estate of the deceased employee by such other person as the industrial tribunal may appoint being either—

(*a*) a person authorised by the employee to act in connection with the proceedings before the employee's death; or

(*b*) the widower, widow, child, father, mother, brother or sister of the deceased employee,

and references in this Schedule to a personal representative shall be construed as including such a person.

(2) In such a case any award made by the industrial tribunal shall be in such terms and shall be enforceable in such manner as may be provided by regulations made by the Secretary of State. [**579**]

4.—(1) Subject to any specific provision of this Schedule to the contrary, in relation to an employee or employer who has died—

(*a*) any reference in the relevant provisions to the doing of anything by or in relation to an employee or employer shall be construed as including a reference to the doing of that thing by or in relation to any personal representative of the deceased employee or employer; and

(*b*) any reference in the said provisions to a thing required or authorised to be done by or in relation to an employee or employer shall be construed as including a reference to any thing which, in accordance with any such provision as modified by this Schedule (including sub-paragraph (*a*) above), is required or authorised to be done by or in relation to any personal representative of the deceased employee or employer.

(2) Nothing in this paragraph shall prevent references in the relevant provisions to a successor of an employer from including a personal representative of a deceased employer. [**580**]

Rights and liabilities accruing after death

5. Any right arising under any of the relevant provisions as modified by this Schedule shall, if it had not accrued before the death of the employee in question, nevertheless devolve as if it had so accrued. [**581**]

6. Where by virtue of any of the relevant provisions as modified by this Schedule a personal representative of a deceased employer is liable to pay any amount and that liability had not accrued before the death of the employer it shall be treated for all purposes as if it were a liability of the deceased employer which had accrued immediately before the death. [**582**]

Death during protected period

7. Where an industrial tribunal makes a protective award under section 101 above and an employee of a description to which the award relates dies during the protected period, the award shall be treated in his case as if it specified a protected period of such length as to end on the date of his death. [**583**]

COMMENCEMENT

This Schedule came into force on 8th March and 20th April 1976 by the Employment Protection Act 1975 (Commencement No. 2) Order 1976, S.I. 1976 No. 144, to the extent that s. 110 came into effect, i.e. so far as it relates to ss. 99–107 and 63–69.

PARA. 1: SO MUCH OF THE 1974 ACT AS RELATES TO UNFAIR DISMISSAL

See the note "Provisions . . . relating to unfair dismissal" to s. 50, *ante*.

PARA. 3: INDUSTRIAL TRIBUNAL

See the note to s. 6, *ante*.

PARA. 7: PROTECTED PERIOD

See s. 101 (5), *ante*.

DEFINITIONS

By virtue of s. 126 (1), *ante*, for "employer", see the definition inserted in the Trade Union and Labour Relations Act 1974, s. 30 (1), by s. 125 (1), *ante*, and Sch. 16, Part III. para. 7 (2), *post*, and s. 30 (2) (*b*) of that Act; and for "employee", see s. 30 (1) of that Act. As to "the relevant provisions", note para. 1 above.

REGULATIONS UNDER THIS SCHEDULE

At the time of going to press no regulations had been made under para. 3 (2) above.
As to the making of regulations generally, see s. 123, *ante*.

PART II

UNFAIR DISMISSAL

8. In this Part of this Schedule "the unfair dismissal provisions" means so much of this Act (including this Schedule) and the 1974 Act as relates to unfair dismissal. **[584]**

Death during notice period

9. Where an employer has given notice to an employee to terminate his contract of employment and before that termination the employee or the employer dies, the unfair dismissal provisions shall apply as if the contract had been duly terminated by the employer by notice expiring on the date of the death. **[585]**

10. Where the employee's contract of employment has been terminated by the employer and by virtue of paragraph 5 (6) of Schedule 1 to the 1974 Act a date later than the effective date of termination as defined by sub-paragraph (5) of that paragraph is to be treated as the effective date of termination for the purposes of certain of the unfair dismissal provisions, and before that later date the employee or the employer dies, the said sub-paragraph (6) shall have effect as if the notice referred to in that sub-paragraph as required to be given by the employer would have expired on the death. **[586]**

Remedies for unfair dismissal

11. Where an employee has died, then, unless an order for reinstatement or re-engagement has already been made, the unfair dismissal provisions relating to reinstatement and re-engagement shall not apply; and accordingly if the industrial tribunal finds that the grounds of the complaint are well-founded the case shall be treated as falling within section 72 (5) above as a case in which no order is made under section 71 above. **[587]**

12. If an order for reinstatement or re-engagement has been made and the employee dies before the order is complied with—

(*a*) if the employer has before the death refused to reinstate or re-engage the employee in accordance with the order, section 72 (2) and (3) above shall apply and an award shall be made under section 72 (2) (*b*) above unless the employer satisfies the tribunal that it was not practicable at the time of the refusal to comply with the order;

(*b*) if there has been no such refusal, section 72 (1) above shall apply if the employer fails to comply with any ancillary terms of the order which remain capable of fulfilment after the employee's death as it would apply to such a failure to comply fully with the terms of an order where the employee had been reinstated or re-engaged. **[588]**

COMMENCEMENT

See s. 129 (3), *ante*.

SO MUCH . . . AS RELATES TO UNFAIR DISMISSAL

See the note "Provisions . . . relating to unfair dismissal" to s. 50, *ante*.

DEFINITIONS

By virtue of s. 126 (1), *ante*, for "employer", see the definition inserted in the Trade Union and Labour Relations Act 1974, s. 30 (1), by s. 125 (1), *ante*, and Sch. 16, Part III, para. 7 (2), *post*, and s. 30 (2) (*b*) of that Act, and for "employee", see s. 30 (1) of that Act. As to "the unfair dismissal provisions", note para. 8 above.

SCHEDULE 13

Section 114

AMENDMENTS OF THE EMPLOYMENT AGENCIES ACT 1973

1. In sections 1 and 2, for the words "licensing authority", wherever they occur, substitute the words "Secretary of State". [**589**]

2. In section 1 (2) (*b*) for the words from "time for appealing" to the end, substitute the words "refusal is notified to him in accordance with section 3 (10) of this Act". [**590**]

3.—(1) After section 2 (3) insert the following subsection—

"(3A) A licence may be revoked by the Secretary of State on any of the grounds specified in subsection (3) of this section."

(2) Section 2 (4) is hereby repealed.

(3) In section 2 (5) omit the words "under the subsequent provisions of this Act" and for the words from "time for appealing" to the end, substitute the words "refusal is notified to him in accordance with section 3 (10) of this Act". [**591**]

4. For sections 3 and 4, substitute the following section—

"3. Right to make representations

(1) Where the Secretary of State proposes to refuse or to revoke a licence he shall notify the applicant for or the holder of the licence of—

(*a*) the proposal and the reason for it; and
(*b*) his right under this section to make written representations relating to that proposal and the time within which that right maybe exercised.

(2) A person who receives a notification of a proposal such as is mentioned in subsection (1) of this section may make written representations about it to the Secretary of State.

(3) Written representations in relation to a proposal to refuse or revoke a licence must be received by the Secretary of State within 21 days of the receipt of the notification of that proposal.

(4) If the Secretary of State receives such representation within the time specified in subsection (3) of this section, he shall consider them and—

(*a*) if he decides not to proceed with the proposal, and accordingly decides to grant or not to revoke the licence, shall notify the applicant or holder of his decision;
(*b*) in any other case, shall appoint a person to consider the representations on his behalf, and shall notify the applicant or holder of that appointment and of the name of the appointed person, and shall require the applicant or holder to state within 14 days whether he wishes to make oral representations to the appointed person.

(5) If a person who receives such a notification as is mentioned in subsection (4) (*b*) of this section expresses, within the time mentioned in that paragraph, a wish to make oral representations to the appointed person the Secretary of State shall give the former written notice of the place, date and time of the hearing.

(6) A notice under subsection (5) of this section shall not specify a date

for the hearing earlier than 21 days from the date of the notice, unless the person who wishes to make representations has agreed to an earlier hearing.

(7) The appointed person shall, in accordance with the notice given under subsection (5) of this section, afford to the person who wishes to make oral representations an opportunity to do so, either in person or by any person authorised by him in that behalf.

(8) The appointed person shall consider the written representations referred to in subsection (4) of this section and any oral representations made under subsection (7) of this section, and shall make a report to the Secretary of State giving his findings of fact and his recommendations.

(9) Where representations relating to a proposal have been made under this section, the Secretary of State may make a final decision relating to that proposal only after receiving and considering the report on it of the appointed person.

(10) The Secretary of State shall notify the applicant, or holder, of his decision and the reasons for it and shall send him a copy of the appointed person's report." [**592**]

5. Section 8 is hereby repealed. [**593**]

6.—(1) In section 9 (1) for the words "of a licensing authority duly authorised by them in that behalf" substitute the words "duly authorised in that behalf by the Secretary of State".

(2) In section 9 (1) (*c*) for the words "licensing authority" and "their" substitute respectively the words "Secretary of State" and "his".

(3) In section 9 (4) (*a*) sub-paragraphs (ii) and (iii) are hereby repealed, sub-paragraphs (iv) and (v) shall be renumbered as, respectively, sub-paragraphs (ii) and (iv), and after the renumbered sub-paragraph (ii) there shall be inserted the following sub-paragraph—

"(iii) by the Secretary of State, or an officer or servant appointed by, or persons exercising functions on behalf of, the Secretary of State to the person carrying on or proposing to carry on the employment agency or employment business concerned, to any person in his employment or, in the case of information relating to a person availing himself of the services of such an agency or business, to that person; or",

and in sub-paragraph (iv) (as renumbered) for the words from "on an appeal" to the end, substitute the words "under section 3 (7) of this Act". [**594**]

7. In section 13 (1), the definition of "licensing authority" is hereby repealed. [**595**]

COMMENCEMENT

This Schedule was brought into force on 1st January 1976 by the Employment Protection Act 1975 (Commencement No. 1) Order 1975, S.I. 1975 No. 1938.

SCHEDULE 14

Section 115

Amendments of the Employment and Training Act 1973

1. For section 1 (7) substitute the following subsections—

"(7) The functions of the Commission and of the Agencies and of their officers and servants shall be performed on behalf of the Crown.

(8) For the purposes of any civil proceedings arising out of those functions, the Crown Proceedings Act 1947 and the Crown Suits (Scotland) Act 1857 shall apply to the Commission and the Agencies as if they were government departments within the meaning of the said Act of 1947 or, as the case may be, public departments within the meaning of the said Act of 1857." [**596**]

2.—(1) In section 5 (1), for the words from "providing" onwards substitute—

"(*a*) providing temporary employment for persons in Great Britain who are without employment;

(*b*) securing a temporary continuation of employment for persons in Great Britain who in his opinion would otherwise be likely to be dismissed by reason of redundancy; and

(*c*) obtaining employment for any description of persons in Great Britain who in his opinion would, because of their special circumstances and a high or increasing level of unemployment in Great Britain, otherwise have or be likely to have difficulty in obtaining employment;

and any such arrangements may include arrangements for the making by the Secretary of State of payments by way of grant or loan to employers or other persons in order to facilitate the carrying out of the arrangements".

(2) Paragraphs (*b*) and (*c*) of the said section 5 (1) shall cease to have effect on the expiration of the period of eighteen months beginning with the commencement of this paragraph unless continued in force by an order under this paragraph.

(3) The Secretary of State may by order—

(*a*) provide that the said paragraph (*b*) or the said paragraph (*c*) or both paragraphs, shall continue in force for a period not exceeding twelve months from the expiration of the period mentioned in sub-paragraph (2) above; and

(*b*) from time to time extend or further extend the period for which either or both of those paragraphs is or are to continue in force by a further period not exceeding twelve months.

(4) Any arrangements made before the expiration of the said paragraphs (*b*) or (*c*) shall continue in force after its expiration and may be enforced and otherwise implemented accordingly.

(5) No order shall be made under this paragraph unless a draft of the order is laid before and approved by a resolution of each House of Parliament. [**597**]

3. After section 13 (1) insert the following subsection—

"(1A) Any reference in this Act to redundancy shall be construed as a reference to the existence of one or other of the facts specified in section 1 (2) (*a*) and (*b*) of the Redundancy Payments Act 1965." [**598**]

4. In Schedule 1, after paragraph 10 insert the following paragraph—

"10A. The Commission shall pay to the Minister for the Civil Service, at such times in each accounting year as may be determined by that Minister subject to any directions of the Treasury, sums of such amounts as he may so determine for the purposes of this paragraph as being equivalent to the increase during that year of such liabilities of his as are attributable to the provision of pensions, allowances or gratuities to or in respect of persons who are or have been in the service of the Commission in so far as that increase results from the service of those persons during that accounting year and to the expense to be incurred in administering those pensions, allowances or gratuities.". [**599**]

5. In paragraph 13 of Schedule 1 for the words "or employee" substitute the words "officer or servant". [**600**]

6. The following provisions and passages are hereby repealed—

Section 7.

In section 13 (1), in the definition of "employee" the words ", except in Schedule 1,", and in the definition of "employment" the words ", except in section 7 and Schedule 1,".

Section 13 (5).

In section 15 (3), the references to paragraphs 5 and 13 of Schedule 3.

In Schedule 1, in paragraph 10 (1) the words from "and any" to the end, paragraphs 10 (2), 11, 12 and 16.

In Schedule 3, paragraphs 5 and 13. **[601]**

COMMENCEMENT

This Schedule was brought into force on 1st January 1976 by the Employment Protection Act 1975 (Commencement No. 1) Order 1975, S.I. 1975 No. 1938.

ORDERS UNDER THIS SCHEDULE

At the time of going to press, no order had been made under para. 2 (3) above.

As to the making of orders generally, see s. 123, *ante*.

SCHEDULE 15

Section 116

Amendments of the Health and Safety at Work etc. Act 1974

1. In section 1 (2) omit the words "and agricultural health and safety regulations". **[602]**

2. In section 2, omit subsection (5) and in subsection (7) for the words "subsections (4) and (5)" substitute the words "subsection (4)". **[603]**

3. After section 10 (7) insert the following subsection—

"(8) For the purposes of any civil proceedings arising out of those functions, the Crown Proceedings Act 1947 and the Crown Suits (Scotland) Act 1857 shall apply to the Commission and the Executive as if they were government departments within the meaning of the said Act of 1947 or, as the case may be, public departments within the meaning of the said Act of 1857.". **[604]**

4. In section 11, in subsection (1) omit the words "except as regards matters relating exclusively to agricultural operations", and in subsection (2) omit the words "except as aforesaid". **[605]**

5. In section 14 (2), omit the words from "but shall not do so" to "agricultural operations". **[606]**

6. In section 15, for subsection (1) substitute—

"(1) Subject to the provisions of section 50, the Secretary of State, the Minister of Agriculture, Fisheries and Food or the Secretary of State and that Minister acting jointly shall have power to make regulations under this section for any of the general purposes of this Part (and regulations so made are in this Part referred to as "health and safety regulations".)". **[607]**

7. In section 16 (1), omit the words "and except as regards matters relating exclusively to agricultural operations". **[608]**

8. In section 18, in subsection (3) omit the words "or agricultural health and safety regulations", and in subsection (5) omit the words "the appropriate Agriculture Minister". **[609]**

9. In section 28, after subsection (8) insert the following subsection—

"(9) Notwithstanding anything in subsection (7) above, a person who has obtained such information as is referred to in that subsection may furnish to a person who appears to him to be likely to be a party to any civil proceedings arising out of any accident, occurrence, situation or other matter, a written statement of relevant facts observed by him in the course of exercising any of the powers referred to in that subsection.". **[610]**

10. Sections 29, 30, 31 and 32 are hereby repealed. **[611]**

11. In section 33, in subsection (1) (*c*) omit the words "or agricultural health and safety regulations", and in subsection (4) (*a*) omit the words "or the appropriate Agricultural Minister". **[612]**

12. In section 43, in subsection (3) omit the words "the Minister of Agriculture, Fisheries and Food" and for subsections (6) and (7) substitute—

"(6) The power to make regulations under this section shall be exercisable by the Secretary of State, the Minister of Agriculture, Fisheries and Food or the Secretary of State and that Minister acting jointly.". [**613**]

13. In section 44, in subsection (1) omit the words "agricultural licences and", and in subsection (7) (*a*) for the words "an agricultural licence or nuclear site licence" substitute the words "a nuclear site licence". [**614**]

14. In section 47, in subsection (2) omit the words "or agricultural health and safety regulations", in subsection (3) omit the words "or, as the case may be, agricultural health and safety regulations" and in subsection (5) omit the words "or, as the case may be, agricultural health and safety regulations". [**615**]

15.—(1) In section 49, in subsection (1) for the words "The appropriate Minister may by regulations amend" substitute the words "Regulations made under this subsection may amend", in subsection (2) for the words "appropriate Minister" substitute the words "authority making the regulations", in subsection (3) omit the words "by the appropriate Minister" and for the words "if the appropriate Minister" substitute the words "if the authority making the regulations".

(2) For subsection (4) of that section substitute—

"(4) The power to make regulations under this section shall be exercisable by the Secretary of State, the Minister of Agriculture, Fisheries and Food or the Secretary of State and that Minister acting jointly.". [**616**]

16.—(1) In section 50, for subsection (1) substitute—

"(1) Where any power to make regulations under any of the relevant statutory provisions is exercisable by the Secretary of State, the Minister of Agriculture, Fisheries and Food or both of them acting jointly that power may be exercised either so as to give effect (with or without modifications) to proposals submitted by the Commission under section 11 (2) (*d*) or independently of any such proposals; but the authority who is to exercise the power shall not exercise it independently of proposals from the Commission unless he has consulted the Commission and such other bodies as appear to him to be appropriate.".

(2) In subsection (2) of that section, for the words from "Secretary of State" to "preceding subsection" substitute "authority who is to exercise any such power as is mentioned in subsection (1) above proposes to exercise that power".

(3) In subsection (3), for the words "to the Secretary of State" substitute the words "under section 11 (2) (*d*)".

(4) Subsections (4) and (5) are hereby repealed. [**617**]

17. In section 52, for subsections (3) and (4) substitute—

"(3) The power to make regulations under subsection (2) above shall be exercisable by the Secretary of State, the Minister of Agriculture, Fisheries and Food or the Secretary of State and that Minister acting jointly.". [**618**]

18.—(1) In section 53, in subsection (1) omit the definitions of "agriculture", "the Agricultural Ministers", "agricultural health and safety regulations", "agricultural licence", "agricultural operation", "the appropriate Agriculture Minister", "forestry", "livestock" and "the relevant agricultural purposes" and in the definition of "the relevant statutory provisions" omit the words "and agricultural health and safety regulations".

(2) Subsections (2) to (6) of that section are hereby repealed. [**619**]

19. In section 80, for subsections (4) to (6) substitute—

"(4) The power to make regulations under subsection (1) above shall be exercisable by the Secretary of State, the Minister of Agriculture, Fisheries and Food or the Secretary of State and that Minister acting jointly; but the authority who is to exercise the power shall, before exercising it, consult such bodies as appear to him to be appropriate.

(5) In this section 'the relevant statutory provisions' has the same meaning as in Part I." [**620**]

20. In section 84 (1) (*a*), omit the words "or 30". [**621**]

21. Schedule 4 is hereby repealed. [**622**]

COMMENCEMENT
This Schedule was brought into force in two stages on 1st January and 1st March 1976 by the Employment Protection Act 1975 (Commencement No. 1) Order 1975, S.I. 1975 No. 1938.

SCHEDULE 16

Section 125

Minor and Consequential Amendments

Part I

Redundancy Payments Act 1965

1. In section 1 (1) (general right to redundancy payments) at end add "and Schedule 4 to the Employment Protection Act 1975." [**623**]

2. For subsections (3) to (5) of section 2 (disentitlement to redundancy payment where employee unreasonably refuses offer of renewal of contract or re-engagement) substitute the following subsections—

"(3) If an employer makes an employee an offer (whether in writing or not) before the ending of his employment under the previous contract to renew his contract of employment, or to re-engage him under a new contract of employment, so that the renewal or re-engagement would take effect either immediately on the ending of his employment under the previous contract or after an interval of not more than four weeks thereafter the provisions of subsections (5) and (6) of this section shall have effect.

(4) For the purposes of the application of the last preceding subsection to a contract under which the employment ends on a Friday, Saturday or Sunday—

(*a*) the renewal or re-engagement shall be treated as taking effect immediately on the ending of the employment under the previous contract if it takes effect on or before the next Monday after that Friday, Saturday or Sunday; and

(*b*) the interval of four weeks shall be calculated as if the employment had ended on that Monday.

(5) If an employer makes an employee such an offer as is referred to in subsection (3) of this section and either—

(*a*) the provisions of the contract as renewed, or of the new contract as to the capacity and place in which he would be employed, and as to the other terms and conditions of his employment, would not differ from the corresponding provisions of the previous contract; or

(*b*) the first mentioned provisions would differ (wholly or in part) from those corresponding provisions, but the offer constitutes an offer of suitable employment in relation to the employee;

and in either case the employee unreasonably refuses that offer, he shall not be entitled to a redundancy payment by reason of his dismissal.

(6) If an employee's contract of employment is renewed, or he is re-engaged under a new contract of employment, in pursuance of such an offer as is referred to in subsection (3) of this section, and the provisions of the contract as renewed, or of the new contract, as to the capacity and place in which he is employed, and as to the other terms and conditions of his employment, differ (wholly or in part) from the corresponding provisions of the previous

contract but the employment is suitable in relation to the employee, and during the trial period referred to in section 3 of this Act the employee unreasonably terminates the contract, or unreasonably gives notice to terminate it and the contract is thereafter, in consequence, terminated, he shall not be entitled to a redundancy payment by reason of his dismissal from employment under the previous contract.". [**624**]

3. For section 3 (dismissal by employer) substitute the following section—

"3. Dismissal by employer

(1) In this Part of this Act, "dismiss" and "dismissal" shall be construed in accordance with the provisions of this section and the next following section.

(2) Subject to the following provisions of this section and to the next following section, an employee shall be treated as dismissed by his employer, if, but only if—

(*a*) the contract under which he is employed by the employer is terminated by the employer, whether it is so terminated by notice or without notice, or

(*b*) where under that contract he is employed for a fixed term, that term expires without being renewed under the same contract, or

(*c*) the employee terminates that contract, with or without notice, in circumstances (not falling within section 10 (4) of this Act) such that he is entitled to terminate it without notice by reason of the employer's conduct.

(3) If an employee's contract of employment is renewed, or he is re-engaged under a new contract of employment in pursuance of an offer (whether in writing or not) made by his employer before the ending of his employment under the previous contract, and the renewal or re-engagement takes effect either immediately on the ending of that employment or after an interval of not more than four weeks thereafter, then, subject to subsections (5) to (8) of this section, the employee shall not be regarded as having been dismissed by his employer by reason of the ending of his employment under the previous contract.

(4) For the purposes of the application of the last preceding subsection to a contract under which the employment ends on a Friday, Saturday or Sunday—

(*a*) the renewal or re-engagement shall be treated as taking effect immediately on the ending of the employment if it takes effect on or before the Monday after that Friday, Saturday or Sunday, and

(*b*) the interval of four weeks referred to in that subsection shall be calculated as if the employment had ended on that Monday.

(5) If in a case to which subsection (3) of this section applies, the provisions of the contract as renewed, or the new contract, as to the capacity and place in which the employee is employed, and as to the other terms and conditions of his employment, differ (wholly or in part) from the corresponding provisions of the previous contract, there shall be a trial period in relation to the contract as renewed, or the new contract (whether or not there has been a previous trial period under this section).

(6) The trial period shall begin with the ending of the employee's employment under the previous contract and end with the expiration of the period of four weeks beginning with the date on which the employee starts work under the contract as renewed, or the new contract, or such longer period as may be agreed in accordance with the next following subsection for the purpose of retraining the employee for employment under that contract.

(7) Any such agreement shall—

(*a*) be made between the employer and the employee or his representative before the employee starts work under the contract as renewed or, as the case may be, the new contract;

(*b*) be in writing;

(*c*) specify the date of the end of the trial period; and

(*d*) specify the terms and conditions of employment which will apply in the employee's case after the end of that period.

(8) If during the trial period—

(*a*) the employee, for whatever reason, terminates the contract, or gives notice to terminate it and the contract is thereafter, in consequence, terminated; or

(*b*) the employer, for a reason connected with or arising out of the change to the renewed, or new, employment, terminates the contract, or gives notice to terminate it and the contract is thereafter, in consequence, terminated,

then, unless the employee's contract of employment is again renewed, or he is again re-engaged under a new contract of employment, in circumstances such that subsection (3) above again applies, he shall be treated as having been dismissed on the date on which his employment under the previous contract or, if there has been more than one trial period, the original contract ended for the reason for which he was then dismissed or would have been dismissed had the offer (or original offer) of renewed, or new, employment not been made, or, as the case may be, for the reason which resulted in that offer being made.

(9) Subject to the next following subsection and to the next following section, in this Part of this Act, "the relevant date", in relation to the dismissal of an employee—

(*a*) where his contract of employment is terminated by notice, whether given by his employer or by the employee, means the date on which that notice expires;

(*b*) where his contract of employment is terminated without notice, means the date on which the termination takes effect;

(*c*) where he is employed under a contract for a fixed term and that term expires as mentioned in subsection (2) (*b*) of this section, means the date on which that term expires; and

(*d*) where he is treated, by virtue of subsection (8) of this section, as having been dismissed on the termination of his employment under a previous contract, means—

(i) for the purposes of section 21 of this Act, the date which is the relevant date as defined by paragraph (*a*), (*b*) or (*c*) of this subsection in relation to the renewed, or new, contract, or, where there has been more than one trial period, the last such contract; and

(ii) for any other purpose, the date which is the relevant date as defined by paragraph (*a*), (*b*) or (*c*) of this subsection in relation to the previous contract, or, where there has been more than one trial period, the original contract.

(10) Where the notice required to be given by an employer to terminate a contract of employment by section 1 (1) of the Contracts of Employment Act 1972 (minimum period of notice) would, if duly given when notice of termination was given by the employer, or (where no notice was given) when the contract of employment was terminated by the employer, expire on a date later than the relevant date as defined by the last preceding subsection, then for the purposes of section 8 (1) of, and paragraphs 1 (1) and 5 (7) of Schedule 1 to, this

Act, that later date shall be treated as the relevant date in relation to the dismissal.". [**625**]

4. In section 5 (2) omit the words "(calculated in accordance with Schedule 2 to this Act)" and after that subsection insert the following subsection—

"(2A) For the purposes of Part II of Schedule 4 to the Employment Protection Act 1975 as it applies for the calculation of a week's pay for the purposes of the last preceding subsection, the calculation date is the day immediately preceding the first of the four or, as the case may be, the six weeks referred to in section 6 (1) of this Act.". [**626**]

5.—(1) In section 8 (1) for the words "one hundred and four weeks" substitute the words "two years".

(2) In section 8 (3) for the words "3 (2)" substitute the words "3 (3)".

(3) After section 8 (3) insert the following subsection—

"(3A) Where by virtue of section 3 (10) of this Act a date is to be treated as the relevant date for the purposes of subsection (1) of this section which is later than the relevant date as defined by subsection (9) of that section, then in determining for the purposes of section 1 (1) of this Act whether the employee has been continuously employed for the requisite period, the period of the interval between those two dates shall count as a period of employment notwithstanding that it does not count under that Schedule."

(4) In section 8 (4) for the words "sections 17 and 24" substitute the words "sections 17, 24 and 24A". [**627**]

6. For section 12 there shall be substituted the following section—

"12. Claims as to extension of terms and conditions

(1) A claim under paragraph 1 of Schedule 11 to the Employment Protection Act 1975 (claims as to recognised terms and conditions and general level of terms and conditions) may be reported to the Advisory Conciliation and Arbitration Service in accordance with that Schedule, and may be referred by the Service to the Central Arbitration Committee, and the Committee may make an award under that Schedule, notwithstanding that the terms and conditions which it is claimed that the employer is not observing consist of or include terms and conditions as to payments to be made to employees in the circumstances specified in paragraph (*a*) or paragraph (*b*) of section 1 (1) of this Act, or in similar circumstances, and that provision for redundancy payments is made by this Act.

(2) Where a claim which is reported to the Service under the said paragraph 1 is founded upon recognised terms and conditions and relates to an agreement in respect of which an order under section 11 of this Act is for the time being in force, and the Committee makes an award in pursuance of that claim, section 11 (3) of this Act shall have effect in relation to all persons in respect of whom the employer is required by that award to observe the recognised terms and conditions, whether they are persons to whom section 11 (3) of this Act would apply apart from this subsection or not.". [**628**]

7.—(1) In section 13 (2) for the words "section 3 (2)" substitute the words "subsections (3) to (10) of section 3".

(2) In section 13 (3) omit the words from "but the employee" to the end of the subsection and insert the words "subsections (3) to (6) of section 2 of this Act shall have effect, subject to the next following subsection, in relation to that offer as they would have had effect in relation to the like offer made by the previous owner.".

(3) In section 13 (4) for the words "subsection (3) or subsection (4)" substitute the words "subsections (3) to (6)" and at the end of paragraph (*b*) insert the words "or, as the case may be, whether the employee acted reasonably in terminating the

renewed, or new, employment during the trial period referred to in section 3 of this Act.". [**629**]

8. For section 17 (3) to (6) (computation of period of employment as respects employment wholly or partly abroad) substitute the following subsections—

"(3) Subject to the following provisions of this section, in computing, in relation to an employee, the period specified in section 8 (1) of this Act, or the period specified in paragraph 1 of Schedule 1 to this Act, a week of employment before 6th April 1975 shall not count if—

(*a*) the employee was employed outside Great Britain during the whole or part of that week, and

(*b*) no employer's contribution in respect of him was paid in respect of the corresponding contribution week,

unless an employer's contribution in respect of him was payable (though not in fact paid) in respect of the corresponding contribution week.

(4) For the purposes of the application of the last preceding subsection to a week of employment where the corresponding contribution week began before the 5th July 1948, an employer's contribution shall be treated as payable as mentioned in that subsection if such a contribution would have been so payable if the statutory provisions relating to national insurance which were in force on 5th July 1948 had been in force in that contribution week.

(4A) Subject to the following provisions of this section, in computing, in relation to an employee the period specified in section 8 (1) of this Act or the period specified in paragraph 1 of Schedule 1 to this Act, a week of employment after the 6th April 1975 and before the day appointed for the coming into force of paragraph 8 of Part I of Schedule 16 to the Employment Protection Act 1975 shall not count if—

(*a*) the employee was employed outside Great Britain during the whole of part of that week; and

(*b*) he was not during that week an employed earner for the purposes of the Social Security Act 1975.

(4B) Subject to the following provisions of this section, in computing in relation to an employee, either of those periods, a week of employment after the day so appointed shall not count if—

(*a*) the employee was employed outside Great Britain during the whole or part of that week; and

(*b*) he was not during that week an employed earner for the purposes of the Social Security Act 1975 in respect of whom a secondary Class 1 contribution was payable under that Act (whether or not such a contribution was in fact paid).

(5) Where by virtue of subsection (3), (4A) or (4B) of this section a week of employment does not count in computing such a period as is mentioned in those subsections, the continuity of that period shall not be broken by reason only that that week of employment does not count in computing that period.

(6) Any question arising under this section—

(*a*) whether an employer's contribution was paid, or was or would have been payable, as mentioned in subsection (3) or (4) of this section; or

(*b*) whether a person was an employed earner for the purposes of the Social Security Act 1975 and if so whether a secondary Class 1 contribution was payable in respect of him under that Act,

shall be determined by the Secretary of State; and any legislation (including regulations) as to the determination of questions which under that Act the Secretary of State is empowered to determine (including provisions as to the reference of questions for decision, or as to appeals, to the High Court or the

Court of Sessions) shall apply to the determination of any question by the Secretary of State under this section.". **[630]**

9. Renumber section 21 (claims for redundancy payments) as subsection (1) of that section, and at the end add—

"or

(*d*) a complaint relating to his dismissal has been presented by the employee under paragraph 17 of Schedule 1 to the Trade Union and Labour Relations Act 1974.

(2) An employee shall not by virtue of the preceding subsection lose his right to a redundancy payment if, during the period of six months immediately following the period mentioned in that subsection, the employee—

(*a*) makes such a claim as is referred to in paragraph (*b*) of that subsection,

(*b*) refers to a tribunal such a question as is referred to in paragraph (*c*) of that subsection, or

(*c*) makes such a complaint as is referred to in paragraph (*d*) of that subsection,

and it appears to the tribunal to be just and equitable that the employee should receive a redundancy payment having regard to the reason shown by the employee for his failure to take any such step as is referred to in paragraph (*a*), (*b*) or (*c*) of this subsection within the period mentioned in the preceding subsection, and to all the other relevant circumstances.". **[631]**

10.—(1) In section 22 (1) at the end insert the following words "and in particular the provisions of section 3 of this Act shall apply accordingly.".

(2) For section 22 (2) substitute the following subsection—

"(2) Where the preceding subsection applies, and the employee's contract of employment is not renewed, and he is not re-engaged under a new contract of employment, so as to be treated, by virtue of section 3 (3) of this Act as not having been dismissed, he shall, without prejudice to section 3 (8) of this Act, be taken for the purposes of this Act to be dismissed by reason of redundancy if the circumstances in which his contract is not so renewed and he is not so re-engaged are wholly or mainly attributable to one or other of the facts specified in paragraphs (*a*) and (*b*) of section 1 (2) of this Act.".

(3) For section 22 (4) substitute the following subsection—

"(4) In this section any reference to section 3 (3) of this Act includes a reference to the said section 3 (3) as applied by section 13 (2) of this Act or as so applied and, where appropriate, modified by section 13A (2) of this Act, and where section 3 (3) applies with modifications in accordance with the said section 13A (2) the references in subsection (2) of this section to renewal of or re-engagement under a contract of employment shall be construed as including references to renewal of or re-engagement in employment otherwise than under a contract of employment.". **[632]**

11. In section 25 (2) for the words "3 (4)" substitute the words "section 3 (9) and (10)". **[633]**

12.—(1) In section 30 (1) (*c*) for the words "Industrial Court" substitute the words "Central Arbitration Committee".

(2) After section 30 (2), insert the following subsection—

"(2A) The Secretary of State may if he thinks fit pay a rebate to an employer who has paid an employee a redundancy payment in circumstances in which, owing to section 21 of this Act, the employee had no right to, and the employer had no liability for, the payment, if the Secretary of State is satisfied that it would be just and equitable to do so having regard to all the relevant circumstances.". **[634]**

13. In section 31 (4) (repayment from Redundancy Fund in certain cases) for

the words "the appropriate allocation to the Redundancy Fund" substitute the words "the amount paid into the Redundancy Fund from the appropriate employment protection allocation." [**635**]

14. In section 32 (5) (definition of insolvency), at the end of paragraph (*a*) insert the words "or a receiving order is made against him". [**636**]

15. (*Applies to Scotland.*) [**637**]

16. In section 34 after subsection (3) insert the following subsection—

"(3A) Where, in any case to which section 30 (2A) of this Act applies, the Secretary of State refuses to pay a rebate, the employer may appeal to a tribunal; and if on any such appeal the tribunal is satisfied that it is just and equitable having regard to all the relevant circumstances that a rebate should be paid, the tribunal shall determine accordingly, and the Secretary of State shall comply with any such determination of a tribunal.". [**638**]

17. In section 35 (2) (limit on advances from the National Loans Fund to the Redundancy Fund) for the words "£8 million" and "£20 million" substitute respectively the words "£16 million" and "£40 million". [**639**]

18. For section 48 (associated companies) substitute the following section—

"48. Associated employers

(1) Any reference in Part I of this Act to re-engagement by the employer shall be construed as a reference to re-engagement by the employer or by any associated employer, and any reference in that Part of this Act to an offer made by the employer shall be construed as including a reference to an offer made by an associated employer.

(2) The preceding subsection shall not affect the operation of section 13 of this Act in a case where the previous owner and the new owner (as defined by that section) are associated employers; and where that section applies, the preceding subsection shall not apply.

(3) Where an employee is dismissed by his employer and—

(*a*) neither of the conditions specified in paragraphs (*a*) and (*b*) of section 1 (2) of this Act is fulfilled, but

(*b*) one or other of those conditions would be fulfilled if the business of the employer together with the business or businesses of his associated employers were treated as one business,

that condition shall for the purposes of Part I of this Act be taken to be fulfilled in relation to the dismissal of the employee.

(4) For the purposes of this section any two employers are to be treated as associated if one is a company of which the other (directly or indirectly) has control, or if both are companies of which a third person (directly or indirectly) has control; and the expression "associated employer" shall be construed accordingly.". [**640**]

19. In paragraph 1 (1) of Schedule 1 (computation of period of employment for calculating redundancy payments) in paragraph (*a*) omit the word "and", and after paragraph (*b*) insert the following paragraph—

"and

(*c*) the period of any such interval as is referred to in section 8 (3A) of this Act counted as a period of employment notwithstanding that it does not count under that Schedule.". [**641**]

20. In paragraph 1 (2) of Schedule 1 for the words "or section 24" substitute the words ", section 24 or section 24A". [**642**]

21. For paragraph 5 of Schedule 1 (computation of and limit on a week's pay for calculating redundancy payments) substitute the following paragraph—

"5.—(1) For the purposes of Part II of Schedule 4 to the Employment Protection Act 1975 as it applies for the calculation of a week's pay for the purposes of this Schedule, the calculation date is, subject to sub-paragraph (3) below, the date on which notice would have been given by the employer had the conditions referred to in the next following sub-paragraph been fulfilled (whether those conditions were in fact fulfilled or not).

(2) Those conditions are that the contract was terminable by notice and was terminated by the employer giving such notice as is required to terminate that contract by section 1 (1) of the Contracts of Employment Act 1972 (minimum period of notice) and that the notice expired on the relevant date.

(3) Where by virtue of section 3 (10) of this Act a date is to be treated as the relevant date for the purposes of certain provisions of this Act (which do not include this sub-paragraph) which is later than the relevant date as defined by subsection (9) of that section, then, for the purposes of Part II of Schedule 4 to the Employment Protection Act 1975 as it applies for the calculation of a week's pay for the purposes of this Schedule, the calculation date is the relevant date as defined by the said subsection (9).

(4) Notwithstanding anything in the said Part II of Schedule 4, the amount of a week's pay for the purpose of calculating a redundancy payment shall not exceed £80.

(5) The Secretary of State may, after a review under section 86 of the Employment Protection Act 1975, vary the limit referred to in the preceding sub-paragraph by order made by statutory instrument in accordance with that section.

(6) An order under this paragraph may contain such transitional and incidental provisions as appear to the Secretary of State to be necessary or expedient, and may be varied or revoked by a subsequent order made thereunder.

(7) Without prejudice to the generality of the power under the last preceding sub-paragraph to make transitional provision in an order under this paragraph, such an order may provide that it shall apply in the case of a dismissal in relation to which the relevant date for the purposes of this sub-paragraph falls after the order comes into operation, notwithstanding that the relevant date for the purposes of other provisions of this Act falls before the order comes into operation.". [**643**]

22. In paragraph 9 of Schedule 1 after the word "week" insert the words ", except in the expression "a week's pay,"" and omit the words from "and" to the end. [**644**]

23. For paragraphs 3 and 4 of Schedule 4 (renewal of employment by personal representative of deceased employer) substitute the following paragraphs—

"3. Where by virtue of subsection (1) of section 22 of this Act the death of the deceased employer is to be treated for the purposes of this Act as a termination by him of the contract of employment, section 3 of this Act shall have effect subject to the following modifications:—

(*a*) for subsection (3) there shall be substituted the following subsection—

"(3) If an employee's contract of employment is renewed or he is re-engaged under a new contract of employment, by a personal representative of the deceased employer and the renewal or re-engagement takes effect not later than eight weeks after the death of the deceased employer, then, subject to subsections (5) and (8) of this section, the employee shall not be regarded as having been dismissed by reason of the ending of his employment under the previous contract.".

(*b*) in subsection (4) paragraph (*a*) shall be omitted and in paragraph (*b*) for the words "four weeks" there shall be substituted the words "eight weeks";

(*c*) in subsections (7) and (8) references to the employer shall be construed as references to the personal representative of the deceased employer.

4. Where by reason of the death of the deceased employer the employee is treated for the purposes of this Act as having been dismissed by him, section 2 of this Act shall have effect subject to the following modifications—

(*a*) for subsection (3) there shall be substituted the following subsection—

"(3) If a personal representative of the deceased employer makes an employee an offer (whether in writing or not) to renew his contract of employment, or to re-engage him under a new contract of employment, so that the renewal or re-engagement would take effect not later than eight weeks after the death of the deceased employer the provisions of subsections (5) and (6) of this section shall have effect.";

(*b*) in subsection (4) paragraph (*a*) shall be omitted and in paragraph (*b*) for the words "four weeks" there shall be substituted the words "eight weeks";

(*c*) in subsection (5) the reference to the employer shall be construed as a reference to the personal representative of the deceased employer.". **[645]**

24. In paragraph 5 of Schedule 4 at the end insert "or, as the case may be, whether the employee acted reasonably in terminating the renewed, or new, employment during the trial period referred to in section 3 of this Act". **[646]**

25. Paragraph 6 of Schedule 4 is hereby repealed. **[647]**

26. In paragraph 7 of Schedule 4 for the words from "as mentioned" to "Schedule" substitute the words "by a personal representative of the deceased employer". **[648]**

27. Paragraph 12 of Schedule 4 is hereby repealed. **[649]**

28. Renumber paragraph 16 of Schedule 4 (death of employee during notice period) as sub-paragraph (1) of that paragraph and after that sub-paragraph insert the following sub-paragraph—

"(2) Where the employee's contract of employment has been terminated by the employer and by virtue of section 3 (10) of this Act a date later than the relevant date as defined by subsection (9) of that section is to be treated as the relevant date for the purposes of certain provisions of this Act, and before that later date the employee dies, the said subsection (10) shall have effect as if the notice referred to in that subsection as required to be given by an employer would have expired on the employee's death.". **[650]**

29. Renumber paragraph 17 of Schedule 4 (death of employee after offer of alternative employment) as sub-paragraph (1) of that paragraph. **[651]**

30. In that sub-paragraph for the words from "subsection (3)" to the end substitute the words "subsection (5) of section 2 of this Act shall apply as if for the words "the employee unreasonably refuses" there were substituted the words "it would have been unreasonable on the part of the employee to refuse."." **[652]**

31. After that sub-paragraph insert the following sub-paragraph—

"(2) Where an employee's contract of employment has been renewed, or he has been re-engaged under a new contract of employment, and during the trial period the employee dies without having terminated or having given notice to terminate the contract, subsection (6) of that section shall apply as if for the words from "and during the trial period" to "terminated" there were substituted the words "and it would have been unreasonable for the employee, during the trial period referred to in section 3 of this Act, to terminate or give notice to terminate the contract". **[653]**

32. After paragraph 17 of Schedule 4, insert the following paragraph—

"17A. Where an employee's contract of employment has been renewed, or he has been re-engaged under a new contract of employment, and during the trial period he gives notice to terminate the contract but dies before the expiry of that notice sections 2 (6) and 3 (8) (*a*) shall have effect as if that notice had expired and the contract had thereby been terminated on the date of the employee's death.". [**654**]

33. Renumber paragraph 20 of Schedule 4 as sub-paragraph (1) of that paragraph and—

(*a*) in that sub-paragraph after the words "relevant date" insert the words "subsection (1) of"; and

(*b*) after that sub-paragraph insert the following sub-paragraph—

"(2) In relation to the making of a claim by a personal representative of a deceased employee who dies after the end of the period of six months beginning with the relevant date and before the end of the following period of six months, subsection (2) of section 21 of this Act shall apply with the substitution, for the words "six months", of the words "one year".". [**655**]

34. After paragraph 21 of Schedule 4 insert the following paragraph—

"21A.—(1) If there is no personal representative of a deceased employee, tribunal proceedings arising under any of the provisions of this Act (or proceedings to enforce a tribunal award made in any such proceedings) may be instituted or continued on behalf of the estate of the deceased employee by such other person as the tribunal may appoint being either—

(*a*) a person authorised by the employee to act in connection with the proceedings before the employee's death; or

(*b*) the widower, widow, child, father, mother, brother or sister of the deceased employee,

and references in this Part of this Schedule to a personal representative shall be construed as including such a person.

(2) In such a case any award made by the tribunal shall be in such terms and shall be enforceable in such manner as may be provided by regulations made by the Secretary of State.

(3) Section 122 of the Employment Protection Act 1975 shall apply to this paragraph as if it were a provision of that Act.". [**656**]

COMMENCEMENT

Paragraph 17 was brought into force on 1st January 1976 by the Employment Protection Act 1975 (Commencement No. 1) Order 1975, S.I. 1975 No. 1938.

PART II

CONTRACTS OF EMPLOYMENT ACT 1972

1. In sections 1 (1) to (3) and 2 (minimum period of notice) for the words "thirteen weeks", wherever they occur, substitute the words "four weeks". [**657**]

2. In section 1 (1) for paragraphs (*b*) to (*e*) substitute the following paragraphs—

"(*b*) shall be not less than one week's notice for each year of continuous employment if his period of continuous employment is two years or more but less than twelve years; and

(*c*) shall be not less than twelve weeks' notice if his period of continuous employment is twelve years or more.". [**658**]

3. In section 1 (4) (contract for a term certain to be treated in certain cases as a contract for an indefinite period) for the words "thirteen weeks" substitute the words "twelve weeks". [**659**]

4. In section 4 (1) (written statement of terms of employment),—

(*a*) after the words "the date when the employment began", insert the words "stating whether any employment with a previous employer counts as part of the employee's continuous period of employment with him, and if so specifying the date on which the continuous period of employment began"; and

(*b*) after paragraph (*e*) insert "and

(*f*) the title of the job which the employee is employed to do:". **[660]**

5. In section 4 (2) (written particulars to contain note about grievance procedure)—

(*a*) at the beginning insert the words "Subject to subsection (2A) of this section"; and

(*b*) for paragraphs (*b*) and (*c*) substitute the following paragraphs:—

"(*a*) specifying any disciplinary rules applicable to the employee, or referring to a document which is reasonably accessible to the employee and which specifies such rules;

(*b*) specifying, by description or otherwise—

(i) a person to whom the employee can apply if he is dissatisfied with any disciplinary decision relating to him; and

(ii) a person to whom the employee can apply for the purpose of seeking redress of any grievance relating to his employment,

and the manner in which any such applications should be made; and

(*c*) where there are further steps consequent upon any such application, explaining those steps or referring to a document which is reasonably accessible to the employee and which explains them,". **[661]**

6. After section 4 (2) insert the following subsection—

"(2A) The provisions of paragraphs (*b*) to (*d*) of subsection (2) of this section shall not apply to rules, disciplinary decisions, grievances or procedures relating to health or safety at work.". **[662]**

7. In section 4 (7) (part-time employment)—

(*a*) at the beginning insert the words "Subject to the following provisions of this section,"; and

(*b*) for the words "twenty-one hours" substitute the words "sixteen hours". **[663]**

8. After section 4 (7) insert the following subsections—

"(8) If the employee's relations with his employer cease to be governed by a contract which normally involves work for sixteen hours or more weekly and become governed by a contract which normally involves employment for eight hours or more, but less than sixteen hours, weekly, the employee shall nevertheless for a period of twenty-six weeks computed in accordance with the next following subsection be treated for the purposes of the foregoing subsection as if his contract normally involved employment for sixteen hours or more weekly.

(9) In computing the said period of twenty-six weeks no account shall be taken of any week—

(*a*) during which the employee is in fact employed for sixteen hours or more;

(*b*) during which the employee takes part in a strike (as defined in paragraph 11 of Schedule 1 to this Act), or is absent from work because of a lock-out (as so defined) by his employer; or

(*c*) during which there is no contract of employment but which, by virtue of paragraph 5 (1) of Schedule 1 to this Act, counts in computing a period of continuous employment.

(10) An employee whose relations with his employer are governed by a

contract of employment which normally involves employment for eight hours or more, but less than sixteen hours, weekly shall nevertheless, if he has been continuously employed for a period of five years or more (computed in accordance with Schedule 1 to this Act) be treated for the purposes of subsection (7) of this section as if his contract normally involved employment for sixteen hours or more weekly.". [**664**]

9. In section 5 (4) (written statement of change in terms of employment), after the word "but" insert the words "subject to subsection (5) of this section", and after that subsection insert the following subsection—

"(5) A written statement under this section which informs an employee of such a change in his terms of employment as is referred to in subsection (4) (*b*) of this section shall specify the date on which the employee's continuous period of employment began.". [**665**]

10. In section 9 (excluded categories of employees)—

(*a*) after subsection (2) insert the following subsection—

"(2A) Section 1 of this Act shall not apply to a person employed under a contract made in contemplation of the performance of a specific task which is not expected to last for more than twelve weeks, unless the employee has been continuously employed for a period of more than twelve weeks (computed in accordance with Schedule 1 to this Act)."; and

(*b*) in subsection (3) for the words from "father" to "daughter" substitute the words "husband or wife". [**666**]

11. For section 10 (power to vary number of weekly hours of employment necessary to qualify for rights) substitute the following section—

"10. Power to vary number of weekly hours of employment necessary to qualify for rights

(1) The Secretary of State shall have power by order to provide that this Act shall have effect as if—

(*a*) for each of the references to sixteen hours in section 4 (7) to (10) of this Act and in paragraphs 3, 4, 4A, 4B and 4C of Schedule 1 to this Act there were substituted a reference to such other number of hours less than sixteen as may be specified in the order; and

(*b*) as if for each of the references to eight hours in section 4 (7), (8) and (10) of this Act and in paragraphs 4B and 4C of the said Schedule there were substituted a reference to such other number of hours less than eight as may be specified in the order.

(2) An order under the foregoing subsection shall affect the operation of Schedule 1 to this Act as respects periods before the order takes effect as well as respects later periods.

(3) An order under this section may contain such transitional and other supplemental and incidental provisions as appear to the Secretary of State to be expedient, and may be varied or revoked by a further order so made.

(4) An order under this section shall be made by statutory instrument, but no such order shall be made unless a draft of the order has been laid before Parliament and approved by resolution of each House." [**667**]

12. For paragraph 1 (1) of Schedule 1 (computation of period of employment) substitute the following sub-paragraph—

"(1) Where an employee's period of employment is, for the purposes of any enactment (including any enactment contained in this Act), to be computed in accordance with this Schedule, it shall be computed in weeks, and in any such enactment which refers to a period of employment expressed in years, a year means 52 weeks (whether continuous or discontinuous) which count in computing a period of employment.". [**668**]

13. In paragraph 3 and 4 of Schedule 1 for the words "twenty-one hours" wherever they occur substitute the words "sixteen hours". [**669**]

14. After paragraph 4 of Schedule 1 insert the following paragraphs—

"4A.—(1) If the employee's relations with his employer cease to be governed by a contract which normally involves work for sixteen hours or more weekly and become governed by a contract which normally involves employment for eight hours or more, but less than sixteen hours, weekly, and but for that change the later weeks would count in computing a period of employment, or would not break the continuity of a period of employment, then those later weeks shall count in computing a period of employment or, as the case may be, shall not break the continuity of a period of employment, notwithstanding that change.

(2) Not more than twenty-six weeks shall count under this paragraph between any two periods falling under paragraph 4 of this Schedule, and in computing the said figure of twenty-six weeks no account shall be taken of any week which counts in computing a period of employment, or does not break the continuity of a period of employment, otherwise than by virtue of this paragraph.

4B.—(1) An employee whose relations with his employer are governed, or have been from time to time governed, by a contract of employment which normally involves employment for eight hours or more, but less than sixteen hours, weekly shall nevertheless, if he satisfies the condition referred to in the next following sub-paragraph, be treated for the purposes of this Schedule (apart from this paragraph) as if his contract normally involved employment for sixteen hours or more weekly, and had at all times at which there was a contract during the period of employment of five years or more referred to in the next following sub-paragraph normally involved employment for sixteen hours or more weekly.

(2) The foregoing sub-paragraph shall apply if the employee, on the date by reference to which the length of any period of employment falls to be ascertained in accordance with the provisions of this Schedule, has been continuously employed, within the meaning of the next following sub-paragraph, for a period of five years or more.

(3) In computing, for the purposes of the foregoing sub-paragraph, an employee's period of employment the provisions of this Schedule (apart from this paragraph) shall apply but as if, in paragraphs 3 and 4, for the words "sixteen hours" wherever they occur, there were substituted the words "eight hours".

4C.—(1) If an employee has, at any time during the relevant period of employment, been continuously employed for a period which qualifies him for any right which requires a qualifying period of continuous employment computed in accordance with this Schedule, then, he shall be regarded for the purposes of qualifying for that right as continuing to satisfy that requirement, until the condition referred to in sub-paragraph (3) of this paragraph occurs.

(2) In this paragraph the relevant period of employment means the period of employment ending on the date by reference to which the length of any period of employment falls to be ascertained which would be continuous (in accordance with the provisions of this Schedule) if at all relevant times the employee's relations with the employer had been governed by a contract of employment which normally involved employment for sixteen hours or more weekly.

(3) The condition which defeats the operation of sub-paragraph (1) of this paragraph is that in a week subsequent to the time at which the employee qualified as referred to in that sub-paragraph—

(*a*) his relations with his employer are governed by a contract of employment which normally involves employment for less than eight hours weekly; and

(*b*) he is employed in that week for less than sixteen hours.

(4) If, in a case in which an employee is entitled to any right by virtue of sub-paragraph (1) of this paragraph, it is necessary for the purpose of ascertaining the amount of his entitlement to determine for what period he has been continuously employed, he shall be regarded for that purpose as having been continuously employed throughout the relevant period.". **[670]**

15. In paragraph 5 (1) of Schedule 1 after paragraph (*c*) insert the following paragraph:—

"or

(*d*) absent from work wholly or partly because of pregnancy or confinement,"

and for the words "or paragraph 4" substitute the words ", 4 or 4A." **[671]**

16. In paragraph 5 (2) of Schedule 1, after the words "paragraph (*a*)" insert the words "or, subject to paragraph 5A below, paragraph (*d*)", and for the words "two periods falling under paragraphs 3 and 4" substitute the words "periods falling under paragraph 3, 4 or 4A". **[672]**

17. After paragraph 5 of Schedule 1, insert the following paragraph:—

"5A. If an employee returns to work in accordance with section 49 of the Employment Protection Act 1975 after a period of absence from work wholly or partly occasioned by pregnancy or confinement, every week during that period shall count in computing a period of employment, notwithstanding that it does not fall under paragraph 3, 4 or 4A of this Schedule.". **[673]**

18. In paragraph 6 (1) of Schedule 1, for the words "paragraph 4 or paragraph 5", substitute the words "4, 4A, 5, or 5A". **[674]**

19. For paragraph 10 of Schedule 1, substitute the following paragraph:—

"10.—(1) If an employee of an employer is taken into the employment of another employer who, at the time when the employee enters his employment is an associated employer of the first mentioned employer, the employee's period of employment at that time shall count as a period of employment with the second mentioned employer and the change of employer shall not break the continuity of the period of employment.

(2) For the purposes of this paragraph, any two employers are to be treated as associated if one is a company of which the other (directly or indirectly) has control, or if both are companies of which a third person (directly or indirectly) has control; and the expression "associated employer" shall be construed accordingly.". **[675]**

COMMENCEMENT

See s. 129 (3), *ante*.

PART III

TRADE UNION AND LABOUR RELATIONS ACT 1974

1. In sections 8 and 11, and in Schedule 2, for the words "Registrar of Friendly Societies" and "Registrar" wherever they occur substitute the words "Certification Officer". **[676]**

2. In section 8, after subsection (6) insert the following subsection:—

"(6A) The Certification Officer shall remove the name of an organisation from the relevant list—

(*a*) if he is requested by the organisation to do so, or

(*b*) if he is satisfied that the organisation has ceased to exist.". **[677]**

3. For section 8 (7) substitute the following subsection:—

"(7) Any organisation aggrieved by the refusal of the Certification Officer to enter its name in the relevant list or by a decision of his to remove its name from that list may appeal, in accordance with section 88 (3) of the Employment Protection Act 1975, to the Employment Appeal Tribunal; and on any such appeal the Tribunal, if satisfied that the name should be or remain so entered, shall declare that fact and give directions to the Certification Officer accordingly.". **[678]**

4. In section 8 (9), for the words from "Chief Registrar" to the end of the subsection substitute the words "Certification Officer under paragraph 13 (2) of Schedule 1 to the Employment Protection Act 1975.". **[679]**

5. In section 8 (10), for the words from the beginning to "employers' associations" substitute the words "The fact that the name of an organisation is included in the list of trade unions or employers' associations shall be evidence (and in Scotland sufficient evidence) that the organisation is a trade union or, as the case may be, an employers' association, and on the application of the organisation", and omit the words from "and that the organisation" to the end. **[680]**

6. Renumber section 17 (Restriction on grant of ex parte injunctions and interdicts) as subsection (1) of that section and at the end of that section insert the following subsections:—

"(2) It is hereby declared for the avoidance of doubt that where an application is made to a court, pending the trial of an action, for an interlocutory injunction and the party against whom the injunction is sought claims that he acted in contemplation or furtherance of a trade dispute, the court shall, in exercising its discretion whether or not to grant the injunction, have regard to the likelihood of that party's succeeding at the trial of the action in establishing the matter or matters which would, under any provision of section 13, 14 (2) or 15 above, afford a defence to the action.

(3) Subsection (2) above shall not extend to Scotland." **[681]**

7.—(1) In section 30 (1), after the definition of "act" and "action" insert—

"Certification Officer" means the officer appointed under section 7 of the Employment Protection Act 1975;".

(2) In that subsection, after the definition of "employee" insert—

" 'employer' (subject to subsection (2) below)—

(*a*) where the reference is to an employer in relation to an employee, means the person by whom the employee is (or, in a case where the employment has ceased, was) employed, and

(*b*) in any other case, means a person regarded in that person's capacity as one for whom one or more workers work, or have worked or normally work or seek to work;".

(3) In that subsection, at the end of the definition of "independent trade union" insert "and 'in relation to a trade union' "independence" and "independent" shall be construed accordingly;".

(4) In that subsection, after the definition of "individual proprietor" insert—

" 'job', in relation to an employee, means the nature of the work which he is employed to do in accordance with his contract and the capacity and place in which he is so employed;".

(5) In that subsection, after the definition of "1971 Act", insert—

" 'officer', in relation to a trade union or an employers' association includes any member of the governing body of that union or association and any trustee of any fund applicable for the purposes of that union or association;". **[682]**

8. In paragraph 5 (3) of Schedule 1 (meaning of dismissal), omit the words "obligatory" and "in writing". **[683]**

9. Omit paragraph 5 (4) of Schedule 1. **[684]**

10. After paragraph 5 (5) of Schedule 1 insert the following sub-paragraph—

"(6) Where the notice required to be given by an employer by section 1 (1) of the Contracts of Employment Act 1972 (minimum period of notice) would, if duly given when notice of termination was given by the employer, or (where no notice was given) when the contract of employment was terminated by the employer, expire on a date later than the effective date of termination as defined by sub-paragraph (5) above, that later date shall be treated as the effective date of termination in relation to the dismissal for the purposes of paragraph 10 (*a*) below and of sections 70 (2), 74 (3) and 75 (6) of the Employment Protection Act 1975 (written statement of reasons for dismissal and calculation of basic award of compensation for unfair dismissal).'. [**685**]

11. After paragraph 6 (4) of Schedule 1, insert the following sub-paragraph:—

"(4A) In sub-paragraph (4) above, "appropriate time" in relation to an employee taking part in the activities of a trade union, means time which either—

(*a*) is outside his working hours, or

(*b*) is a time within his working hours at which, in accordance with arrangements agreed with or consent given by his employer, it is permissible for him to take part in those activities;

and in this sub-paragraph "working hours", in relation to an employee, means any time when, in accordance with his contract of employment, he is required to be at work.". [**686**]

12. After paragraph 6 (5) of Schedule 1 (dismissal in closed shop situation), insert the following sub-paragraph:—

"(5A) For the purposes of sub-paragraph (5) above a union shall be treated as specified for the purposes of or in relation to a union membership agreement (in a case where it would not otherwise be so treated) if—

(*a*) the Service has made a recommendation for recognition covering the employee in question which is operative within the meaning of section 15 of the Employment Protection Act 1975; or

(*b*) the union has referred a recognition issue (within the meaning of that Act) covering that employee to the Advisory, Conciliation and Arbitration Service under section 11 of that Act and the Service has not declined to proceed on the reference under section 12 of that Act, the union has not withdrawn the reference, or from the reference, and the issue has not been settled or reported on under that section.". [**687**]

13. For paragraphs 7 and 8 of Schedule 1 (dismissal in connection with industrial action) substitute the following paragraph:—

"7.—(1) The provisions of this paragraph shall have effect in relation to an employee who claims that he has been unfairly dismissed by his employer where at the date of dismissal—

(*a*) the employer was conducting or instituting a lock-out; or

(*b*) the employee was taking part in a strike or other industrial action.

(2) In such a case an industrial tribunal shall not determine whether the dismissal was fair or unfair unless it is shown—

(*a*) that one or more relevant employees of the same employer have not been dismissed, or

(*b*) that one or more such employees have been offered re-engagement, and that the employee concerned has not been offered re-engagement.

(3) Where it is shown that the condition referred to in paragraph (*b*) of sub-paragraph (2) above is fulfilled, the provisions of paragraph 6 above and of section 34 of the Employment Protection Act 1975 shall have effect as if in that paragraph and that section for any reference to the reason or principal

reason for which the employee was dismissed there were substituted a reference to the reason or principal reason for which he has not been offered re-engagement.

(4) Paragraph 21 (4) below shall apply in relation to a complaint to which sub-paragraph (3) above applies as if for references to the effective date of termination there were substituted a reference to the first date on which any relevant employee was offered re-engagement.

(5) In this paragraph—

(*a*) "date of dismissal" means—

(i) where the employee's contract of employment was terminated by notice, the date on which the employer's notice was given, and

(ii) in any other case, the effective date of termination.

(*b*) "relevant employees" means—

(i) in relation to a lock-out, employees who were directly interested in the trade dispute in contemplation or furtherance of which the lock-out occurred, and

(ii) in relation to a strike or other industrial action, employees who took part in it; and

(*c*) any reference to an offer of re-engagement is a reference to an offer (made either by the original employer or by a successor of that employer or an associated employer) to re-engage an employee, either in the job which he held immediately before the date of dismissal or in a different job which would be reasonably suitable in his case.". **[688]**

14.—(1) In paragraph 9 (1) of Schedule 1—

(*a*) omit paragraph (*a*);

(*b*) in paragraph (*b*), omit the words "or a close relative"; and

(*c*) omit paragraphs (*e*) and (*f*).

(2) Omit paragraph 9 (4) of Schedule 1. **[689]**

15. In paragraph 11 (1) of Schedule 1 for the words "Paragraphs 9 (1) (*a*) and 10" substitute the words "Paragraph 10". **[690]**

16. In paragraph 17 (1) of Schedule 1 omit the words "or by a person acting on the employer's behalf" (which are unnecessary). **[691]**

17. For paragraph 20 of Schedule 1 substitute the following paragraph:—

"20.—(1) The amount of compensation awarded to a person under section 72 (1) of the Employment Protection Act 1975 or of a compensatory award to a person calculated in accordance with section 76 of that Act shall not exceed £5,200.

(2) The Secretary of State may by order increase the said limit of £5,200 or that limit as from time to time increased under this sub-paragraph, but no such order shall be made unless a draft of the order has been laid before Parliament and approved by a resolution of each House of Parliament.

(3) It is hereby declared for the avoidance of doubt that the limit imposed by this paragraph applies to the amount which the industrial tribunal would, apart from this paragraph, otherwise award in respect of the subject matter of the complaint after taking into account any payment made by the respondent to the complainant in respect of that matter and any reduction in the amount of the award required by any enactment or rule of law.

(4) Section 123 of the Employment Protection Act 1975 shall apply to this paragraph as if it were a provision of that Act.". **[692]**

18. In paragraph 21 (3) of Schedule 1, after the words "paragraph 17 above"

insert the words "or any other enactment in relation to which there is provision for conciliation,". [**693**]

19. After paragraph 21 (3) of Schedule 1 insert the following sub-paragraph:—

"(3A) In relation to proceedings under paragraph 17 above—

(*a*) where the employee has expressed a wish to be reinstated or re-engaged which has been communicated to the employer at least seven days before the hearing of the complaint; or

(*b*) where the proceedings arise out of the employer's failure to permit the employee to return to work after an absence due to pregnancy or confinement,

regulations shall include provision for requiring the employer to pay the costs or expenses of any postponement or adjournment of the hearing caused by his failure, without a special reason, to adduce reasonable evidence as to the availability of the job from which the complainant was dismissed, or, as the case may be which she held before her absence, or of comparable or suitable employment.". [**694**]

20. In paragraph 21 (4) of Schedule 1, at the beginning insert the words, "Subject to sub-paragraph (4A) below", and for the word "within" in the second place in which it occurs substitute the words "before the end of". [**695**]

21. After paragraph 21 (4) of Schedule 1 insert the following sub-paragraph:—

"(4A) An industrial tribunal shall consider a complaint under paragraph 17 of Schedule 1 above if, where the dismissal is with notice, the complaint is presented after the notice is given notwithstanding that it is presented before the effective date of termination and in relation to such a complaint the provisions of this Act and of the Employment Protection Act 1975, so far as they relate to unfair dismissal, shall have effect—

(*a*) as if references to a complaint by a person that he was unfairly dismissed by his employer included references to a complaint by a person that his employer has given him notice in such circumstances that he will be unfairly dismissed when the notice expires;

(*b*) as if references to reinstatement included references to the withdrawal of the notice by the employer;

(*c*) as if references to the effective date of termination included references to the date which would be the effective date of termination on the expiry of the notice; and

(*d*) as if references to an employee ceasing to be employed included references to an employee having been given notice of dismissal.". [**696**]

22. In paragraph 21 (5) of Schedule 1, in paragraph (*c*) for the words "be seriously prejudicial to the interests of" substitute the words "cause substantial injury to". [**697**]

23. After paragraph 21 (5) of Schedule 1 insert the following sub-paragraph:—

"(5A) The regulations may include provision authorising or requiring an industrial tribunal, in circumstances specified in the regulations, to send notice or a copy of any document so specified relating to any proceedings before the tribunal, or of any decision, order or award of the tribunal, to any Minister, government department or other person or body so specified.". [**698**]

24. In paragraph 26 (3) of Schedule 1—

(*a*) in paragraph (*a*) omit the words "his engagement";

(*b*) for paragraph (*b*) substitute—

"(*b*) where the complainant does not wish to be reinstated or re-engaged, or where reinstatement or re-engagement is not practicable,"; and

(*c*) for the word "they" substitute the words "the parties". [**699**]

25. After paragraph 26 (4) of Schedule 1 insert the following sub-paragraph:—

"(4A) In proceeding under sub-paragraphs (2) to (4) above a conciliation officer shall where appropriate have regard to the desirability of encouraging the use of other procedures available for the settlement of grievances.". [**700**]

26. In paragraph 27 (1) of Schedule 1, after the words "this Schedule" insert the words "and sections 33, 34, 51 and 71 to 80 of the Employment Protection Act 1975". [**701**]

27. In paragraph 27 (2) of Schedule 1, for the words from "paragraph 19" to the end of the sub-paragraph substitute:—

"(*a*) section 72 (2) (*b*) of the Employment Protection Act 1975 shall have effect as if for the words "not practicable to comply" there were substituted the words "not practicable for the local education authority to permit compliance"; and

(*b*) section 76 (5) of the said Act of 1975 shall have effect as if any reference to the employer were a reference to the local education authority.". [**702**]

28. In paragraph 28 (2) of Schedule 1 for the word "claimant" substitute the word "complainant". [**703**]

29. After paragraph 30 (1) of Schedule 1 insert the following sub-paragraph:—

"(1A) Where by virtue of paragraph 5 (6) above a date is to be treated as the effective date of termination for the purpose of paragraph 10 (*a*) above which is later than the effective date of termination as defined by paragraph 5 (5) above, then in determining for the purpose of paragraph 10 (*a*) above for what period an employee has been continuously employed, the period of the interval between those two dates shall count as a period of employment notwithstanding that it does not count under the said Schedule 1.". [**704**]

30. In paragraph 30 (3) of Schedule 1, for the words from "section 24" to the end of the sub-paragraph substitute:—

"sections 24 and 24A of the Redundancy Payments Act 1965 (which require the continuity of a period of employment to be treated as broken for the purposes of that Act where a redundancy payment or an equivalent payment is paid to an employee and he is subsequently re-engaged) subject to the recovery of any such payment,

in cases where, in consequence of action to which sub-paragraph (4) below applies, a dismissed employee is reinstated or re-engaged by his employer or by a successor or associated employer of that employer.". [**705**]

31. In paragraph 31 (1) (*b*) of Schedule 1 (nominations by members of trade unions) for the words "£500" substitute the words "£1,500". [**706**]

32. In paragraph 31 of Schedule 1, for sub-paragraphs (4) and (5) substitute the following sub-paragraph:—

"(4) Sub-paragraph (1) (*b*) above shall be included among the provisions with respect to which the Treasury may make an order under section 6 (1) of the Administration of Estates (Small Payments) Act 1965, substituting, for references to the amount for the time being provided for, references to such higher amount as may be specified in the order.". [**707**]

33. In paragraph 33 (2) of Schedule 1, after the words "government department" insert the words "or any officer or body exercising on behalf of the Crown functions conferred by any enactment", and in paragraph 33 (3) (*e*) of that Schedule, after the word "department" in the second, third and fourth places where it occurs insert the words, "officer or body". [**708**]

34. After paragraph 33 (4) of Schedule 1, insert the following sub-paragraph:—

"(4A) For the purposes of the application of the provisions of this Act in relation to employment by any such body as is referred to in sub-paragraph

(4) (*a*) above, any reference to redundancy shall be construed as a reference to the existence of such circumstances as, in accordance with any arrangements for the time being in force as mentioned in section 41 (3) of the Redundancy Payments Act 1965, are treated as equivalent to redundancy in relation to such employment.". **[709]**

35.—(1) For the avoidance of doubt it is hereby declared that the change of name of the Industrial Court to the Industrial Arbitration Board originally effected by section 124 (2) of the Industrial Relations Act 1971 and continued in force, so far as the Industrial Courts Act 1919 is concerned, by paragraph 3 of Schedule 3 to the 1974 Act, shall, as respects the relevant period, be taken not to have divested that body of any functions under any other enactment or any instrument notwithstanding that after the repeal by the 1974 Act of the said section 124 (2) references in any such other enactment or any such instrument to the Industrial Court were no longer expressly directed to be construed as references to the Industrial Arbitration Board.

(2) In this paragraph "the relevant period" means the period beginning with 16th September 1974 (the day appointed for the coming into operation of the said Schedule 3) and ending with the repeal by this Act of Part I of the Industrial Courts Act 1919. **[710]**

COMMENCEMENT

Paragraphs 5, 6, 7 (2) and (5), 11, 18, 23, 25, 31, 32 and 33 were brought into force on 1st January 1976 and paras. 1, 2, 3, 4, 7 (1) and (3), 12 and 35 on 1st February 1976 by the Employment Protection Act 1975 (Commencement No. 1) Order 1975, S.I. 1975 No. 1938.

Part IV

Miscellaneous Amendments

House of Commons Offices Act 1846 (*c.* 77)

1. In section 5 of the House of Commons Offices Act 1846, after the words "the said first-recited Act" insert the words ", the Employment Protection Act 1975,". **[711]**

The Trade Union Act 1913 (2 & 3 *Geo.* 5 *c.* 30)

2.—(1) The Trade Union Act 1913 shall be amended in accordance with the following provisions of this paragraph.

(2) In sections 3 to 5 for the words "Registrar of Friendly Societies" and "Registrar" wherever they occur substitute the words "Certification Officer".

(3) After section 5 insert the following section—

"5A. Appeals

An appeal shall lie, in accordance with section 88 (2) of the Employment Protection Act 1975, to the Employment Appeal Tribunal on any question of law arising in any proceedings before or arising from any decision of the Certification Officer under section 3, 4 or 5 of this Act.".

(4) For section 7 substitute—

"7. Definition of Certification Officer

In this Act references to the "Certification Officer" are references to the officer appointed under section 7 of the Employment Protection Act 1975.". **[712]**

The Industrial Courts Act 1919 (*c.* 69)

3.—(1) The Industrial Courts Act 1919 shall be amended in accordance with the following provisions of this paragraph.

(2) The following provisions and passages are hereby repealed:—

Sections 1, 2 and 3

In section 4 (1), the words "whether or not the dispute is reported to him under Part I of this Act".

In section 7, the words "of the Industrial Arbitration Board and".

In section 9, the words "before the Industrial Arbitration Board, before an arbitrator or".

Sections 11 and 12.

(3) For section 8 substitute—

"8. Interpretation

In this Act the expressions "trade dispute" and "worker" have the same meaning as in the Trade Union and Labour Relations Act 1974.".

(4) For section 10 substitute—

"10. Employment under the Crown

(1) Subject to the following provisions of this section, the provisions of this Act shall have effect in relation to Crown employment and to workers who are Crown employees as they have effect in relation to other employment and to other workers.

(2) In this section "Crown employment" means, subject to subsection (3) of this section, employment under or for the purposes of a government department or any officer or body exercising on behalf of the Crown functions conferred by any enactment.

(3) This section does not apply to service as a member of the naval, military or air forces of the Crown or of any women's service administered by the Defence Council, but does apply to employment by any association established for the purposes of the Auxiliary Forces Act 1953.

(4) A Minister of the Crown may exempt from the provisions of this section employment of a specified description or the employment of a particular person by certificate stating that such exemption is required for the purpose of safeguarding national security; and any document purporting to be such a certificate shall, unless the contrary is proved, be deemed to be such a certificate.". [**713**]

Road Haulage Wages Act 1938 (*c.* 44)

4.—(1) The Road Haulage Wages Act 1938 shall be amended in accordance with the following provisions of this paragraph.

(2) In sections 4 and 5 for the word "Minister" substitute the word "Service" and in section 15 (1) after the definition of "Road haulage work" and "Road haulage worker" insert—

" 'Service' means the Advisory, Conciliation and Arbitration Service.".

(3) In sections 4, 5 and 8 for the words "Industrial Court" and "Court" wherever they occur substitute respectively the words "Central Arbitration Committee" and "Committee".

(4) In section 4 (6) for the words "the Industrial Courts Act, 1919" substitute the words "section 3 of the Employment Protection Act 1975".

(5) Section 5 (5) is hereby repealed. [**714**]

Civil Aviation Act 1949 (*c.* 67)

5. In section 15 of the Civil Aviation Act 1949, in subsection (2) for the word "Minister" substitute the words "Advisory, Conciliation and Arbitration Service", and in subsections (2) and (3) for the words "Industrial Court" and "Court" wherever they occur substitute respectively the words "Central Arbitration Committee" and "Committee." [**715**]

Public Records Act 1958 (*c.* 51)

6. In Part II of the Table at the end of paragraph 3 (2) of Schedule 1 to the Public Records Act 1958 insert at the appropriate place in alphabetical order the following entry—

"Commission on Industrial Relations.". **[716]**

Road Traffic Act 1960 (*c.* 16)

7. In section 152 of the Road Traffic Act 1960,—

(*a*) for subsection (2) substitute the following subsection:—

"(2) Any organisation representative of the persons engaged in the road transport industry may make representations to the Advisory, Conciliation and Arbitration Service to the effect that the wages paid to, or the conditions of employment of, any persons employed by the holder of a road service licence are not in accordance with the requirements of the foregoing subsection, and if the matter in dispute is not otherwise disposed of it shall be referred by the Service to the Central Arbitration Committee for settlement."; and

(*b*) in subsections (3) and (4) for the words "Industrial Court" and "Court", wherever they occur, substitute respectively the words "Central Arbitration Committee" and "Committee". **[717]**

Films Act 1960 (*c.* 57)

8. In section 42 of the Films Act 1960 for the words "Minister of Labour" substitute the words "Advisory, Conciliation and Arbitration Service" and for the words "industrial court" and "court" wherever they occur substitute respectively the words "Central Arbitration Committee" and "Committee". **[718]**

9. (*Applies to Scotland.*)

The Trade Union (Amalgamations, etc.) Act 1964 (*c.* 24)

10.—(1) The Trade Union (Amalgamations, etc.) Act 1964 shall be amended in accordance with the following provisions of this paragraph.

(2) In sections 1, 4, 6 and 7 (and the Schedules), for the word "Registrar" wherever it occurs substitute the words "Certification Officer", and in section 9 (1) after the definition of "the amalgamating unions" and "the amalgamated union" insert—

" 'Certification Officer' means the officer appointed under section 7 of the Employment Protection Act 1975.".

(3) For section 4 (8) substitute the following subsection—

"(8) An appeal shall lie, in accordance with section 88 (2) of the Employment Protection Act 1975, at the instance of the complainant or the trade union to the Employment Appeal Tribunal on any question of law arising in any proceedings before, or arising from any decision of, the Certification Officer under this section.". **[719]**

Remuneration of Teachers Act 1965 (*c.* 3)

11.—(1) The Remuneration of Teachers Act 1965 shall be amended in accordance with the following provisions of this paragraph.

(2) In section 3 (3) for the words "Minister of Labour" substitute the words "Advisory, Conciliation and Arbitration Service"; and references in any arrangements made by the Secretary of State under section 3 (1) to the Minister of Labour shall be construed as references to the Service.

(3) In section 3 (3), the words from "and, where arbitrators" to the end, and section 6 (*d*) are hereby repealed. **[720]**

12.—(*Applies to Scotland.*) **[721]**

Equal Pay Act 1970 (*c.* 41)

13.—(1) The Equal Pay Act 1970 shall be amended in accordance with the following provisions of this paragraph.

(2) In sections 3, 4, 5, 7 and 10, for the words "Industrial Arbitration Board" (being words substituted by Part I of Schedule 1 to the Sex Discrimination Act 1975), wherever they occur, substitute the words "Central Arbitration Committee".

(3) In sections 4, 5 and 10 for the word "Board" (being a word so substituted), wherever it occurs except in the expression "Agricultural Wages Board", substitute the word "Committee".

(4) In section 3 (1), for the words "Part I of the Industrial Courts Act 1919" there shall be substituted the words "section 10 of the Employment Protection Act 1975".

(5) In section 3 (2), for paragraph (*b*) substitute the following paragraph—

"(*b*) if an award or determination is, or has been, made under any enactment requiring an employer to observe the collective agreement, that award or determination shall have effect by reference to the agreement as so amended.".

(6) In section 4, in subsections (1) and (2), for the words "wages regulation order" wherever they occur there shall be substituted the words "order under section 11 of the Wages Council Act 1959".

(7) In section 4 (1) for the words from "the Secretary of State" in the second place where they occur to the end there shall be substituted the words "it shall be the duty of the wages council or statutory joint industrial council, by a further order coming into operation not later than five months after the date of the Committee's decision, either to make those amendments in the order referred to by the Committee or otherwise to replace or amend that order so as to remove the discrimination.".

(8) In section 4, after subsection (1) there shall be inserted the following subsection—

"(1A) Where a wages council or statutory joint industrial council certifies that the effect of an order under section 11 of the Wages Councils Act 1959 is only to make such amendments of a previous order as have under this section been declared by the Central Arbitration Committee to be needed, or to make such amendments as aforesaid with minor modifications or modifications of limited application, or is only to revoke and reproduce with such amendments a previous order, then the wages council or statutory joint industrial council may instead of complying with subsections (3) and (3A) of the said section 11 give notice of the proposed order in such manner as appears to the council expedient in the circumstances, and may make the order at any time after the expiration of seven days from the giving of the notice.".

(9) In section 4, for subsection (2) there shall be inserted the following subsection—

"(2) An order under section 11 of the Wages Councils Act 1959 shall be referred to the Central Arbitration Committee under this section if the Secretary of State is requested so to refer it either—

(*a*) by an employers' association for the time being entitled to nominate for membership of the wages council or statutory joint industrial council in question persons representing employers (or, if provision is made for any of the persons representing employers to be elected instead of nominated, then by a member or members representing employers); or

(*b*) by a trade union for the time being entitled to nominate for membership of the wages council or statutory joint industrial council in question persons representing workers (or, if provision is made for any of the persons representing workers to be elected instead of nominated, then by a member or members representing workers);

or if in any case it appears to the Secretary of State that the order may be amendable under this section." .

(10) In section 4 (3), after the words "12 (1)" wherever they occur there shall be inserted the words "or (1A)" and for the words "11 (7)" there shall be substituted the words "11 (8)".

(11) Section 4 (4) is hereby repealed. [**722**]

Tribunals and Inquiries Act 1971 (*c.* 62)

14. Section 13 of the Tribunals and Inquiries Act 1971 (which, among other things, makes provision for appeals from and the statement of cases by industrial tribunals to the High Court or the Court of Session) shall, in its application to industrial tribunals, be taken as referring to those tribunals only when exercising jurisdiction other than under the Acts referred to in section 88 (1) above. [**723**]

Independent Broadcasting Authority Act 1973 (*c.* 19)

15. In section 16 of the Independent Broadcasting Authority Act 1973 for the words "Secretary of State" wherever they occur substitute the words "Advisory, Conciliation and Arbitration Service" and for the words "Industrial Arbitration Board" and "Board" wherever they occur substitute respectively the words "Central Arbitration Committee" and "Committee". [**724**]

House of Commons Disqualification Act 1975 (*c.* 24)

16.—(1) The House of Commons Disqualification Act 1975 shall be amended in accordance with the following provisions of this paragraph.

(2) In Part II of Schedule 1 (bodies of which all members are disqualified under that Act), insert, at the appropriate places in alphabetical order, the following entries:—

"The Central Arbitration Committee."
"The Council of the Advisory, Conciliation and Arbitration Service."
"The Employment Appeal Tribunal."
"The Employment Service Agency."
"The Training Services Agency."

(3) In Part III of Schedule 1 (other disqualifying offices), insert the following entry at the appropriate place in alphabetical order—

"Certification Officer or assistant certification officer appointed under section 7 of the Employment Protection Act 1975." [**725**]

Social Security Pensions Act 1975 (*c.* 60)

17. After section 31 (8) of the Social Security Pensions Act 1975 there shall be inserted the following subsection:—

"(9) A trade union shall be treated as recognised for the purpose of this section not only if it is recognised for the purpose of collective bargaining, but also if the Advisory Conciliation and Arbitration Service has made a recommendation for recognition under the Employment Protection Act 1975 and that recommendation is operative within the meaning of section 15 of that Act.". [**726**]

The Sex Discrimination Act 1975 (*c.* 65)

18.—(1) The Sex Discrimination Act 1975 shall be amended in accordance with the following provisions of this paragraph.

(2) In section 65 (2), for the words "amount for the time being specified in paragraph 20 (1) (*b*)" substitute the words "limit for the time being imposed by paragraph 20".

(3) In the Equal Pay Act 1970 as set out in Part II of Schedule 1 to the Sex Discrimination Act 1975 there shall be made the same amendments as are made to the former Act by paragraph 13 of this Part of this Schedule. [**727**]

COMMENCEMENT

This Schedule was brought into force in two stages on 1st January and 1st February 1976 by the Employment Protection Act 1975 (Commencement No. 1) Order 1975, S.I. 1975 No. 1938, with the exception of paras. 9 and 18 (2).

SCHEDULE 17

Section 125

TRANSITIONAL PROVISIONS

1. Subject to any express provision made in any of the following paragraphs of this Schedule, in so far as anything done or treated as done under any enactment replaced or amended by any provision of this Act, could have been done under that provision or, as the case may be, that enactment as amended, then it shall on the commencement of that provision have effect as if done under that provision or, as the case may be, that enactment as so amended. [**728**]

2. Where any action has been taken by a conciliation officer under paragraph 26 (2) to (5) of Schedule 1 to the 1974 Act before the commencement of section 2 above, that action shall on the commencement of that section be treated as if it had been taken by a conciliation officer appointed under that section. [**729**]

3. Any matter which immediately before the commencement of section 10 (2) above stood referred to the Industrial Arbitration Board under section 2 (2) of the Industrial Courts Act 1919 or section 13 of the National Health Service (Amendment) Act 1949 shall be treated as if it had been referred to the Committee by the Service under section 3 (1) above. [**730**]

4.—(1) The Code of Practice in effect under Part I of Schedule 1 to the 1974 Act immediately before the repeal of that Part by this Act shall remain in effect and shall be taken into account in industrial tribunal proceedings in accordance with paragraph 3 of that Schedule, notwithstanding that repeal, until it is superseded in accordance with sub-paragraph (2) below by one or more Codes of Practice issued by the Service under section 6 above.

(2) If on issuing any Code of Practice under section 6 above the Service is of the opinion that the code of practice continued in effect by sub-paragraph (1) above, or any part of that code, should cease to have effect by reason of being superseded by the provisions of the Code of Practice under section 6 above, the Service shall state in the new Code of Practice that the old code, or a specified part is so superseded and that old code, or part, shall cease to have effect on the date on which the new Code comes into effect in pursuance of an order by the Secretary of State under section 6 (8) above.

(3) Without prejudice to any other power to make transitional and other supplementary or incidental provisions in an order under the said section, such an order may contain such transitional provision or savings as appear to the Secretary of State to be necessary or expedient in connection with any provisions of the code of practice under Part I of Schedule 1 to the 1974 Act which ceases to have effect on the day appointed by that order. [**731**]

5.—(1) Anything done before the commencement of section 7 above by, to or in relation to the Chief Registrar of Friendly Societies or any assistant registrar under any of the Acts referred to in section 7 (2) above, shall be treated on the commencement of that section as having been done by, to or in relation to the Certification Officer.

(2) In particular, sub-paragraph (1) above applies to the following things done under any such Act, that is to say,—

any complaint presented;

any application, determination, registration, order, entry, return, report, or requirement made;

any certificate, approval, notice, direction or exemption given. [**732**]

6. Anything done before the commencement of section 10 (2) above by, to or in relation to the Industrial Arbitration Board under any enactment in which by virtue

of that subsection references to the Industrial Arbitration Board (whether by that or any other name) are to be construed as references to the Central Arbitration Committee, shall be treated after the commencement of that subsection as if they had been done by, to or in relation to the Committee. [**733**]

7.—(1) Sections 29 (4), 33, 34, 51 and 71 to 80 above and the provisions of Part III of Schedule 16 to this Act so far as they amend Schedule 1 to the 1974 Act as respects the law relating to unfair dismissal, shall apply to a dismissal where the effective date of termination in relation to that dismissal falls on or after the commencement of the relevant provision.

(2) The provisions of paragraphs 17 (2) and (3) and 19 of Schedule 1 to the 1974 Act shall, notwithstanding the repeal of those provisions by this Act, continue to apply to dismissals where the effective date of termination falls before the commencement of sections 71 to 76 above.

(3) Where the notice required to be given by an employer to terminate a contract of employment by section 1 (1) of the Contracts of Employment Act 1972 (minimum period of notice) would, if duly given when notice of termination was given by the employer, or (where no notice was given) when the contract of employment was terminated by the employer, expire on a date later than the effective date of termination as defined by paragraph 5 (5) of Schedule 1 to the 1974 Act, that later date shall be treated as the effective date of termination—

(*a*) for the purposes of sub-paragraph (1) above as it applies to sections 34 and 71 to 80 above, and the provisions of Part III of Schedule 16 referred to in that sub-paragraph; and
(*b*) for the purposes of sub-paragraph (2) above. [**734**]

8. The provisions of sections 64 and 65 above shall apply in relation to an employer who becomes insolvent (within the meaning of those sections) after the commencement of those sections, and shall in such a case apply to any debts mentioned in section 64 above and to any unpaid relevant contribution (within the meaning of section 65 above), whether falling due before or after the commencement of those sections. [**735**]

9. An appeal arising out of any proceedings before or any decision of an industrial tribunal under any of the Acts referred to in section 88 (1) above which immediately before the commencement of that section is pending in the High Court or the Court of Session shall be transferred by virtue of this paragraph on the commencement of that section to the Employment Appeal Tribunal. [**736**]

10. An appeal arising out of any proceedings before or any decision of the Chief Registrar of Friendly Societies or any assistant registrar under any of the enactments referred to in section 88 (2) or 88 (3) (*a*) above which immediately before the commencement of that section is pending in the High Court or the Court of Session shall be transferred by virtue of this paragraph on the commencement of that section to the Employment Appeal Tribunal. [**737**]

11.—(1) An order under section 11 of the Wages Councils Act 1959 which is in force immediately before the commencement of Schedule 7 to this Act shall, notwithstanding that it was made by the Secretary of State, continue to have effect after the commencement of that Schedule as if it had been made by a wages council under that section as substituted by that Schedule and may be amended or revoked under that section accordingly.

(2) Anything done with a view to the making of an order under the said section 11 immediately before the commencement of the said Schedule, that is to say, any proposals published and any notice published and representations made with respect thereto, shall notwithstanding that it was done with a view to an order being made by the Secretary of State, have effect after the commencement of that Schedule as if it had been done under that section as substituted by that Schedule.

(3) A person who is, on the commencement of the said Schedule, a member or

officer of a wages council or central co-ordinating committee shall be treated as if he had been appointed under Schedule 2 to the said Act of 1959, as substituted by that Schedule, and accordingly shall continue in office, and in particular, a member appointed to represent employers or workers shall be treated as if he had been appointed by a nominated employers' association or trade union, as the case may be. **[738]**

12. An order under section 11 of the Wages Councils Act 1959, section 3 of the Agricultural Wages Act 1948 or section 3 of the Agricultural Wages (Scotland) Act 1949 (as substituted, in each case, by this Act) which may have effect as from a date earlier than the date of the order, shall not have effect from a date earlier than the commencement of the provision of this Act effecting that substitution. **[739]**

13.—(1) Any award made under section 8 of the Terms and Conditions of Employment Act 1959 which is in force immediately before the commencement of Schedule 11 to this Act shall continue to have effect after that commencement, notwithstanding the repeal of that Act, as if it had been made under the said Schedule and may be superseded or varied accordingly.

(2) Any claim reported to the Secretary of State or referred to the Industrial Arbitration Board under the said section 8 which immediately before the commencement of the said Schedule was pending before the Board shall be treated on that commencement as if it had been reported to the Service or referred to the Committee under Part I of the said Schedule. **[740]**

14. Where any provision of this Act increases the penalty for an offence under any other enactment, that increase shall not have effect in relation to an offence committed before the commencement of the relevant provision. **[741]**

15. The repeals effected by section 111 above—

(*a*) in the case of subsection (1) of that section, shall not confer or affect any right to unemployment benefit in respect of any day before the commencement of that subsection, and

(*b*) in the case of subsection (2) of that section, shall not affect the manner in which any person's requirements or resources are to be ascertained in relation to any period beginning before the commencement of that subsection. **[742]**

16.—(1) Any provision of Part I of Schedule 16 to this Act so far as it amends the Redundancy Payments Act 1965 as respects entitlement to or the computation of a redundancy payment or to the reference of questions to industrial tribunals concerning such entitlement or computation, shall, subject to sub-paragraph (2) below, have effect in relation to dismissals and to lay-off or short-time where the relevant date falls after the commencement of the relevant provision.

(2) Where the notice required to be given by an employer to terminate a contract of employment by section 1 (1) of the Contracts of Employment Act 1972 (minimum period of notice) would, if duly given when notice of termination was given by the employer, or (where no notice was given) when the contract of employment was terminated by the employer expire on a date later than the relevant date as defined by section 3 (9) of the said Act of 1965, that later date shall be treated as the relevant date for the purposes of sub-paragraph (1) above. **[743]**

17. The provisions of this Act which affect the computation of an employee's period of continuous employment for the purposes of this Act or any other Act shall have effect in relation to any week or event, whether falling or occurring (wholly or partly) before or after the commencement of the relevant provision, where the computation falls to be made after the commencement of that provision. **[744]**

18. Any enactment or document which refers, whether specifically or by means of a general description, to an enactment which is replaced or amended by any provision of this Act, shall, except so far as the context otherwise requires, be construed as referring or as including a reference, to that provision. **[745]**

19. Nothing in this Schedule shall be construed as prejudicing section 38 of the Interpretation Act 1889 (effect of repeals). **[746]**

COMMENCEMENT

Schedule 17 was brought into force as follows: paras. 1, 2, 4, 11, 12, 14, 15, 18 and 19 on 1st January 1976, and paras. 3, 5, 6, 9 and 10 on 1st February 1976 by the Employment Protection Act 1975 (Commencement No. 1) Order 1975, S.I. 1975 No. 1938, and para. 8 on 20th April 1976 by the Employment Protection Act 1975 (Commencement No. 2) Order 1976, S.I. 1976 No. 144.

PARA. 2: CONCILIATION OFFICER

As to the designation of such an officer to perform functions specified in any enactment, see s. 2 (4), *ante*.

PARA. 7: CHIEF REGISTRAR OF FRIENDLY SOCIETIES

As to this officer, see the Friendly Societies Act 1974, s. 1 (1) and the notes to that section.

CERTIFICATION OFFICER

That officer is appointed under s. 7, *ante*.

PARA. 6: INDUSTRIAL ARBITRATION BOARD

See the note to s. 10, *ante*.

PARA. 9: INDUSTRIAL TRIBUNAL

See the note to s. 6, *ante*.

EMPLOYMENT APPEAL TRIBUNAL

That body is established under s. 87, *ante*.

PARA. 11: WAGES COUNCIL

Such councils are established under the Wages Councils Act 1959, s. 1.

CENTRAL CO-ORDINATING COMMITTEE

Such committees are established under the Wages Councils Act 1959, s. 7 (1), as substituted by s. 89 (3), Sch. 7, Part IV, para. 3 (1), *ante*.

NOMINATED EMPLOYERS' ASSOCIATION OR TRADE UNION

As to the nomination of such bodies, see the Wages Councils Act 1959, Sch. 2, para. 1 (2), as substituted by s. 89 (2) and Sch. 7, Part III, *ante*.

PARA. 17: COMPUTATION OF . . . PERIOD OF CONTINUOUS EMPLOYMENT

As to the enactments having effect for the purposes of such computation, see s. 126 (5), *ante*. As to the provisions affecting such computation, see the amendments to the Contracts of Employment Act 1972, Sch. 1, contained in Sch. 16, Part II, paras. 12–19, *ante*, and the amendments to the Trade Union and Labour Relations Act 1974, Sch. 1, para. 30, contained in Sch. 16, Part III, paras. 29, 30, *ante*.

DEFINITIONS

By virtue of s. 126 (1), *ante*, for "employer", see the definition inserted in the Trade Union and Labour Relations Act 1974, s. 30 (1), by s. 125 (1) and Sch. 16, Part III, para. 7 (2), *ante* and s. 30 (2) (*b*) of that Act; for "trade union", see s. 28 of that Act and for "dismissal" and "effective date of termination", see Sch. 1, para. 5, to, that Act; for "the Service", see s. 1 (1), *ante*; for "the Committee", see s. 10 (1), *ante*; and for "employers' associations", see s. 126 (2) *ante*.

SCHEDULE 18

Section 125

ENACTMENTS REPEALED

Chapter	Short Title	Extent of repeal
1896 c. 30	The Conciliation Act 1896	The whole Act.
2 & 3 Geo. 5 c. 30	The Trade Union Act 1913	In section 3 (2), the words from "shall be binding" to "restrainable by injunction, and" and the words "and 'interdict' shall be substituted for 'injunction' ".

Chapter	Short Title	Extent of repeal
1919 c. 69	The Industrial Courts Act 1919	Part I. In section 4 (1), the words "whether or not the dispute is reported to him under Part I of this Act". In section 7, the words "of the Industrial Arbitration Board and". In section 9, the words "before the Industrial Arbitration Board, before an arbitrator or". Sections 11 and 12.
1938 c. 44	The Road Haulage Wages Act 1938	Section 5 (5).
1948 c. 67	The Agricultural Wages Act 1948	In section 12 (5), the words from "and in any such civil proceedings" onwards. In Schedule 4, in paragraph 6, the words from the beginning to "holidays".
1949 c. 30	The Agricultural Wages (Scotland) Act 1949	In section 12 (4), the words from "and in any such civil proceedings" onwards. In Schedule 3, in paragraph 6, the words from the beginning to "holidays".
1949 c. 93	The National Health Service (Amendment) Act 1949	Section 13.
1958 c. 51	The Public Records Act 1958	In Schedule 1, in Part II of the Table at the end of paragraph 3, the entries relating to the Employment Service Agency, the Manpower Services Commission and the Training Services Agency.
1959 c. 26	The Terms and Conditions of Employment Act 1959	The whole Act, so far as unrepealed.
1959 c. 69	The Wages Councils Act 1959	Section 9 (1). In section 23, the words "a commission of inquiry". In section 24, the definitions of "wages regulation order" and "wages regulations proposals'. Schedule 4.
1960 c. 37	The Payment of Wages Act 1960	Section 2 (4) to (8). In section 4 (2), the words from "and, at or before" to the end. In section 4 (3), the words from "and, at or before" to the end. Section 7 (3). The Schedule.

Chapter	Short Title	Extent of repeal
1962 c. 47	The Education (Scotland) Act 1962	In section 85, subsection (3) and in subsection (5) the word "(3)". In section 123 (2), in the proviso, the words from "and", where secondly occurring, to the end.
1964 c. 24	The Trade Union (Amalgamation, etc.) Act 1964	In section 7 (1) (*c*), the words "or by any assistant registrar". In section 9, the definitions of "assistant registrar" and "Registrar".
1965 c. 3	The Remuneration of Teachers Act 1965	In section 3 (3), the words from "and, where arbitrators" to the end. Section 6 (*d*).
1965 c. 62	The Redundancy Payments Act 1965	In section 5 (2) the words "(calculated in accordance with Schedule 2 to this Act)". Schedule 2. In Schedule 4, paragraphs 6 and 12. In Schedule 5, in paragraph 1 the words from "and paragraph 5" onwards; and paragraph 13.
1966 c. 20	The Supplementary Benefit Act 1966	In section 10 (2), in paragraph (*a*), the words "or financing" and the word "and" and paragraph (*b*).
1967 c. 36	The Remuneration of Teachers (Scotland) Act 1967	In section 3 (3), the words from "and, where arbiters" to the end. Section 7 (*c*).
1968 c. 73	The Transport Act 1968	Section 35 (3) (*b*).
1970 c. 41	The Equal Pay Act 1970	Section 4 (4).
1972 c. 11	The Superannuation Act 1972	In Schedule 1, the entries relating to the Manpower Services Commission, the Employment Service Agency and the Training Services Agency.
1973 c. 35	The Employment Agencies Act 1973	Section 2 (4). In section 2 (5), the words "under the subsequent provisions of this Act". Section 8. In section 9 (4) (*a*), sub-paragraphs (ii) and (iii). In section 13 (1), the definition of "licensing authority".
1973 c. 38	The Social Security Act 1973	In Schedule 27, paragraph 54.
1973 c. 50	The Employment and Training Act 1973	Section 7. In section 13 (1) in the definition of "employee" the words "except in Schedule 1"; and in the definition of "employ-

Chapter	Short Title	Extent of repeal
1973 c. 50—*cont.*	The Employment and Training Act 1973—*cont.*	ment" the words "except in section 7 and Schedule 1". Section 13 (5). In section 15 (3), the words "5" and "13". In Schedule 1, in paragraph 10 (1) the words from "and any" to the end, and paragraphs 10 (2), 11, 12 and 16. In Schedule 3, paragraphs 5 and 13.
1974 c. 37	The Health and Safety at Work etc. Act 1974	In section 1 (2) the words "and agricultural health and safety regulations". Section 2 (5). In section 11, in subsection (1), the words "except as regards matters relating exclusively to agricultural operations"; and in subsection (2), the words "except as aforesaid". In section 14 (2), the words from "but shall not do so" to "agricultural operations". In section 16 (1), the words "and except as regards matters relating exclusively to agricultural operations". In section 18, in subsection (3), the words "or agricultural health and safety regulations"; and in subsection (5), the words "the appropriate Agriculture Minister". Section 29, 30, 31 and 32. In section 33, in subsection (1) (*c*), the words " or agricultural health and safety regulations"; and in subsection (4) (*a*), the words "or the appropriate Agriculture Minister". In section 43 (3), the words "the Minister of Agriculture, Fisheries and Food". In section 44 (1), the words "agricultural licences and". In section 47, in subsection (2), the words "or agricultural health and safety regulations"; in subsection (3), the words "or, as the case may be, agricultural health and safety regulations"; and in subsection (5), the words "or, as the case may be, agri-

Chapter	Short Title	Extent of repeal
1974 c. 37—*cont.*	The Health and Safety at Work etc. Act 1974—*cont.*	cultural health and safety regulations". In section 49 (3), the words "by the appropriate Minister". Section 50 (4) and (5). In section 53 (1), the definitions of "agriculture", "the Agriculture Ministers", "agricultural health and safety regulations", "agricultural licence", "agricultural operation", "the appropriate Agriculture Minister", "forestry", "livestock" and "the relevant agricultural purposes"; and in the definition of "the relevant statutory provisions", the words "and agricultural health and safety regulations". Section 53 (2) to (6). In section 84 (1) (*a*), the words " or 30". Schedule 4.
1974 c. 39	The Consumer Credit Act 1974	In section 16 (3) (*b*) the words "or (*c*)".
1974 c. 52	The Trade Union and Labour Relations Act 1974	In section 8 (1), the words in brackets. Section 8 (8). In section 8 (10), the words from "and that the organisation" to the end. In section 30 (1), the definition of "Registrar". In Schedule 1, Part I; in paragraph 5 (3), the words "obligatory" and "in writing"; paragraph 5 (4); in paragraph 9 (1), paragraphs (*a*), (*e*) and (*f*) and in paragraph (*b*) the words "or a close relative"; paragraph 9 (4); in paragraph 17 (1), words from "or by a person" onwards; paragraphs 17 (2) and (3), 19 and 26 (1); in paragraph 26 (3) (*a*) the words "his engagement"; and paragraph 29. In Schedule 3, paragraphs 2 (6), 3, 8, 9 (4), (6) and (7), 10 (4), and (6) and 15.
1975 c. 14	The Social Security Act 1975	In section 19 (1), in paragraph (*a*), the words "or financing" and the word "and", and paragraph (*b*).

Chapter	Short Title	Extent of repeal
1975 c. 18	The Social Security (Consequential Provisions) Act 1975	In Schedule 2, in paragraph 19 the words "17 (3) and (4A) and", and paragraph 20.
1975 c. 24	The House of Commons Disqualification Act 1975	In Part II of Schedule 1, the entry relating to the Industrial Arbitration Board. In Part III of Schedule 1, in the entry relating to members of Wages Councils and other persons appointed under the Wages Councils Act 1959, the words "or a member of a Commission of Inquiry appointed under paragraph 1 (*a*) of Schedule 4 to that Act".
1975 c. 25	The Northern Ireland Assembly Disqualification Act 1975	In Part II of Schedule 1, the entry relating to the Industrial Arbitration Board. In Part III of Schedule 1, in the entry relating to members of Wages Councils and other persons appointed under the Wages Councils Act 1959, the words "or a member of a Commission of Inquiry appointed under paragraph 1 (*a*) of Schedule 4 to that Act".
1975 c. 65	The Sex Discrimination Act 1975	In section 82 (1), the definition of "conciliation officer". In Schedule 5, paragraph 4.

[**747**]

COMMENCEMENT

Some of the provisions of Sch. 18 were brought into force by the Employment Protection Act 1975 (Commencement No. 1) Order 1975, S.I. 1975 No. 1938 as follows: on 1st January 1976 the repeals relating to the Conciliation Act 1896, the Agricultural Wages Act 1948, the Agricultural Wages (Scotland) Act 1949, the Public Records Act 1958, the Wages Councils Act 1959, the Equal Pay Act 1970, the Superannuation Act 1972, the Employment Agencies Act 1973, the Employment and Training Act 1973, section 2 (5) of the Health and Safety at Work etc. Act 1974, section 8 (10) of, paragraph 26 (1) of Schedule 1 to, and paragraph 9 (4), (6) and (7) of Schedule 3 to the Trade Union and Labour Relations Act 1974, Part III of Schedule 1 to the House of Commons Disqualification Act 1975 and Part III of Schedule 1 to the Northern Ireland Assembly Disqualification Act 1975 and the Sex Discrimination Act 1975; on 1st February 1976 the repeals relating to the Trade Union Act 1913, the Industrial Courts Act 1919, the Road Haulage Wages Act 1938, the National Health Service (Amendment) Act 1949, the Trade Union (Amalgamations, etc.) Act 1964, the Remuneration of Teachers Act 1965, the Remuneration of Teachers (Scotland) Act 1967, the Transport Act 1968, the Consumer Credit Act 1974, sections 8 (1), 8 (8) and 30 (1) of, and paragraphs 2 (6), 3 and 10 (4) and (6) and 15 of Schedule 3 to the Trade Union and Labour Relations Act 1974, Part II of Schedule 1 to the House of Commons Disqualification Act 1975, and Part II of Schedule 1 to the Northern Ireland Assembly Disqualification Act 1975; and on 1st March 1976 the remaining provisions relating to the Health and Safety at Work etc. Act 1974.

INDEX

References are to paragraph numbers.

References are to paragraph numbers.

References are to paragraph numbers.

References are to paragraph numbers.

References are to paragraph numbers.

References are to paragraph numbers.

References are to paragraph numbers.

References are to paragraph numbers.

Printed in Great Britain by offset lithography by
Billing & Sons Ltd, Guildford, London and Worcester